Watchdog Journalism

Watchdog Journalism

THE ART OF INVESTIGATIVE REPORTING

Stephen J. Berry

UNIVERSITY OF IOWA

New York   Oxford
OXFORD UNIVERSITY PRESS
2009

Oxford University Press, Inc., publishes works that further Oxford University's
objective of excellence in research, scholarship, and education.

Oxford   New York
Auckland   Cape Town   Dar es Salaam   Hong Kong   Karachi
Kuala Lumpur   Madrid   Melbourne   Mexico City   Nairobi
New Delhi   Shanghai   Taipei   Toronto

With offices in
Argentina   Austria   Brazil   Chile   Czech Republic   France   Greece
Guatemala   Hungary   Italy   Japan   Poland   Portugal   Singapore
South Korea   Switzerland   Thailand   Turkey   Ukraine   Vietnam

Copyright © 2009 by Oxford University Press, Inc.

Published by Oxford University Press, Inc.
198 Madison Avenue, New York, New York 10016
http://www.oup.com

Oxford is a registered trademark of Oxford University Press

Library of Congress Cataloging-in-Publication Data

Berry, Stephen J., 1948–
Watchdog journalism : the art of investigative reporting / Stephen J. Berry.
   p.   cm.
Includes bibliographical references and index.
ISBN-13: 978-0-19-537402-5 (alk. paper)   1. Investigative reporting.   I. Title.
PN4781.B395 2009
070.4'3—dc22   2008004998

Printing number: 9 8 7 6 5 4 3 2 1

Printed in the United States of America
on acid-free paper

To Cheryl and Richard
In memory of my parents, Charles and Marjorie Berry,
and Mimmie, a loving matriarch to the Berry family

CONTENTS

PREFACE

In selecting the stories for this book, my methodology was not very methodical. Although the daily newspapers and several media contests are filled with many excellent projects, it would have been impossible to review them all. I selected the Pulitzer as a good minimum qualification for consideration, because journalists recognize it as the most coveted award.

From that pool, I picked stories that I liked because of the quality of work that I sensed was there the first time that I read them. Before I started reading, I wrote down a few guidelines. The most general guide was to find stories that depended on hard work and the fundamental journalistic practices that I believe everyday readers have a right to expect from their news organizations and exuded courage and exemplary writing. To make those judgments, I drew on my 33 years of practicing journalism at small, medium-sized, and large dailies and four years of studying and teaching basic and investigative reporting. I liberally detail that background—personal and professional—in Chapter 1. As I read and reread these projects, I gradually began to see stories that I thought would resonate with reporters who work at the type of small to huge newspapers that had formed my experience. I wanted to give reporters at all levels a chance to read and enjoy good work and see things that could work for them.

After settling on those broad goals, I gave much thought to what I did not want. I did not want stories that relied totally on anonymous sources. I did not want stories that required a whole squad of reporters, because I hoped to isolate individual work. Nor did I want stories that required more than a year of work from idea to publication. I also did not want stories that were wholly dependent on big bucks or big media power.

Relying on the Pulitzer website, Pulitzer.org, which carries the stories in each project going back to 1995, and the news organizations' archives, I started reading. I read every winner in the public service, investigative reporting and national reporting categories from April 2007 back to 1993. A couple that I selected violated some of my own criteria. For example, big media is represented in my choices, but the quality of the work drew primarily on the qualities of the individual journalists rather than on the resources and power of their employers. One of the projects lasted for more than 12 months, but the reporters wrote dozens of related spot news and enterprise stories as they investigated their topic. I chose my own project because it was an opportunity to provide the most detailed and introspective account of what we did and what we were thinking. It is included in Appendix A. The other projects are available at Pulitzer.org.

My reporting consisted of interviews and archival research. I conducted face-to-face, tape-recorded interviews mostly in the journalists' newsrooms or cafeterias. I did one at Ronald Reagan National Airport in Washington, D.C., and another at a coffee shop in Los Angeles. I followed up on most of the face-to-face interviews with quite a few e-mails and telephone conversations. The face-to-face interviews lasted anywhere from two hours to two days. Except for one, I interviewed the journalists, including reporters in partnerships, separately. I also used the newspapers' electronic archives to study the papers' coverage of the topic before and after publication of the series, sometimes going back more than 20 years and forward as many years as it took to see the resolution.

To help re-create the dialogue and thought processes that the journalists in these pages recalled from memory or from their notes, I frequently employed a device that I call a quote without quote marks. Although the passages are presented in the format of dialogue, the words could not be presented verbatim, because the journalists relied on memory. They are reconstructions that I asked the journalists to re-create to reflect the content as accurately as their memories would allow. At the time of my interviews, my primary purpose was to prompt careful and conscientious thought for the sake of accuracy. Use of the quote without the quote marks device was an afterthought that occurred to me as I transcribed the tape recordings and was struck by how much detail and feeling the journalists conveyed during our conversations. For guidance in its use, I then read several other works in search of authors who employed a similar device. Two of those books are *All the President's Men,* by Bob Woodward and Carl Bernstein, and *Tiger Force: A True Story of Men and War,* by Michal D. Sallah and Mitch Weiss, who are two of the reporters who appear in this work.

Discussion Questions

In the case study approach to teaching investigative journalism, taking students step-by-step through portions of the investigation is a good way to generate stimulating discussions and a strong desire among the students to read the entire project. The method allows instructors to present reporting problems that would have confronted the reporters and to ask the class to figure out ways to solve them. The ensuing discussion often becomes like a game in which students try to figure out a puzzle. By the end of this preliminary discussion, you have students pleading to read the entire project. As they do, the students are more likely to read it as professional journalists would, noticing reporting tactics, analyzing writing techniques and looking for reporting holes.

For journalism instructors, discussion questions are on a companion website for this book. For each chapter, the discussion questions are divided into two groups. The first group is for discussion before the students read the chapter, and the second is for afterward.

The stories are available at Pulitzer.org, except for "Tainted Cash or Easy Money?" which is reproduced in Appendix A.

ACKNOWLEDGMENTS

As a journalist who is deeply passionate about journalism, I found that the most refreshing and inspiring part of this project was the time I spent with reporters and editors whose every word revealed a passion matching my own. After four years in the academy, I needed that. I am deeply grateful to all of these professionals. They were generous with their time so that others could enjoy and learn from the fascinating back stories to their incredible adventures. They include John Carroll, Tracy Weber, Charles Ornstein, Julie Marquis, Mitchell Landsberg, Steve Hymon, Nigel Jaquiss, Mark Zusman, Richard Meeker, Clifford Levy, Joe Sexton, Mitch Weiss, Michael Sallah, Ron Royhab, John R. Block, Allan Block, Gary Cohn, Will Englund, Rebecca Corbett, Jeff Brazil, Michael Ludden, Eric Nalder, Deborah Nelson, Scott Higham and Sari Horwitz. Their dedication to the mission of journalism and their faith in its ability to make society a better place will be reassurance to all readers and an inspiration to young journalists.

I owe a special debt to Mike Ludden, whose advice and support on this project and on others during my career has been valuable to me.

I also owe a debt of gratitude to Oxford University Press for seeing the value of this work and for giving me—a first-time book author—the opportunity to embark on this adventure. I thank the following proposal and manuscript reviewers: Cole C. Campbell, University of Nevada, Reno; Ira Chinoy, University of Maryland, College Park; Richard Craig, San José State University; Douglas J. Fisher, University of South Carolina; William C. Gaines, University of Illinois at Urbana-Champaign; Suzanne McBride, Columbia College Chicago; Brian L. Massey, Salisbury University; David T.Z. Mindich, Saint Michael's College; and Mary Kay Quinlan, University of Nebraska-Lincoln.

I thank the University of Iowa's School of Journalism and Mass Communication for its financial assistance and express my gratitude to my faculty colleagues for their support, particularly, Professor Carolyn Dyer for her advice and very detailed editing in preparing my original book proposal. Arlecia Simmons, a doctoral candidate in our school, provided valuable copy editing assistance on this project.

To my five brothers and sisters—Bob, Mike, Jenny, Tracy and Gail—thank you for putting up with my long obsession with career and projects that never seem to end.

Finally, and most important, I am and will forever be eternally and lovingly beholden and dedicated to my wife Cheryl, whose editing, support and encouragement made this project possible and whose unconditional love has been the foundation of my life for more than three decades.

Watchdog Journalism

Introduction

The reporting part of journalism often is an ugly sight, as are the writing and the editing. Yet, practitioners like to describe what they do as a craft. In reality, there is little that resembles craftsmanship. It is, instead, a chaotic wonder that sometimes produces stories that are craft-like. But within journalism, a special genre—called investigative reporting—perhaps comes closer to craftsmanship. Although still not a thing of beauty, investigative reporting produces work that usually reflects the best that journalism has to offer, and it often prompts change in society and in people's lives. It is how journalism should work when editors and reporters, in the words of several in this book, want "to get it right."

This book, in a figurative way, takes readers into the newsroom, out into the field and into interviews to show them what doing it right looks like. You will not see everyday journalism and ordinary journalists. You will see some of the best of both. The work revealed in these pages is not neat and clean, because that's not journalism, even at this craftsman-like level. Some of it, in fact, may make you wince, and perhaps even raise an eyebrow. Some of it will make you laugh.

Each chapter is a backstory of six Pulitzer Prize–winning investigative projects and the journalists who produced them. In these chapters, the stories serve a measure of suspense, a bit of character study, and a dash of fun in a quirky concoction containing a healthy dose of serious discourse. These reporters and editors show what journalism is like in the trenches, down where they stumbled miserably or succeeded ecstatically, down where they found the records and the sources and down into the messy, ego-sapping, nitty-gritty of the editing process. Some of the reporters described it as a chaotic process, but, somehow, it produced powerful and accurate stories that anger, disgust, sadden and sicken. In one case, the project takes the readers into what a source called one of Dante's circles of hell.

Why do this book now? What is the news peg? There is a good reason people need to know how journalism should work, and it is not much different from the reason they need to know how government and business works:

it affects their daily lives. To know if journalism is working the way it should, they need to know how it works when it is running on all cylinders.

The idea for this book is rooted in my personal reaction to the rash of major media failings, particularly in the coverage of this country's march to war in Iraq in 2002 and early 2003. *The New York Times'* stunningly detailed mea culpa concerning its shocking mistakes in covering the run-up to the war was a wake-up call for me, a lifelong admirer of that great journalistic institution. Missteps at other well-respected news organizations followed, such as CBS, where broadcasting icon Dan Rather muffed the story about President George Bush's National Guard record. The failings were massive. Some violated or confused core principles of journalism.

In the interim, studies about what went wrong poured forth, and the burgeoning industry in media criticism flourished. It has done a thorough job of tracking journalism's miscues, and now the media has become a major item on the public's agenda, alongside all of the other institutions that claim to serve society. The watchdogs watching the watchdogs are quite good at mobilizing public opinion to call media giants to account. Many news organizations now have full-time reporters covering the press. Blogs and websites thrive on media mistakes, and media watchdog organizations churn out calls to action every week. In broadcast, the media is a daily target on Fox News, MSNBC, radio talk shows and even on Comedy Central. All in all, yammering about press folly has become good sport.

The impact on the public and on journalism is still playing out. So far, people who care about public affairs are becoming well versed on how the press *is not* supposed to work, with little or no opportunity to know how it *is* supposed to work. As for the practitioners, they may be feeling a bit weak in the knees and fuzzy in the head trying to sort out the studies. This book's relevance to the public, to journalists and to educators and its role in these confusing times is clear; by simply showing journalists doing their jobs on projects ranked among the best in journalism, it can bring some clarity to the murkiness created by conflicting notions of good public affairs reporting.

Part of the confusion arises from the seismic technological changes roiling the profession. The worrisome part of the discourse on these changes suggests that we have learned nothing from the failings of our recent history. The focus now is not on the quality of journalism, but the technology of it. With this technology, reporters can blog, update every hour, do stand-ups for television and grab some audio.

At some point, though, they are supposed to find time to do some hard reporting. In this milieu, the public good seems to take a back seat to the public's tastes. The desire to keep pace with the marvels of new media can lead us to mistake good journalism for servile deference to public whim: giving the audience what it wants, when it wants it and through whatever new, technological device that comes down the pike. Instead, professional leaders and journalism educators should focus less on the devices and more on giving people what they need to know to object to a government misadventure or to simply serve as informed citizens in a democratic society. New technology is welcome, but the focus of discussion on what it means for journalism should turn to how it can be harnessed to serve quality journalism. Visuals and inter-active venues are indeed captivating, and serving the perceived public desire for instant gratification seems to be conventional wisdom among many in journalism. Millions of readers and listeners, however, still hunger for serious, thorough and careful public affairs journalism that remains the profession's core mission.

The work of the reporters in this book—even with their missteps—provides a frame of reference for readers in seeing how good, but real, journalism is practiced in the pursuit of real stories intended for the public's good. For daily journalism, these backstories reveal much that can apply every day on every story. In comparison to the hurly-burly of daily news reporting, investigative journalism provides reporters the opportunity to marshal all of their skill, creativity and writing talent. Reporters and editors can experiment with different techniques and approaches to interviewing, finagling documents out of the grasp of bureaucrats and persuading frightened sources to talk and rewriting their stories until the prose is as close to perfect to as they can make it. Under these conditions, reporters have no excuse for taking shortcuts or failing to verify the accuracy of what people tell them. They are expected to do whatever is ethically necessary to get the story. Because much is at stake with such projects, nothing but the best can be accepted as par for the course.

The lessons that emerge from their work have immense implications for the public and journalism. For one, the quality of the reporting found in the Pulitzer Prize–winning projects is not the preserve of investigative reporting. After all, in many of these projects, the knowledge, skills and intense personalities reflect what the authors brought from their pasts, from the days when they were doing daily journalism. Moreover, several of the journalists in these chapters were daily reporters.

In this book I do not preach, criticize or promote. Nor do I tell you how journalism is supposed to work. I let the journalists *show* you how it worked on their stories and reveal what they were thinking while they worked. Although I give up center stage after Chapter 1, I am always close by, and at the end of each chapter, I offer some "lessons learned" from the experiences the reporters generously shared with me for the public. Finally, I offer a few discussion prompts for each chapter that are designed to spark discourse in the classroom or wherever the topic of "the media" may emerge.

For those who care about public affairs enough to read the news each day and who keep the legions of media critics in business on the air and in cyberspace, I hope these stories entertain. Simultaneously, I hope they inform and contribute to the public body of knowledge about how journalism works when its practitioners operate at peak performance.

For journalists and educators, the value of seeing how these reporters and editors made decisions, did their jobs and overcame their mistakes goes beyond learning tricks of the trade, although their stories offer much at that level. Indeed, the reporters and editors talked colorfully and candidly about writing, interviewing, handling sensitive interviews, working anonymous and on-the-record sources, working with partners and editors, and surviving the grueling editing process. More than that, though, their work and their mental approach to it reveal a distinctive view of journalism and its mission in society. They, in many ways, reveal a faith in journalism that is refreshingly idealistic and passionate for a profession where jaded skepticism is too often the depressingly dominating persona.

Perhaps that—rather than the power and cachet of big media—is the fire that can spark good journalism and fuel public debate about the affairs of society. My contention is that their work provides a model at any level of journalism, down to the classroom level in America's schools of journalism.

CHAPTER 1

Investigative Mentality Exposes Cash Seizure Abuse

Drug Scare, Street Justice and the Press

Sheriff's Sgt. Bobby Jones sat in the driver's seat peering intently at every driver who whisked through the 40-foot-wide band of light from the high beams of his patrol cruiser. On that warm central Florida night in Volusia County, Jones had parked perpendicular to Interstate 95 in the wide grassy median separating motorists heading north from those bound south. He was locking on to the southbound drivers, knowing that the next traffic violator he spotted could be what he was looking for—a drug trafficker.

As a reporter for *The Orlando Sentinel*, I sat beside Jones, gazing into the glow just as intently. In that split second, the human eye and mind sees and records a wondrous amount of detail: stuff on the dash, whether the drivers are large or small, men or women, young or old, alone or with a passenger, and, most interestingly to me, whether they were black or white.

In the back seat, a *Sentinel* photographer chattered as he leaned forward, resting his arms on the back of the front seat. Like me, he was looking for drug couriers. Neither of us knew what they looked like. Jones did, though. We had been told he was so well trained, he could spot one in an instant. Jones talked about a few of his tricks, and I jotted notes. The cars whizzed by. Our heads went back and forth. The photographer droned on.

"What's all this stuff about you guys stopping only black people out here?" the photographer blurted.

"Damn," I cursed to myself. I was busted. I wanted the answer to that question, too, but I did not want Jones to know that. Not at that moment. I wanted to see for myself what he and the Volusia County Sheriff's Department were really up to in the wee hours of the night out on I-95.

"What are you talking about, man? I haven't seen anything like that out here," I said, desperately trying to mitigate the blunder. I didn't dwell on the topic and probably quickly changed the subject. Jones was the field commander of the elite I-95 drug interdiction squad of Sheriff Bob Vogel, one of the most popular and well-known law enforcement officers in the state. Vogel had become the proverbial folk hero in the battle to stop illegal narcotics trafficking.[1] The five-person squad's sole mission was to stake out this Miami-to-Maine coastal highway and find drug couriers. I wanted to see how they did it and whether they were targeting minorities for traffic stops and searches for drugs. According to the clips, they took big wads of cash if they found any, even if they could not find enough evidence to arrest the motorists. It was supposed to be perfectly legal under a much-ballyhooed state law called the Florida Contraband Forfeiture Act.

At the time of the photographer's indiscreet comment, Jones had pulled over several black and Hispanic motorists, which was not yet a pattern of targeting minorities, but it was at least the beginning of one. From then on that night, I saw nothing else in Jones' pullover choices that would sustain our suspicion during that long, boring ride-along.

The remark was just a minor annoyance during the first month of a project that would dominate my life and the lives of my partner, Jeff Brazil, and our editor, Mike Ludden, for more than a year. There would be others. At that point, we knew we had a lot of work ahead of us, but we did not know it would become so all-consuming. Nor were we sure that the evidence that we had just started uncovering would confirm what our preliminary findings suggested: that Vogel's vaunted drug interdiction program was targeting minorities and punishing innocent people, that it was more about raising money than catching drug traffickers. For me, it was another one of those "just too good to be true" stories, and like most others I had chased in my career, this one eventually either would fall apart or become confusingly fuzzy.

Sun, Fun and the War on Drugs

Interstate 95 is the perfect narco-trail, a coastal asphalt strip where evil blends with innocence. It slices through the heart of Sheriff Vogel's domain, providing a connection for drug couriers heading south to Miami with huge stashes of cash and for drug mules heading north carrying their illicit product. But I-95 also carries Mom, Dad and the kids to the long stretch of beach along the Atlantic coast or to Disney World and Sea World in Orlando. Volusia County itself draws sun worshipers and spring breakers to Daytona Beach, bikers to Bike Week and NASCAR fans to the famed Daytona 500 stock-car race. For two years, *The Orlando Sentinel*, *The Daytona Beach News-Journal* and especially Orlando television stations in neighboring Orange County had followed Sheriff Vogel's drug war on I-95. The story line was simple, colorful and great for visuals.

As the vacationers and drug dealers sped by, Sgt. Jones and his specially trained Selective Enforcement Team (SET) would lie in wait, always looking for out-of-state drivers committing the slightest traffic violation. That's all they needed to pull someone over so they could switch on their K-9ish instincts to alert them to the tell-tale demeanor and manner of a typical drug dealer. Almost anything—a furtive look, a shaky voice, a Crown Royal bag—could cause them to perk up like the drug-sniffing dogs that are just a radio call away. As the officer chatted up the suspect, his busy eyes and ears tracked appearances or mannerisms. Whenever something set off their internal alarms, the deputies asked for permission to search the motorists' cars. Invariably, they found drugs or "drug money." It was always suspiciously large amounts of cash, usually stashed in some cleverly contrived secret compartment behind the dash or in the gas tank or beneath the raised truck bed or maybe just stuffed in the spare tire. The motorists were given case numbers and told they could return to Volusia County and try to prove that their money was not drug money. Of course, it was drug money, and they were drug dealers, and the deputies usually never heard from them again. So the story line went.

Hot Story Trumps Real Story

The Central Florida press coverage of the I-95 drug interdiction program—intentionally or not—played to the public's support for law enforcement's battle against drug crimes. No stories had examined the program in detail to see how it worked. None had followed its paper trail. None were exploring the fundamental question: How can a law enforcement program that is supposedly governed by a system of laws countenance the taking and keeping of someone's property or cash based on mere suspicion without proving that the suspect had broken the law? Occasionally, news stories allowed an American Civil Liberties Union spokesman to decry the seizures.

Even the more pedestrian reporting questions received scant attention. Why would a traffic violator's shaky voice or money in a Crown Royal bag be suspicious? Since when has carrying a large amount of money been against the law? How were cash-seizure cases litigated from beginning to end? What was the sheriff doing with all of that money and how was he accounting for it? The department had seized about $8 million over the 3.5 years.[2]

In the early 1990s milieu of that coverage, political, government and civic leaders had started calling the enforcement of laws against the illegal use and sale of narcotics a "war on drugs." The public fear of drugs and drug-related crimes ran rampant in the 1980s and early 1990s. In polls, the public had consistently listed illegal drugs as the number one crime problem facing the country.[3]

So a drug bust or a cash seizure on the grassy shoulders of I-95 in Volusia County was a victory story that people longed to read. Vogel knew that, and in journalism, those drug busts and seizures became good stories. Vogel didn't have to frame the issue for the press, but his fearmongering played nicely in a story that entertained the public and fit the profession's definition of news.

"There's no secret we live in the drug capital of the world," Vogel once said.[4]

Prime Time for a Crusader

Vogel was the resourceful crusader making a feared enemy look silly. At one point, he posted signs on I-95 warning that a narcotics traffic stop was ahead, and his deputies chased down any car that attempted to turn around. The public loved it. Vogel was in the trenches, leading the troops in battle to wipe out the scourge that was ripping through the country.[5] And he was getting results. So what if, in this life-or-death struggle for the future of our children and the safety of our communities, he tromped on a few constitutional rights of drug dealers? Who cared?

For Vogel, the times were prime time. He had been sheriff for three years. His drug enforcement crusade had made him a hero throughout Florida and his star was getting brighter. Vogel had earned his stripes in the drug war a few years earlier when he launched a one-man crusade while prowling I-95 as a state trooper. He had built a reputation as a drug-busting cop whose experience and study had sensitized him to the body language, mannerisms and practices of drug couriers. He had won so many state commendations for his drug busts that the head of the state highway patrol finally had a special commendation stamp made for him.[6] Vogel even caught the attention of CBS's *60 Minutes* when he was a state trooper. He was Buford Pusser with a radar gun, or, as one headline in *The Orlando Sentinel* said, "The Mayor of I-95."[7]

In 1988, he ran for sheriff of Volusia County. Vogel was the dream candidate: a fit, handsome, likeable, articulate ex-Marine. He wore nice suits and had learned to work the public with the aplomb of a man who seldom faced press or professional criticism. He took office in 1989 and immediately established the five-man Selective Enforcement Team to do what he had perfected as a state trooper. By 1990, ABC News featured him on *20/20*.

Big Haul Stirs Press

By early 1992, Vogel's I-95 program, although at its peak, had become an old story. On Jan. 30, 1992, however, Sgt. Jones unknowingly put the drug interdiction program on the paper's front burner when he stopped a van on I-95 and found $697,599 hidden in a secret compartment under the vehicle floor. It was a record and brought the total seizure amount since the program's inception to $7.7 million.[8] That caught a lot of people's attention, including Ludden's. In February of that year, Brazil, who worked in the paper's bureau in Volusia County, was told to take a look at the program. He initially examined a sampling of records for about a dozen cases and saw something that could shatter the public's perception of Vogel's I-95 antidrug campaign. "It was not what the program had appeared to be before—kicking ass in the drug business," Brazil recalled.[9] Most of the motorists and their passengers were either Hispanic or black. Equally intriguing was the fact that Vogel had struck deals with several of them in which he returned a portion of the money to persons Vogel had claimed were drug dealers in exchange for their written promise not to sue the department for confiscating their cash. Those files, although interesting, only suggested a pattern; they did not establish it. "We knew we were going to have to look at every single case," Brazil said.[10] That's when Ludden pulled me out of Lake County, where I was working on a project about assisted-care living facilities, to work with Brazil.

A Partnership Takes Shape

Brazil and I had met in 1989 when we worked together in the Lake County bureau. Lake is an orange-growing and retirement community northwest of Orlando. We would soon begin an on-and-off partnership that would last through a half-dozen investigative projects and continue later at the *Los Angeles*

Times. Our partnership worked well, particularly on this project, because we brought such widely different backgrounds, talents and interests to each story. We had come from opposite ends of the continent. I arrived from *The Greensboro* (NC) *News & Record*, where for 17 years I had covered beats and done a few investigative projects.

I had grown up in the Deep South, mostly in Dothan, Ala., in the heart of George Wallace country. I was part of a large, white middle-class family, during one of the most tumultuous periods of the civil rights movement. My parents, the products of two respected families in Dothan, were Wallace–Goldwater conservatives. Even so, overt, white supremacist demagogues such as Bull Connor embarrassed them, and we were taught the quickest way to hell was to say you hated somebody. Nevertheless, I never heard them question the morality of segregation. We were the quiet, polite segment of Southern society. "Our kind" do not use the N-word, my grandmother always said. In the neighborhood, the term "nigra" was the social compromise between "goody-goody" and street corner, where racial jokes and the N-word littered the chatter of many children. Segregation was deeply entrenched in Dothan, which is so deep in the South, school integration did not touch our schools until my senior year in 1966, and, even then, only a few minorities attended.

My late mother, Marjorie, like most moms in those days, was a homemaker. Of course, with six children, she had no other choice. The daughter of a car-dealership owner, she had been a member of the quintessentially in-crowd at Dothan High School. My late father, Charles, was an only child. When he was a small boy, his father, a grocery wholesaler, died of tuberculosis. My father was an ROTC graduate of Alabama Polytechnic Institute (now Auburn University) and a World War II veteran. After 13 years in the military, he resigned for a reason that still remains unclear. He struggled in the civilian world for many years before he finally landed a job as a case worker for the Alabama welfare department. He hated the Vietnam War—"we have no business in that god-forsaken hell hole"—and abhorred the policies of Lyndon Johnson—"that sanctimonious [expletive deleted]." He never missed *Meet the Press* or *Face the Nation* on Sunday mornings, especially when Wallace was railing against liberal bureaucrats who probably carried nothing but "peanut-butter-and-jelly sandwiches" in their fancy briefcases. The few times I saw him laugh came when we watched those shows together.

He was a disciplinarian and spare with praise. Not one to accept excuses for doing something incorrectly, he was just as tough with himself. Once during my pre- and early teens, he had to suspend our allowances—but not the chores assigned that went with them—for several years because of hard times. He kept track of every dollar he owed us in a gray and dark red ledger book and eventually repaid us with interest. He was a perfectionist and had no patience for quitters, which, in his mind, included anyone who stopped trying before every conceivable alternative had been explored. His mantra was to go all out on anything you try, and do not stop until you get it right. He insisted that his three sons take advanced math and science courses in high school, and then he expected good grades, which, to his disappointment, we never achieved. His discipline and common sense served me well. Although a conservative, he was open minded, welcomed lively debate about politics, government, and social mores, and had a talent for asking penetrating questions. He had pushed us toward liberal arts educations.

I gravitated toward English, political science and international relations at the University of Montevallo, a small liberal arts college near Birmingham, and graduated in 1970. After a year at *The Dothan Eagle,* I landed a reporting job at *The Greensboro Daily News* (later *The News & Record*) in Greensboro, N.C. Greensboro, a clean, well-governed city, was the home of the notorious Woolworth's store, where a greasy-spoon lunch counter became the birthplace of the civil rights sit-in strategy.

In Greensboro, I built a modest portfolio of investigative clips, including a securities fraud scheme, dangerous laxity in fire inspection efforts in the public schools, problems with the housing inspection program, a complex and racially sensitive controversy over a proposed merger of three independent school systems, and several more. In most of them, I did the bulk of the reporting on an as-time-permitted basis, gaining the luxury of full-time work on them during the sprint-to-the-end stage. But I was predominantly a local government, spot news reporter whose primary duty was to churn out four or five stories every week. I covered cops, government, the courts, general assignments, and state and local education.

In hindsight, the mix of investigative and spot news and beat reporting was the perfect foundation for the future course of my career. I had come to feel at home in the legal, law enforcement and bureaucratic worlds, a comfort zone that I found to be transferable wherever I went. Moreover, the intensely local reporting experience provided an excellent opportunity to intimately understand the interplay between those worlds and the public, particularly how the former reacted to and influenced the latter. Finally, because my editors were so thoroughly versed in community affairs, the level of accountability they imposed on their reporters was excruciatingly demanding.

In 1981, I entered graduate school at the University of North Carolina at Greensboro, where I studied American history. I specialized in the civil rights movement, and, for the first time in my life, I was forced to analyze and study my own history. My thesis on "The Birmingham Movement," had a reportorial, revisionist quality, but my thesis committee also wanted a long first-person preface on growing up as part of the quiet, white middle class in the midst of a decade of racial turmoil. I rationalized my own apolitical, teenage silence, but could not explain my father's. My only memory now is that the politics of fear and status quo played eloquently and loudly back then. Few in that age of conformity, especially those with a military mentality like my father, even thought about publicly challenging it.

I held on to my job at the paper while working on my master's degree, which I earned in 1984. By 1989, I was becoming increasingly interested in long-term project reporting, and I wanted to focus entirely on investigative and explanatory reporting. I moved on to *The Orlando Sentinel,* hoping to earn a spot as a projects reporter.

Brazil and I joined the *Sentinel* at the same time, and Ludden, then the regional editor, hired us both for reporting jobs in the Lake County bureau. Although I did not know what the *Sentinel's* bureau system was like in years past, it impressed me when I arrived there in 1989. In Greensboro, I had been a "bureau chief" in two assignments, but that was a joke; I was the only reporter in each. At the *Sentinel*'s Lake County Bureau, I was one of 10 or 12 reporters, plus an array of stringers who contributed reams of copy every day. We had two photographers, two editors, an advertising department and our own newspaper, *The Lake Sentinel,* which came with the main newspaper. The paper's mission was to cover that county so massively that the residents would see us, rather than the local *Daily Commercial,* as the hometown newspaper. "We were the growth part of the company," Ludden said, referring to the *Sentinel*'s far-flung regional bureau system. "I was trying to bring in high-class people, and we were doing more and better stuff than before."[11] My bureau colleagues were not novices. I was the most experienced among them, but all of us were veterans, and most of us had been hired by Ludden. We were a close-knit group and we lived for three things: to kick *The Daily Commercial*'s ass, get our stuff in the main sheet and get downtown.

Before his editing days at the *Sentinel,* Ludden did investigative reporting and clearly wanted his bureaus to follow suit. In our recruiting conversation, I told Ludden of my ambition to focus entirely on project reporting. "We do that out here," he said. That's all I recall of his response, but I believed him. A few weeks later, when I got the go-ahead for a big race relations project that I had proposed, I knew I had made the right decision to join the *Sentinel,* even if it was a bureau job.

Brazil had been a general assignment reporter with the now-defunct *Peninsula Times Tribune* in Palo Alto, Calif., when he arrived in Lake County. Initially, I, like a true-blue Southerner, expected to meet one of those snooty, left-coasters who never saw a Southerner who wasn't a hick.

In Lake County, though, we were both out of our element. The county was a throwback to the 1950s. I had spent most of my adult life in an image-conscious city proud of its cultural and intellectual atmosphere and its five universities and eager to show the world that racism was a thing of the past, that it was a leader in the New South. For me, fresh from graduate school, living in Lake County was like stepping back into my childhood years and into the history that I had just studied for three years at the University of North Carolina at Greensboro. With its oppressive heat and humidity, monster roaches, low-wage orange-growing economy and violent racial history, Lake County was a culture shock for Brazil and his family. Brazil was at his best when things got tough, as if the prospect of not succeeding at something—whether on a story or in a pickup basketball game—opened a spigot of adrenaline. He was mentally quick, and I was captivated by his extraordinary sense of humor. He often spotted humor in what others saw as ordinary, and he laughed hysterically at *Seinfeld* episodes. Although short, Brazil was tough as nails. On the football field, he flattened opponents twice his size and got up unscathed. He exuded an air of extreme confidence. His favorite line was, "I may be wrong, but I'm never in doubt."

Although a bearded, wine-sipping, Bay Area Californian, Brazil was fun-loving, with a frat-boy spirit, and he professed conservative social and religious views to the right of my own. His wife, Louanne, was a stay-at-home mom who held strong antiabortion beliefs. About our partnership, he liked to joke that "you were the reasonable and rational one, and I was the asshole and unpredictable one." He was right about the unpredictable part, and that, plus his creativity, is what made our combination an effective one. I, like most of his colleagues, respected his writing talent, and I learned a lot from it. I identified with his never-give-up persistence.

In Lake County, my growing interest in civil rights issues brought us together on the race relations project. I had proposed it as a two-person endeavor just two weeks after I joined the paper. It eventually ensnared Brazil and three or four other reporters at various stages. It was on that project that I also began forging a long relationship with Ludden.

Ludden is a tall, taciturn man and a big-picture thinker. Because of a habit of thinking out loud, he's given to long, drawn-out answers to questions that often start with seemingly unrelated anecdotes, but that invariably become sharply relevant. Conversations with him take time and undivided attention, but they're worth it.

He also was an aggressive journalist. During the eight years I worked with him, he frequently displayed absolutely no patience with public officials who hinted at withholding public records or closing meetings. His message was simple: Give us the records now or we will see you in court. Florida has the most open sunshine laws in the country, and Ludden milked them for everything he could squeeze out of them. He joined the *Sentinel* in 1980, also in the Lake County bureau as a reporter, but quickly became a regional projects reporter. He took on a project about the Mariel boatlift that ran for 10 days. He wrote about refugees, the space shuttle, prisons, the death penalty, piracy in the Caribbean and drug smuggling. The *Sentinel* nominated him twice for the Pulitzer Prize, once for "The New Immigrants" and the other for the first launch of the space shuttle. His management career started in 1983 when he became editor of the *Sentinel*'s Osceola bureau, which led to his position as regional editor in 1986. Projects he edited collected another nine Pulitzer nominations and a string of national awards.[12]

He was an aggressive writing editor as well, which rubbed some reporters wrong. For me, Ludden was an important influence on my journalistic thinking, which had always been expansive on the reporting side but constricted by a nuts-and-bolts writing mentality. In the early 1980s, I had one Greensboro editor who had started broadening that view, but he didn't stay at the *News & Record* long. Although his coaching was cut short, he planted a seed of thought that at least opened my mind to the notion of writing with power and confidence. Ludden would help that thought take root. When I went to Orlando, I was still governed in daily practice by a very narrow understanding of what journalists could do in the writing process. In the Lake County race relations project, Ludden forced me to step back from my reporter's notebooks and analyze the larger meaning of their contents, to be more bold about drawing conclusions from the mountains of facts and figures that I had so diligently accumulated. The first draft of the day-one story on that project came back from him with very little editing, but a daunting message: Great stuff. Now, tell me what it all means; think bigger in the writing and you need to bump it up a notch or two; the language needs to reach "a higher plane." It suddenly reminded me of and resonated with that long-forgotten Greensboro editor's way of thinking. It was quite liberating and helped make the project a success.

In the meantime, Brazil completed an exhaustive, explanatory series on the endangered manatees, a project that earned him the Scripps Howard Foundation's

Meeman Award for environmental reporting. While the Lake County race relations project was still lurching through the editing process, Brazil was transferred to the Volusia County bureau. In late 1991, he was assigned to pursue another Vogel controversy unrelated to I-95 and drugs. It was a seemingly unjustified shooting by Vogel's SWAT deputies of a recently widowed and apparently mentally ill farmer, Helen McConnell, in rural Volusia County. Ludden pulled me out of Lake County temporarily to rejoin Brazil for a few stories on that shooting. Ludden was unrelenting in a public records battle with Vogel during the SWAT team story.

A few months later, Ludden sent me back to Volusia again to join Brazil to investigate Vogel's I-95 operation. By then, Ludden had worked successfully with us individually and as a partnership on difficult projects. Ludden knew the Vogel project would be record-intensive, long and complex and that it would require veteran reporters who could work together efficiently.[13] He had seen us work foolishly long hours before. On many occasions, Brazil and I pulled repeated all-nighters working on stories for the race relations project while still managing some fairly intense discussions about religion, politics, family, raising children, the nature of friendship and sports. He and I and our families had grown close over the years. At critical points in our work and at our own expense, we sent them packing—Cheryl and our 14-year-old son Richard back to North Carolina and Louanne and their one child (at the time) to San Francisco—so we could "zone out" on the project at hand.

Ludden became deeply involved in the project, despite his responsibilities as regional editor. "It was not the kind of thing where I felt I needed to be looking over your shoulders to make sure nothing bad happened," he said. "It was really that I felt it was as much my project as yours, and it was really important to me. It was a labor of love for me, just as it was for you."

Getting on the Paper Trail

Brazil and I went after the sheriff's I-95 seizure records as soon I as got up to speed. The files were called forfeiture cases because the department had to petition a civil court to order that the seized cash be forfeited to the department. We focused on 199 cases in which the deputies seized the motorists' cash, but did not arrest them. In 62 additional cash-seizure cases, the deputies found enough evidence to make arrests. It seemed logical to concentrate on the 199 cases to find out how they justified seizing the cash without making arrests.

Getting into the files was surprisingly easy. Although we had a right to the forfeiture files under Florida's Sunshine Law, Vogel could have seriously delayed our investigation by forcing us to initiate legal action and throwing up administrative procedures that would slow our search considerably or allow him to carefully monitor every record we wanted.

Our strategy was to gain full and free access without showing our hand. We wanted to avoid another records battle, and I carried a streak of paranoia that made me worry that someone in Vogel's office would start pulling documents from the files or altering them if they knew what we suspected. We gave Vogel and his attorney no reason to think that we wanted to search his records to see if the pattern Brazil had seen in that file sampling was indicative of the entire program. Being vague without lying, we told department officials we were fascinated by the program's success and the deputies' uncanny ability to sense who was a drug dealer. We said we wanted to talk to the SET deputies, spend a night riding along with one on I-95 and do a thorough in-depth story about it. That apparently satisfied him.

In hindsight, I suspect Mike Ludden's aggressiveness in the SWAT team story a year earlier may have played a major role in getting those file drawers opened up so easily. Brazil believes that Vogel simply thought we were going to write a glowing story and that no one in Vogel's office really knew what was in those records. The overwhelming majority of press coverage had been positive, often openly laudatory, so Vogel could well have thought we would "lead that parade," Brazil said.[14] Ludden and I, viewing the situation with the knowledge gained afterward, believe Vogel was blinded by his zealotry, his unquestioning faith in the rightness and righteousness of that drug interdiction program.[15] He firmly believed that he was simply taking money only from drug dealers and no one else and putting a huge dent in the drug trade. He also believed that even before we started viewing the files that we were personally opposed to the forfeiture law.[16] At that moment, I did not know enough about how the law was working to form an opinion, but after our investigation I saw numerous ways the law could be improved. Nevertheless, Vogel's staff gave us total access to the forfeiture files, which they said contained all closed cases (we were not allowed to examine pending cases). His staff simply stayed out of our way. They showed us the file drawers and said have at it. They even let us use their copying machines, which meant no one in the office would know which documents we were copying.

We spent two weeks, working six to eight hours each day working that copy machine. Ludden told us to work nonstop. Don't read anything, he said. Don't talk to anyone; don't even take bathroom breaks; just get in and get out. "I was completely nervous about losing access," Ludden said.[17] So, we flipped pages, cleared paper jams, stacked and stuffed and pushed that copy button a million times as fast as we could, fearing that at any moment someone would get nervous and pull the plug. When the paper began to pile up, we would cart the stack out the door and lock it in our car trunk. Brazil and I were two obsessed, copying fools, copying everything—scraps of paper, sticky notes, extra copies of documents, message slips, things that we were not supposed to copy, and even the file folders themselves. The longer we stayed, the more curious deputies and sheriff's staffers became and the more conspicuous I felt. We seldom saw Vogel. Occasionally, we had to discreetly cover documents when an employee needed to use the copy machine, but we worked undisturbed for the most part. When we finished, Brazil and I had duplicated Vogel's forfeiture files in all cases in which no one was arrested. I had never before or since enjoyed such convenient, unfettered, unmonitored access to public records.

As Ludden suggested, we did not stop to ponder what we copied, but we caught snatches of what the records contained. We did not need to dwell on a file to see instantly whether the motorist was a minority. Virtually every non-arrest seizure case involved a minority. The amounts of money involved also were readily decipherable, because it was on the folder tab, and we were astonished to see so many cases involving very small amounts. It was more than a smoking gun. "It was a smoking arsenal," Brazil recalled. "And you could have seen it from space."[18]

Getting the records turned out to be the easy part. Completely understanding them would take more time. We had to know what we were looking for. To figure out whether the law was abused, we had to clearly understand precisely how it was supposed to work. We also had to understand officialdom's explanations about the program's purpose and successes. So, many of our questions during the first weeks of the investigation were mostly informational, an effort to view the program solely from the sheriff's department's perspective. Sgt. Jones and Melvin Stack, a local attorney hired by Vogel to handle the legal end of the forfeiture cases, were good sources for that.

We immersed ourselves in the legal nuances of the state seizure law, the case law that interpreted it and a national law on which it was modeled. The seizure act was written to use against criminals to deny them the fruits of their illegal acts. And the courts said its procedural provisions—although weak—afforded people whose cash or property was seized a sufficiently fair legal process. We also had to become versed on the concept of being innocent until proven guilty, Fourth Amendment provisions against warrantless searches and seizures, and 14th Amendment protections against deprivation of property without "due process of law." We interviewed legal experts on the rights of the officers and motorists. We studied case law on racial profiling, the definition of consent to search and the criteria for establishing probable cause. Because the seizures were civil matters rather than criminal cases, we brushed up on the nuances separating the legal meanings of the various standards of proof. Most readers understood the concept of proving something beyond a reasonable doubt, which is the criminal court standard of proof. It became the basis for explaining the lower standard of proof that applied to forfeiture cases—the preponderance of the evidence—if a motorist chose to challenge the cash seizure in a civil court trial. If an arrest was made along with the cash seizure, the deputies filed a separate criminal case as well as the civil forfeiture case.

Probe Reveals Charm-and-Pounce Tactic

With that background work and the copies of Vogel's forfeiture files, we were off to a stunningly fast start. I felt we had control of most everything we would need to discover what was going on out on I-95. I knew we could get a story out of this effort, but I did not know what that story would be. In my experience, the original hypothesis had never survived an investigation without being disproved or significantly altered. I have chased so many supposedly promising tips that did not pan out or could not be proven with tangible evidence, my biases are usually against the validity of the tip. My initial response to so-called hot tips is "That's too good to be true." So, on the Vogel story, I, in a sense, wiped the slate clean as we began working the I-95 operation.

My ride-along with Sgt. Jones was part of an effort to see the program in the field in whatever way they chose to present it. Although the squad would be on its best behavior in front of a reporter, I hoped its members had not yet figured out what our line of questioning was. I was not too concerned about seeing a show, because I knew the forfeiture files eventually would reveal how the system really worked.

Although the photographer's careless comment probably alerted Jones to our suspicions, it may have even diverted his attention from other areas that I was interested in. The ride-along provided some key evidence. The fact that Jones shined his car lights across the lanes to watch motorists speed by was circumstantial evidence that he was looking for more than a traffic violation; he was trying to identify the race of the drivers, an allegation he and Vogel always denied. What I observed that night and what we learned later from the department's files revealed how deputies used charm and trickery to win the motorists' cooperation.

Here's is how a typical stop worked. The deputy stopped motorists for very minor traffic infractions—burned out tag lights, driving five miles over the speed limit, following too closely—ones that would justify warnings rather than citations. Jones also said seeing a motorist drive precisely at the speed limit became a suspicious element to him. It was as if any innocent act, in itself, became a suspicious one, an action meant to cover illegal activity. Every gray was seen as black. All the team needed was three or four such interpretations, and they had established a pattern that created the probable cause they were seeking to justify confiscation at the roadside stage of the legal process.

After the stop, the deputy became an actor. He was paternal and friendly, an officer who was merely worried about the drivers' safety. He gave no indication that he considered them drug suspects. As he examined their licenses, he chatted and laughed with the motorists. He admired their vehicles and called their children "precious." The charmed motorists made off-the-cuff small talk, unaware that the deputy's tape recorder was running and that he could and would use their chatter against them. Deputies often selected comments that the officers would later describe as contradictory to comments they had extracted from an equally unsuspecting traveling companion. After returning their licenses and urging them to drive carefully, the deputy and the motorists would turn and start walking back to their vehicles. Then, with timing honed by repetition and synchronized to seize the perfect instant of stunned confusion that freezes prey under surprise attack, the deputy would stop, turn, and with two or three short, fast questions, score what he wanted all along—consent to search:

> By the way, Mr. Smith, you aren't carrying any bombs, guns or drugs are you?
> No, no. I don't have anything like that.
> You don't mind if I take a quick look, do you?
> No, I don't mind. You just go right on.
> Thanks, I appreciate that. Why don't you just take a seat in my car? You'll be a lot more comfortable.

As the motorists sat in the cruiser, a hidden tape recorder rolled to catch any incriminating comments. Through the front windshield, they watched as the deputy, joined by other deputies, swarmed their car. The quick look had turned into an invasive search and detention, a vehicular ransacking. The motorists watched helplessly as the uniformed strangers opened their luggage and rifled through their clothing, toiletries, and other personal, perhaps embarrassing, items that might turn up. The officers would sift through glove compartments, pull things from under the seats, take out the spare tires, open the hood, check the wheel wells, bang on the tires. If they found money, the once friendly, neighborly deputy, who had now turned into a cop out to make a case, confronted the motorists.[19]

In one stop, the officer's tape recorder captured the dénouement, this one of Selena Washington, a Miami-bound Charleston woman. "Right now, we believe this is drug money," the deputy, who had just found $19,000, said to Washington, who, stunned and scared, sat in the back seat of the officer's cruiser with her cousin. As the owner of several homes in Charleston, she explained that one had been severely damaged recently by Hurricane Hugo. The money was from loans from family members to pay for construction materials in Miami to repair her home. Price gougers all along the Carolina coast had sent the price of construction materials skyrocketing, and she was going to Miami where relatives could help her find lower prices and where she presumed she would need cash to buy supplies. She pleaded with the deputies to call her hometown to verify her information:

> "You can go and call back to Charleston and ...," she began, before the deputy interrupted her.
> "Well, we can't do that tonight. So just let me finish my investigation."
> "Oh, OK. I'm sorry."

The deputy leaves, and the woman starts frantically reciting the 23rd Psalm over and over. The deputy finally returns.

> "We believe this is drug money right now."
> "No sir, whatever you want to do, we can do. You look through my papers and see who I is [sic]."
> "We'll do that."[20]

The deputy consults with other deputies and returns to the motorist asking for proof. She gives him several names of people he can call to verify her story, but the deputy declines the invitation. "He [another deputy] feels this is drug money. He's going to confiscate it. You have a right to follow us [back to the station] to get a receipt." Despite repeated protests, the deputy takes the money.[21]

That cash seizure was larger than most, but they usually took most anything the deputies discovered by declaring it suspected drug proceeds. Nearly one-fifth was less than $5,000. Often they took less than $2,000; sometimes they took as little as $300. Those details of the traffic-stop process became a key part of the story.[22]

Records: A "Trove of Truth"

The forfeiture files were a gold mine, a "treasure trove of truth," as Brazil recalled.[23] The department's entire case against the motorists was in those files. From those papers, we could document the deputies' reasons for pulling a motorist over, their interpretations of the motorists' words and actions, and everything the deputies found inside the vehicles. The files also contained the reports of detectives who conducted an investigation after the seizure and records showing whether the motorists had criminal histories. Those files, in conjunction with the legal research, helped us figure out precisely how Vogel adhered to the letter of the law, manipulating it in such a way that he was able to take money from innocent people with scanty evidence that fell far short of proving that the money was illegal.

The law's flimsy standard of proof gave Vogel's deputies carte blanche to take any amount of money from just about any motorist for almost any reason. In their view, the standard, known as "probable cause" in legal parlance, let them take the money if they could list three or four observations or facts that they considered evidence of illegal activity. According to those files, the incriminating evidence included traces of cocaine on the money, nervousness, too much luggage, too little luggage, a wrinkled military uniform, the way the money was folded, if the money was packaged in $100 denominations, if the money was in $20 denominations, if the money was packaged in small denominations, if the statements of the vehicles' occupants conflicted with one another, if the origin of the trip was from a city known as a drug center, if the destination was to a city known as drug center, and if the money was carried in a Crown Royal bag, which is considered a common way drug dealers carry money. Hiding the money in a safe place became suspicious.[24]

Just having what the deputies believed was a large amount of cash was an element of suspicion. Although carrying a wad of money conflicts with the credit-card culture of the educated middle class, it is not unusual to run across many people who carry cash for a variety of reasons. Many don't trust the banks because of bad financial experiences in their pasts or their fear of the free-spending allure of credit cards. We ran across people who had cash because they pay their employees in cash. I knew a woman in our Lake County bureau and her husband who kept money buried in a hole in the backyard. Later in our investigation, we ran across a state legislator who pulled a roll of $100 bills out of his pants pocket. I have encountered numerous off-the-grid survivalist and militia types who eschew the institutional and governmental connections that a cashless culture entails.

The Contraband Forfeiture Act was clearly intended to give law enforcement a tool to deny real criminals the fruits of their crime. It also provided officers a way to counter drug traffickers' common practice of hiring "mules" to carry huge amounts of money but who knew nothing about the crime that produced the cash. Our reporting recognized the tactics of drug traffickers and the law's value in dealing with them. But our reporting also saw how Vogel's drug interdiction program bent the law beyond its purpose.

They interpreted virtually any amount of money as suspicious. The law did not require them to show a direct connection between the motorists' allegedly suspicious actions and the money or to any specific criminal violation. Any suspicious action, regardless of what may have motivated the action, was seen as one piece of the overall picture that painted the motorists' money as drug money.

Once the deputies made that determination, a momentous legal shift, one that upended a basic principle of American jurisprudence, occurred: The motorists—based on the weakest of evidence—were presumed guilty until they could prove themselves innocent. It was a reversal of a legal right that even the most heinous criminals enjoy, the right to be presumed innocent until proven guilty by due process of law. The motorists had to prove they were not drug dealers, and, unlike the meager burden imposed on the deputies, they would be required to build a solid, evidentiary case.

After the roadside seizure, a detective would take over the case and launch an investigation to seek incriminating information that could be used if the motorist challenged the seizure in court. As it turned out, our reporting showed that the detectives seldom found additional evidence that tied the money to a drug deal or gave them a basis for filing criminal charges in these cash-only cases. Nevertheless, the lack of evidence didn't matter, because the legal sparring that would follow kept it out of the courtroom.

The motorists, through their attorneys, engaged in that sparring with Vogel's forfeiture attorney, Melvin Stack. Stack was a private lawyer hired on a retainer to work exclusively on cash-seizure cases. Vogel's full-time in-house attorney worked on the department's other legal matters. In the legal fight, the motorists' lawyers exchanged letters with Stack and submitted financial documents and other evidence to try to show the money was not contraband. These exchanges lasted for six or more months. When the case got close to trial, the forfeiture attorney would offer an out-of-court settlement in which he would agree to return a portion of the seized cash in exchange for the motorist signing a waiver agreeing not to sue the sheriff. By then the motorist had little choice except to agree. To fight on eventually would have consumed the entire amount of the seizure in legal expenses.

Although they probably would have been victorious in court, motorists would not likely win suits to force Vogel to pay their legal expenses. To accomplish that, they would have to prove that the seizing deputy did not have enough evidence on the roadside to show he had probable cause to believe that the money was contraband. Because very little evidence is needed to meet such a low standard of proof, the court probably would have sustained the deputies' roadside decisions to seize the money.[25] So Vogel had devised a way to seize millions of dollars from motorists, often on nothing more than suspicion that they were drug couriers.

Making Your Own Luck

The forfeiture files contained dozens of cases we could have used to illustrate the unfairness of Vogel's use of the law. But to show that an abuse of power often ensnares the innocent, we wanted to focus on motorists with unblemished criminal records. A lucky break helped us do that. As we started investigating individual cash seizure cases and tracing the criminal backgrounds of individual motorists, we realized that one of our lucky breaks had occurred early in the investigation when we arranged to copy Vogel's files. Vogel's in-house attorney decided not to take the time to screen the folders for legally confidential material, so she did not remove FBI rap sheets and records from the state's computer network or redact notes between deputies and the forfeiture attorney that were scrawled in the margins of public records in the file. The in-house attorney said she was going to leave the confidential material in the file and "trust us" not to look at or use it. She tossed that concession out unexpectedly, and we were caught flat-footed. We didn't know what to say. So we didn't say anything, and, inexplicably, she didn't demand a response. We copied every single confidential document. Although FBI rap sheets are often incomplete, they helped us immensely, because they revealed everything the detectives knew about the motorists' criminal backgrounds.

In case after case, the detectives' investigations failed to come up with any evidence linking the seized money to illegal drugs or any illegal activity. The detectives' reports also were important for what they said about many of the motorists—their records were clean. In three or four files, we found documents that bore some handwritten marginal notations to the forfeiture attorney that strongly suggested their interest was in seizing money even when the evidence favored the motorist. One such notation was about the results of a detective's investigation in a cash seizure:

"Mel: Paul indicated pretty strongly that they can turn up nothing concrete on this guy."

Nevertheless, the department kept the $19,000 seizure for six months, at which point the sheriff's department agreed to return 75 percent in return for the driver's written promise not to sue. The driver's attorney got a portion of the returned money as legal fees. In those cases, the seizures and final decisions to keep the money rested on deputies' suspicions, assumptions and opinions and a totally negative interpretation of every action and statement.[26]

Culling the Cases

The forfeiture files contained thousands of pages of documents. We picked through the files one by one. Although we worked separately, we decided on a long list of facts we would extract from each folder, such as the race and name and other identifying facts about the motorists, their criminal records, amount of money they lost, their lane of travel, the deputies' names, the mile marker where the stop occurred, the traffic violation for which they were stopped and whether their vehicle was a rental, privately owned and out-of-state. We would put that information in a paper database. Although the *Sentinel* had a computer-assisted reporting capability then, it wasn't available to us. Our database management system consisted of a hand calculator and four white posterboards taped together and covered with a dizzying magic-marker grid filled with the data plucked from the forfeiture files. We also used a five-star rating system to symbolize our initial assessment of each case based on the information in the files. Five stars represented cases with the weakest evidence justifying confiscation of the motorists' cash. As each of us came upon a case that seemed promising, Brazil and I often discussed it to determine whether it merited further investigation into the motorist's background. We eventually went through all 199 cash-seizure cases in which no one was arrested, conducting [27]more in-depth investigations on dozens of them separately. At first we decided not to go through files for the arrest cases. The motorists in those cases were caught with drugs, so we didn't see any reason to question those seizures.

As we plowed through file after file and filled up our posterboard database, we searched for motorists who had no criminal record or anything suspicious in their backgrounds so that we could track them down for interviews. In one case, a deputy seized $3,989 from a black Navy reservist from Savannah, Ga., who said he was heading to school in Miami. The deputy seized the cash, because he thought the motorist acted nervous, wasn't carrying enough luggage, had folded the money in groups of $100, and had left a wrinkled uniform and scuffed shoes in the trunk, which, in the deputy's opinion, was something a legitimate military man would never allow. But the motorist produced Navy pay stubs and a résumé showing steady employment. His record contained no criminal charges. The margin space on one of the documents contained a note from a detective to the forfeiture attorney suggesting that the seizing officer, Sgt. Bobby Jones, the SET field commander, had doubts about the seizure. The note read: "Bobbie [sic] Jones doesn't care if the money is returned."[28]

The evidence mounted daily. In file after file, the pattern held firm: Vogel's deputies were abusing the Contraband Seizure Act, violating people's rights, acting as judge and jury on the roadside of I-95, targeting minorities and taking money from innocent people as well as drug couriers. In all of the investigative projects I had worked in the past and since, the initial hypothesis underwent many changes as the evidence came in. But in this one, a clear pattern consistent with the original hypothesis emerged early in the file search and never deviated. Almost all of the motorists who lost their cash to the SET deputies were black or Hispanic. Cash seizures over $100,000 were rare. They made arrests in only one out of every four seizure cases. Even rarer was the existence of real traffic law enforcement; the deputies wrote no more than one traffic citation every four months. They frequently let serious traffic violators, including drunken drivers, drive away. In another tell-tale development, we found that instead of quickly and passively disappearing as a drug dealer might be expected to do, most of the motorists went home, hired lawyers, gathered evidence and fought for months to get their money back. Only about a fourth gave up without a fight. In almost every challenged seizure, the sheriff's department and the motorists' lawyers fought for six to eight months until shortly before a trial became imminent, when the department made the settlement offer.[29]

Confronting Big Story Bias

As the weeks passed and the number of five-star cases mounted and the picture remained sharp, I sensed we had a big, successful story. I think the sensation hit me somewhere just past the halfway point in the forfeiture files when we saw that the statistical pattern was remaining intact and the behavior of the deputies was continuing in its script-like way. I was getting excited, but at that moment, the thought of a big award like the Pulitzer didn't occur to me. At that stage of my career, my level of thinking was that you had to work for *The New York Times* or *The Washington Post* to get that. At some point toward the end of the reporting but before the writing started, I remember hearing a colleague in the bureau— not Brazil—allude to something about "avoiding the P word." I had to ask what the P stood for. The superstition was something to the effect that if you say the P word before you finish the project, it won't happen. I don't remember my reaction (I hope I rolled my eyes).

Brazil and Ludden say the Pulitzer never crossed their minds. Brazil recalls that the first time anyone broached the subject to him came after he let another journalist read an early draft and the colleague's reaction was: "You guys are going to win the Pulitzer."[30]

For me and for so many other journalists I have known, the tantalizing feeling that you are on to a big story is more influential than political or ideological bias. I haven't met many reporters who would back off of a good story because it might conflict with their political leanings. In fact, the drive to get the story is, itself, a bias, which is why I value partners and editors. The good ones keep you honest with their devil's advocate role. In this story, Ludden said he felt part of his role as editor was "to try to prove Vogel was right."[31] But editors' responses depend on the information reporters give them. So Brazil and I were the first line of defense against bias.

Finding the Keeper Cases

The give-and-take among us produced the keeper cases. Those were the cash-seizure anecdotes that would get in the story. Selecting them would be crucial if we expected all of our work to do any good. The seizure law was written to prevent guilty people from getting rich from crime. Because most readers probably had not committed any serious crimes in their lives, we decided not to use any cases in which the motorists' criminal record contained a felony or serious misdemeanor before or after the seizure. From the strictly legal perspective of judges, defense lawyers and civil libertarians, violating the rights of someone with a criminal record is as egregious as violating the rights of someone with no prior record. But we were not writing for lawyers. In the drug-scare frenzy of the time, readers were in no mood for a lecture on an abstraction about how governments that are allowed to violate the rights of criminals will soon proscribe the rights of innocent people. "You can argue principle on people who are dirty, but not in the court of public opinion," Brazil said. "The strongest way to make the case was to choose people who we honestly believed had done nothing wrong, and we worked really hard to find those people."[32]

With that notion in mind we decided that even if motorists had clean records at the time of the seizure, we would not use them in the story if we found any record of criminal behavior after the seizure. Ludden believed "it would have been a lazy workaround" to highlight a motorist who had committed a crime after the seizure and defend it by saying Vogel's deputies didn't know about those crimes when they took their money. "We wanted grandmas," Ludden said. Although we would never call them innocent in the story, we wanted to satisfy ourselves as far as humanly possible that they were at least innocent in the public records at the time of publication.[33]

Finding that kind of satisfaction was the most difficult, grueling and worrisome part of the investigation. "I thought it was a huge risk to hold somebody up for exoneration whose past could come back to bite us," Ludden said. "That was the most troubling thing I could think of in terms of reporting."[34] In other words, let us make sure one of our victim-motorists does not turn out to be serial killer. In the early 1990s, without access to online records, we had no foolproof, systematic way to ensure that we didn't miss an arrest or conviction on the records of any of the motorists who we were going to hold up for exoneration. The FBI rap sheets were helpful, but their value ended at the date of the seizure, and even up to that date we were not entirely confident of the completeness of their contents. So our investigation had to confirm their information and pick up where they left off. With the identification information in the files and rap sheets and our newspaper librarian's research, we managed to get a fairly good record of all of the towns and counties where the motorists in our most promising cases lived. To get the information, we groveled to court clerks. We talked to local police chiefs, detectives, prosecutors and the motorists' neighbors. We checked prison records to make sure none of our most promising motorists had served time.

The prison check's importance emerged when I was investigating one of my favorite cases. The SET deputies had stopped a black man, who was with his wife and several other people, including some children. He was carrying a small amount of money considering the carload of people with him, and the justification for the seizure seemed minor. In the follow-up probe, the detective found no evidence that the money was contraband. The rap sheet contained no other convictions or arrest. It appeared to be the perfect case.

I spent a week trying to locate him. I left several messages at addresses that showed up in the forfeiture files. His attorney was no help. I talked to local law enforcement in several towns where he had lived. He had not run afoul of the law at any of those locations. It was like he had fallen off the face of the earth. Finally, just as an afterthought, I called the state prison in one of the states where he had lived. There he was. He was serving a short sentence on an unrelated felony drug arrest that had occurred several months after his encounter with SET deputies in Volusia County. Although the cash seizure still was unjustified based on the evidence the deputies had found, we dropped him from our list of candidates for sidebar and anecdotal cases.

At times, we eliminated motorists with pristine records because somebody didn't feel comfortable about the person. Brazil and I played devil's advocate with each other. Then the three of us discussed each case that Brazil and I proposed for use in the story. Ludden examined the documentation. Brazil or I or both of us would defend the motorist and Ludden tried to punch holes in our case. "If I shot holes in it, we threw it out," Ludden recalled. We tossed one case simply because Ludden thought the motorist's car was too expensive for his financial means. My prisoner case probably would have been eliminated even if I had not tracked him to a penitentiary, because his apparent disappearance into oblivion was suspicious. By the time we finished investigating each case, Ludden was convinced that even if the sheriff's department later found some criminal action that we missed, we could legitimately argue that the department went searching for the information long after the seizure and solely as part of an effort to rebut our stories, not because they knew anything about the motorists' behaviors when they confiscated the money.

In the writing process, we employed another technique designed to present the case to the readers in a neutral way. It reminded me of people who like to resolve a tough decision by drawing a line down the middle of a piece of paper and listing the pros in one column and the cons in the other. In a similar style, we presented case study sidebars in a list-like way, in which we reported evidence pointing to a motorist's innocence and evidence pointing to guilt. As example, consider the case of Jorge Nater, 48, and a friend, Francisco Muriel, who were pulled over on Feb. 4, 1991, for following too closely by Deputy Ray Almodo-var. Almodovar searched Nater's car and seized $36,990. Nater told Almodovar he had sold an apartment complex in Puerto Rico and was headed to Brevard County, where four of his sons lived. He said he was going to Pompano Beach to buy a home. We wrote:

> Pointing to Nater's guilt:
> He was more nervous than the average person, Almodovar said. When asked where he was going, he had to look up the address.
> Finally when Nater and Muriel were asked to wait in a patrol car during the search, a hidden microphone recorded Nater saying to Muriel that, if they were allowed to leave, maybe they should hide the money in the tire.
> Pointing to his innocence:
> Documentation confirming his real-estate transaction, including sworn affidavit from the buyer; no criminal record; testimonial letters from the mayor, police chief and a priest in his hometown.

Nater tried for nine months with the help of a lawyer to recover the money, but finally gave up and reached a settlement agreement requiring him to give the sheriff $6,000 and a written waiver of his right to sue. He had to pay his law-yer 25 percent of the amount he recovered. He said he realized that even if he won in court, he couldn't recover the cost of going to court.[35]

We used the same technique in the case of Edwin Johnson, who lost his $38,923, which had been profit from two Miami businesses, Ed's Lawn Services and Thirst Quenchers. He said he had owned the latter enterprise for eight years. He said he didn't use banks because of a bad experience from a wage garnish-ment following a lawsuit in 1985.

> Pointing to his guilt:
> Johnson, who is black, was nervous. He didn't carry enough luggage. When asked to specify the amount of cash, he said, "30-some thousand," not the actual amount.
> Pointing to his innocence:
> Johnson's attorney, David Raben, provided accounting documents, tax forms, canceled checks, testimonial letters from Johnson's clients, records verifying the wage-garnishment story and a resume detailing Johnson's work record.

The sheriff's department found no criminal history, except an old misde-meanor that the department's attorney dismissed as insignificant. After a six-month legal battle, Johnson agreed to a settlement that forced him to give up $10,000. And he had to pay his attorney a third of the amount he got back.[36]

"What we were saying to readers [in using that technique] is that the cops should see some gray to this case," Ludden explained. Instead, the deputies concluded emphatically that the motorists were drug couriers.[37]

The Confrontation

About a month to six weeks before publication, we completed our records search and case studies and took our preliminary findings to Vogel. It was not pleas-ant. Each of us took turns asking questions about the individual cash seizures we investigated and the broader issues. He refused to respond to the specific cases, but willingly discussed all other questions. I focused on the racial targeting issue, asking specifically whether his team was targeting minorities, while Brazil grilled him about the practice of taking people's money without showing any tangible evidence that they had committed a crime.

Vogel was clearly, in Brazil's words, "taken aback by our posture and tone." We knew more about the specific cases than he did. Brazil described him as "antagonistic."[38] For his part, Vogel inaccurately wrote in his 2001 autobiography, *Fighting to Win*, that Brazil started early "hurling questions like 'why are you a racist?'" He called our questions "absurd and uncomfortable" that we posed in an "accusatory" manner and insisted that we had already written the story before we interviewed him.[39]

The story had not been written, but the evidence we had gathered was strong statistically. In many very specific cases, we wanted him to challenge our evidence, but we knew more about the individual cases than he did. Vogel continually reverted to his central contentions: his deputies randomly selected traffic violators for stops; every motorist whose money was seized was a drug dealer; the I-95 program was a resounding success that hit drug dealers where it hurt the most—in their pocketbooks. Not to be outdone by his repetitious answers, we kept repeating our central question: Don't your cash seizures essentially assume everybody is guilty until proven innocent, thereby turning a key principle of American jurisprudence upside down? At one point Vogel snapped, "Are you suggesting that we let them go and not seize the illegal drug money? If you don't like the statutes... then get the doggone statutes changed. We don't have to prove that they are guilty."[40]

Show and Tell

From the beginning of this long process, we had committed to relying on tangible evidence to make our case, to being transparent about our methods and to avoiding inconclusive he-said/she-said segments. We certainly did not want any anonymous sources in the story. We would use quotes, but only to punctuate or emphasize a fact based on tangible evidence. Although the story was about civil liberties and race, we did not use a lot of outrage quotations from the American Civil Liberties Union and the NAACP. We didn't need them. The evidence was outrageous without getting somebody to describe it as such. We also wanted to rely on original research as much as possible, even when secondary sources would suffice.

In keeping with that mode of thinking, near the end of the investigation somebody hit on the idea of the money test. Early in our study of the forfeiture files, we saw that SET deputies repeatedly cited the existence of traces of cocaine on currency as evidence that the motorist was a drug courier. They made that determination using a drug-sniffing dog, which wagged its tail or barked or alerted in some other characteristic manner when it detected cocaine. Additionally, in the rare instance when a motorist refused to give consent for a search, the deputies would bring the dog, which could supposedly alert to microscopic traces of a drug hidden anywhere in a vehicle and thus give the deputies probable cause to search the car without permission.

We knew about recent studies showing that trace amounts of cocaine could be found on virtually any bill that had been in circulation for awhile. Such findings, if accepted, rendered the traces on money useless as evidence of wrongdoing. Rather than relying on a study to raise questions about the evidentiary value of cocaine traces on dollar bills, we conducted our own test. We circulated throughout central Florida, and, without warning, went to people and asked them to exchange the money in their wallets for our money.

Our money test started with the editor of the *Sentinel,* John Haile. We got money from the chairwoman of the Volusia County Board of Commissioners, a circuit court judge, a Catholic priest, a small-town mayor, a community college president, a conservative strongly pro-law-enforcement state senator who pulled a thick roll of $100 bills from his pocket, the cash drawer of a Publix supermarket, the chief of the Leesburg Police Department, and others. We sealed the currency in separate bags and labeled them.

We went back to Sheriff Vogel to see if he would let us test the money in his wallet.

"That strikes me as somewhat offensive," he said.

We asked him to let us borrow one of his K-9s for a sniff test with our currency samples, and one of the department's representatives refused.

We hired a toxicologist to run tests on the money. He was a certified court expert and until recently had worked for the Florida Department of Law Enforcement. The tests found that all of the bills, except those that had recently gone into circulation, carried microscopic traces of cocaine easily detectible to a K-9. Haile's money had the most cocaine on it. We wrote a sidebar reporting the results, revealing our study methods in detail and reporting reactions of some of the participants when told of what we found on their money.

"I think you are on to a good story," the Leesburg police chief said.[41]

Tying Up Loose Ends

As we were wrapping up the loose ends, a gut feeling that had nagged me earlier started worrying me again. I had not paid much attention to it or even discussed it with Brazil, because more important and pressing demands kept it buried. It was about our decision months earlier not to examine forfeiture files in which drugs had been found and the motorists arrested. The decision seemed to make sense. If drugs were found and the motorist arrested, the cash seizure would be legitimate on its face, so examining those files seemed like a waste of time. We already knew the total number of arrests from statistics that the department had given us.

By not examining the case files, however, we would not be able say whether the patterns we found in the nonarrest cases continued in the arrest cases. Late in the investigation, with all of the nonarrest data safely tucked away, we decided to examine the arrest cases to see if they followed the same pattern we had found in the nonarrest cases. Brazil remembers the arrest cases did not seem important at first, because it was only over time that we began to see the overwhelming racial injustice in the program. "So, in the beginning we were just focusing on the nonarrest cases. Then the whole race issue became huge."[42]

Whatever the explanation, I returned to the sheriff's department to start plowing through arrest cases. The reception at headquarters was a bit cooler than it was during our previous visit months earlier. I did not get to use their copy machine. But I got through 46 of the 63 arrest cases before Vogel's in-house attorney threw up a roadblock. There would be no more carte-blanche access to the documents. This time, she insisted on culling all of the confidential documents from the files, an action that would have delayed publication. Nevertheless, because we had the total count of arrests, and I had managed to get through two-thirds of the arrest files, we decided to go with what we had rather than delay publication. In our story, we explained those circumstances to the reader.

As we wrapped up the reporting, I felt that the only possible wiggle room for Vogel was the fact that we had no data showing specifically what percentage of the motorists that he targeted for pullovers were minorities. Our statistics showed what happened only after the motorists had been pulled over—that among an undetermined number of traffic stops, blacks and Hispanics made up 91 percent of those in which the deputies seized cash but made no arrests. Vogel claimed he did not keep records of stops in which no one was arrested or cash seized, thus preventing us from determining what percentage of the total traffic stops involved minorities.

Taking advantage of that bit of statistical space, Vogel insisted that his deputies paid no attention to the race of the drivers when they selected traffic violators for stops. In fact, he argued that our findings just proved that among those motorists who were stopped, 90 percent of those who exhibited the mannerisms of drug couriers happened to be minorities. His deputies could not be blamed for that, he said. We did not think the public would buy that argument, but it was an out for Vogel, and, given his folk-hero status and the drug-war hysteria, it might be all the sheriff needed to diminish the impact of our findings.

Getting Scooped

About a week before publication of the three-day series, we suffered what we thought then was the reporter's worst nightmare—getting scooped. Somebody told *The Daytona Beach News-Journal* about our investigation and they published a quick story that seemed clearly designed to trump our work. Although it did not come close to the quality or depth of our work, it captured the gist of our findings. Brazil and I were stunned, but we were too busy trying to make deadline to dwell on it. They had he-said/she-said; we had evidence, I thought. But it ruined Ludden's day: "As soon as the story hit, a bunch of people showed up at my door," he said, noting that the managing editor was among the first. But the damage was more psychological—"to take the wind out of our sails"—than real, Ludden said. "It would have bothered me much more than it did if it had come anywhere close to the quality of what we were doing." To Ludden, the *News-Journal* bombshell was a strong sign that someone in the sheriff's department sat their reporters down and revealed everything that we had done just to undercut us. "Maybe they thought that would be a death blow to us," he said. We had done all of the reporting and the interviews by then, and Vogel's staff knew from our detailed questions what the stories were going to report.[43]

Our series started running in the *Sentinel* on June 14, 1992, and the *News-Journal* story was quickly forgotten. Under a banner headline that read "Tainted Cash or Easy Money?" the series began this way:

Volusia County Sheriff Bob Vogel's elite Interstate 95 drug interdiction squad has taken tens of thousands of dollars from motorists against whom there was no evidence of wrongdoing nor any criminal record.

In one case, a woman lost part of an emergency loan to fix her hurricane-damaged home. On another occasion, grandparents lost part of their retirement.

And in virtually every case, the people stopped and stripped of their cash were either black or Hispanic. Seizing cash from drug dealers is nothing new. But a review of records by *The Orlando Sentinel* raises questions about tactics and about the ethics of allowing this free-wheeling drug squad to beef up the sheriff's budget with selective traffic stops of people never charged with a crime.

The story listed a series of bullets summarizing the major findings from the 262 cases: 90 percent of the motorists who lost their money were black or Hispanic; to avoid court, Vogel's department struck a bargain with motorists, including some who were clearly drug dealers; and that the practice of using a drug-sniffing dog was questionable because most Florida currency carried traces of cocaine.[44]

It was an enormous success. Our work produced 12 stories plus charts, graphics, information boxes and photos. Gov. Lawton Chiles held a press conference to express his outrage at the abuses and to announce a task force to investigate Vogel's department, determine if other departments were abusing the law and recommend legislative reforms. That was an encouraging result. But we weren't finished yet.

The Investigation Continues

Shortly after the series ran, a lawyer called the office with some information that prompted another investigation. It revealed another missed opportunity in our initial probe. However, it also helped us with the one reporting hole that our first package had not completely filled.

The lawyer had represented one of the few I-95 motorists who had been charged and convicted of a drug offense. During the discovery process in that case, the prosecution had to turn over the evidence it would use to prosecute him. Had we investigated the criminal court files of the arrest cases, we would have discovered what the defense lawyer was bringing to our attention. Also, a video camera may have been in Sgt. Jones' cruiser the night I rode along with him, but if it was, I didn't see it.

Among the evidence that the prosecution turned over to the lawyer was a videotape showing the traffic stop in which his client had been arrested. But his client's stop wasn't the only one on that tape; there were nearly 30 more stops, in which the motorists' vehicles were stopped and searched and then allowed to drive away. Almost all of those motorists were either black or Hispanic. The videotapes, I realized, could be Brazil's "smoking arsenal," something that could establish beyond question that Vogel's deputies were targeting minorities instead of randomly selecting traffic violators for traffic stops. To Ludden, the videotapes meant Vogel had purposefully misled us when he denied earlier that they did not have any records on stops that did not yield a cash seizure or arrest.

If there was one tape for one case, there had to be more tapes for other cases, and there was. We discovered that Vogel, using dash-mounted cameras in some of the patrol cars, recorded traffic stops in which the deputies arrested the motorists, seized cash, or both. The video recordings were made to provide proof—if ever needed in court—that the motorists consented to the search.

After another public records skirmish, we got access to the tapes. Brazil and I developed a data form, enlisted the help of four other reporters and started watching videos. For the next six weeks, we watched 148 hours of video involving 1,084 stops. There could have been thousands of additional stops, but the deputies had recorded over many of the tapes, erasing the stops that had been on them originally. The story explained that caveat, but more than 1,000 stops was a healthy sampling, which we felt presented strong evidence of which drivers the deputies focused on.

In August, the *Sentinel* published a fourth package, this one with a lead story headlined, "Color of Driver Is Key to Stops in I-95 Videos." The opening went like this:

> Videotapes obtained by *The Orlando Sentinel* offer the most compelling evidence to date that Volusia County Sheriff Bob Vogel's drug squad uses skin color to decide whom to stop and search for cash on Interstate 95.
>
> There is the bewildered black man who stands on the side of the roadside trying to explain to the deputies that it is the seventh time he has been stopped.
>
> And the black man who shakes his head in frustration as his car is searched; it is the second time in minutes he has been stopped.
>
> They are among more than 1,000 people whose roadside stops are shown on videotapes obtained from the Sheriff's Office by the *Sentinel* through the state's public records law.

The bulleted items followed a few paragraphs later. One reported that almost 70 percent of the motorists targeted for stops were minorities, which we described as "enormously disproportionate, because the vast majority of interstate drivers are white." Another reported that 80 percent of the searches were of blacks and Hispanics. A third disputed the deputies' contentions that they only stopped people for legitimate traffic violations by noting they wrote just nine traffic tickets for the 1,084 drivers they pulled over.

We also compiled a sampling of the videotapes and submitted them to a law professor, a former prosecutor and two defense lawyers who had won landmark state Supreme Court cases challenging seizures under the state's forfeiture law. They concluded the seizures appeared illegal.

Gov. Chiles' general counsel described the tapes as "worse than Nixon's," a reference to President Nixon's Watergate tapes.[45]

Vogel declined to comment for the story. Much later, he dismissed the significance of the tapes, arguing that they did not cover all of the squad's stops.

Postscript

Overall, Vogel's comments in follow-up news stories and in his 2001 autobiography suggested he felt like the persecuted warrior in the war on drugs. He challenged our statistics, and he never deviated from his contention that every motorist his team took money from was a drug dealer, despite the fact that he could not find enough evidence to arrest them.

Several months after the series ran, I once stopped him coming out of a courtroom to ask for a comment about the proceedings. It was my first face-to-face encounter with him after the stories were published. I approached him from behind and called his name. He stopped abruptly and turned to face me. As I asked the question, he looked straight into my eyes. After I finished the question, a silent pause followed but he continued looking directly into my eyes. Then he responded, never turning away as he spoke, but punctuating his comment with another silent stare before turning and leaving. I do not remember what he said now, but I found it hard to forget the penetrating eye contact and the pauses.

The public reaction to the stories astounded us. Despite Vogel's best effort to dismiss them as a liberal onslaught against law enforcement, the strength of our evidence simply lifted our findings out of the liberal-versus-conservative theme. Although our findings prompted a considerable amount of hateful calls and letters to the paper from Vogel's supporters and allies, they also sparked outrage at his practices from conservatives as well as liberals. Nevertheless, they did not prompt a viable candidate to run against Vogel in the November 1992 election. So he sailed to victory on the Republican Party ticket against a weak Democratic Party candidate. Four years later, he barely squeaked past his Democratic opponent in an intensely disputed vote count that swung Vogel's way after election night when absentee ballots were tallied.

But civil suits, investigations and legislative controversy shadowed the four years of his second term. Then–Attorney General Janet Reno announced that the Justice Department would launch a criminal civil rights investigation. Several private civil rights suits were filed, the most significant of which was by the NAACP on behalf of two motorists highlighted in the stories.

Both of the legal efforts seemed doomed to failure, unless they unearthed evidence we missed. Our work showed that the problem was rooted in a law that could be easily, but legally, abused. Vogel had been very careful to stay within its confines. The videotapes showed that each stop was for a traffic violation and that the searches were legal.

Making civil or criminal cases seemed impossible absent tangible evidence, such as a written order or policy, that Vogel instructed deputies to target minorities. A civil plaintiff or a criminal prosecutor would need an admission by a believable current or former SET deputy that he made a conscious decision to stop and search motorists because of their race and that he had orders to do so. The statistics we gathered were powerful, but numbers cannot prove that an individual deputy acted in a specific case to commit a specific crime. We never found any written orders from Vogel or departmental policies that ordered deputies to target minorities and to trump up probable cause evidence to seize their money. All SET deputies denied the allegations.

Although we had followed up on a few tips about deputies willing to give statements alleging the team targeted minorities, they either decided not to talk or we felt their credibility was questionable. There was talk of a written order, but we never found it. Later, an order supposedly posted on a squad room bulletin board making a reference to stopping "ethnics" surfaced, but it was vague language on plain paper with no letterhead and no signature. Anyone with a grudge against Vogel could have written it to cast suspicion on him.

The Justice Department investigated for four years before deciding not to seek indictments, but its investigation corroborated our findings. Long after I had left the *Sentinel*, the federal prosecutor who supervised the probe wrote a stinging 33-page report to a congressional committee that was studying seizure law reform and furnished it to the *Sentinel* in response to a Freedom of Information Act request. She said the investigation found statistical, anecdotal and direct evidence that skin color was the primary reason for stopping motorists, searching their cars and taking money officers thought was suspicious. But it wasn't enough for a conviction.[46]

In his autobiography and press statements, Vogel appeared to miss the meaning of the story. His program had targeted minorities, presumed them guilty without proving it and then forced them to prove their innocence. In his book, he acted deeply and personally wounded that federal prosecutors would go after him, a Vietnam veteran and officer of the law who was dedicated to doing good and getting drug dealers. He could only guess, Vogel wrote, that they went after him because he was a Republican. He said they pursued him long after they had determined there was no evidence that he had committed a crime, because they presumed him guilty, and, now "we had to prove ourselves innocent." Bemoaning his plight, Vogel wrote he now was curious how many others had fallen victim to the system, "hounded by someone in power that had virtually every means at his or her disposal with which to turn up the heat."[47]

In the NAACP suit, a federal judge had little choice but to dismiss the case in January 1995 without submitting it to the jury, because the plaintiffs could not provide any direct evidence that the deputies who stopped them did so because of their race. The judge said they had failed to disprove the seizing deputies' contentions that they had stopped the two motorists because of the traffic law violations.[48]

The civil and criminal cases had negative and positive results. Vogel used their failure to say he had been vindicated and to claim they proved that our series was wrong.[49] On the positive side, the start of the investigation underlined the seriousness of what our series had found and pressured the legislature to act. Without them, the politicians could not have withstood the immense opposition from law enforcement to any effort to reform seizure laws.

In Washington, our series and a motorist we wrote about played a role in congressional hearings on a reform measure sponsored by U.S. Rep. Henry Hyde, R-Ill., a conservative with strong law-and-order credentials. Indicative of how the issue crossed the political spectrum, Rep. John Conyers, a liberal Democrat from Michigan, chaired the hearing and strongly supported reforms. Despite law enforcement's strong opposition, Congress passed the Civil Asset-Forfeiture Reform Act in August 2000.[50]

In Florida, the legislature wrestled with several bills calling for some tough reforms, such as prohibiting any seizures unless they are accompanied by an arrest or requiring officers to gather more evidence to justify a seizure. Another would have required the seizing agency to pay the motorists' legal bills as well as return the cash if the agency failed to prove the money was contraband.

But such measures sparked an all-out law-and-order lobbying campaign by the Florida Sheriff's Association, which argued that the reforms would emasculate a law that had proven to be a valuable tool in the war on drugs. The debate dragged on for two sessions.[51]

Meanwhile, Gov. Chiles' task force worked throughout the first of those two sessions. It never investigated Vogel's program, and confined its work to holding hearings in Tallahassee, the state capital. But again, the weight of the Sheriff's Association was heavy. The task force made several recommendations for reform, the most important being a provision to require the prevailing side in a cash seizure trial to pay the other side's legal bills. Even reformers opposed that suggestion, arguing that it would discourage motorists from challenging the seizure in court.[52]

In the meantime, as the investigations and reform efforts got under way, our series won the Pulitzer Prize for investigative reporting in April 1993. It was the paper's first reporting Pulitzer. In the middle of the newsroom celebration, I called my father in Prattville, Ala., to tell him the news. He had already learned about it. When he answered the phone, he had the encyclopedia out, and in the middle of the popping champagne corks, I listened to him read from the encyclopedia about Joseph Pulitzer. That was his way of saying he was proud. He had a heart attack about a week before the ceremony at Columbia University, but my grandmother and siblings insisted I go, that he would be upset if I missed it. The day we returned to Orlando, I called home as soon as we got back to the *Sentinel* office, where we had left our cars. I was told he was fading fast, that I should come home immediately. I went straight back to the airport, but I was too late. He had died a few hours earlier. He was 70.

About two years later, the legislature began debating a compromise to reform the state's contraband forfeiture law. It would require deputies to prove during a preliminary hearing that the preponderance of evidence showed that the money was illegal contraband. Failing that burden, they would return the money, and the agency would pay the motorists' legal fees up to $1,000. If the seizure case survived the preliminary hearing, the seizing agency would have to go to trial and meet a higher standard of proof, which is called "clear and convincing evidence," that the money was contraband. That standard is just below the burden of proof required in a criminal case, which is "beyond a reasonable doubt."[53]

The compromise passed; Chiles signed the measure; the *Sentinel* wrote about it the next day, June 14, 1995, the third anniversary of the publication of our series.

The project produced an immense impact on all of our careers. Brazil and I launched another project—this one on felony drunken drivers. But I finished that one alone, because he went to work for the *Los Angeles Times*, a paper he had longed to join for many years. He left the paper in 2000 and took a job as communications director at Mariners Church and Ministries in Irvine, Calif. He later did freelance work and media consulting for churches and other faith-based groups. Ludden became deputy managing editor for local news and later moved to Atlanta where he became senior writer for CNN Headline News' *Prime News* program. I was promoted to senior writer and assigned full-time as the projects reporter at the *Sentinel*. I remained there for about three years after publication. In 1996, perhaps needlessly worried about the future of investigative reporting at the *Sentinel,* I joined Brazil at the *Times* where we continued our partnership for one more major investigative project that kept up us together through early 1998. I remained at the *Times* until I exchanged my professional career for an academic one in the fall of 2003.

Epilogue to "Tainted Cash or Easy Money?"

The "Tainted Cash or Easy Money?" project was a pivotal event in my career and a formative period in the development of my approach to journalism. Although I had completed quite a few projects over the years, this one had harnessed many aspects of my upbringing, professional experience and education. But, more pertinent to this book, it prompted considerable introspection and the beginning of years of reflection on the mission of investigative reporting and its value at all levels of journalism.

"Tainted Cash or Easy Money?" appeared on my agenda when my interest in minority affairs, civil and human rights, constitutional issues and the legal system had reached a peak. The influence of my early journalistic thinking and background, particularly my upbringing in the Deep South during a tumultuous historical era, had been playing out in a latent sort of way since graduate school. Studying American history at UNC-Greensboro had forced me to examine a historical period that I had experienced and then to view it from my socioeconomic perspective. It was a task that turned into a cauldron of complexity that, nevertheless, powerfully demonstrated the unique value that one's background and experiences can contribute to the pursuit of knowledge. For the first time, I understood how the prism formed by one's individuality is a valued perspective in the search for truth when allied with other perspectives that the effort to report objectively can reveal.

For years afterward, the view through that prism fueled a fascination with any vestige of the age of de jure and de facto discrimination and certainly directed my attention to events, issues, actions and attitudes—large and small— that otherwise may have slipped by. In covering education in the mid-1980s, I wondered whether parents' defensive and repeated, but seemingly innocent, allusions to "neighborhood schools" in connection to a school district merger debate was code for de facto segregation, a notion that opened up new lines of inquiry. In studying *The Orlando Sentinel*'s journalism while considering its job offer in early 1989, the discovery of several spot news stories about isolated race-related incidents in Lake County made me wonder about underlying causes and eventually produced the race relations project. My years of exposure to issues of constitutional rights and fairness initially raised my sensitivity to the fundamental problems embedded in the laws that produced Sheriff Vogel's cash-seizure program. When the pattern of overt racial injustice slowly emerged from our investigation, my background allowed me to consider meanings and context that may not have occurred to others or even to me at any other period. Seeing and documenting law enforcement actions focused and targeted at the simplest of human activities—driving along I-95 or carrying money in a Crown Royal bag—again yields new lines of inquiry about new subjects, such as the racial disproportionality of the prison population.

More broadly significant, "Tainted Cash or Easy Money?"—more than any other project before or since—provided the experience from which my notion of and questions about investigative reporting took root. As I moved on to the *Los Angeles Times* and to other projects, where I learned from other reporters and editors, those notions matured and developed as did my skills and knowledge of the craft as a practitioner. One day, it dawned on me that my interest in investigative reporting grew out of what I had been trying to do while I was a beat reporter, and that what I was doing as a projects reporter is not much different from what I was trying to do as a beat reporter. And, to some modest extent, I had successfully completed investigative projects as a beat reporter. So, was I indeed an "investigative" reporter or just another reporter who enjoyed the cachet of the title? And, what does that tell me about investigative and everyday beat reporting?

Now, I am looking at this craft from yet another perspective—that of an educator who is trying to make sense of it for students who know no more about journalism than I did when I started, which was nothing.

After three years of teaching, I began the reporting for this book. As I visited newsrooms across the country, I pursued a twofold mission. I wanted to make these highly accomplished journalists, all of whom work from instincts sharpened by years of experience, think about what they did in pursuing their stories and to explain it in a way that nonjournalists can understand and enjoy. And, I wanted to use these journalists to vet notions that had been forming for more than a dozen years about the mission of investigative reporting and its value as an approach for daily journalism at all levels.

To the general reading public, who might worry that an academic treatise is about to unfold, I am not an academic. I am a journalist, who only knows how to write for readers, and who interviewed other journalists who are guided by the same star. They understood why I was asking some of the seemingly purposeless questions and they graciously answered them all.

Thanks to their patience, I can now let their individual stories do the heavy lifting.

Lessons

BACKGROUNDS, BIASES AND JOURNALISM

Lesson Learned: As with anyone, journalists' educational and personal backgrounds and values will affect their perspective. It influences what interests them, their biases and motivations. Rather than considering such influences as negatives, conscientious journalists try to recognize them and be wary of them, but then learn to mine them to reveal ideas and avenues of inquiry that others with different influences will be unable to see.

How It Applied: Ever since those mentally exhausting childhood discussions with my father, a latent inquisitiveness had driven my reporting style. Overwhelmed by the hurly-burly of daily news and beat demands, it did not surface in a recognizable form until graduate school while studying American history and the civil rights movement.

The most memorable professors were the quiet, unassuming ones whose methodical and unemotional way of presenting historical evidence, evaluating facts and the sources of those facts, and raising questions always revealed fascinating new perspectives on what had been a narrow view of the past. During those years of studying history, the basic how and why questions in the practice of journalism took on a deeper meaning. Those history professors pushed my journalistic inquisitiveness deeper, to a level that inevitably led me to look backward when trying to learn how things get the way they are today. "Nothing happens in vacuum," I tell my students. "Look back, move forward, see the chronology." From those professors, I began to believe a good approach to investigative journalism should be one that is less targeted at nailing somebody or some agency in a wrongdoing and more about understanding the how and why—then and now. Often, the latter, which is the current wrongdoing, becomes the by-product of trying to understand what happened, why and how it came about.

Less difficult to fathom was the origin of my consuming interest in minority affairs, civil and human rights and the legal system at that time. That fascination clearly goes back to my childhood and educational and professional experiences. In contrast to nonjournalists, I, as do all reporters, carry a professional responsibility to recognize those factors and to see them as one of many prisms through which they can evaluate facts and situations.

The pursuit of objectivity is intellectually liberating, and journalism's requirement that reporters try to view things objectively sets them apart from their readers. Their pasts clearly influence the way they view facts as they appear, but the rigor of journalistic objectivity demands that they try to identify that view and challenge it, a process that opens new perspectives and avenues of inquiry that otherwise would have remained closed. My father, for example, was a conservative and a disciplinarian—a tandem that, to many people, would brand him as narrow and closed-minded. Yet it was not until I learned to challenge things the way he challenged so many of my youthful notions—with cold, unemotional, merciless logic that became a fountain of penetrating questions—that I was able recognize and articulate the many flaws in his thinking and in my own. He, like many bright people not in a profession that demands efforts to be objective, could challenge others' views, but not his own.

Objectivity and the Big-Story Bias

Lesson Learned: The desire to get a story, especially the "big one" or the one vested with time, resources and high expectations, poses the biggest danger to journalists' efforts to evaluate facts objectively. Reporters and editors from the top down have to recognize the danger of becoming personally and emotionally vested in the outcome of a story.

How It Applied: After Brazil and I were well into the investigation, each of us, probably at different points, began to sense the story was turning into something stronger than we had imagined.

It is in such circumstances that the effort to be objective faces the supreme test. In competitive journalism, the pressure to find the big story and to find it first is immense. When the scent of the blockbuster became strong and the evidence seemed clear and irrefutable, I felt I had to be on high alert in "Tainted Cash or Easy Money?" In almost any story—whether an investigative project or a spot news article—I worried more about the big-story bias to my objectivity than political or philosophical beliefs. I try to understand the difference between becoming personally obsessive about the topic, which I welcome, and becoming personally vested in it, which I avoid. And I like to have partners and good editors to ensure the two never mix.

INVESTIGATIVE MENTALITY AS A DAILY ROUTINE

Lesson Learned: In the routine coverage of government, journalism should bring to bear investigative reporters' intense, critical thinking attitude on everyday official action, especially when new laws are enacted and programs launched, such as Sheriff Bob Vogel's I-95 drug interdiction campaign.

How It Applied: Immediately after Vogel deployed his Selective Enforcement Team to I-95 in early 1989, the *Sentinel* began covering the drug and cash seizures on the highway. The early stories carried quotes from defense lawyers and civil liberties advocates raising lawyerly, general objections to what they perceived as violations of the motorists' rights. Many of the other issues that the *Sentinel*'s 1992 investigation explored in its thorough and methodical manner also were broached in those early stories. There were several references to Vogel's practice of entering into settlements in which he would return portions of the alleged drug dealers' money. Lawyers back then also questioned the lack of evidence connecting the seized money to drugs and Vogel's practice of considering the existence of trace amounts of drugs on the seized cash as bogus evidence.[54]

But those objections apparently did not claim a high measure of news value during the so-called war on drugs, because they were usually found deep in a story and treated as reactions in a story that headlined another victory. The *Sentinel* covered two seizure cases in 1989 that went to court, including one involving only $1,800 that was in the possession of two men. In neither case did the motorists challenge the seizures in hearings, so the evidence and the legal issues were never thoroughly explored.[55] From then on, the official line was that the program had withstood careful court scrutiny. In those early years, the parts of the story that resonated with the public, that influenced news judgments, that provided the color and suspense were the huge hauls of money and drugs that deputies found in cleverly hidden compartments in the motorists' vehicles, not the legal debate. So, Brazil, Ludden and I were not the first ones to reveal the problems of the interdiction program. The issues we explored in 1992 could have been explored in 1989. The only difference is that in 1992, we examined them with our investigative headgear in place, an approach no one else had employed.

Time has blurred our memory of precisely what eventually prompted our investigation. But all three of us recall that there was a single, record-breaking, attention-grabbing seizure, which a quick clip search traces to the name of Sgt. Bobby Jones. It occurred just before our investigation started, and it probably prompted the decision to take a closer look at the program. Even if our memories are deceiving us on that point, the scenario would have been typical in daily reporting. Daily reporting should bring the investigative mentality into play systematically and not rely on such hit-or-miss prompts like the Jones seizure.

What if Jones had missed that historic seizure? How many more years would we have let that program run without seeing the need to take a close look? Would we have ever written "Tainted Cash or Easy Money?"

Borrowing language from the day one package of the "Tainted Cash or Easy Money?" series, the lesson from this story seems to "hit like a hammer": The investigative mentality needs to be so thoroughly drilled into the minds of journalism students that it becomes an instinctive part of the craft everyday for every reporter on every story.

War and the Watchdogs

Lesson Learned: Because fear or patriotism or both often lead to unwise policy decisions during times of hot war—like the war in Iraq—or slogan war—like the war on drugs or the war on terror—the unemotional, aggressive questioning of government policy and decision making by journalists becomes more critical than ever. At no other time in a country's history does the public need cold, unemotional reporting based on disciplined and conscientious efforts to be objective and questioning. Not only should it question decisions before they are made, but it should closely examine the unintended consequences of those decisions after they are made.

How It Applied: In covering the I-95 drug interdiction program, in the early 1990s, much of the central Florida press, including *The Orlando Sentinel*, focused most of its reporting on the seizures without digging into the constitutional issues and examining the program in a questioning manner. Media critics may offer a variety of opinions (i.e., it let Vogel frame the issue, it was gullible to believe that he was targeting only drug dealers, it bought into the "war on drugs"). Whatever the actual reason, the clips show that in the middle of a drug hysteria, the press's stories seldom advanced much beyond the basic requirements of spot news reporting for more than three years—answering the six basic questions—who, what, when and where, with a doff of the hat to the why and how—and they all relied primarily on the programs' administrators or enforcers to meet those requirements. The end result was shallow reporting that essentially played to the audience's wants—colorful, entertaining stories, a folk hero, fighting the war on drugs—rather than to what it needs—a hard, unemotional, critical examination of a program of questionable value and fraught with enormously serious constitutional questions and the potential for violating basic human rights. Instead of advancing the story, the stories simply repeated the previous day's stories with a few different details.

5W + H = Story: A Failing Formula

Lesson Learned: The time-worn formula postulating that the sum of the variables who + what + when + where + why + how equals a story should be abandoned. In practice, the nature of journalism with its emphasis on speed, brevity, moving on to the next story and now "backpack" journalism does not foster thoughtful use of those questions (besides, "what" and "why" should cover the other four). In place of those six questions, journalists would produce better stories by substituting six penetrating what and why questions. Adding an "impact" question to the list of basic queries would add an informative dimension to most stories. It is certainly more probing and consequential than when, where and who, all of which are usually answered by default in the process of discovering what and why. The impact question would explain the impact of a decision or action on people. They are as integral to most stories about events and policies and actions as the official sources. Those who feel the impact of a program or action are first to feel the unintended consequences and are more likely to raise the probing questions that would escape anyone, including reporters, who do not share their perspective.

How It Applied: The press's coverage of the drug interdiction program was common, usually acceptable daily journalism. But it reflects a basic shortcoming of the traditional mantra that every story should answer who, what, when, where, why and how. "Tainted Cash or Easy Money?" showed that after three years of coverage, the press still had not answered those questions adequately, and the *Sentinel* had to write 16 stories in hundreds of additional inches of copy to fill all the reporting holes.

THE I-95 DRUG INTERDICTION "BEAT"

Lessons Learned: Before an investigative reporter can determine whether someone or some agency is doing something wrong or whether a law is being abused, the reporters have to get an education. That is, they have to learn how the system or law is supposed to work before they can determine if it is broken. They have to learn who the major and minor players are. And they have to know how the program works out in the field. In short, investigative reporters essentially have to do what every beat reporter does: learn their beat.

How It Applied: In the beginning, Brazil and I knew nothing about Sheriff Bob Vogel's drug interdiction program except what we had occasionally read in our own newspaper or seen on television. In a way, we were like beat reporters on the first day of covering any beat, such as the school board or city hall. Like them, we studied the clips to find out how our beat—the I-95 drug interdiction program—works. There was no departing I-95 beat reporter to brief us on how the drug interdiction program worked and how the money was budgeted, approved and spent. But the clips revealed a key source, a lawyer named Melvin Stack, who was often quoted in the clips and appeared to be the nuts and bolts guru of the entire program. So Brazil interviewed him and got an A-to-Z explanation about how the I-95 drug interdiction program should work from the roadside to courtroom. No city charter governed the I-95 operation, but the Contraband Forfeiture Act, civil and criminal court procedures, constitutional provisions such as being innocent until proven guilty and the right to be free from warrantless searches were ground rules for the drug interdiction program. There were no minutes to record the decisions and actions of the I-95 program, but there were forfeiture files that, figuratively speaking, were the minutes of the drug interdiction program. On the drug interdiction beat, there was no city council proceedings to attend to watch the government in action, but the Selective Enforcement Team was out on the interstate pulling cash and drugs out of car trunks, and the sheriff was happy to let us ride along and watch those proceedings. Later, the videos provided revealing candid-camera moments.

Within a very short time, we had learned our beat. We knew from the clips how the sheriff's department had presented the program to the public. We knew what the law and the U.S. Constitution allowed in the type of law enforcement practices that the Selective Enforcement Team employed. We had the official administrator of the program on record in an interview explaining how the program worked. And we knew the legal parameters from our study of the law and the case law.

ESTABLISHING TANGIBLE CRITERIA

Lesson Learned: In project reporting, the goal is to dig deeper than the surface facts. Investigative journalists have to research below the he-said/she-said quotes and answers and to deliver enough information so that readers can get to the bottom of something in a dispute. But the project has to do more than dump volumes of information into the public domain. It has to give the readers tangible criteria to use as a standard against which the readers can judge the actions and decisions of the subjects of the investigation.

How It Applied: In "Tainted Cash or Easy Money?" some of the tangible criteria emerged from the clips. The clips showed how the program had been presented to the public by official sources: the field deputies, the public relations office, the forfeiture-case attorney in charge of administering the program. It was a very positive picture. The law provided another guideline for readers to use to determine whether the drug interdiction was a good program. The U.S. Constitution and the basic principle of American jurisprudence that every accused person has the right to be presumed innocent until proven guilty by due process of law were two more criteria. The forfeiture attorney's detailed explanation of how the program is supposed to work in the field and in the courts provided the sheriff's department's official policy. Finally, we provided Sheriff's Vogel's criteria: If the SET squad determined someone was a drug dealer, the motorist must be a drug dealer and any money found in the car was fair game. With all of those criteria, our investigation simply had to document what actually happened out on the highway and compare those actions with the criteria we provided.

RECORDS STRATEGY

Lesson Learned: Although a straightforward and open approach to gaining access to records works in many investigative projects, reporting routines seldom apply in cookie-cutter fashion. Reporters cannot lie, pose or violate laws and ethical standards, but they are not required to reveal their suspicions until they have been substantiated. Many situations require reporters to be more discreet about fully disclosing the nature of their inquiry in the early stages of the investigation.

How It Applied: The "Tainted Cash" investigation demonstrated how the source's degree of knowledge of our investigation directly affected his willingness to provide access to records that were legally in the public domain. During the previous year, Vogel had resisted records requests from the *Sentinel* when the tactics of his SWAT team came under question in the Helen McConnell SWAT shooting. That was an instructive lesson for the "Tainted Cash" investigation. Before Sheriff Vogel realized that we were investigating whether he was abusing the seizure laws, he was totally cooperative. But weeks later, after we presented our preliminary findings to him and then went back to his headquarters to review more forfeiture files and view the videotapes, his office threw up road-blocks and challenged our public records request.

RESPECTING YOUR AUDIENCE

Lesson Learned: Some media commentators and scholars like to refer to journalists' audience as "news consumers," which is an extraordinarily disrespectful way to refer to the people who read or listen to the stories that journalists report and write. "We're not selling toasters here," John Carroll, the former editor of the *Los Angeles Times*, often says. Readers aren't buying toasters when they read a story. To avoid the cheapening of news in the consumerist view of readership, journalists have to respect the audience rather than play to it like a salesperson hawking toasters when they select, report and write stories.

How It Applied: Although the journalistic mantra to "show, rather than just tell" motivated much of the investigative work Brazil and I did, respect for the readers is the reason journalists have to work so hard to fulfill that mission. Brazil, Ludden and I understood that abuse of a law is serious even when it just violates the rights of a criminal. But respect for our readers required us to work very hard to investigate the backgrounds of dozens of motorists so that we could show how the same abuses can victimize the innocent, people like the majority of our readers.

Notes

1. Charles Fishman, "A Few Moments With: Sheriff Bob Vogel—He's the Mayor of I-95, and a Terror to Drug Smugglers," *Orlando Sentinel*, August 11, 1991, p. 6; Jeff Brazil, "Bob Vogel—Lightning Rod in U.S. Debate," *Orlando Sentinel*, December 20, 1992, p. A1.

2. Kevlin Haire, "I-95 Deputy Racks Up Numbers in Drug War," *Orlando Sentinel*, January 31, 1992, p. B1.

3. Jonathan P. Caulkins et al., *How Goes the Drug War: An Assessment of U.S. Drug Problems and Policy* (Santa Monica, CA: Rand Corporation, 2005), 1. It reported since 1985, the $60 billion-a-year illegal drug industry touched people as young as 12. One month after Vogel took office in 1989, the White House released its first National Drug Control Strategy targeting drug users.

4. Jeff Brazil and Steve Berry, "Tainted Cash or Easy Money?" *Orlando Sentinel*, June 14, 1992, p. A1.

5. Beth Taylor, "Public Support Solid for Vogel," *Orlando Sentinel*, May 28, 1989, p. A1.

6. Brazil and Berry, "Tainted Cash or Easy Money?"

7. Fishman, "A Few Moments With"; Taylor, "Public Support Solid."

8. Taylor, "Public Support Solid."

9. Interview, Jeff Brazil, via telephone, September 5, 2006.

10. Ibid.

11. Interview, Mike Ludden, Atlanta, Ga., January 13–14, 2006.

12. Mike Ludden, e-mail message, September 14, 2007.

13. Interview, Ludden, January 13–14, 2006.

14. Interview, Brazil, September 5, 2006.

15. Interview, Ludden, January 13–14, 2006.

16. Bob Vogel and Jeff Sadler, *Fighting to Win* (Paducah, KY: Turner, 2001), 133.

17. Interview, Ludden, January 13–14, 2006.

18. Interview, Brazil, September 5, 2006.

19. Brazil and Berry, "Tainted Cash or Easy Money?"; Brazil and Berry, "Color of Driver Is Key to Stops in I-95 Videos," *Orlando Sentinel*, August 23, 1992, p. A1.

20. Jeff Brazil and Steve Berry, "Deputies Take $19,000 and Leave Woman in Despair," *Orlando Sentinel*, June 14, 1992, p. A16.

21. Ibid.; Jeff Brazil and Steve Berry, "Many Black or Hispanic Drivers Feel They Are Singled out, Tapes Show," *Orlando Sentinel*, August 23, 1992, p. A10.

22. Brazil and Berry, "Tainted Cash or Easy Money?"

23. Interview, Brazil, September 5, 2006.

24. Brazil and Berry, "Tainted Cash or Easy Money?"

25. Ibid.

26. Ibid.

27. Ibid.

28. Ibid.

29. Ibid.

30. Interview, Brazil, September 5, 2006; Interview, Ludden, January 13–14, 2006.

31. Interview, Ludden, January 13–14, 2006.

32. Interview, Brazil, September 5, 2006.

33. Interview, Ludden, January 13–14, 2006.

34. Ibid.

35. Jeff Brazil and Steve Berry, "How Could They Say They Treated Me Fairly?" *Orlando Sentinel*, June 15, 1992, p. A17.

36. Jeff Brazil and Steve Berry, "I Could Win the Battle but Lose the War," *Orlando Sentinel*, June 15, 1992.

37. Interview, Ludden, January 13–14, 2006.

38. Interview, Brazil September 5, 2006.

39. Vogel and Sadler, *Fighting to Win*, 135.

40. Brazil and Berry, "Tainted Cash or Easy Money?"

41. Jeff Brazil and Steve Berry, "You May Be Drug Free, but Is Your Money?" *Orlando Sentinel*, June 15, 1992.

42. Interview, Brazil, September 5, 2006.

43. Interview, Ludden, January 13–14, 2006.

44. Brazil and Berry, "Tainted Cash or Easy Money?"

45. Brazil and Berry, "Color of Driver Is Key."

46. Ludmilla Lelis, "Feds Had Evidence on Vogel; Prosecutors Didn't Think Case Was Strong Enough to Win," *Orlando Sentinel*, October 3, 1997, p. A1.

47. Vogel and Sandler, *Fighting to Win*, 186–87.

48. Steve Berry, "Vogel Breezes Through Minorities' Challenge," *Orlando Sentinel*, January 15, 1995, p. A1.

49. Ibid.

50. Stephen Labaton, "Congress Raises Burden of Proof on Asset Seizures," *New York Times*, April 12, 2000, p. 1.

51. Cory Jo Lancaster, "Sheriff's Influence Kills Cash-Seizure Bill," *Orlando Sentinel*, March 22, 1995, p. C1; John Kennedy, "Changes to Cash-Seizure Law May Be Lacking Support," *Orlando Sentinel*, March 10, 1995, p. D5.

52. Steve Berry, "Seizure Reforms Rejected," *Orlando Sentinel*, February 26, 1993, p. B1; Jeff Brazil and Craig Quintana, "Vogel Panel Disbands: 'He's Cleaned Up His Act,'" *Orlando Sentinel*, February 27, 1993, p. A1.

53. Mike Griffin, "Forfeiture Reform Bill Becomes Law," *Orlando Sentinel*, June 14, 1995, p. C1.

54. Beth Taylor, "Volusia Cash Seizures Go to Court; Law Officers Await Verdict on Taking Money Without an Arrest," *Orlando Sentinel*, June 11, 1989, p. B1; Taylor, "Public Support Solid." These are a sampling of numerous articles about Vogel's cash seizures that were published in *The Sentinel* between 1989 and 1991 in which some of the major constitutional questions were first mentioned.

55. Beth Taylor, "Judges Okay Deputy Taking Cash on I-95," *Orlando Sentinel*, June 13, 1989, p. B1; Craig Quintana, "2nd Judge Lets Volusia Sheriff Seize Cash from I-95 Motorists," *Orlando Sentinel*, September 15, 1989, p. D6

Selected Bibliography

Articles

Brazil, Jeff, and Steve Berry. "Tainted Cash or Easy Money?" [Part one of three-part series]. *Orlando Sentinel*, June 14–16, 1992.

Brazil, Jeff, and Steve Berry. "Color of Driver Is Key to Stops in I-95 Videos." [Main story of three-story package]. *Orlando Sentinel*, August 23, 1992.

Book

Vogel, Bob, and Jeff Sadler. *Fighting to Win*. Paducah, KY: Turner Publishing, 2001.

Correspondence

Ludden, Michael, e-mail message to Berry, September 14, 2007.

Interviews

Brazil, Jeff, September 5, 2006, by telephone.
Ludden, Michael, Atlanta, GA, January 13–14, 2006.

Report

Caulkins, Jonathan P., et al. *How Goes the Drug War: An Assessment of U.S. Drug Problems and Policy*. Santa Monica, CA: Rand, 2005.

News Archives and News Search Services

Access World News, NewsBank, Inc., Naples, FL.
New York Times Archives, http://nytimes.com
Orlando Sentinel Archives, http://pqasb.pqarchiver.com/orlandosentinel/search.html.

CHAPTER 2

Secret Sources, Documents Unlock Dark Secret

When a Rumor Is Not Just a Rumor[1]

Willamette Week editor Mark Zusman still remembers the day investigative reporter Nigel Jaquiss entered his office to tell him about a rumor he had just picked up.

Guess what I just heard, Jaquiss said.

It was a sordid tale that involved a 30-year-old secret, a 14-year-old baby-sitter and the most powerful man in Oregon—former Democratic governor and behind-the-scenes kingmaker Neil Goldschmidt.

You're sick, Zusman said. And you're crazy. I would have known about that if it was true. Now, get out of my office.

The day was March 11, 2004, and the 50-year-old Zusman was joking with Jaquiss, but he had good reason to believe such an egregious story would have reached him before then. He had been editor and co-owner of the weekly since 1983, and Zusman probably knows Portland better than most. He knows its players, and Goldschmidt was one of the most important. Zusman had covered him when Goldschmidt was governor. He had also done his share of investigative reporting during his 26 years in journalism. He once interned with one of the best in the business, the late Jack Anderson.[2]

He also had a lot respect for Nigel Jaquiss. Nigel Jaquiss is no novice. The 42-year-old alumnus of the prestigious Columbia Graduate School of Journalism had worked with the *Willamette Week* since 1998, and he was not one to chase frivolous rumors.

After leaving Zusman's office, Jaquiss walked to the fax machine and grabbed a four-page document. He had been expecting it. On its face, the document would have meant nothing. The pages of legalese were part of a probate record that was 10 years old covering something that was—even at that point—ancient history.[3] The 1994 record showed someone had agreed to pay a woman $1,500 a month as a settlement for her claim that she suffered personal injuries from 1975 through 1978 (see Appendix B). A conservator had been appointed for the woman, because she had sustained "psychological injury."[4]

It wasn't much. The name of the plaintiff didn't ring a bell. The pages revealed nothing about the personal and psychological injuries. And besides, lawyers throw those words around to cover anything from coffee burns to near-death experiences. The papers were filed in neighboring Washington County, and the rest of the file was gathering dust in the archives of the probate department. It would take time to go to there and examine it. Jaquiss is only one of five reporters for the *Willamette Week*, and at a busy weekly, everyone has to churn out stories. They do not have a lot of time to chase leads as spare in detail as the fax Jaquiss held in his hands.

Jaquiss decided to look a little further. The name of the defendant didn't appear, and that was a bit strange. And one key detail was consistent with the ugly backstory that came with the fax—Goldschmidt had engaged in sex with the underage babysitter starting during a period when he was mayor of Portland, which was 1973 to 1979. And besides, the *Willamette Week* was not some wimpy weekly; it was an aggressive, irreverent, but well-established alternative newspaper serving 90,000 readers with newsroom archives full of kick-butt journalism. Jaquiss took the fax to Mark Zusman.

Drop everything else, Zusman said.[5]

A Story That Has to Be Right

In Oregon politics, most anyone who was anybody, including the current governor, had Goldschmidt to thank. Goldschmidt had been a progressive, wildly popular, two-term mayor, the U.S. Secretary of Transportation for President Jimmy Carter in 1979–1980, a top executive for Nike, the governor from 1987–1991 and was now a lobbyist and consultant for some of the biggest corporate names in the state.[6]

At the *Willamette Week*, taking on "sacred cows" was nothing new to Zusman and the paper's co-owner and publisher, Richard H. Meeker. Advertisers had boycotted them before, targets of their stories had sued and a bomb threat had once cleared the building.[7]

But this story was different. "It was like we were heading into a Category 5 hurricane," Meeker said, evoking the image of storms that destroy cities. Although he did not think Goldschmidt would react vindictively, he feared what his powerful friends might do out of personal loyalty. "This guy is so powerful, has so many friends in so many places that they could have cut the oxygen off for this newspaper," he said. "We've pledged our lives and houses to this newspaper. I prepared myself emotionally for battening down the hatches and going to borrow money from people. If we had been wrong that might have been the end of this paper." Said Zusman, "It is certainly the story that I have lost the most sleep over. It was clearly a huge, huge story. It was one we wanted to do right."[8]

Doing it right was not going to be easy. Jaquiss would have to draw on the best interviewing and record-searching magic he could conjure up. It would require seven-day work weeks, reneging on a promised vacation with his family, scrupulous and careful reporting and writing, and smart planning and strategizing. At times, the investigation would feel like a one-on-one competition with Goldschmidt. Recalling one such moment, Zusman said, "Part of our problem was that we were in a chess game with a guy who I knew was a lot smarter than I was. So how do we beat him in this chess game?"[9]

The pressure in that game would be immense. They were chasing a story that could be the biggest of their careers. And there would be times when Jaquiss would feel it slipping away from him.

The Goldschmidt Touch

Jaquiss would soon discover that the interviews would be the trickiest part of his investigation, because Goldschmidt's reach seemed unlimited. It was everywhere. It had even touched the life of his publisher, Richard Meeker. Meeker openly acknowledges his acquaintanceship with Goldschmidt; his wife, state Appeals Court Judge Ellen F. Rosenblum, got her start on the bench when Goldschmidt appointed her Multnomah County district judge in 1989. The Meeker family went to the same temple as Goldschmidt. Meeker also had a close relationship with at least two men who had been in Goldschmidt's inner political circle and who were still deeply devoted to him. Moreover, he has publicly acknowledged a great admiration for Goldschmidt's work over the decades.

Meeker's links to Goldschmidt began forming indirectly almost as soon as he moved to Portland in the early 1970s. He had grown up in Washington, D.C., graduated from Amherst College and earned a law degree at the University of Oregon. Instead of practicing law, he went to work as an investigative reporter for Ron Buel, a former campaign manager for Goldschmidt and a city hall aide, who had recently started the *Willamette Week*. Meeker and Zusman, who had arrived in 1980, bought the paper in 1983. Meeker also was close to Alan Webber, a former mayoral aide to Goldschmidt. He describes Webber as one of his best friends. Webber was still close to Goldschmidt while Jaquiss was investigating the story.

Goldschmidt's influence on Meeker's way of thinking had been immense. "He was as an amazing mayor for this city as anybody could have been or could ever again be," Meeker said. "I try as publisher, as so far as I can, to make this a paper that promotes a vision of Portland that I learned from Neil," Meeker said, noting that he had revealed these sentiments to his readers in a column.[10]

With Goldschmidt's personality and circle of admirers reaching so far and wide and even into the leadership of the newspaper, would the reporter assigned to investigate him hold back? Would Jaquiss sense an unspoken message—this man's friends controls the oxygen supply to the paper, my boss respects him immensely, so back off?

Despite Goldschmidt's connection to Meeker and his power to inflict damage on the small newspaper he and Zusman had built their lives around, Jaquiss says the two owners gave him free reign to investigate.[11] In the weeks ahead, their actions would show their impact on the story.

From Oil Trading to News Reporting

By the time Meeker and Zusman were making the tough decisions on the Goldschmidt story, Nigel Jaquiss had earned his stripes in their estimation.

"Nigel had already demonstrated many times over before this story began what his investigative skills were," Meeker said. Added Zusman: "If he interviews you and it's an adversarial interview, you can be sure he is going to have his documents with some numbers, and you are going to say, 'this guy has done his homework.'"[12]

Jaquiss' roots in Portland were not as deep as those of his bosses. He is a tall, unsmiling man, given to wearing small, rimless glasses. He speaks in a low, emotionless monotone. He grew up in the southern Indiana farm town of New Harmony, population 950. The son of an organic chemist for a General Electric plant, Jaquiss graduated from Dartmouth College in 1984 with a major in English and then worked as an oil trader for 11 years on Wall Street and in Singapore.

The money was good in the oil trade, and he and his wife, Meg Remson, his college girlfriend, were living a comfortable life. "But I wasn't consumed by it like other guys were. Your sole focus as a trader is to make money. Your interests are money, golf and Republican politics. I was apolitical. I was interested in making money as a benchmark, but I wasn't that interested in spending it. My wife and I were interested in books, going to movies and eating out, but that didn't take a lot of money."

In the mid-1990s, Jaquiss went through a series of "life-changing events." His dad died of an unexpected heart attack at the age of 57. A couple of years later, his mother died of lung cancer. Then three uncles died in the same period of time. He started having second thoughts about his career choice. "I was pretty conscious of the fact that I could continue doing what I was doing and live a rich, happy, unexamined and unfulfilling life. I felt that essentially, my only function in life was to make money. I had no connection to anybody in the community. I don't think I even voted until I was in my 30s." By the time his first son was born in 1995, it was clear to Jaquiss he needed to get out of "the New York rat race." He quit his job and spent a few months writing a novel about the Russian mob and sent it out. "It was uniformly rejected for very valid reasons," he said.

Jaquiss enrolled at the Graduate School of Journalism at Columbia University in New York, counting on the prestige of that school to open the way for a quick transition from oil trading to news reporting. "The first half of school was like a boot camp," Jaquiss recalled. Several journalism professors made a lasting impression. One was LynNell Hancock, a reporter and writer specializing in education and child and family policy issues and the author of or contributor to four books. "She was very tough, very commanding, and she had very high standards and all of that was perfect for me." Jaquiss readily acknowledged that he could not dispute her essential notion—"You don't know anything, and I'm going to teach you, and I'm going to fill your papers with red so the next paper will be better"—and he responded positively to her criticism and submitted to her "strong management."

Another was Sandy Padwe, a former deputy sports editor for *The New York Times* and senior editor for *Sports Illustrated*. "I liked him, because he was no-nonsense, a real hard-ass," Jaquiss recalled. "Padwe gave me a sense of journalism as a disciplined craft, that if you set about it methodically you could do it. I guess in a way I saw trading in the same way, that if you have a goal and a task and if you apply principles and learn some skills you can be successful about it." Jaquiss said he struggled in journalism school. "But I loved it and could see

I had made the right choice." He graduated in 1997, and he and his wife chose to live in Portland, where his brother lived.[13]

Words of J-School Professors Key

After reading a few issues of the *Willamette Week*, Nigel Jaquiss thought that paper's work, rather than *The Oregonian*'s, which was the more well-known and prestigious mainstream newspaper, meshed with what had interested him at Columbia University. Jaquiss remembered something Hancock told him. She had worked at *Newsweek* and the *New York Daily News*, but she said she had the most fun while working for an alternative paper—*The Village Voice*. He also recalled a lesson from a class on long-form writing that had made an impression. "I came to see how you base stories on public records and documents," he said. "Regardless of whether people will talk to you, public records can become a powerful tool to write any story anywhere. Those were the two overarching lessons I took away from journalism school, and then to come here and see there was a paper interested in investigative reporting that would let a young reporter write 3,000–4,000 words was really compelling to me."

Nevertheless, Jaquiss had to consider applying at *The Oregonian*, because it seemed the logical choice. "With my background, I could get a job on its business desk, write small stories and in five years, if I proved myself, I could write big stories," Jaquiss said. "Or, I could try to get a job at the *Willamette Week* and start writing big stories right away, and so that's what I did."

Jaquiss went to work in 1998. Instead of feeling like the proverbial fish out of water, the erstwhile oil trader found that the journalistic environment played to his strengths. "The process is quite similar to what a trader does, which is sort of like being a catfish sitting at the bottom of a river sifting all the stuff that drifts by and trying to figure out what is usable. What he liked about trading and reporting is that both fed what he described as his curious nature. "I like to know why things happen, how things work and who really affects change."[14]

Jaquiss has flourished at the *Willamette Week*. One of his first stories revealed how a high school was letting a star basketball player continue to play despite the facts that his grade point average was near zero and he was causing problems in school. Jaquiss became a thorn in the side of the local utility, Portland General Electric. He revealed how a college president was feathering his own nest with school money, forced the closure of a middle school after he found that a deadly, odorless gas was poisoning its air, discovered "ghost fans" at the PGE Baseball Park, and exposed plagiarism by a top editor of a rival newspaper.

Jaquiss began circling Goldschmidt in 2003 when the former governor plunged into a highly visible effort to block the public purchase of Portland General Electric. He succeeded and then led a private group of Texas investors that itself planned to buy the utility. In the meantime, Goldschmidt also had accepted an appointment to the Oregon State Board of Higher Education from Gov. Ted Kulongoski, a close ally, who rose to power with Goldschmidt's help. In early January 2004, Jaquiss began inquiring about Goldschmidt's consulting firm. He was interested in the immense influence Goldschmidt had been exerting on the political life of Oregon. It wasn't long before the salacious stories about Goldschmidt floated Jaquiss' way.[15]

Rumors of womanizing had always dogged Goldschmidt, who was married and the father of two children. Zusman and Meeker had heard them for years.[16] The rumors had followed him through his single term as governor. In February 1990 when he announced he would not seek a second term as governor, Goldschmidt cited marital problems as one reason.

Rumor, Records Show Paper Trail

Jaquiss was not interested in those tabloid-type stories when his morning began on March 11, 2004, the day he walked into Zusman's office to tell him about the babysitter rumor. He was entirely focused on Goldschmidt's business activities, and he had called a state legislator looking for information on Goldschmidt's dealings with the state. The lawmaker had been one of the few daring enough to publicly criticize Goldschmidt. Jaquiss had never talked to this source before, but he knew she had objected to a very lucrative consulting and lobbying deal he had obtained from the state's retirement system. He did not know that his source once was a victim of sexual abuse. He thought she might have collected some other information. The exchange that set the babysitter investigation in motion was simple. "I asked her what else she knew about him that was of substance."

There was a woman and an affair, she said.

Not interested, he told her.

But this one was an underage babysitter when he was mayor.

There always have been rumors about him and women, Jaquiss replied. I am not willing to spend any time on them unless there are some documents.

Well, I may have something that could help, she said, referring to the Washington County conservatorship record.

That got Jaquiss' attention. The legislator said she didn't know what to make of the documents, but the rumor behind them was that the plaintiff in the document did babysitting for Goldschmidt when he was mayor. There are some serious impediments to proving anything, she told Jaquiss. She had heard the woman, who would now be in her mid-40s, wouldn't talk or was mentally ill.

Why don't you fax it over right away, Jaquiss said.[17]

The record consisted of two documents that were brief, but enough to give Jaquiss something to follow. One was a November 1994 court order revealing the plaintiff's name, which Jaquiss refers to with the pseudonym Susan. The judge noted Susan would be filing suit claiming someone inflicted personal injuries on her nearly 20 years earlier, from 1975 through 1978. In addition to appointing the conservator for Susan, he ordered that settlement proceeds be deposited in an interest-bearing account. Three months later, Susan's conservator was back in court seeking permission to start withdrawing $1,500 a month from the account on her behalf, according to the second document.[18]

Separating Fact From Rumor

Although those sparse facts proved nothing about Goldschmidt, Jaquiss understood the rumors about him having illicit sex with a babysitter gave them a dark context. The alleged offenses occurred in the 1970s when Goldschmidt was mayor, and a judge in 1994 had concluded Susan was suffering a psychological injury. Although the order didn't specifically say the psychological injury originated from the 1970s, the wording and syntax could imply a connection, which would be consistent with the latent effects of childhood sexual abuse. The rumor could also color two key facts in the documents. For one, the name of Jeffrey Foote, one of the most prominent plaintiffs' attorneys in Oregon, was stamped on the document, a fact suggesting this case was no small matter. And second, the stamped filing dates on the documents showed that this had been settled in less than three months. That is lightning speed for personal injury cases, which frequently drag on for years. Such expeditiousness could certainly suggest someone—probably the defendant because he or she was not identified in the papers—wanted this case settled without the usual depositions, interrogatories and other discovery procedures that could reveal a lot of information. Possible translation: Someone wanted this case hushed up.

Nevertheless, Jaquiss still had serious doubts about the rumor. Zusman's initial incredulous reaction had articulated one of them—Goldschmidt had been the most covered public figure for two decades. So how, Jaquiss asked himself, could the press not have heard about this? Second, Jaquiss doubted that a man as brilliant and ambitious as Goldschmidt would take such a foolish, personal risk.[19]

Tips about public officials' affairs are fairly routine in journalism. Most are either not true, not worth pursuing, useless because they cannot be proven or are unimportant even if provable. But this one was different, and not just because it involved Neil Goldschmidt. This was more than just another rumor; it came with an official public record as a starting point. It was more than just another salacious sex story; it was statutory rape, a third-degree felony punishable by up to three years in the state penitentiary. And, it was even more than a serious felony; it was a felony that had been covered up for more than 30 years.

Records Leave Footprint of a Life

At the very least, this tip deserved a due diligent effort, and Jaquiss began the investigation in a routine way—he ran the woman's name through public records indexes. He was hoping the woman had left footprints of her life on a paper trail that he could follow. He wanted to find out everything he could, starting with her date of birth. That would let him calculate whether she would have been under the age of 16—the age of consent—between 1975 and 1978, the period mentioned in the court records. She would have been 14 in 1975. The date of birth also would help him confirm that other records bearing the same name applied to her.

He also put in a records request with the Washington County courts for the original case file to see what other records it might contain. About a week later he had the file. The settlement was huge. The $1,500 monthly annuity was just half the total settlement. She also would get $30,000 up front, and the annuity was to run for 10 years starting in March 1995. At that point, Susan would receive the first of three $50,000 lump sum payments, with final two coming in 2010 and 2020. In return, the woman and all of her family members had to keep quiet about the deal. The total would amount to about $350,000.[20]

Jaquiss found the new information interesting, but the full document didn't contain much else that was helpful. Goldschmidt's name was not mentioned. Moreover, the settlement apparently precluded Susan from filing suit, which at least would have included a formal complaint outlining details of the charges and the defendant's name. Even worse, a confidentiality agreement effectively silenced everyone involved.

In the meantime, Jaquiss had started pulling all the public records he could find that mentioned her name: property, police files, criminal and civil court records, state archives, a high school yearbook, reverse directories from all surrounding counties. Gradually, a circumstantial case began to form. The yearbook gave him the names of friends and teachers, the beginnings of a source list.

Important tidbits emerged. He found that Susan had lived just three doors down from Goldschmidt's home, a fact that gave the "babysitter" element of the rumor some plausibility.[21] The sources identified her mother, and Meeker, the weekly's publisher, recognized her as a former mayoral aide to Goldschmidt. "I knew her very well in the 1970s," Meeker said. Now, a link between Goldschmidt and Susan seemed more than just plausible.[22]

The records, the yearbook and the files were paying off. The story of Susan's life was taking shape, and it was beginning to look like hers was spiraling downward while Goldschmidt's was heading for the stratosphere. By the 1980s, Susan had started on a long police record involving drugs and drunken driving arrests. From them, Jaquiss learned about many of her hangouts and more names to add to his source list.

One record revealed more than just background on Susan. It was a police report on a 1986 drunken driving arrest. Leaving one of her favorite haunts after an afternoon swilling champagne and brandy, Susan drove out of a parking garage and clipped the bumper of a parked truck. The police came and Susan grew petulant with the arresting officer.

"I will personally make sure you get shit for this," she swore. "Neil Goldschmidt is my best friend." He had hit pay dirt.[23]

Competitor Leaves Sign, Pressure Builds

For Jaquiss, finding that stack of records produced a bittersweet moment that often confronts investigative reporters on the chase. The police report was important, because it was the first time Goldschmidt's and Susan's names surfaced in the same public record. But there was something sitting on top of the pile of records that worried him mightily: an e-mail from a reporter for a competing newspaper, *The Portland Tribune*, requesting the records he was looking at. His heart sank. "I thought at that point, I was beat for sure."[24]

Jaquiss had good reason to worry. He assumed the rumor mill was working overtime. After all, he himself was on the story because of it. Moreover, at that moment, he did not know that the original source of the Washington County conservatorship record that had piqued his interest was *Tribune* reporter Phil Stanford.[25] Nor did he know Stanford had interviewed Susan the month before. Or that a former Goldschmidt speechwriter had given *The Oregonian* Susan's name plus a detailed account of the rumor and a list of sources who could confirm it.[26] Even without that specific knowledge, fear of the competition was driving Jaquiss to work double-time. He was worried sick about *The Oregonian*, with its huge resources, its cadre of strong reporters and its deep institutional knowledge of Portland and its major players. "I was working continuously, seven days a week," Jaquiss said. "I was tremendously fearful we would get beat. At some point we figured where the [Portland] *Tribune* was, but I never figured where *Oregonian* was on the story, if anywhere. So, I was pushing to go to print much before we did. The editors and the lawyer were more cautious."[27]

The Oregonian was still living with the humiliation of getting scooped by *The Washington Post* on a story about former Oregon Sen. Bob Packwood sexually harassing women. Jaquiss suspected its editors were not about to let that ever happen again. "I knew there was no chance they wanted to get beat by us on a story of consequence like that," Jaquiss said. "I was in kind of a state of paranoia."

Jaquiss and Zusman worked as quietly as possible. For weeks, no one else in the newsroom other than Zusman and former Managing Editor John Schrag knew what Jaquiss was up to. His byline disappeared from the paper, which is unusual at such a small weekly. His colleagues seldom saw him in the office, and when he did make an appearance he was behind closed doors with Zusman and Schrag. When someone asked, they learned nothing. "I can't tell you what I am working on," he told them.[28]

Their in-house strategizing was intense. They figured Goldschmidt had gotten wind of what they were doing by late March, probably as soon as Jaquiss asked for Goldschmidt's papers at the state archives. "We were constantly weighing what we thought the competition would do and what Neil was going to do," Zusman said, referring to Goldschmidt. Their reporting strategy called for them to move through what Zusman referred to as "three concentric circles." In the first circle, Jaquiss would fan out all over the surrounding area searching all the records he could find for anything that related to Susan and Goldschmidt. In the second circle, Jaquiss would talk to the "friendlies," the people Jaquiss and Zusman believed were Susan's close friends, boyfriends, roommates or acquaintances, people who they hoped would corroborate the tip and not run to Goldschmidt to reveal their line of questioning. Finally, they would go to the inner circle, the people directly connected to Susan and Goldschmidt.[29]

Seattle Rape Record Yields Breakthrough

Jaquiss had already moved into the circle of "friendlies" in late March when he discovered the quintessential breakthrough document—another drunken driving arrest record. This arrest happened in Oregon City in Clackamas County, and Susan had missed some court dates in the case. It would lead to something no other reporter had discovered.

In one of the filings, her lawyer revealed that in December 1988 while living in Seattle, Susan had been abducted at knifepoint and forced to drive to her apartment, where her attacker brutally raped her for hours. The lawyer argued she was suffering post-traumatic stress disorder from the attack, and he included an excerpt of testimony from the rape trial (in which the defendant was found guilty and convicted) to prove his point. Susan had moved to Seattle, Jaquiss later learned, to get a fresh start, and Goldschmidt had gotten her a job at a law firm there. Jaquiss hoped the records in that case would contain some clues that would help his case. With that goal in mind, he enlisted a trusted former *Willamette Week* colleague, who was living in Seattle that March, to plow through every document in the file.

It contained more than 1,000 pages, including a trial transcript. Although the case did not involve Goldschmidt, it paid off in a major way. It revealed that Susan had been sexually abused from 1975 through 1978. In the rape case, Susan also said the abuser was a neighbor, a trusted family friend and 21 years her senior. Jaquiss was ecstatic. "It was a perfect match," he said. "That rape case file was crucial."[30]

His investigation had come a long way from its start: a mere rumor. Now, after a few weeks of work and relying strictly on the public record, here is what Jaquiss had: Susan lived three doors down from Goldschmidt and was the daughter of one of his aides; that she called him "her best friend"; that she was 21 years younger than him; that she had been sexually abused in the 1970s by a neighbor and family friend 21 years older than she; that the abuse occurred between 1975 and 1978 when she would have been 14 to 17 and Goldschmidt would have been mayor of Portland; and that she had received about $350,000 in a hastily arranged settlement that forestalled a suit and swore the victim and her family to secrecy. Jaquiss was glad he had not dismissed the original rumor out of hand.

Editors, Reporters and the Big-Story Bias

Despite the encouraging turn, Jaquiss didn't have enough. The public records, at best, provided a weak circumstantial case. At that point, he had to assume—for planning purposes—that Goldschmidt would vehemently deny the charges and that Susan and her mother probably would never confirm the story. The two women had nothing tangible to gain from even risking an interview with Jaquiss and tens of thousands of dollars to lose. He needed more evidence, and it was going to have to come from interviews, primarily with the friendlies in the "second concentric circle" of Editor Mark Zusman's depiction of the investigative strategy.

The story had become all-consuming for Jaquiss and Zusman. Jaquiss was drawing heavily on Zusman's judgment. In describing their collaboration, they talked like they were practically joined at the hip. "Oh God, you can imagine," Zusman said. "We would talk at night and we would talk at home. We were living and breathing this."[31]

Investigative reporters on most stories often go for days without giving progress reports to their editors, but the collaboration between Zusman and Jaquiss on this one was closer than most. Editors seldom pitched in on the reporting as Zusman did. "There was a variety of points along the way where we sort of split up the reporting," he said. Jaquiss also kept Zusman in the loop constantly. "Whenever he would report [gather information], he would tell me what he reported, and we would talk about what is the next step." At one point, Zusman made a key contact with a woman he says he still cannot identify. "We had a phone conversation with a woman who convinced me we had a story. It was not her mother." Zusman was very mysterious about this. He wouldn't say anything else about her, how she knew. "The level of specificity she had was compelling," he said.

At times, his collaboration with Jaquiss got down to the nitty-gritty level. He and Jaquiss would talk about who to interview and in what order, whether he or someone else rather than Jaquiss would be better off calling a source. He said they discussed detailed tactics for an interview, such as whether to ask only half of the questions in one interview and the other half in a later one or what the best process was to get people to open up about a subject they had not been willing to discuss earlier.

For his part, Jaquiss came to value his editor's investigative experience and knowledge of Portland and the people who ran it. "He knows all of the players," Jaquiss said. "And he's pretty strategic, helping me think about things like what order we are going to talk to people in."[32]

Working the Anonymous "Friendlies"

For Jaquiss, getting enough information sometimes would test his patience and determination. Sources' loyalty or fear of Goldschmidt ran deep. Gaining their trust would not be automatic; gleaning usable information would be tricky.

Some people accused him of spreading rumors about a man who—in what was becoming common parlance—"has done so much for our community." Others tried to scare him off. "You're walking on thin ice," they warned. To this day, some of his formerly valued professional contacts will not speak to him. Those who talked would not do it on the record. Many were simply too frightened, and they had good reason. Lawyers who had dated the woman and heard her firsthand accounts realized the next judge who tried their cases would likely be a Goldschmidt appointee, Jaquiss said. To Jaquiss, it seemed, half the judiciary and the prosecution owed Goldschmidt.[33]

Goldschmidt's reach was so extensive that one source who lived close to the homeless fringe apparently believed the ex-governor's reach could even find him. That interview bordered on the comic when Jaquiss pulled out a time-worn interviewing tactic to pull information out of him. Jaquiss had heard that this source was a boyfriend of Susan's in the early 1990s, a key point in Susan's life and for Jaquiss' story. In that period, Goldschmidt completed his gubernatorial term and was building a highly lucrative consulting and lobbying business. Meanwhile, Susan's life was spiraling further out of control. After the 1988 rape in Seattle, Susan had moved back to Portland suffering emotional turmoil, undergoing counseling and turning heavily to cocaine and alcohol. From 1991 to 1994, she was arrested nine times, including once in 1992 for a probation violation in a cocaine case that sent her to federal prison in 1993 for five months. She got out in 1994, the year she went to Jeffrey Foote, the prominent plaintiff's attorney, to discuss taking action against whoever abused her from 1975 to 1978. Jaquiss had heard the boyfriend might know something about her decision to take legal action.[34]

After considerable effort, Jaquiss tracked him down to an address in downtown Portland and drove there unannounced. It was a dump, making Jaquiss think "flophouse." He didn't know what to expect when he knocked on the door, except that he was warned the guy suffered from severe attention deficit hyperactivity disorder. A man, looking almost destitute, answered to the knock. Jaquiss mentioned Susan's name, but not Goldschmidt's. It had become his common practice in these interviews to start only with Susan's name. In this case, the boyfriend looked wary when he spoke her name. He said he didn't want to talk.

That's OK, Jaquiss said, but you look like you could use a cup of coffee, so let's go get something to eat.

They walked across the street to a Starbucks, and the conversation went on and on. The source's mannerisms appeared to confirm what Jaquiss had heard about him. He talked erratically. He was shaky and nervous. It was clear to Jaquiss that he was suffering from something. But he knew a lot about Susan, enough to convince Jaquiss that Susan could have confided in him. The source described her as beautiful woman, a music lover who had been a friend of the late, Seattle-based rocker Kurt Cobain, all of which was irrelevant but tracked with what Jaquiss already knew. He described Susan as someone who had been damaged mentally because of a previous relationship and said she drank too much—all because of what happened to her in the past.

The source finally broached the subject that interested Jaquiss. "I know what you want, and I am not going to talk about that," he said. With his motive out on the table, Jaquiss decided to press. He assured the source that he understood that he was in a vulnerable position and that he was afraid. But Jaquiss said he had an idea.

He would write the initials of the guy he wanted to talk about down on a piece of paper and push it across the table. If the initials were those of the man Susan had been involved with, he could circle them and push the paper back to Jaquiss.

That way, Jaquiss told him, you will always be able to deny that you said anything and you will be able to say you didn't use his name, Jaquiss told the source.

Jaquiss wrote "NG" in his reporter's notebook and slid over to the source. He looked at it and crossed his arms across his chest.

Nope, I am not going to do that, he said.

Oh, come on, Jaquiss whined.

Then the source took his napkin, wadded it up and pointed across the coffee shop to the trash can. I am going to throw this, and if it goes in, I'll tell you what you want to know, he said. The source tossed the napkin, and Jaquiss watched its flight across the coffee shop as it hit the edge of the can and dropped to the floor.

Oh come on, Jaquiss protested. You've got to tell me.

No, I told you I am not going to tell you, he said, and I am *not* going to tell you, the source responded emphatically.

Although disappointed, Jaquiss said he understood the man's fear. "Look, if you know Goldschmidt is the most powerful guy in the state, and you are like this quasi-homeless, paranoid and mentally ill man, what possible benefit could accrue to you by confirming something? People are afraid of powerful people," he said. Nevertheless, Jaquiss said he found the encounter interesting and even useful in that it helped him form a picture of Susan's life and made him feel more confident about the validity of the rumor. "I think that was an example of how seeing people in person gets you stuff you couldn't possibly get any other way," he said.[35]

You Can't See a Red Face Over the Phone

The phone is so easy to use. E-mail is even easier. They are such tempting devices. They're efficient, quick and essential tools of the journalistic trade. The impulse to grab the phone or shoot an e-mail when a question pops up is almost irresistible. But they are also impersonal and prevent reporters from reading nonverbal messages that an interviewee often conveys. When he approached interviewees to talk about Susan and Goldschmidt, he never mentioned Goldschmidt's name at first, primarily for fear of unfairly spreading rumors. "But it was another way to test people's reaction and body language," Jaquiss said. "You know something if, when you mention the girl's name but you don't mention his name, you get a strong reaction."

Early in the second phase of his investigation—interviewing the friendlies—Jaquiss decided to touch base with Susan's lawyer Jeffrey Foote. Instead of going to see him personally, he picked up the phone. He knew Foote was bound by the confidentiality agreement, but he figured Foote would be sympathetic to the story. He should be willing to confirm things that were in the public record, Jaquiss thought. He picked up the phone and asked if he could come over and talk to him.

What about? Foote asked. Jaquiss told him he wanted to talk about Susan.

I won't talk to you about that, he said.

What would you do if you were me, Jaquiss asked Foote, hoping for a lead to other sources or public records. At least, he hoped for a veiled signal that he was on the right track.

I would forget all about it, Foote replied. It was clear, Foote wouldn't play the game.

Jaquiss' ploy is common, and often fruitful. He had used it before. "A lot of lawyers take their ethical responsibility to clients very seriously, so I am looking for ways to get these signals that they will feel comfortable with," he said. "It is always some variation of 'Who else should I talk to?'" Was his execution in this interview a mistake? "Yeah," he said. "I should have gone to him in person. So I got off the phone with him and said to Mark, 'Well, that was a fuck up.'" Zusman, not one to dwell on second-guessing, was more interested in "what's next."[36]

If the key players in the settlement had not already heard about Jaquiss' investigation, his phone call to Foote certainly ensured word would soon spread. Jaquiss and Zusman agreed he should move immediately to approach Susan's other lawyers before Foote called them to try to "shut them down." But this time, they would do it in person.

Jaquiss remembered that Zusman knew Susan's conservator, Portland lawyer Doreen Margolin. He and Zusman had teamed up on an earlier story, and he thought that experience had worked out well. In that earlier interview, they fell into the good-cop/bad-cop tactic. Jaquiss is usually the good cop, Zusman the tough cop. "He's a very aggressive, pugnacious interviewer, and I am not," Jaquiss explained. "I don't know if I really have a style; I would say low key, I guess." The important result was that their team effort worked in that case.

You know Doreen Margolin, Jaquiss told Zusman, so why don't you come with me and we'll go see her.[37]

Zusman agreed, and the two journalists walked the five or six blocks to her office. She welcomed them warmly. "She's a very tall, elegant woman, and we just talked for awhile," Zusman said. Margolin's husband is an author of thrillers and she and Zusman discussed that briefly. They chatted about a few other topics. Then Zusman got down to business.

"The reason I am here…," Zusman began. As soon as he mentioned Susan's name, Margolin's demeanor changed, he recalled.

This conversation is over, she said standing up.[38]

To Jaquiss, the dramatic change in demeanor was overwhelming. She had seemed so polite and congenial. "What was memorable was her body language, her face turning a very, bright red, her immediate lightning bolt of discomfort, the tenor of her voice. It just turned icy. I don't remember her exact words, but it was something to the effect that she was not going to discuss Susan, and you need to leave right now."[39]

But Zusman, the bad cop, wasn't done.

Doreen, this leads us to conclude that we are on to something, Zusman said, trying to bait her.

I am not going to play that game, she said.[40]

Zusman and Jaquiss left, but they didn't tarry. Their excitement running high, they immediately drove to a second lawyer's office, Jana Toran, who was an associate of Foote and was listed as one of the lawyers involved in the settlement. But she was less help than Margolin, and they left. "There is a high level of adrenalin at a time you are with the people, so when you leave them you sort of have to decompress," Jaquiss said, recalling the aftermath of the confrontations with Foote, Margolin and Toran. "That's another reason to have two people at an interview, because you can compare what you each see and what you think it meant or whether you heard something different." Moreover, the encounters clearly demonstrated the value of person-to-person interviews. Margolin's body language spoke volumes; Foote's may have as well, but Jaquiss wasn't sitting in front of him to see it. "You cannot see somebody's face turn red on the telephone," he said.

As he and Zusman "decompressed," they talked about what they had seen and heard. They focused on Margolin's dramatic reaction and on what the three lawyers did not say, Jaquiss said. "What none of them said was, 'Gee, you are both out of your mind, you are wasting time,' or, 'Why don't you tell me what you think happened, and I will tell you why you are wrong.'" Jaquiss also thought Foote's advice to "forget all about it" was significant. To him, those words meant exactly the opposite of their literal meaning. "He could have said 'I can tell you about 20 other cases that are more interesting,' Jaquiss said. By then, Jaquiss was fairly certain the sexual abuse story was true, yet he conceded: "It's possible I am seeing more than was there."[41]

Finding the "Friendlies"

Other interviews produced more, albeit not for attribution. As the days went by, Jaquiss figured out where Susan's turf had been and went there to hang out. He hit the bars and restaurants that she frequented or worked at in the 1980s and early 1990s. He was looking for friends and boyfriends and roommates, people in whom she may have confided. Gradually, a picture started taking shape. Jaquiss said he talked to one friend who had worked with Susan as a waitress and who he described now as a solid, middle-class citizen. Susan had told her about Goldschmidt.

"I didn't believe her," Jaquiss recalled the former co-worker saying.

Jaquiss asked why.

If it were true, she said, it would have been in the paper by now, and she was kind of crazy and drunk.

Nevertheless, her story was useful to Jaquiss, because her account of Susan's relationship with Goldschmidt tracked precisely with what others had told him about her lifestyle. Other than occasional waitress jobs, Susan seldom worked, although friends described her as smart and charming. But her self-esteem was shockingly low. She spent a lot of time at the bars. She was drinking and partying heavily with barflies, lawyers, developers, musicians and dope dealers.[42]

Inevitably, after a few drinks, Susan would tell a story about her early- and mid-teen years, when the young, handsome, popular and progressive mayor of Portland turned his attention to her. She told Jaquiss' sources that she and Goldschmidt had sex in many different places, such as the basement of her parents' home, at a hotel and other private spots. Much of it happened when she was 14 and 15, which would constitute statutory rape in Oregon. One friend told Jaquiss that at times she talked as if she was proud of the relationship, at other times as if she was angry and bitter. Sources told him she occasionally would try to call Goldschmidt, even when he was in the governor's office.[43]

The interviews, although anonymous, began to pile up, and their stories were remarkably similar. By then, Jaquiss believed the rumor was true.

"I was convinced he had done it, but the question was how are we going to get it in the paper, because these people were all speaking off the record, and even if they were on the record, they were not exactly the most reputable people around," he said.

After several of these interviews, Jaquiss started pushing to interview Susan, who had moved to Las Vegas. But Zusman held him back. "He kept saying, 'You don't have enough yet,'" Jaquiss recalled.[44]

While Jaquiss worked the "friendlies," Zusman began trying to track down Susan's mother. She was working for the U.S. Department of State and she was stationed abroad. Zusman finally found her in Ankara, Turkey.

Zusman didn't expect the mother to openly acknowledge the relationship because of the confidentiality restrictions. He was hoping for private confirmation. The interview started cordially, and it would last for more than three hours. "Part of that was because I was trying to get her comfortable so she would talk about it," Zusman said. "I had never met her before." The opening was odd, and Zusman remembered it:

Q. This is Mark Zusman, and I am the editor of the *Willamette Week*.

A. Oh, I know you.

Q. I know this is kind of strange, but I'm calling about a very difficult subject. I am calling about your daughter and Neil Goldschmidt.

A. Well, what do you want to talk about?

Relieved that she did not hang up, Zusman soon realized she was willing to talk as long as he wanted to stay on the phone. "It was amazing," he said. "We had done a fair amount of reporting, and so my guess is that she had been alerted to what we had been up to and so she probably was not in a complete surprise."Instead of posing a blunt question about a sexual relationship between Susan and the ex-governor, Zusman moved slowly, letting the interview become a conversation. "I said, 'Let me tell you how I got to the point of calling you.'" At that point, Zusman told her about the Washington County court records and chronologically took her through the investigation. But she denied a sexual relationship occurred between Susan and Goldschmidt.

The conversation meandered, with Zusman repeatedly steering it to the central question. "We sort of go in and out," he said. But each time she would deny it happened. She talked about her work for Goldschmidt, and she discussed at length her high regard for him. "She would say what a great man he was and what a contribution he made," Zusman said. The conversation moved on to Susan. She told him about her troubled life. "At several points, I said you mean to be telling me you are denying the fact this happened," Zusman said. He brought up the court settlement and how Susan was getting lots of money from someone.

Q. It has to come from somewhere, and you are saying it is not Neil?

A. I am not going to go there.

She never relented, but she never cut him off. At times, Zusman felt she tacitly acknowledged the abuse of her daughter. "It was almost along the lines that if he had done this, it's an old story, and it is really not worth your and your paper's time given the enormous contributions he had made."

Nevertheless, Zusman clearly understood her bottom-line answer: "She denied it; flat-out denied it."

Zusman tried to talk to her twice more. In one call she acknowledged her "daughter was a wreck," and on the final one she became angry, Zusman recalled:

I am getting tired of this, she said. I am worried you are going to do a story that is going to do harm to my daughter.[45]

Goldschmidt: Let's Do Lunch

In early April, the story would take another strange twist, one that forced them to deal with Goldschmidt face-to-face when they were not ready for him. By then, Jaquiss was trying to arrange an interview with Susan, and word had probably gotten back to Goldschmidt, Zusman said. Deciding when to talk to the subject of an investigation is not always easy. Circumstances in each story vary so much, routines don't apply. Although such encounters often become contentious, they sometimes turn into a confrontation akin to a showdown. Reporters often like to have their "ducks in a row" when they go to such interviews. That was the plan for Zusman and Jaquiss. But Goldschmidt apparently heard what the *Willamette Week* was doing. He picked up the phone and called the paper's publisher, Meeker.

Meeker was not in when the call came. But he, Zusman and Jaquiss have listened to Goldschmidt's phone message and subsequent phone-tag exchanges many times.

"Richard, this is Neil. I'm calling, because I was wondering if you and me and Mark can get together for lunch."[46]

They would be glad to meet, Meeker responded with his own phone message, asking about the nature of what of he wanted to discuss.

"There was no agenda," Goldschmidt said in a return message. "It's just that you guys are doing good journalism, and I'm involved in some interesting things, and I just think it would be fun."

Zusman and Meeker were puzzled. They felt sure he knew about Jaquiss' investigation. Why else would he invite Zusman? "I know him," Zusman said. "I've interviewed him, been with him, but I don't have casual lunches with this guy. This guy, you know, travels at a very high altitude."

He and Zusman set the meeting for April 5—two days before Jaquiss was scheduled to meet with Susan—not knowing whether he would bring up Topic A but sure that they would not introduce it. Either way, they were not going to talk about it. They met at the Carafe Restaurant, a swanky establishment that serves wine from Goldschmidt's own winery. Goldschmidt's longtime business partner, Tom Imeson came with him. Imeson looked clueless, Zusman recalled. Goldschmidt was charming, fascinating, the usual raconteur. He talked about Oregon's higher education system, about the public electrical utility and about a variety of other issues. But not one word about Jaquiss' investigation. He once asked what they were working on. Are you working on anything interesting, he asked? Meeker and Zusman didn't tell him about the Susan story.

The conversation continued pleasantly for more than an hour. Zusman remembers his strange emotions. He was partly intrigued, but at the same time he was thinking: "What the hell is going on here? On the one hand, it was an incredibly pleasant conversation. On the other hand, it felt like there was this fifth person at the table, and it was Susan's story, and no one dares speak its name."

The conversation came to an end and the foursome stepped outside. Zusman and Meeker turned to head back to the office. Goldschmidt stopped Zusman, grabbed his hand, looked at him with cold steely eyes and said, "Go get 'em."

He knows; he absolutely knows, Zusman told Meeker. Meeker agreed. "It was like a challenge."[47]

When Delicacy Matters

Zusman's present-day thoughts about the parting handshake, the look and the implicit challenge at the Carafe Restaurant may well benefit from hindsight, but more surprises and the toughest challenges lay just ahead.

Jaquiss had been working more of Susan's former friends. Although the interviewing had been tough, by the first week of April, Jaquiss was sure Goldschmidt had sexually abused Susan. About a half-dozen or more witnesses had independently told Jaquiss what Susan had told them about having sex with Goldschmidt. Each had heard her tell the story directly, and their accounts of what she had told each one were remarkably alike. He had discovered some of the worst and most intimate details of her life, but he also heard she was a smart, charming and beautiful woman. Had she chosen education and career over partying and abusing alcohol and drugs, she could have been a successful person. Jaquiss was eager to meet the woman whose life had so consumed his since early March. For weeks, he had been pressing to interview her. Finally, Zusman gave the go-ahead.[48]

Zusman and Jaquiss discussed the best way to approach the woman. She could well be still be coping with psychological problems; yet it was the most important interview to date. For his part, Zusman sensed it would not be easy. As he pondered the interview, Zusman said he tried to empathize with Susan and calculate whether a female reporter should make the first contact with her and then go with Jaquiss for the interview. "Women are less likely to talk about sexual abuse with men than they are with women, because men's interview styles tend to be more aggressive and less emotional, less sympathetic."

Jaquiss is not an aggressive interviewer; he has a "very matter of fact interviewing style," Zusman said. He relies enormously on records, because he believes records don't lie. He goes to interviews thoroughly prepared. "He is not necessarily the kind of reporter who is going to convey [to an interviewee] 'Oh shucks, you're a good guy, and I'm a good guy, so let's talk.' That is not his style. He isn't the guy who is going to go down to Vegas and get this woman to feel like this is a shoulder she can cry on and get her to tell him her story."[49]

Jaquiss understood the delicacy of the interview. He said he and Zusman thought about the horrific experiences she had had with men. "We knew by then that she was pretty fragile and that she had already refused to talk to Phil Stanford [the *Tribune* reporter]," Jaquiss said. "If she's been raped; if she's been abused by Goldschmidt and in a lousy existence, to have a male reporter call and say we're anxious for you to tell us all the gory details of your life is not a good idea." So Zusman enlisted the help of Ellen Fagg, the *Willamette Week*'s arts and culture editor. Zusman felt that Susan perhaps would come to feel that "this is a woman with whom I could unburden myself with."[50]

Jaquiss said that without Ellen's help he probably would have never gotten the interview.[51]

Zusman and Jaquiss had been journalists long enough to know that even the best plans and the most thorough planning can go awry. At best, planning can only reduce the amount of spontaneous mental and tactical adjustments that most interviews require. This one would be no exception.

Susan agreed to an interview on April 7, just two days after Meeker and Zusman chatted pleasantly over lunch at the Carafe Restaurant. Susan wanted to meet in a sports bar.

Governed by a confidentiality agreement, Susan would not be able to talk on the record, but Jaquiss hoped she would at least privately acknowledge what happened. "I had been preparing for weeks, reading documents, talking to friends, learning her early bio. I felt like I knew her very well, as much as anyone else." He had prepared questions, put them in order and assembled his documents "I brought my documents, because I wanted her to see I had done a lot of work and knew what I was talking about," he said. He was ready, but the jitters had set it in. "I was so nervous," he said.

When Susan came to their table, Jaquiss saw a thin and tired-looking woman. She was suffering from insomnia, and wore the demeanor of one who had led a hard life. Susan was shaking and chain smoking. She had trouble lighting her cigarettes. She sat down and pulled out a tape recorder.

Do you mind if I tape this, she asked.

Jaquiss said, OK, thinking if she had nothing to say, she wouldn't be taping this, he thought, jumping to an unlikely conclusion that suited his purpose but, as he later would realize, was probably erroneous. She appeared uncertain how to use it. He had his own tape recorder, but Jaquiss was so nervous he forgot to turn it on.

Jaquiss began the interview gently. For a while, they just talked about her life, her friendship with Kurt Cobain, what she was doing in Las Vegas. Susan told them how she was class president in elementary school and made straight As. She went to Portland's St. Mary's Academy, one of the best schools in Portland, but dropped out when she was a sophomore. She later earned a general equivalency degree and had taken a few courses at Portland Community College. She was married now, worked occasionally as a waitress, loved her two Dalmatians and riding horses with her stepdaughter, and had completed paralegal courses.

Then Jaquiss brought out his documents, put them on the table and got down to business. "For 20 minutes, I am pounding away at her with questions," he said, referring to his notes from that interview. "Here's a document that says this, and here's a document that says that," Jaquiss said, describing his questioning.

No, that didn't happen, Susan said. I have the highest regard for Neil Goldschmidt. He's been nothing but an inspiration.

At one point, he showed her a document from the Seattle rape case in which Susan said she had been abused by a family friend 21 years her senior. Then he asked the question: Neil Goldschmidt is 21 years older than you and a family friend, he began. So isn't the person in this document Neil Goldschmidt?

The ploy didn't work; nothing did.

Jaquiss asked her how could she explain why so many of her friends would tell him that she had confided to them about Goldschmidt's abuse of her.

"It must have been my chemical imbalance," she said. "The state, the county and city owe a debt of gratitude to him."

Jaquiss was getting nowhere. It was now clear why she brought the tape recorder—to prove to Goldschmidt that she had not cooperated.

A cell phone rang and broke the tension. It was Susan's. She excused herself and walked away from the table to answer it.

What do think? Fagg asks Jaquiss.

"I said, 'I think she's a fucking liar,'" Jaquiss answered.

What do you mean?

"Every...thing out of her mouth is a lie."

No sooner had those foul words escaped his mouth than he saw Fagg motioning downward with her hand toward the table.

What? Jaquiss asked. Fagg silently mouthed words he didn't want to hear.

"Tape turning," she said.

Her words hit hard.

"Not only was I not getting any cooperation, but I had just called her a liar on her own tape recorder," Jaquiss said.

So when Susan came back to the table, Jaquiss went after her again. "I spent another 20 minutes just pounding away," he said. But she wouldn't back down.

At one point, Susan revealed that she had been molested as a teen and even ear-lier than that by her grandfather but never by Goldschmidt.

The interview was turning into a disaster, and Jaquiss thought of one last desperate ploy. "Look," I told her, "I will leave you alone, and you will never hear from me again, and we will never write a word of this; all you have to do is give me the name of the guy who did it. If I can confirm that, we will drop the story immediately." Once again, Susan gave him an answer he didn't want.

OK, I can do that, she said. She would check with her lawyer get back to him in an hour. The interview ended. Jaquiss and Fagg hung out at a library wait-ing for Susan's call. An hour passed, but Susan didn't call. Fagg finally called her, and Susan backed out of the agreement and threatened to sue them if they bothered her again. Although her offer apparently had been a bluff, Jaquiss was devastated by the interview. He still firmly believed Susan was lying, but her denial was emphatic. "I had a lot to drink that night," he said.[52]

When a Project Reaches the Nadir ...

Jaquiss took an early flight back to Portland and went straight to Zusman's office. "She shut us down," he told Zusman. "She denied this, and we're screwed."

The veteran editor empathized. Zusman sometimes talks about one of his own disastrous interviews with a sexual abuse victim in his reporting days, and the results were worse. "That story ended up getting broken by a female reporter for another newspaper," he said.

With both the victim and her mother denying anything had happened, the investigation had reached a nadir. Neither interview had met even their mini-mal expectations. Zusman saw that Jaquiss was down like never before. He had seen his reporter struggle through other low points, but they didn't last long. "He would get pieces of information and he would come back into my office completely liberated," he recalled. But this time, this was the lowest of the low points. "He was completely down in the dumps. "I said, 'Nigel, if you thought this story was going to be easy, somebody else would have had it by now.' "[53]

... "Try to Make Something Happen"

Jaquiss also remembers Zusman giving him a verbal kick in the rear. "He said, and I remember this clearly, 'you are in a reporter's worst nightmare; you've got the biggest story of your career and you may not get it in the paper unless you make something happen.' "

To Jaquiss, the challenge meant that it was time to journalistically "shake the bushes." The time for being subtle was over. He was going to start visiting Goldschmidt's people openly and in person. He would go to their offices or homes unannounced, ask to talk to them about Susan and broach specific issues and reveal that he had very detailed knowledge. Essentially, he wanted to make some noise to get the message out to Goldschmidt that there was no doubt he was pursuing the story and pursuing it hard. "I assumed these people would call him and say Nigel has been here and seems to have some specific informa-tion about this specific issue with a specific person," Jaquiss said.

At the same time, working from the legal advice of the paper's longtime lawyer, he started making the story trial proof. He went back to the friendlies who had confirmed Susan's story. Some agreed to a sign an affidavit for use if the case ever went to court. With other sources, he took advantage of a state law that allowed him to record his phone conversations without disclosing it. He called them back, got them to confirm the content of their earlier interview and recorded the affirmation.[54]

More important, Jaquiss continued searching for more sources for more confirmation. One was one of Susan's former roommates. She told Jaquiss that Susan once stole her credit card and ran up a huge bill. When she threatened to file charges if Susan didn't repay her, Susan's roommate got a call from a man who identified himself as Bob Burtchaell and said he would take care of the charges Susan had put on the credit card. Jaquiss later learned Burtchaell was a Goldschmidt confidante who acted as an intermediary between him and Susan.[55]

Another key source was a lawyer. He was a prominent lawyer who defends many capital murder cases. But in the early 1990s, he had been in a long-term romantic relationship with Susan, which is why Jaquiss wanted to talk to him. Although Jaquiss doubted he would cooperate (because of an unrelated legal conflict between the lawyer and the *Willamette Week*), he had to try. "I was at the point where I knew I was not going to get this story in the paper if I didn't make something happen." Astoundingly, when Jaquiss called and mentioned Susan's name, the lawyer told Jaquiss to come over and he would clear his calendar all day for him. Like so many others, he insisted on remaining anonymous. Jaquiss attributed his reticence to the fact that most of the judges and prosecutors he faced in court were Goldschmidt appointees.

It was one of the strangest interviews in Jaquiss' career. The lawyer was careful and cryptic. Jaquiss sensed he desperately wanted to confirm the story, but was afraid. He was careful to put every response in hypothetical terms. At one point, Jaquiss described the rumor and the $350,000 settlement. "He said, 'If it were the case that this happened, and, if it were the case that this guy reached this settlement, that would be a hell of a story.'" At times Jaquiss would ask bluntly: Are you telling me that it is true? His answer again was positive but hypothetical: "If I were to ask her that question, and she denied the truthfulness of the accusation, I would want to think about why she might do that." He asked him if he was living with Susan around the time of the settlement and if he suggested that she hire Jeff Foote. His answer: Jeff Foote is one of the finest lawyers I have ever come across. Jaquiss revealed several other oblique answers that taken together spelled a single message to him—confirmation.[56]

Jaquiss showed up at another source's home unannounced at 9:30 on a Saturday morning. She had interviewed Susan and had direct knowledge of her ordeal. He got her name from the court records. "I knocked on the door and said 'I'm here to talk about Neil Goldschmidt abusing this woman.'" She looked at him and told him to wait there. She went back inside the house. Her reaction puzzled Jaquiss. About 10 minutes later, she reappeared. "I can't talk to you," she said. Jaquiss was undeterred. Indeed, he interpreted her momentary retreat into her home as an encouraging sign, that it was a stall to figure out a way to share information with him. So he plowed ahead:

Jaquiss: If I were to write the story would I be wrong?

Source: I can't talk to you.

Jaquiss: You realize if I write this story, and I am wrong, I will get sued and I will lose my job and I've got three kids.

Jaquiss wasn't serious. He was just trying to lighten the moment. "My goal is to always keep people talking, to try and make a connection with these people. If I invoke my children, I would do so only humorously, you know, 'Don't let me hang myself here, I've got kids to feed.' It's humorous, but it is a way to try and get people to confirm things that they are not able to confirm. Sometimes asking for indirect confirmation pays off for him. "You call somebody up and they say 'I can't speak for the record,' and you say 'If I print the fact that you just reached a $15 million out-of-court settlement, will I be wrong, and would I be making a mistake?'" Sometimes it works, sometimes it fails.

In this case the woman who was close to Susan could not speak about the case, nor would she.

I can't talk to you, but I am looking forward to reading your story, she said.

Are you sure? Jaguiss asked. Nobody will ever know; nobody knows that I am even here; nobody knows who you are.

The source didn't give in, but Jaquiss interpreted the one positive answer and the lack of any negative answers as good sign.[57]

"Something" Happens: Goldschmidt Side Reaches Out

In the meantime, Richard Meeker, the publisher, got pulled into the reporting process. In early May, Goldschmidt's rabbi, Emanuel Rose of Congregation Beth Israel, where Meeker's family also worships, reached out to the publisher. Meeker says he is bound by a confidentiality agreement not to reveal the details of the conversation, and the rabbi declined Jaquiss' attempt to interview him.[58]

Meeker acknowledged he met with a source he described as "somebody who had been on Neil's side." Meeker said, "Somebody said to me can't you avoid the humiliation, and write about the other women, not the girl. That was the first and only confirmation we got from the Goldschmidt side and that's my only real contribution to the whole process." Meeker adamantly refused to say whether that person was the rabbi. "I can't tell you any more about that conversation," he said repeatedly.

The conversation occurred in the first week of May, shortly before a crucial in-house meeting on May 5, 2004, with the paper's lawyer to decide whether they had enough to publish over the denials from Susan, her mother and the expected denial or no comment from Goldschmidt. Except for hearing Goldschmidt's explanation for the evidence they had turned up, the reporting was complete. Meeker was at the meeting. For the most part, Jaquiss and Zusman updated Rod Lewis, the paper's lawyer. Meeker told them about his secret conversation.[59]

Although most of their sources were anonymous, Zusman said they had made their case ironclad. "If I could divulge three of them to you, you would understand why I felt as comfortable as I did of the truthfulness of this story," he said. "It is a helluva story and maybe when they are all dead, I will feel like

I am not violating them. These people are scared shitless to this day." Lewis was satisfied from a legal perspective and gave them the go-ahead.[60]

There were no high-fives or celebrating after the May 5 meeting, but everyone knew what it meant. Unless Goldschmidt produced incontrovertible counterevidence at the last minute, a story accusing the most powerful man in Oregon of sexually abusing a 14-year-old girl 30 years ago was going to get into the paper.

"We just started, in a real workmanlike way, planning what we were going to do next," Meeker recalled. They prepared a letter detailing the allegations and the evidence and sent it to Goldschmidt and his lawyers. It said: "Our investigation has led us to believe the story of your relationship with [Susan] is true. If you deny the story, we want to give you the opportunity to provide information to us to support your denial." Goldschmidt had eight days to answer.[61]

Meeker said he had no doubts about publishing the story. Meeker himself was a lawyer. He also had been an investigative reporter and an editor. Lewis had represented the paper for decades, guided it through many legal issues and shown Meeker that he was a very careful lawyer. Jaquiss had long since proven his mettle. Meeker considered Zusman experienced, knowledgeable and "the best editor" in the state. "It was a pretty seasoned group of people actually making very calculated, very deliberate decisions," he said.

Nevertheless, Meeker pondered what was at risk and girded for the worst that could happen. "If we had been wrong, we could have been in very serious trouble. He fully expected Goldschmidt would deny the story, and he worried how the paper could survive if Goldschmidt's powerful friends declared all-out war on the *Willamette Week*, a paper that did not have bountiful resources. Although the paper had survived economic retaliation before, this story had Meeker more on edge than usual. As publisher, Meeker felt it was his job to try to prepare for what could happen after publication. "I really felt helpless," he said. "I would have this disconcerting sense that in addition to doing good journalism, we were also driving off of a cliff. I was thinking what can I do to help protect us from the potential fallout, and there was nothing that I could do. He decided not to convey his worries to Zusman and Jaquiss.

Did he ever think about not publishing the story? "The thought never crossed my mind. It's not that I am some kind of fearless person; but this is the kind of work I did; this is the kind of work we run this newspaper for. To say no to publication in the face of a completed and properly done story would have undercut everything this paper was about."[62]

Goldschmidt's Flanking Move

Meeker would not have much time to agonize, because events would unfold faster than any of them imagined and force them into a frantic effort to prevent the occurrence of what they had feared since mid-March—getting beat on the story by another news organization. The day after Jaquiss sent the letter to Goldschmidt, Craig Bachman, the former governor's attorney, called him and Zusman to his office, where they encountered the first of a series of surprises: Susan's lawyer, Jeff Foote, was there. Jaquiss was stunned, and the lawyers understood how the scene must look to the two journalists.

"They were like 'don't read anything into the fact that we are here together; it is not an admission.' I mean it was crazy. I was stunned by it."

Did Jaquiss read anything into the scene?

"Of course. What do these two men have in common?"[63]

Bachman had more surprises in store for Jaquiss and Zusman. He said Goldschmidt was going to make a public statement within 24 hours resigning from several public positions, including chairman of the Oregon Board of Higher Education, and take a leave from his consulting firm. He also said Goldschmidt would acknowledge the sexual relationship with an underage girl in his past and express contrition. He asked the paper to consider not publishing the story. Foote urged them not to use Susan's real name if they did run the story. Zusman and Jaquiss asked Bachman for an interview with Goldschmidt, and he agreed to pass their request along.[64] The two journalists left the office, expecting that the next step would be Goldschmidt's answer to their request for an interview.[65]

By noon, less than 15 minutes after the meeting ended, Goldschmidt issued a press release announcing his resignation and attributing his decision to ill health only. Jaquiss felt deceived. The statement was four pages long, and he believed that it had been prepared before their meeting with Bachman. And, it contained no reference to his abuse of a 14-year-old girl.

Despite the shocking sequence of events, Jaquiss and Zusman were ready to move. By 1:47, the paper posted on its website a summary of what it planned to publish a week hence in the weekly print edition of the paper. Broadcast news organizations statewide picked up the *Willamette Week*'s brief story.

But Goldschmidt would make another move. Shortly after the paper posted the summary, Jaquiss learned that Goldschmidt was going to meet with *The Oregonian* that afternoon.[66]

Now, Jaquiss was worried. "I was a wreck," he said. He thought he was about to lose his exclusive story.[67] Later, Jaquiss learned that Goldschmidt had confessed to his rival. Jaquiss had already been working on a draft of the story, so by 5 p.m. he had posted a fuller story on the website outlining more details of Goldschmidt's 30-year secret. Not until three hours later was *The Oregonian* able to post its story of Goldschmidt's confession to it.[68] The *Willamette Week* had beaten *The Oregonian* on one of the biggest stories in Oregon's history.

The following Wednesday, the *Willamette Week* ran a longer story, beginning with an editor's note explaining the events of the past week and that the story would not include all the details and evidence supporting its allegations of Goldschmidt's abuse of the girl because his confession had made those details unnecessary. Jaquiss also wrote a story explaining partly how Goldschmidt managed to keep it secret by using Burtchaell, the intermediary between him and Susan.

In the weeks ahead, Jaquiss continued investigating to find more details on how Goldschmidt was able to keep the secret for nearly three decades and who knew the secret. As his work continued, other formerly secret sources spoke on the record to Jaquiss, including Mark Smolak, who Jaquiss said was the criminal defense attorney who had spoken in cryptic code to try to indirectly confirm Jaquiss' information during his initial investigation. In June 2004, State Sen. Vickie Walker, a Democrat, who publicly acknowledged years earlier that she had been a child victim of sexual abuse, announced she was the source of Washington County court record that precipitated Jaquiss' investigation.[69] That month

Rabbi Rose wrote a commentary in *The Oregonian* extolling Goldschmidt's virtues, bemoaning the continuing coverage. "Enough is enough," he wrote.

By early November, Jaquiss produced a third major story revealing the names of more than a dozen people, including a former sheriff, and Goldschmidt's former secretary, who knew about Susan. He also presented on-the-record allegations that the current governor and Goldschmidt confidant Ted Kulongoski knew about it when he was Goldschmidt's attorney general, a charge the governor has denied. He also revealed *The Oregonian* first learned of the rumors in the mid-1980s and that as late as 2003, a former Goldschmidt speechwriter had leaked details of the affair and gave them a list of sources who could confirm it.

Postscript—The Aftermath

The stories were bombshells. Reader reaction was instantaneous with hundreds of letters pouring into the paper, most of which condemned Goldschmidt's behavior. The stories permanently changed the political landscape. Goldschmidt, a force to contend with for so long, had left a power vacuum. In the state capitol, Goldschmidt's portrait had been removed from a wall bearing the portraits of other Oregon governors. By early 2007, it still was not there.

Jaquiss continued writing about Goldschmidt's last business and political cause—Portland General Electric and the group of Texas investors trying to buy it. The effort would finally fail. Kulongoski was re-elected in 2006 despite his ties to Goldschmidt.

Goldschmidt sold his Oregon winery. He began spending a lot of time in France, where he bought another winery. He still is seen in Portland periodically, dropping in at Starbucks for coffee or at the RiverPlace Athletic Club to work out. Zusman also works out there and ran into him in the locker room in late December 2006. They shook hands and exchanged holiday greetings. "I haven't seen him since," Zusman said.[70]

Opinions differed as to whether Goldschmidt would try to make a comeback. Jaquiss and Zusman said they thought he would try to find a way back. Meeker doubted it. "He probably doesn't care," Meeker said. Goldschmidt was 67 in 2007 and financially secure.[71]

Susan had not publicly come forward at this writing, but Jaquiss' sources told him she was back in Portland. Her mother was still defending Goldschmidt. Zusman said he got call from her in late 2004 saying she was disappointed in the story.[72]

As for *The Oregonian*, it had to face a humiliating reality. It had suffered another ignominious defeat more shameful than the Packwood debacle—this time, not by one of the big boys like the *Washington Post*, but by the tiny, but feisty *Willamette Week*. It came under a considerable amount of criticism. Many critics felt it had failed to adequately follow up on key tips that it had received in the mid-1990s and again in late 2006, well before Jaquiss started working on the story. Moreover, they felt it had soft-pedaled the story and showed disregard for the seriousness of Goldschmidt's sexual relationship with Susan by using a headline that called it an "affair."

At the *Willamette Week*, its staff luxuriated in the afterglow of its journalistic feat. The accolades poured in. It was the greatest feat in its 30-year-history, and on April 4, 2005, the national journalism community gave the paper its due—the Pulitzer Prize for investigative reporting.

The next day, Jaquiss was back in the newsroom. By midafternoon, he wasn't doing much work, just sitting at his desk "staring into space." He was still in shock from the Pulitzer win and a bit hung over from the celebrations. At 3:30, his phone rang.

"Come on downstairs," a voice said. "I want to shake your hand."

Jaquiss recognized it instantly. It was Neil Goldschmidt.

He was standing on the sidewalk outside the paper's former offices when Jaquiss went down. Goldschmidt looked him in the eye when they shook hands. They talked for about five minutes. Things had been tough, Goldschmidt said, and he regretted what had happened. He mentioned that he had heard from several people who knew Jaquiss.

They said you are a pretty decent guy, Goldschmidt said.

Jaquiss thanked him.

I did not get any pleasure out of reporting the story, he said. I came to understand through the course of reporting how influential you had been in the success of the city, and I would like to talk to you at greater length someday about that.

Was Goldschmidt's congratulatory gesture sincere?

"I had done a number of follow-ups that were not very flattering," Jaquiss said. "I think he wanted some closure—to close the loop by talking to me, and, maybe to some extent, for me to leave him alone."[73]

Lessons

WEATHERING A "CATEGORY 5 HURRICANE"

Lesson Learned: A small, moderately financed paper can practice aggressive, irreverent journalism without falling victim to economic retaliation for several reasons: a long tradition of watchdog journalism; a record of resisting economic retaliation; and establishing itself as a vital part of the charitable, social and cultural scene.

How It Applies: The *Willamette Week*, a for-profit newspaper that relies on small advertisers, took on the most powerful force in the state and subjected him to an aggressive probe. The *Willamette Week* goes to about 90,000 readers, mostly in the coveted 18–34 age range. Its owners are satisfied with a profit margin that huge corporate chains would not consider acceptable, editor and co-owner Mark Zusman said.[74]

In pursuing a career-destroying story about Goldschmidt's sexual abuse of an underage girl, Meeker said the paper was risking retaliation from Goldschmidt loyalists that included a web of powerful bankers, businessmen, lawyers, developers and realtors. Although the danger became moot when Goldschmidt publicly confessed to the allegations after the *Willamette Week* had scheduled publication, the paper had expected Goldschmidt to deny the charges and was prepared to publish the story regardless.

Publisher Richard Meeker acknowledged there wasn't much he could do to stave off a financial assault. But in hindsight, he points to a number of factors that he feels greatly lessened the risk of running the story, even over the expected Goldschmidt denial. He counts the journalistic quality of the reporting as the most important factor. Despite the story's heavy reliance on anonymous sources, Meeker said several were so strong and irrefutable that he had absolute certainty that the story was accurate. Accuracy substantially mitigates the financial repercussions that a suit would impose.

The *Willamette Week* also may be less vulnerable to economic retaliation than typical mainstream papers because of the variety and number of its advertisers. The paper does not rely on a few huge advertisers such as big-box stores and car dealerships. The average major advertiser spends only $192 a week, and the biggest advertiser provides only 3 percent of the company's total revenue.[75]

People have tried advertising boycotts before, and they didn't work. One of the most memorable occurred several years ago when the *Willamette Week* reported that a popular and highly regarded director of a homeless shelter was forcing homeless boys to have sex with him in exchange for shelter.[76] Meeker said he received death and bomb threats, and someone hired a private detective to follow him. When the director vehemently denied the charges, the gay community swung into action in support of him and launched an advertising boycott that cost the *Willamette Week* $100,000 in advertising. "The amount of revenue we lost was greater than whatever profit we had that year," Meeker said.

Meeker believed his paper's long history, reputation and community involvement also helps it withstand retaliation. He said community business leaders have learned that advertising boycotts will not influence editorial decisions. Moreover, the company has made itself an integral part of the community's charitable, cultural and social scene. "If we were just publishing a newspaper and nothing else, we would be on hard times," Meeker said, speculating that readership and interest in the paper would have declined.[77]

DEALING WITH APPARENT CONFLICTS OF INTEREST

Lesson Learned: Journalists must always avoid getting involved in stories in which they have any involvement, personal or pecuniary. Sometimes, however, reporters unavoidably become involved in a story, and when they do, full disclosure to the readers is mandatory.

How It Applied: In "The 30-Year Secret," Richard Meeker, the co-owner and publisher of the *Willamette Week* was an acknowledged admirer of Goldschmidt, and wrote effusively about Goldschmidt's public service contributions to Oregon and Portland. Moreover, Goldschmidt had appointed his wife to the court bench and they attended the same synagogue. He had close personal friendships with some of Goldschmidt's strongest supporters. However, he openly revealed all of this to the paper's readers and his involvement in the reporting on the Goldschmidt story. Ultimately, there was no evidence that his relationship with Goldschmidt had any restrictive impact on the work of Nigel Jaquiss or editor Mark Zusman.

ALL REPORTERS ARE INVESTIGATIVE REPORTERS

Lesson Learned: In daily news reporting, the investigative mentality should drive every reporter on every story.

How It Applied: With just a handful of reporters, the *Willamette Week* regularly turns out hard-hitting stories and a steady diet of solid investigative work, as exemplified in Jaquiss' Pulitzer Prize–winning project. Editor and co-owner Mark Zusman believes daily reporters "can and do" produce investigative work. "All of our reporters are working on stories that they won't see for six months," he said. "That's the idea. Every reporter has the ability to do that."

Zusman does not subscribe to the notion that investigative reporting is the "province of a few special people." At the *Willamette Week* every reporter is expected to do investigative work, which he defines as probing beneath the surface and "connecting the dots."

"That is a term we use a lot around here, which means to place things in a larger context and to understand what is really going." In Zusman's view, any news organization can do that kind of work if the organization makes it the mission.[78]

RUMORS AND TIPS: WHEN TO IGNORE, NIBBLE OR BITE

Lesson Learned: An unsubstantiated rumor earns attention when a pertinent document contains details that are consistent with the rumor, even if those details are sparse.

How It Applied: This project began with four pages of a conservatorship court file that were so factually thin and dated, they would not have caught Jaquiss' attention without the salacious rumor that went with them. On the flip side, Jaquiss would never have put the rumor on his to-do list without the four pages of records that came with it. Jaquiss was wise to put the rumor and the document together and conclude that the rumor at least deserved some preliminary checking. For veteran reporters such decisions are more instinctive rather than calculated, but Jaquiss' choice provides a good lesson for younger journalists.

THE RUMOR FILE: "PAPER, PLEASE"

Lesson Learned: Establish a paper file in which to deposit any notes about all rumors or tips, no matter how weak or unlikely they may be.

How It Applied: Let's be honest. We, as journalists, love the lowly rumor. We salivate on juicy scuttlebutt. We are among the few people on this planet who welcome those who monger in rumors. That does not mean we plop them in the paper, but we listen. A reporter with a thick rumor file is a reporter who is out beating the bushes. Good journalists, who constantly work their sources and hang out on their beats, hear rumors and tips every day. You can't chase all of them. You have to be like Jaquiss' metaphorical catfish sitting at the bottom of a river waiting for the good stuff to float by. Picking the good stuff means first keeping a rumor file (a paper file is preferable to an electronic file). Every rumor and tip you hear should go in your rumor file. If you didn't take notes when you first heard the rumor, scribble a reminder on the first scrap of paper you find and drop it in the file. Most of the notes will languish there forever. But as more information about a particular rumor floats by, snap it up and attach it to the rumor. Filing a handwritten rumor note helps plant it firmly in your memory where it may later provide context for new information that otherwise would have no meaning.

THE FUTURE FILE: THINGS WORTH CHECKING

Lesson Learned: When the lowly rumor accumulates more details and solid information, consider it for a promotion in status.

How It Applied: If you are a good reporter, your rumor file will become a bulging mess fairly quickly, which is why you should always keep a future file. Once a rumor accumulates a modicum of substance, give the rumor a bump; advance it to your future file—the electronic one you should start on the same day you hang a rumor folder in your desk drawer. At this point, the lowly rumor has earned a place somewhere on your daily or weekly to-do list, maybe even on your electronic calendar, depending on its urgency and degree of substance. You may relegate it to the bottom of that list, but it is at least on your agenda.

Lesson Learned: A good, well-maintained future file is key to setting the agenda on your beat; it also can shield you from ribbon-cutting assignments and other "scut" work.

How It Applied: A future file is a very useful organizational tool that will keep you constantly busy working on stories that interest you rather than on an assigned story that any other warm body in the newsroom could handle. With a well-maintained future file and to-do list, you will always have a ready answer when an editor hits you with the dreaded question—"What are you working on today?"—which is usually a prelude to "I need you to cover a ribbon-cutting." Your editor may growl and grouse at the moment but will love you later when the story from your future file makes him or her look like a genius.

More important, a future file and to-do list enables you to plan how you want to cover your beat or specialty and establish your priorities. By becoming the readers' expert on the topic, you are better equipped to identify the most important and most interesting stories for them. A welcome, in-house by-product of this practice is that your editors will soon realize that you know what you are doing and they will leave you alone to let you do it. You will have established your signature on the beat, and it will identify you as clearly as your byline does.

ANONYMOUS SOURCES

Lesson Learned: Anonymous sources are valuable, but using their information imposes immense responsibility on the reporter to confirm its accuracy. Such confirmation requires multiple independent sources and probing interviewing techniques to determine how the source obtained the information.

How It Applied: Although public records provided the foundation of Jaquiss' story, anonymous sources made it publishable even if Goldschmidt had not confessed. The records provided a circumstantial case, which would have been too weak for publication without the interviews. Ordinarily information from anonymous sources also is weak, because readers have no way of gauging the credibility or authority of the source. When reporters report information provided by anonymous sources, they are, in effect, asking readers to trust their judgment of the source's reliability and to believe that information from the source is accurate. Aware of the risk of using anonymous sources, reporters have to develop ways to measure the reliability of a source and test the accuracy of the information they provide.

Jaquiss said he had more than a dozen anonymous sources for the story, and Zusman noted that there were three who—if he could identify them publicly—would show clearly why he would have been so confident of the validity of the story even if Goldschmidt had not confessed.

However, the sources as described in the story did not appear to be as solid individually; their credibility rested in the number of them. Jaquiss relied heavily on the "friendlies," who were Susan's friends, co-workers, roommates and boyfriends who gave him information they received directly from Susan. Although the information from them was firsthand, he still had to be careful in using it. He had to make sure these sources were in a position to hear these stories and determine whether their relationship was such that Susan could be reasonably expected to confide in them. He had to consider that much of the information these sources provided to him came to them while they and Susan were drinking. Some sources said she was bitter toward Goldschmidt, which cast doubt on what she told Jaquiss' sources. The sources were relying on their memories, and those memories were of conversations that occurred 10 to 20 years ago. Some had become very close to Susan and thus may have had a prejudice against Goldschmidt.

The reporting and the story itself, however, dealt with these weaknesses in several ways. From the outset of the story, Jaquiss made no secret of his methodology. The nature of the information from these sources was clearly apparent to the readers. Jaquiss reported that he had more than a dozen independent sources recount Susan's story with remarkably similar detail. In some cases, public records, such as yearbooks and court records, led him to her friends.

More important, interviewing skill played a key role in helping him determine the reliability of their information. He asked a number of questions designed to confirm the validity of their relationship with Susan and the information they provided in a number of ways. In his interviews, he listened for personal details that matched details others had provided to help him decide whether they were in a position to have known her. "The more detail the person knows, the more likely it is going to be true," he said. Asking these sources "How do you know that?" was often as important as "What do you know?" He asked them to tell where they were when they heard Susan tell her story, who else was around when she told the story. He looked for sources who knew her at different times in her life. He looked for sources close to her when she was a child and when she was an adult and sources who were close to her parents when she was a child.

Jaquiss also went back to most of these sources to go over their information again. In some cases, sources signed affidavits, which is evidence that they would be willing to go on the record if the case went to court.[79]

Although Goldschmidt himself provided the ultimate confirmation, the fact that the reporting convinced him that he had no choice provides testament to the thoroughness of the journalists' efforts to test the accuracy of their sources' information.

THE REPORTING STRATEGY

Lesson Learned: Developing an overall strategy is a crucial part of reporting, especially in long-term investigative projects. It keeps the reporting on target while helping you effectively analyze new leads.

How It Applied: In explaining their strategy, editor Mark Zusman talked about three phases, which he referred to as "concentric circles": the circle of public records, the circle of "friendlies" or people close to Susan, and finally the subjects of the story, who were Goldschmidt and his supporters and Susan, her mother and lawyers. The concentric circles are not definitive boundaries because they often overlap and Jaquiss darted back and forth through the rings as much as the reporting trail required.

Although strategy is a guide—not a policy manual—it is a crucial part of project reporting. In longer term investigative stories, reporters sometimes spend weeks circling in the outer ring doing desk research, following the paper trail and talking to peripheral experts to develop expertise and a source list. Gradually, their circling constricts; the reporting pace accelerates as the information gathering trail takes them closer and closer to the center where the subjects of their investigation reside.

Although such a process is one of many that reporters use, it is a classic investigative strategy. Many reporters believe the longer they can work quietly, under the radar, there is less chance that the subjects of their investigation will try to obstruct their work by pulling crucial documents from the record, pressuring sources not to cooperate or fabricating a common response theme ("getting their stories straight"). Moreover, such a strategy is sometimes necessary for competitive reasons similar to what Zusman and Jaquiss faced: to reduce chances that rival news organizations will hear about your work and break the story first. But more often reporters engage in such sub-rosa strategies because the more time they can devote to becoming educated about their topic, the more effective they will be when interviewing the subjects of their investigation or other key sources.

Developing an overall reporting strategy helps reporters work methodically and efficiently. Reporting on a long-term project without an overall strategy is like trying to find an address across the country without a roadmap. A strategy keeps you on a course leading to the center of the investigation, minimizes wrong turns and helps you avoid tangential digressions. When you do need to digress, a strategy helps you keep the main road in sight. Because reporting on a long-term project often reveals several tantalizing digressions, an overall strategy helps you select only those that are likely to loop back to the main road. Moreover, a project often starts as a local story, but your reporting reveals the local problem is symptomatic of a state or national problem.

EDITOR–REPORTER RELATIONSHIPS

Lesson Learned: Experience, detachment from the story and broad community knowledge provide frontline editors the ability to give reporters perspective, leadership, guidance and emotional support at all levels of the reporting process. They come into play in long-range strategizing and in the nuts-and-bolts of reporting.

How It Applied: Jaquiss and his editor, Mark Zusman, worked closely on this story, at times sharing reporting duties. Their collaboration was closer than what is customary in reporter–editor relationships.

Ordinarily, editors—even line editors, those who work directly with reporters—prefer to keep a measure of distance from the reporting. Distance helps them see factual holes in the reporting. It also helps them protect their reporters from the big-story bias.

The editor's role as the reporter's backstop, leader, supporter and resource becomes especially crucial in stories as difficult, frustrating and sensitive as the one Jaquiss was investigating. Despite Zusman's deep involvement in the reporting, Jaquiss has noted several times when Zusman provided "the cooler head." Zusman reined in his eagerness to interview Susan before building a strong body of evidence that could be of use to him in pulling information from her. Although Zusman was as eager for the story as Jaquiss, Jaquiss was ready to publish the story long before Zusman was satisfied with the evidence to support it. And when Jaquiss returned from the disastrous interview with Susan in Las Vegas, it was Zusman who called the interview "just a bump in the road" and challenged him "to make something happen," which he did.

Zusman's long standing in the community also played an important role when he dropped into the reporting trenches. Although Zusman did not personally know Susan's mother when he interviewed her, both had lived in Portland for years and found conversational commonalities that helped break the ice. "Oh, I know you," she told Zusman when he first introduced himself. Likewise, Zusman's previous acquaintance with Doreen Margolin was an important factor when he and Jaquiss confronted her. Even Richard Meeker, the publisher, which is a position almost never involved with reporting, found himself contributing because of his long-standing community knowledge.

TIMING THE SHOWDOWN

Lesson Learned: Although reporters differ on when to interview the subject of the investigation, delaying it until you have gathered all of the information and developed preliminary conclusions is a common and effective strategy.

How It Applied: In "The 30-Year Secret," Goldschmidt and Susan were the subjects of the *Willamette Week*'s investigation, but Jaquiss and Zusman delayed interviewing them until late in the reporting. Although Goldschmidt called Zusman and Meeker to a lunch meeting at the Carafe Restaurant, they had decided not to discuss the investigation even if Goldschmidt broached the subject.

The delay strategy didn't help much in interviews with Susan and her mother, but it apparently was resoundingly successful with Goldschmidt. Although Jaquiss and Goldschmidt never revealed all of their evidence to Goldschmidt, they learned that he had been aware of their reporting for weeks. When Jaquiss sent him an outline of their evidence, he apparently realized they had enough to publish and confessed.

THE DELICATE INTERVIEW

Lesson Learned: Like all important interviews, conducting delicate ones with sources laboring under various mental or emotional vulnerabilities requires thorough preparation and knowledge of the subject and the interviewee. But in these types of interviews, success often relies on sensitivity and psychology.

How It Applied: In preparing for the interview with Susan, Jaquiss and Zusman attempted to take her emotional vulnerability into account. Zusman delayed the interview until Jaquiss had compiled at least a half-dozen accounts of Goldschmidt's sexual abuse of her. Recognizing her experiences with men had been sadly tragic, Zusman decided to enlist a female colleague to make the attempt to arrange the interview. Meanwhile, Jaquiss decided he would have to set his sights low. He realized he faced an incredibly difficult interview. Not only was Susan legally bound to confidentiality, but she was a victim of sexual abuse twice during her childhood and of a brutally violent, life-threatening rape in adulthood. Under such circumstances, Jaquiss felt that if he could win her trust enough to get a confidential confirmation, the interview would be a success.

The first part of the plan worked: Arts and culture editor Ellen Fagg succeeded in landing the interview for Jaquiss.

For his part, Jaquiss had prepared thoroughly. He compiled and ordered a list of questions. And he gathered compelling circumstantial evidence from public records and detailed accounts of what she had told former friends and boyfriends about what Goldschmidt had done to her when she was 14–17 years old. "I knew her as well as anyone could know her," he said. He was hoping the stack of records and the detailed accounts from her friends would show her that he knew what he was talking about and encourage her to relent. His questions were direct, and he confronted her with the evidence from his records and from his interviews. Nothing worked.

In hindsight, Jaquiss said he made several mistakes. For one, Jaquiss said he did not do any research on victims of sexual abuse or consult with experts on how to talk with them. "I didn't and I should have," he said. "I think I probably would have been less direct. I knew she was mentally fragile and had been for a long time. A softer approach might have been more effective."

He also thinks that in preparing his list of questions for the interview, he should have constructed more questions that could have gained confirmation in a subtle but definitive way. The idea is to construct a question that assumes the fact you are trying to confirm is correct. For example, if your goal is to find out whether someone committed a certain act, you would not ask "Did you do it?" but you would ask "How did you do that?" In a real interview situation, the questions would have to be much more subtle. "With a hostile source, each question can be a little brick," Jaquiss said. The goal for each question is to orient the source toward acknowledging that "something happened," with each subsequent question repeatedly containing the assumption that "something happened" as a premise to the question. If the source repeatedly accepts the assumption without challenge, it eventually becomes an acknowledged fact in the conversation, at which point you are safe to probe the acknowledged fact directly.[80]

Notes

1. The interviewees listed here are the sources for their direct and indirect quotes; reconstruction of interviews between themselves and their sources; and depictions of their conversations, thoughts and actions that are not referenced in the text:

Richard Meeker, Portland, OR, January 3, 2007; June 5, 2007, by telephone.
Nigel Jaquiss, Portland, OR, January 3, 2007; June 6, 2007, by telephone.
Mark Zusman, Portland, OR, January 3, 2007.
Some material from these sources is individually referenced where necessary to ensure clarity.

2. Interview, Mark Zusman, editor and co-owner, *Willamette Week,* Portland, OR, January 3, 2007.

3. Interview, Nigel Jaquiss, reporter, *Willamette Week,* Portland, OR, January 3, 2007.

4. Circuit Court, Washington County, Department of Probate. The copy in Appendix B was provided to the author. Although the document is a public record, the author is withholding the name and court case number to help protect the victim's privacy.

5. Interview, Jaquiss, January 3, 2007.

6. *The Portland Tribune,* "Neil's Network," May 21, 2004; Nigel Jaquiss, "Goldschmidt's Midas Touch: The Ex-Governor Profited from Ties Made While in Public Office," *Willamette Week,* June 23, 2004; Nigel Jaquiss, "Goldschmidt's Web of Power," *Willamette Week,* March 9, 2005, p. 1.

7. Interview, Zusman, January 3, 2007; Interview, Richard Meeker, publisher and co-owner, *Willamette Week,* Portland, OR, January 3, 2007.

8. Interview, Meeker, January 3, 2007; Interview, Zusman, January 3, 2007.

9. Interview, Zusman, January 3, 2007.

10. Interview, Meeker, January 3, 2007; June 5, 2007, via telephone.

11. Bridget Barton, "Nigel Jaquiss," *Brainstorm Magazine,* April 2005. http://www.brainstorm.com/archive_2005.html.

12. Interview, Zusman, January 3, 2007; Interview, Meeker, January 3, 2007.

13. Interview, Jaquiss, January 3, 2007.

14. Ibid.

15. Ibid.

16. Ibid.; Interview, Meeker, January 3, 2007.

17. Interview, Jaquiss, January 3, 2007.

18. Circuit Court record, Washington County.

19. Interview, Jaquiss, January 3, 2007.

20. Interview, Jaquiss, June 6, 2007.

21. Interview, Jaquiss, January 3, 2007.

22. Interview, Meeker, January 3, 2007.

23. Interview, Jaquiss, January 3, 2007; Jill Rosen, "The Story Behind the Story," *American Journalism Review* [ajr.org], August–September 2004.

24. Ibid.

25. Nigel Jaquiss, "Breaking Silence: The Source of the Goldschmidt Story Steps Forward," *Willamette Week,* June 30, 2004.

26. Fred Leonhardt, "The Goldschmidt Affair: Democrats, Sex and the Press," *Counterpunch,* November 1, 2006. http://www.countepunch.org. Leonhardt was a former speechwriter for Goldschmidt.

Counterpunch is a biweekly political newsletter edited by Alexander Cockburn and Jeffrey St. Clair. Located in Petrolia, CA, it describes itself as a muckraking newsletter with a "radical attitude."

27. Interview, Jaquiss, January 3, 2007.

28. Ibid.

29. Interview, Zusman, January 3, 2007.

30. Interview, Jaquiss, January 3, 2007; Nigel Jaquiss, "Sex Scandal," *IRE Journal,* July–August 2005, 32–33.

31. Interview, Zusman, January 3, 2007.

32. Ibid.; Interview, Jaquiss, January 3, 2007.

33. Interview, Jaquiss, January 3, 2007.

34. Ibid.; Nigel Jaquiss, "The 30-Year Secret," *Willamette Week,* May 12, 2004, pp. 21–23.

35. Interview, Jaquiss, January 3, 2007.

36. Ibid.

37. Ibid.

38. Interview, Zusman, January 3, 2007.

39. Interview, Jaquiss, January 3, 2007.

40. Interview, Zusman, January 3, 2007.

41. Interview, Jaquiss, January 3, 2007.

42. Ibid.

43. Jaquiss, "The 30-Year Secret"; Nigel Jaquiss, "The Goldschmidt Resignation," May 6, 2004. http://wweek.com.

44. Interview, Jaquiss, January 3, 2007.

45. Interview, Zusman, January 3, 2007.

46. Ibid.

47. Ibid.

48. Interview, Jaquiss, January 3, 2007.

49. Interview, Zusman, January 3, 2007.

50. Ibid.; Interview, Jaquiss, January 3, 2007.

51. Jaquiss, "Sex Scandal."

52. Interview, Jaquiss Interviews, January 3, 2007, and June 6, 2007.

53. Interview, Zusman, January 3, 2007.

54. Interview, Jaquiss, January 3, 2007.

55. Ibid.

56. Ibid.

57. Ibid.

58. Jaquiss, "The 30-Year Secret."

59. Interview, Meeker, January 3, 2007

60. Interview, Zusman, January 3, 2007.

61. John Schrag, "The Background," an editor's note to "The 30-Year Secret," *Willamette Week*, May 12, 2004.

62. Interview, Meeker, January 3, 2007.

63. Interview, Jaquiss, January 3, 2007.

64. Schrag, "The Background."

65. Interview, Jaquiss, January 3, 2007.

66. Schrag, "The Background."

67. Jaquiss, "Sex Scandal."

68. Schrag, "The Background."

69. *New York Times,* "Oregon Critic of Ex-Mayor Discloses Role," July 2, 2004.

70. Interview, Zusman, January 3, 2007.

71. Interview, Meeker, June 5, 2007.

72. Interview, Zusman, January 3, 2007.

73. Interview, Jaquiss, January 6, 2007.

74. Interview, Zusman, January 3, 2007.

75. Interview, Meeker, June 5, 2007.
76. Interview, Zusman, January 3, 2007.
77. Interview, Meeker, June 5, 2007.
78. Interview, Zusman.
79. Interview, Jaquiss, June 6, 2007.
80. Ibid.

Selected Bibliography

Articles

Barton, Bridget. "Nigel Jaquiss." *Brainstorm Magazine*, April 2005. http://www.brainstorm.com/archive_2005.html.

Jaquiss, Nigel. "The Goldschmidt Resignation." *Willamette Week*, May 6, 2004. http://wweek.com.

Jaquiss, Nigel. "The 30-Year-Secret." *Willamette Week*, May 12, 2004, p. 1.

Jaquiss, Nigel. "How Gov. Goldschmidt Aided One Man Who Knew." *Willamette Week*, May 12, 2004, p. 18.

Jaquiss, Nigel, "Who New?" *Willamette Week*, December 15, 2004.

Jaquiss, Nigel. "Goldschmidt's Web of Power." *Willamette Week*, March 9, 2005, p. 1. http://wweek.com.

Jaquiss, Nigel. "Sex Scandal." *IRE Journal*, July–August 2005, 32–33.

Leonhardt, Fred. "The Goldschmidt Affair: Democrats, Sex and the Press." *Counterpunch*, November 1, 2006. http://www.counterpunch.org.

"Neil's Network." *Portland Tribune*, May 21, 2004. http://www.portlandtribune.com/news.

Rosen, Jill. "The Story Behind the Story." *American Journalism Review*, August–September 2004. http://www.ajr.org. Article.asp?id=3707.

Interviews

Jaquiss, Nigel, reporter, *Willamette Week*, Portland, OR, January 3, 2007 (tape recording held by author).

Jaquiss, Nigel, June 6, 2007.

Meeker, Richard, publisher and co-owner, *Willamette Week*, Portland, OR, January 3, 2007 (tape recording held by author).

Meeker, Richard, June 5, 2007.

Zusman, Mark, editor and co-owner, *Willamette Week*, Portland, OR, January 3, 2007 (tape recording held by author).

News Archives and News Search Services

Access World News, NewsBank, Inc., Naples, FL.

Willamette Week online archives.

CHAPTER 3

Persistence, Empathy Used in Tracking Tiger Force Terror

History Is News If No One Knows About It[1]

Day after day for nearly five weeks, Mike Sallah, national affairs reporter for *The Toledo* (Ohio) *Blade*, drove to the University of Michigan in Ann Arbor to pick through the private papers of the military's top cop, the late Col. Henry Tufts, during the Vietnam era. Sallah was the first to get access to them, and he was looking for a story. Somewhere in the 25,000 pages there had to be something important and interesting that no one else had revealed. But he was on a deadline. Tufts, commander of the Army Criminal Investigations Division from 1942 to 1974, had appointed his personal friend, Michael Woods, the *Blade*'s science and technology writer, custodian of the papers, and Woods had given his paper exclusive access to them for six months. Then, he would carry out Tufts' instructions to open them to the public, including any other reporter in the country.

Sallah found papers involving a relative of the late William Westmore land, the famed commander of American forces in Vietnam. That might be a decent fallback story if nothing more interesting emerged, Sallah thought. The same was true for papers on Clarence Kelly, the former FBI director. He ran across material with the tantalizing name of the "Khaki Mafia" case. Back in the newsroom in Toledo, his friend and colleague, State Editor Mitch Weiss, did an Internet check on it for him. It was a money laundering case and it had been covered, Weiss reported back. Sallah kept working.

He came to the My Lai massacre of more than 500 unarmed Vietnamese men, women and children by U.S. soldiers in 1968, considered by many historians one of the worst war crimes cases in American history. Sallah spent a week on that case alone, reading each page, and every time he thought he had something new, Mitch Weiss's Internet search turned up old stories on it.

"This went on and on," Sallah said. "I was working sometimes 12 hours a day, and it was a very long and frustrating process. I realized I had put a month into this thing and wasn't sure I would be able to squeeze anything out of it."

Finally, he got to the last box and started digging into it. When he opened a thin file tabbed the "Coy Allegation," his eyes locked on to the first 13 words of a crude spreadsheet: "COY alleged that YBARRA killed a Vietnamese infant by cutting the infant's throat" (see Appendix C). There was more. For page after page, each stamped "FOR OFFICIAL USE ONLY," Sallah read about American soldiers in a unit called the "Tiger Force" committing barbaric acts: killing elderly farmers working in a rice paddy, raping a teenage girl, dropping grenades in underground bunkers where terrified women and children had sought refuge, torturing prisoners, mutilating dead Vietnamese.

"Surely, this had already been thoroughly covered," he thought. He called Weiss and asked him to Google it.

Nothing, Weiss reported back to Sallah.

Weiss checked Lexis-Nexis.

Nothing again.

He looked at other databases.

Still nothing.

"I started looking at books on the Vietnam War," Sallah recalled. He found a few references to Tiger Force. It was an elite platoon of volunteers from the 101st Airborne Division. A Col. David Hackworth created it in 1965 to "out-guerrilla the guerillas." But there was nothing about an investigation into war crimes. This might be the story he was looking for, Sallah thought.

He wrote a memo to his editors outlining possible stories that he could draw from Tufts' papers, and everybody agreed on the Coy Allegation. The case seemed worse than, or at least substantially different from, the My Lai massacre, because the alleged crimes involved a single unit during a sustained rampage over seven months in 1967. Nearly a dozen soldiers were describing atrocities in about two dozen incidents, with most of them involving one or two Tigers and a few involving larger groups. In many cases, more than one soldier had witnessed the atrocities. And finally, the investigation appeared to have lasted about four years, starting in early 1971, and the file did not say whether the military had formally charged the accused soldiers and brought them to trial. The cases may have been ancient history by the here-and-now standards of journalism, but history becomes news if it has never been revealed, especially if the government covered it up.

High Stakes and Getting It Right

When the *Blade* launched its war crimes probe into the Tiger Force in late January 2003, Americans were feeling a mix of fear, pride and patriotism. The terrorist attacks on the World Trade Center and the Pentagon on Sept. 11, 2001, still shadowed the American psyche. But a wave of patriotism and support for the military swept the country as American soldiers battled Taliban in Afghanistan and were assembling near Iraq.[2] President George W. Bush had declared a war on terrorism and had just delivered a militant State of the Union message virtually declaring Iraq the next battleground. "Since when have terrorists and tyrants announced their intentions, politely putting us on notice before they strike?" he asked, referring to Saddam Hussein. "If this threat is permitted to fully and suddenly emerge, all actions, all words, and all recriminations would come too late. . . . Let there be no misunderstanding: If Saddam Hussein does not fully disarm, for the safety of our people and for the peace of the world, we will lead a coalition to disarm him."[3]

That backdrop assured the *Blade* that any story of decades-old war crimes in Vietnam would draw controversy and why-now complaints. Critics would pick it apart line by line looking for weaknesses. Sallah and Weiss, who would soon join the investigation full time, also were thinking about an ongoing controversy over the Associated Press' Pulitzer Prize–winning story in 2000 about American soldiers killing more than 100 unarmed refugees at No Gun Ri bridge in 1950 during the Korean War.[4] If the *Blade* investigation uncovered an important story, they wanted the ensuing public debate to focus on the findings, not on the journalism. So, for this investigation, the paper could spare no effort to do the story right.

That was not going to be easy, despite the trove of leads and names Col. Tufts had buried in his papers. Sallah and Weiss only had last names and vague dates and general locations of the alleged crimes. The information was on a crude 8½-by-14-inch spreadsheet covering 22 pages that appeared to be a summary of an ongoing investigation. The reporters had to assume that the military would not happily release the investigative reports on which that chart was based. They would have to track down surviving members of the Tiger Force, and that would be difficult. After 36 years, they could be anywhere in the world. Many would be dead. Even if Sallah and Weiss found them, what could they possibly gain by talking to two reporters about war atrocities they may have committed? Would Sallah and Weiss be able to break through the legendary bonds among soldiers at war and persuade one Tiger veteran to reveal a heat-of-battle brutality by another, something that soldiers would surely see as betrayal? Even if the Tiger Force members were willing to talk, the reporters would be asking them to accurately recall a part of the long-ago past that they probably would like to forget.

A "Project From Hell"?

It was clear from the start that the Tiger Force probe would be a huge and controversial undertaking for any paper, a commitment that poses many questions. Was a paper the size of the *Blade* up to such a challenge, especially at a time when the paper was dealing with financial problems? Did it have the wherewithal to jump into such a project full bore with enough staff and resources to get into it, get it right and get it into the paper without letting it drag on for a year or more? Or would it become every reporter's nightmare—the project from hell—where one frustrated reporter pecks away at it as time permits, while his or her colleagues roll their eyes every time "The Project" is mentioned. That is often the fate of projects too big for papers where a culture of investigative reporting has not taken hold. The *Blade*'s circulation was less than 150,000. Its newsroom staff numbered around 170—including support personnel—and it was in the midst of budget cuts and a hiring freeze that had started in 2001.[5] The top editors even had to give up one of their cherished perks—their company cars. "We barely had our heads above water," said Allan Block, chairman of the board of Block Communications.

Nonetheless, the *Blade* is one of the few regional, family-owned newspapers that has built a national reputation for investigative reporting. Block's brother,

John Robinson Block, co-publisher and editor-in-chief, traces part of the company's editorial successes to the high salaries mandated in its Guild contract. Although the *Blade* is a low- to midsized paper, its salaries are pegged to the costs of living in Chicago and Detroit, which are significantly higher than that in Toledo. Whereas most papers its size draw reporters either fresh out of journalism school or with very little experience, the *Blade*'s salaries lure veterans. Sallah and Weiss, for example, each had 12 to 15 years of experience, investigative backgrounds and several awards under their belts when they joined the paper. John Block also believes he has more control over the papers than publishers who work for chains. "Those publishers don't have the decision-making power at the local level that I have," he said. "You have business guys in charge [at chains]. I am a journalist. I like good journalism."

Block Communications is a 108-year-old media company that also owns the *Pittsburgh Post-Gazette* and several broadcast stations. Block papers have won nine Pulitzers, including one for the 1938 series revealing the U.S. Supreme Court Justice Hugo Black once belonged to the Ku Klux Klan. At the *Blade*, editors and reporters regularly turn out ambitious investigative or explanatory projects. Former *Blade* Reporter Sam Roe was cut loose for 22 months to investigate how the government and beryllium industry hid workplace dangers in beryllium production for military weapons. Its series was a Pulitzer finalist in 2000. In 2006, the *Blade* published another Pulitzer Prize finalist that revealed state government corruption involving investments in a rare-coin fund. "I guess it comes down to we are guilty of having some pride in this kind of work," John Block said.

That attitude appears to have trickled down throughout the editorial ranks. The executive editor, Ron Royhab, had an investigative pedigree before he joined the *Blade* in 1993. One of the line editors, Dave Murray, ramrodded the beryllium project.

Sallah and Weiss, both of whom moved on to larger papers after the Tiger Force project, said the editors gave them a free rein, and they credit the editor-in-chief for setting the tone at his newspapers. Sallah, now projects editor at the *Miami Herald*, says John Block wanted his papers to compete with *The New York Times* and *The Washington Post*. "He had an open checkbook when it came to big stories." Weiss agrees. "The paper has a culture of great investigative journalism. John Block is a big-league thinker," said Weiss, who later became a business editor at *The Charlotte Observer* in North Carolina. "He was not constrained by the notion that you have to have a 30 percent profit every year." Actually, their notion of profit has been more like single digits without including depreciation, and "not necessarily the high single-digits," said Allan Block, the board chairman.

The Tiger Force investigation once again would require the news organization to devote vast resources that reached into low six-figures counting, salaries.[6] As in past projects, the executives made staff adjustments to accommodate the extra costs. "I have to borrow reporters and shut off other things when we have a big investigation going," John Block said. In letting Sallah and Weiss pursue the story, Royhab, the executive editor, had taken two of the *Blade*'s most veteran journalists out of the daily mix for an indefinite period. Near the end of the project, the paper would assign a third reporter, Joe Mahr, and send Sallah, Weiss and a photographer, Andy Morrison, to Vietnam for 16 days in search of evidence. In freeing Weiss from his duties as state editor, the paper had to pull a state projects reporter out of the reporting mix to fill in for him and postpone other Sunday projects. The paper had relied on Sallah for short-term projects and Sunday stories. Mindful of their paper's austerity mode, Sallah and Weiss said they tried to work frugally but never felt financial pressures limited their reporting.

Weiss, Sallah Draw on Their Pasts

The story came at an unusual point in the two lead reporters' careers: both were planning to leave the *Blade*. Weiss was getting ready to relocate to the North Carolina/South Carolina area, because he recently had promised his wife, whose family lived in Greenville, S.C., that they would move closer to her home. Her father had died in late 2002, and she needed to go back to help take care of her mother. As for Sallah, he was planning to jump to the *Chicago Tribune* and had signed a letter of intent.

Sallah, 47, is a high-energy, animated reporter, whose passion had been known to get him into conflicts with editors.[7] He talks about the need for tough, no-holds-barred reporting while being honest and fair with sources. In conversation, he draws on a huge store of clichés, and speaks so rapidly—especially when talking about investigative reporting—the speediest stenographer would find him a challenge.

Sallah grew up in Toledo, where he attended St. John's Jesuit High School. He traces his interest in the mission of journalism to those high school days. "You got to remember, the Jesuits were burning draft cards back then," he said. "They really stressed social equity. They taught that it is OK to get angry at social injustice. So I gravitated toward journalism even back then and wrote for the high school newspaper."

So he went to the University of Toledo and majored in journalism. Ever since he launched his professional career at the *Boca Raton News* in Florida, Sallah had been doing investigative work. In Florida, he did stories on crack cocaine, local police corruption and white collar fraud. He joined the *Blade* in 1989, starting as a police reporter. He moved on to general assignment, politics and special projects before becoming the national affairs reporter. He investigated police brutality, officer-involved shootings, organized crime and white-collar fraud. He and another reporter won a National Press Club award in 1995 for a series showing that the Lucas County Inspections Department had stopped inspecting restaurants. The Ohio Society of Professional Journalists named him reporter of the year. Entering the Tiger Force project, Sallah had just finished writing an explosive series about the sexual abuse scandal in the Roman Catholic Church in Toledo.[8]

By the time he started sifting through the Tufts papers, Sallah had known Weiss since his friend worked at the AP. After Weiss joined the *Blade* in 1998, he and Sallah had sometimes talked about working on a project together. So Sallah told him about Tufts' papers and wondered if Weiss would like to join him if he uncovered anything worth pursuing. Weiss said yes.

Weiss is viewed by those who know him as the calming force on the duo and the Vietnam expert. "He's more folksy" than Sallah, Royhab said. "He's

quiet, very quick and smart, a good interviewer. He did a lot of the leg work."
Weiss combines a disarming, mild manner with a hard-nosed journalistic attitude. Almost immediately in conversation, his tone of voice and manner suggest
a willingness to listen and a desire to understand. But like his partner, passion
subsumes a kindly demeanor when the conversation turns to investigative
reporting.

Paying the Price, Learning the Ropes

Their partnership worked well in the investigation, because "we are cut from
the same cloth," Weiss said. "We believe in due diligence. . . . You have to look at
every avenue, every document if something doesn't seem right."

Weiss, 44, grew up the youngest of three children in the Bronx, N.Y., home of
a grocery store manager, where politics was a frequent dinner-time topic and an
early influence on how he would one day make his living. Throughout his high
school and college years, he was an avid reader of U.S. history books and classic
American novels, especially the works of Sinclair Lewis and the plays of Eugene
O'Neill. After he won a national high school writing contest, his mother pushed
him toward writing. He took several creative writing courses in college, and
his mother encouraged him to apply to the graduate school at Northwestern
University, where he earned a master's in journalism.

Weiss looks back to his college years to find some of the fundamental lessons
that would serve him as a journalist. During an internship for a congressman,
he investigated constituent complaints. It taught him how to listen and to listen
carefully without prejudging the person or his or her complaint, he said. His
love of history generated the investigative reporter's obsession for answers to
the "why" questions. "From the time I was a kid, I read history books, and I was
always fascinated by the 'why' question, why a certain historical figure did this
or that. Even to this day, I am always preaching that the 'why' in any story is so
important."

His journalism career began with a three-month stint with *The Rockland Journal News*, a small paper serving an area just north of New York City, before he
followed a graduate school friend to *The Greenville News*, a major daily newspaper in South Carolina in 1983. Within two months, he displayed a tough brand of
journalism, twice catching local politicians making derogatory public comments
about Jews and migrants. Although he embarrassed the politicians, they eventually became good sources, teaching him that tough but fair journalism often
opens doors even to those who become its targets.

Later he launched a project on the plight of migrant workers and how crew
leaders had virtually enslaved them. It did not draw much interest from his
editors, because the workers weren't local workers, and the paper had not done
much on the migrant issue. Nevertheless, Weiss pursued the project, much of
it on his own time. Even after the editors read his outline and said they were
not interested, he wrote it anyway. They liked it and published the story. It had
whetted his desire for investigative reporting and taught the green reporter a lot
about the court system, using records, filing public records requests, developing
sources and interviewing. Moreover, he felt a sense of satisfaction over complet-
ing a project against all odds, including the opposition of his editors.

A year later, he was in Columbia, S.C., launching his long career with the Associated Press (AP). He was mostly shagging daily stories and loving it. In 1987, AP's Toledo bureau had an opening, and Weiss snagged it. He got involved in a crack cocaine project, which required him to hang out with a dealer to write a narrative about his transactions with customers throughout one night. He did a project on an agricultural corporation and its poor environmental record. He became an expert on farm issues, including family farms and farm subsidies. He won several awards at AP, but he said, "As a Jewish boy from the Bronx, I was most proud of winning the Ohio Farm Reporter of the Year award from an agricultural group." He also did a project on child labor and another on inmate abuse at a regional jail that housed misdemeanants and people awaiting trial.

In 1998, the *Blade* lured him away to supervise about 10 reporters as state editor. His basic marching order to his reporters was "be aggressive," and soon the state staff was producing investigative stories. One of them grew out of the suicide of a college president's daughter-in-law. It originated from a stringer's tip and started with some preliminary checking by one of Weiss' newest reporters. She learned of rumors that the daughter-in-law had committed suicide out of despair when the college president broke off a 20-year affair with her. The story was too big and sensitive for the new reporter, so Weiss brought in two veterans to help out. One of them was Mike Sallah.[9]

Partnership Forms

Partnerships on a project are often formed ad hoc by an editor, in which case, the two reporters work the project and then go their separate ways. Other partnerships become institutions, such as the one formed by James Steele and Don Barlett, a celebrated investigative reporting team. Frequently, an editor will assign reporters with an investigative bent to work with beat reporters who have discovered a promising project idea on their beat. More often, the partnership takes shape more casually when two reporters discover they each share an interest in a topic or can bring pertinent expertise to the story. That is what brought Sallah and Weiss together on the Tiger Force story.

Sallah knew Weiss loved reading history, that his brother had fought in the Vietnam War and that Weiss was fascinated by the conflict, that he had become an armchair historian on the topic. At first, Weiss helped when he wasn't busy running the state desk, Sallah recalled. "Even the editors didn't know Mitch was involved," he said. "He was a friend who I could kind of bounce things off of. He became sort of an unwitting partner in this even though he was not officially on board and didn't know if he ever would be. He was just glad to do it for me," Sallah said.

Getting Started: Official Silence Speaks Volumes

Soon after the editors gave them the go-ahead, Weiss filed a Freedom of Information Act request with the U.S. Army Criminal Investigations Command for investigative records on the Coy Allegation. Initially, the Army sent 100 heavily redacted pages, but then closed the file, with officials citing the soldiers' privacy rights. Sallah and Weiss appealed to the Pentagon, but lost. The unusual action angered the reporters. "I couldn't believe they wouldn't give us the rest," Sallah said. "My God, why would they have done this if not for a much bigger reason than privacy rights? That's what bothered me."

That is also what raised their suspicions that they were on to a good story.[10] The *Blade* was planning to sue, but the records custodian from the National Archives in College Park, Md., found 600–700 pages on the Tiger Force and would provide access after redacting names and social security numbers, which would take two weeks. In the meantime, Sallah and Weiss had plenty to keep them busy. Their key document was the Coy Allegation spreadsheet from the Tufts papers. Tufts had ordered his staff to compile it in March 1974 from three years' worth of investigative reports.[11] One column listed the allegations and the accusers; another summarized the accusers' most important statements for each allegation and a third capsulized the investigators' remarks on the status of each case.

They found a website on the Tiger Force and sent e-mails to several former members who had posted on the site. Weiss drove to Indianapolis and spent more than three hours with a Tiger who was with the platoon in 1966, the year prior to the abuses in the Coy Allegation. The two reporters did desk research on Vietnam and the war, the Geneva Accord, the military code of justice and post-traumatic stress disorder. They watched nine documentaries on Vietnam. Some of the books on their reading list included Stanley Karnow's *Vietnam: A History*, Col. David H. Hackworth's *About Face: The Odyssey of an American Warrior*, David L. Anderson's *Facing My Lai: Moving Beyond the Massacre*, and Seymour M. Hersh's *My Lai 4: A Report on the Massacre and Its Aftermath*.

From the Coy Allegation, they knew they had to find a soldier identified only as "Carpenter" on the spreadsheet. He was the accuser in about half of the allegations. The spreadsheet said he had seen killings of unarmed prisoners and civilians and mutilations of bodies. Oddly, Spc. William Carpenter found them. He had heard about their interest in the Tiger Force from a Jacksonville veteran who had received one of Sallah's e-mails. He wrote Sallah, explaining he was the "unofficial historian" of the Tiger Force and offering to help. He was living in eastern Ohio in Jefferson County.

Going Eyeball to Eyeball

Sallah called to set up a meeting. He didn't want to interview Carpenter over the telephone. He likes going face-to-face with sources, even when it requires extra work, time and money. "We learned a long time ago in our work, nothing beats face-to-face interviews," Sallah said. "Don't try to do it by phone. Just go there." He reads "their body reaction" and watches their facial expressions and eye contact with him. "You got to go there," Sallah says. "You got to pick up on how direct they are with you face-to-face, eyeball-to-eyeball."

Sallah drove 5½ hours to go eyeball-to-eyeball with Carpenter. He decided to go up a day early and check into a motel so he could be alert and fresh for the conversation.

Sallah had to assume that Carpenter, as the self-described unofficial historian, would spread the word about whatever Sallah knew. Sallah decided he was not going to "show all of my cards" or reveal that he and Weiss had already been working hard on the story.

He also assumed Carpenter would want to know why he was snooping around, so he had to develop an accurate but general story line. He did not want to bluntly bring up the war crimes investigation, fearing such a bull-in-the-china-shop approach would shut him down. He hoped to gradually steer the conversation in that direction and that Carpenter would broach the subject himself. So Sallah decided to explain that he was working on a story about the Tiger Force, that he wanted to know everything, "the good, bad and the ugly." With that approach, he would be telling the truth without saying he was conducting a war crimes investigation. In approaching other Tigers, Sallah said he never misled them. "I never said this was going to be raising the flag at Iwo Jima."

They met at a restaurant, and Carpenter took him to his home for the interview. Tell me about the unit, Sallah began. What was it like? What did you do? What was its origin?

Carpenter started talking about the Tiger Force as if he was taking Sallah on an excursion. Carpenter listed three books that mentioned the Tiger Force. Sallah already consulted two of them but did not reveal that to Carpenter. He still wasn't ready to let him know how much he and Weiss were digging into this topic.

How did everything go over there? Sallah asked. Did you ever run into problems?

Carpenter talked about the Vietnam War in general, showing slides of the Tigers at one point.

I heard you guys were kind of wild, that everything wasn't perfect over there. He mentioned My Lai and said he knew the Tiger Force was controversial.

Carpenter eventually took the bait and started talking about the investigation.

It ruined a lot of careers, he said. They started accusing us of this and this and "it was all bullshit." There was nothing to it. You know, I'd like maybe to go off the record with you on something. Sallah recalled him saying.

Got him, Sallah thought. He's mine; I have him now.

But in a surprising gambit, Sallah asked a strange question. "I think I asked him about the weapons he used," Sallah recalled. He was about to get a big piece of the story—maybe even the full story—from an eyewitness, a Tiger who had participated in battlefield actions where war crimes had occurred, and then Sallah changed the subject. He feared Carpenter was about to get him trapped into a promise he was not ready to give.

"I knew this was the real deal," he said, "and I wasn't going to get compromised on an off-the-record conversation about information that I may not be able to get anywhere else." Sallah figured he could always go back to him, but at that early point in the investigation he did not want to risk getting locked into an anonymous-sources story.

"We had too many other people we had to talk to," Sallah explained. "If he unveiled everything he knew off the record, he would have told everybody else. I didn't want them to know I was under any kind of constraints or compromises with him or anybody else."

Those decisions were complex, considering that he had to make them spontaneously. But Sallah had been through such situations before. "I've been burned before by being compromised with information I was unable to get elsewhere," he said. "Then, I couldn't reveal it, because I had to keep my word. These are things you learn with experience, with talking to people and picking up on what they are about to tell you."

Sallah likes to compare working an interview to playing a card game. "I am not one to show all my cards in an interview," he said. "I may show them an ace or a deuce, but I will not show all five . . . I know this sounds calculating, somewhat Machiavellian, but you have to be that way, to think on your feet. This was a moment where I had to take control of the story. I have watched too many young reporters blow stories that way. I did it too much when I was younger."

So when Sallah steered Carpenter "away from the dark side," the ex-Tiger followed his lead. They did not return to Topic A that day, but Sallah was pleased. "I got what I needed," he said. He had learned about the Tiger Force, the challenges and pressures they faced, a few names of other members, "a feel for the unit." More important, he had opened up a good source. "I knew he was a well I would be coming back to again and again." He would, as did Weiss.

Weiss considered his partner's conversation with Carpenter a key interview, and he eventually established a good relationship with him. "That was really the beginning," he said. "Carpenter was able to get in touch with a lot of Tigers. When someone didn't want to talk to us, Bill would get on the phone and say 'Mike is a good guy or Mitch is a good guy. You can to talk to him.' "

Weiss and Sallah say they tried hard not to come across to Carpenter and other Tiger Force veterans as stereotypical hard-nosed, uncaring reporters.

"We were not the confrontational, mean-spirited reporters," Sallah said. "We were nice guys. We maintained good demeanor." When they discovered new evidence, their approach to Carpenter was to invite cooperation rather than to interrogate. "We would say, this is what we got, now work with us, enlighten us," Sallah recalled.

Weiss said he found it easy to develop a rapport with Carpenter, who was naturally an "outgoing guy." His war comrades called him "good-time Bill." He liked to talk about his sons and hunting and the Tiger Force. He would give the reporters names of other Tigers, some he had lost track of. "He would say, 'Hey if you find Trout, tell him I said hello.' And so I did and then I would call him back." Weiss said that on a few occasions, he put Carpenter in touch with Tigers he had lost track of. "Those things build trust," Weiss said. Carpenter later talked to Weiss about how Lt. James Hawkins, the platoon leader, killed an elderly unarmed Vietnamese man carrying two geese on a shoulder pole and how Pvt. Sam Ybarra sliced off people's ears and scalps. Eventually, Carpenter would tell the reporters he had once killed a wounded elderly villager who had been shot in the mouth by another private on orders from their sergeant.[12]

Some Wells Turn Dry, Others Run Deep

After Sallah interviewed Carpenter, Weiss found Sgt. Harold Trout, who, according to Carpenter, had killed at least one unarmed and wounded Vietnamese and ordered the killing of others (see Appendix C, Coy Allegation, items 6, 11, 13).[13] He talked with him for more than an hour. Trout loved talking about the Tiger Force, but as soon as Weiss mentioned the investigation, that was it. "There was something really bothering him, and he wouldn't tell me about it," Weiss said. But Weiss persisted:

We just want to know whatever happened to the investigation, he said.

That investigation was "bullshit and I don't want to talk about it," Trout responded.

OK, but you know we know about the investigation, because we have some of these documents, Weiss replied.

But Trout wouldn't budge and Weiss decided not to press any further at that point, hoping to keep his line of communication open with the ex-Tiger for later, when he had more information that he could bring up to him. But this particular well ran dry. "He would never talk to us again," Weiss said.

As the reporters waited for the National Archives in February 2003, Sallah found Rion Causey of Livermore, Calif., a former Tiger Force medic. A nuclear engineer now, in the fall of 1967 Causey was a 19-year-old schoolteacher's son from South Carolina. He had been accepted at the University of North Carolina at Chapel Hill and had a dorm room waiting for him but decided to enlist and go to Vietnam instead.[14] Causey's was another name that turned up on the Tiger Force website. There was a cryptic message on the website in which Causey had said bad things had happened in Vietnam and "we all saw," Sallah recalled. Using a database search engines, he found only one Rion Causey and e-mailed him. Causey wrote back, providing his phone number.

Sallah called, using a variation of the story line he used when interviewing Carpenter. He told Causey that this was the 30th anniversary of the Paris Accords ending America's involvement in the war, that he was profiling the Tiger Force, and that he knew it had a little controversy and an interesting history, and he wanted Causey's thoughts about the unit. Sallah reminded Causey of what he had written to other Tigers on the website. "I noticed that you mentioned that things happened that left a deep impression, that 'we can never forget,'" Sallah recalled.

Right away, Sallah sensed Causey wanted to talk. Sallah couldn't clearly explain what he felt, but Causey sounded different from other soldiers, and Sallah detected a variety of emotions—remorse, regret, resignation. This was not an interview that could be conducted effectively over the telephone. "I could tell he wanted to talk, but there was anxiety and stress in his voice," Sallah said. "I could tell I needed to go out there and talk to him."

Managing Editor Kurt Franck told him to work the interview over the phone. Sallah said he didn't fault Franck, because Sallah felt his editor felt the *Blade* had to hold the line on the budget. The investigation had just started.

Nevertheless, Sallah feared Causey needed to talk face-to-face. "I knew in my heart I needed to do this, even if I had to put my own credit card on the line. This was a big story for us. We both knew it. We smelled it. Some people may not have quite seen it the way we did, and so sometimes you have to take the initiative." Sallah said he went to an assistant managing editor, who he knew was in tune with administrative matters. "We could blow this," he explained. "He [Causey] is ready to explode, and I want to go out there and take a chance." The assistant consulted with Franck, and they agreed to let him go.

Sallah and Weiss said they understood the *Blade*'s financial situation and worked on the cheap as much as possible throughout the investigation, husbanding the paper's pennies, because they knew some major expenses lie ahead. For the California trip, Sallah searched for a cheap flight. He paid for his own breakfasts and lunches. Rather than rent a car, he used mass transit and took a cab to Causey's home. They sat in his backyard, and Sallah brought out his tape recorder as he started talking about the Tiger Force.

They chatted for a while before Sallah broached the Coy Allegation. He showed Causey a cover sheet that went with it, and Causey started talking about what the Tigers had done. "He said this is 'something I have been living with a long time,'" Sallah recalled. "To this day, I can remember one of his quotes: 'I still can't figure out how some people sleep even 30 years later. I used to wake up in cold sweats,'" Sallah said. He said Causey opened up entirely.[15]

Causey was with the Tiger Force from October 1967 through March 1968, a period that included the last three months of the unit's rampage through the Central Highlands near Chu Lai. When he joined the unit, he found a stressed out, angry platoon bent on revenge for heavy losses in the previous month. "Everybody was bloodthirsty," he told Sallah. "We just came in and cleared out the civilian population." Causey told him that he counted 120 villagers killed by the Tiger Force in the Chu Lai area of Vietnam in one month. Causey confessed that he clearly knew the killings were wrong but did not condemn them at the time.[16]

The interview was the first clear breakthrough. "He opened the floodgates," Sallah said. Sallah immediately called Weiss. "You won't believe what he just told me," he said. Weiss was astounded and for the first time, he began to realize there was definitely a story and that he was certain they could track it down.

Records Map New Path on Trail of Atrocity

A few days after the Causey interview, the records from the National Archives were ready and Sallah drove to College Park, Md., to get the first batch. Sallah had scheduled a vacation in the Florida Keys with his family, but he took the stack of Tiger Force records with him. Throughout the vacation, he was on the phone daily with Weiss as they plowed through the documents in different parts of the country. "The day we got to Key West was the day we were sending U.S. troops into Bagdad," Sallah recalled.

In April, Weiss and Sallah went back to College Park to get more records. They made seven or eight trips, staying at a Red Roof Inn and sharing a room for $99 a night. They drove each time, using a company car and eating at McDonald's to save money.

The trips were worth the cost. They came back with 600 pages about the Tiger Force and the battalion to which the squad belonged. Although there were lots of missing pages, the documents essentially backed up what was in the Coy Allegation spreadsheet. The reports were detailed and precise. Sallah and Weiss also found radio logs and grid maps, which were crucial in establishing dates and locations for the alleged crimes from May through November 1967. They started thinking about going to Vietnam.

Luckily, the redactions were sloppily done and many names were not blacked out. They could match war crimes in the archives with the Coy Allegations in the spreadsheet. Entire statements were fully intact. It was clear to them that the

Tigers had talked to military investigators at different times in different parts of the country, and they were all independently corroborating each other.

Besides fleshing out the spreadsheet in the Coy Allegation, the records provided more sources, including the name of the chief investigator. Moreover, the records contained no evidence that any of the alleged crimes were ever tried in a court-martial, increasing their suspicion of a cover-up. "We reviewed 241 other war-crime cases unrelated to Tiger Force, and we saw they prosecuted other soldiers," Sallah said, questioning why there was no record of prosecutions in the Tiger Force cases. They had to find out. Finally, on the last trip to the National Archives, they discovered something that opened up a new dimension to their investigation. The Criminal Investigations Command had sent summaries to the top levels of the Nixon administration, to the offices of Secretary of Army Howard "Bo" Calloway, Secretary of Defense James Schlesinger and to White House Counsel John Dean. The implication was mind-boggling: If this case was covered up, it may have gone to the highest reaches of government.

Learning About War Trauma Key

By the time they finished reviewing the National Archives documents, the two reporters knew they had dozens of tough interviews with Tiger Force veterans ahead of them. Getting them to talk about killing unarmed women and children, severing ears from dead people and scalping victims would not be easy. Many of the veterans had suffered post-traumatic stress disorder, an emotional reaction to shocking events that surface in a variety of symptoms such as flashbacks, feelings of guilt, despondency or drug and alcohol dependency. The reporters had learned that it had not been identified as a psychological problem in the 1960s, but later studies revealed that about one out of every six Vietnam veterans suffered from it. It was particularly acute among soldiers who witnessed or participated in needless brutality that violated the moral standards they held before the war.

Sallah said the veterans they interviewed fit what they learned about post-traumatic stress disorder. "They vacillated between being remorseful and justifying what they did," he said. Sometimes they would get angry and say: "Look, I did what we had to do." Some dealt with it "head-on" and succeeded in getting past the emotional suffering, but others were still suffering more than three decades after the trauma.

For example, Weiss encountered one soldier, ex-Tiger medic Barry Bowman, who still seemed to be struggling. Bowman was a 22-year-old patriot who went to Vietnam in 1967 to fight the forces of evil and to save lives, but found himself watching in horror as his own platoon leaders and comrades murdered unarmed elderly villagers and children. The records from the National Archives showed that Bowman would be a key source, and Weiss talked to him by phone seven or eight times.

From the beginning of a two-month relationship, Weiss' approach was "help me understand what went on out there." Weiss also tried to bring him news and contact information about one of his former friends in the Tigers, and then go into a question in a "by-the-way" mode. From one conversation to the next, Weiss didn't know what to expect. "I never knew which Barry Bowman I would get:

the angry Bowman who wanted to talk like he was in a therapy session or the Barry Bowman who was pissed off at me for bringing up all this stuff," Weiss said. Sometimes he was a solid, reflective and quiet man. "He would talk about the birds in Song Ve Valley and how back at home when he hears birds outside, it would take him back there," Weiss said. Other times Bowman complained no one understood "what it was like out there. . . . For that particular interview, there was a lot of regret," Weiss said. The interviews were always long and very difficult and rambling. Often, his answers, rather than being direct responses, were rhetorical: Why do you want to write this, he once asked Weiss. Is this going to be your Pulitzer? Weiss could not detect anger in Bowman's voice because he spoke in monotone, but after a few conversations, he learned to sense when he was about to shut down.

One day, Bowman talked about an incident in August 1967. By then, he had already witnessed three months of killing when the Tiger Force entered a village in the Quang Tin Province and opened fire blindly into some huts in a village, killing and wounding many villagers. Bowman walked over to an elderly man moaning in pain from gunshot wounds that left his intestines exposed. Ordinarily, Bowman would have tried to help the man. But this time everything seemed different, and he went into great detail explaining to Weiss what he was going through. "He said it just annoyed him so much. Everything was going on around him, everything from the moaning, the shrieking in pain to the adrenaline because they had just gone into the village and shot it out. He didn't think twice, and he just blew him away. And once he did it, he said he felt better."

Was that a war crime? Bowman asked, rhetorically. I consider it a mercy killing.

The Geneva Conventions say there is no such thing as a mercy killing, Weiss responded. A long silence followed.

I guess I committed a war crime, then, Bowman said. Bowman said something about joining the Army to save lives and ended up taking them, Weiss recalled. Then the conversation ended abruptly.

Mitch, I am going to get off the line now, Bowman said. Weiss wasn't too concerned. Bowman had done that a couple of times before.

OK, Barry, that's fine, Weiss said, thinking PTSD was kicking in again.

Weiss would give him a few days to settle down, like he had done on other occasions, and call him and he would be ready to talk again. But this time, Weiss had apparently crossed the line.

Within five minutes, Bowman called Royhab, the executive editor.

Please do not have Mitch Weiss call me anymore, he told Royhab.

Can someone else call you, Royhab asked.

No, he said. He didn't want to talk to anybody from *The Toledo Blade* again.

"I honored his request," Weiss said. Although this well had finally run dry, Bowman had been valuable to their investigation.

Why Sources Open Up

Reporters never know when sources will shut down, pour out their souls, or brazenly and unapologetically tell all. Weiss believes reporters are part journalist and part psychologist. He said he cannot be sure why soldiers such as Bowman, Carpenter, Causey and many of the more remorseful soldiers were willing to open up about such emotionally wrenching matters as the slaughter of innocent people. Perhaps his and Sallah's questions simply served as a release valve for long pent-up feelings. Perhaps the news they brought of long-lost comrades-in-arms gave the reporters a link to these veterans and their past that few others in their lives could provide. Or, perhaps a journalist's nonjudgmental and detached tone invites the veteran to revisit suppressed thoughts about the emotional and moral dilemmas they faced in Vietnam, in hopes of understanding how the fear, confusion and horror of war ignited such visceral drives, and that only now—here back in the civilized world, where survival is no longer a daily obsession—do those drives become unrecognizable, inexplicable and abhorrent.

In the Tiger Force investigation, emotionally scarred warriors weren't the reporters' only interviewing challenge. There was an investigator who had spent four years investigating the same subject they were probing; yet they had not been able to determine how it ended. So when Sallah called Warrant Officer Gustav Apsey, he did not know what to expect or what might motivate him to talk. Apsey was the lead military investigator, whose reports created the foundation for the Coy Allegation spreadsheet that Sallah found buried in the Tufts papers. He spent nearly four years investigating the case. His boss had assigned it to him after two others gave it a lackluster effort. Apsey was known as a dogged investigator who sucked up details like a vacuum cleaner. But when he completed the job and recommended criminal charges against several veterans, there were no promotions, no praise. He was shipped out to Seoul, Korea, for his next assignment.

Although not listed as the lead investigator in the records from the National Archives, his name was the only one that appeared at the bottom of every interview report, even those conducted by other investigators. As Sallah searched for him, he knew this man held the key to the entire case. He finally found an Apsey in Washington state and called.

Is this Gustav Apsey? Sallah said when the voice answered the phone.

Yeah, he said, with a little hesitation.

Were you in the Criminal Investigations Command?

Yes, what can I do for you?

Do you remember a case called the Tiger Force case?

Silence. And then:

My God, I cannot believe I am getting this call, Apsey said.

Sallah fought his emotions.

I can't believe you are calling me after all of these years, Apsey continued.

"I remember getting goose bumps," Sallah said. "But I had to contain my excitement. So I just started going through the case and telling him that this looks like pretty serious stuff."

Yes, I investigated that case, and I was able to "substantiate" a lot of things there.

The word "substantiate" hit home for Sallah; he knew what it meant. He and Weiss had learned a lot about the military code and how it applied. They had interviewed experts on military law, including the lead prosecutor in the My Lai case. "Substantiate" in the military system was equivalent to "probable cause" in the civilian system, and it meant Apsey believed he had enough evidence to submit the case to the military judicial system.

Apsey hesitated again, but Sallah sensed he "was wanting to open up." His next comment confirmed it. Apsey was ecstatic that a reporter was taking interest in the case.

Now Sallah's goose bumps were changing to chills. "He could have panned the whole thing and said something like 'yeah, but it never really turned out.'" But that is not what Sallah heard.

I feel "vindicated" after all these years, Apsey said. Somebody is actually looking into this and taking it seriously.

Apsey was going to confirm everything they had been working on, Sallah thought. "Here is this lead agent and he's telling me that this is real serious stuff, that it had consumed his life. When he said he felt vindicated, what else do you need to hear?" But, at that point, Apsey wasn't quite ready to open up completely. Sallah wanted to know if the soldiers Apsey accused of war crimes were prosecuted.

What I am not seeing here, Sallah began, is that there wasn't any military justice carried out. Did this ever go to an Article 32, he asked, referring to a proceeding similar to a civilian grand jury.

I am not going to go into that with you, Apsey said, explaining that he could get called back to active service.

Sallah thought for a moment: How could he get him to confirm indirectly that there were no hearings or trials? By then, he knew how strong Apsey's case was, and he had been around the criminal court system enough to know instinctively about grand juries and trials and that Apsey had more than enough evidence to warrant court proceedings.

Did you ever testify in any proceeding?

No, Apsey said.

The one-word answer spoke volumes. "The lead detective in a case never testified in anything, and later he was shifted to Seoul, Korea? So you tell me what happened. There was a cover-up," Sallah said.

Sallah decided not to press further, again holding back, being satisfied with finding another source who he could tap for more information later. Sallah agreed to keep in touch, to brief him. "I just wanted to keep him in the loop," Sallah said. "There may be questions coming up that I needed to ask him, like I did with Bill Carpenter. So I needed to keep in his good graces. This is going to be long term, and you need to have people's confidence and let them know what you are doing so that they do not shut down on you. It's called investing; investing your time, doing these little things along the way in an investigation."

It paid off for both reporters. Weiss periodically called him to check information he had gathered and sometimes to tell him what had happened to soldiers he interviewed. "It's sort of a courtesy, and it doesn't hurt the story. He is going to help us understand what happened; he is going to let you into his world; he is going to tell us what it was like working for the Criminal Investigations Command and why he made some of the key decisions he made." Apsey had copies of his entire investigative files—some 1,000 pages—that he repeatedly consulted when the reporters called.

Apsey helped Weiss learn about one of the most murderous and brutal Tigers, Sam Ybarra, a seriously disturbed high school dropout from Arizona. Apsey's investigation found Ybarra routinely extracted gold from the teeth of his victims. He severed their ears and carried them around in a ration bag or strung them together and wore them around his neck as a necklace. Ybarra occasionally scalped his victims, and once tied a scalp to the end of his rifle. He was the one suspected of severing the head of a Vietnamese infant.

In Apsey's last interview, he went to see Ybarra in 1975 and found a broken, drunken, dying and dishonorably discharged veteran living in a white-clapboard shack on the San Carlos Indian Reservation. He refused to talk. After Apsey finished his investigation, he never found out what happened to Ybarra until Weiss told him that he got sick and died in 1982 at the age of 36. The once bear of a man had shriveled to 95 pounds.[17]

In the *Blade*'s investigation, Weiss drew the difficult job of learning as much as possible about Ybarra, an interviewing experience that exemplified some of the emotionally wrenching and shocking discoveries that sometimes tested their equanimity. Apsey gave Weiss many compelling details about his visit to Ybarra's shack, but Therlene Ramos, Ybarra's mother, and other family members told him about the life of the son she once thought was a decorated hero.[18] His father was stabbed to death in a bar brawl when Ybarra was only five, and he got into occasional scraps with police, but nothing serious.[19]

Ramos said Ybarra returned from the war a deeply disturbed man who was haunted by what he had done in the war. She said she once found him crying saying, "I killed people, mama. I killed regular people. I shouldn't have. My God, what did I do?" (story, Ybarra sidebar). Weiss discovered that Ybarra had told his family he was honorably discharged and had won the Silver Star, that he was a war hero.

The last conversation with her lasted less than 10 minutes, but it is one Weiss said he can never forget. He called to explain some new information about her son before she read it in the paper. Ybarra was not a holder of the Silver Star, and that he had been court-martialed three times for insubordination for incidents unrelated to the Central Highlands atrocities and dishonorably discharged in 1969.

"She cried like a baby," Weiss said. "She was such a nice woman, and I can still hear her crying." She cried and said "I can't talk any more." Then she hung up the phone. Two minutes later, Weiss' phone rang. Ybarra's sister was calling. She was screaming and cursing Weiss, saying her brother was a hero, that white people were always trying to make Indians look bad and that she was going to put a hex on him. She slammed the phone down. Weiss was shaken by her rants.

"I felt miserable after that," Weiss said. "I remember leaving the office that day, questioning, 'Why am I writing this story?' before reminding myself that if the government can cover this case up, it could do it again." Although Weiss describes himself as an empathetic interviewer, one who succeeds in drawing people out by conversationally bringing himself into the discussion, he could do nothing but express sympathy and let Ybarra's sister vent. Many of Ybarra's relatives did not know about the things he had done, Weiss said.

The pendulum of Weiss' emotions swung the other way when he talked to an unremorseful Sgt. William Doyle, one of Ybarra's commanders. Weiss, as he and Sallah did in many interviews, tape recorded the conversation without advising Doyle, which is permitted under Ohio law.

Weiss knew this was a key interview. Doyle was one of the leaders of the squad, and one of the most brutal and unremorseful. But when Weiss called him, he was not sure of much about Doyle's role. The records they had at the time had not clearly spelled it out. He had no idea what to expect when he placed the call and and Doyle answered the phone:

Is this Bill Doyle, who was with the Tiger Force?

Yeah.

Look, I've been trying to track you down because a lot of members of Tiger Force remember you and this is a story were doing, and I'd like to know what it was like out there and some said you killed a lot of civilians and you know I want to understand what would lead you to this.

Doyle did not know it at the moment, but Weiss turned on a tape recorder to document the grizzled veteran's response.

What followed is one of the most memorable interviews of the investigation. In it, Weiss showed he had mastered a key interviewing lesson: know when to shut up. And when he did ask the key question, his tone was neutral, disarming, not that of an interrogator: It was almost passive, and asked in the grammatical passive voice. In the interview, the 70-year-old former Tiger coldly and profanely recounted the killing of civilians and only regretted that the war didn't last longer so he could have killed more. In contrast, Weiss, although astounded at what he was hearing, remained unflappable and said as little as possible, as Doyle explained how he and other Tigers opened fire on 10 elderly Vietnamese men and women working in a rice paddy and killed four of them.

"Yeah, those sons of bitches should have kept on planting rice," Doyle said. "You don't put your head up and look at somebody when you are planting rice."

"Uh-hmmm," Weiss said.

"You can get killed with a look," Doyle continued.

"Uh-hmmm."

"If the son of a bitch wants to live, he keeps his head down when he's planting rice."

"So they were killed, because they looked at you guys, is that what happened?" Weiss asked.

"Yeah. More or less. If it comes to your attention, you pull the trigger."

"Uh-hmmm."

"If it crosses your mind to pull the trigger and you want to live, you pull it."

"Uh-hmmm."

"Cause if you make a mistake, you want to make it in your own favor."[20]

By the time that conversation occurred, Weiss had learned so much about the savagery of the Tigers, he was more shocked by Doyle's openness than by what he said. He had eluded military investigators in the early 1970s for three years, and when they did catch up with him in Florida in 1975, he declined to comment.[21] But now, retired and out of the military, he was willing to talk.

Making Case for Viet Trip

By late April or early May 2003, the evidence was piling up and pointing toward a strong story, and the reporters decided it was time to ask for the Vietnam trip.

They had been pinching pennies throughout the investigation, and they realized they would be making a very costly request. This was a war crimes investigation, though, and they felt compelled to go to the scene of the crime, to retrace the steps of the suspects and to talk to the victims and survivors. Sallah and Weiss had grid maps and radio logs and, thus, a good chance of tracking down eyewitnesses to the alleged crimes. It would take their investigation beyond what the military had done in the early 1970s.

Despite the importance of such a trip, Sallah believed their request was no small matter. He was prepared to give up his next vacation for the trip. Even working as frugally as possible, the cost of sending them and a photographer to Vietnam, hiring a translator, and flying to the other side of the world for 16 days would come to about $10,000, counting overtime pay. But Sallah may have worried more than was necessary about the cost of going to Vietnam. Neither of the Block brothers said they considered the amount significant in comparison with salary costs. "I would have been more apt to criticize them for not going to Vietnam," John Block, the publisher and editor-in-chief, said. "When you have a big story like this, you do whatever is necessary."

Block met with Sallah, Weiss and executive editor Ron Royhab for about an hour. He brought in David Shribman, the *Post-Gazette*'s executive editor and a former Pulitzer Prize–winning reporter for *The Boston Globe*. Shribman had not been involved in the project, and Block wanted his fresh perspective. Block had not been involved in the project, either. He described the meeting primarily as his opportunity to get an update on its progress. He said he wasn't that concerned about the Vietnam trip. "They would not have had to ask my permission for that," he said.

Nevertheless, Weiss and Sallah were not aware of Block's attitude and went prepared to sell the idea of a trip to Vietnam. "Block wasn't going to just write a check," Sallah said. "Shribman was there as a kind of pit bull. He asked good and tough questions." Sallah and Weiss talked about their interviews with some of the veterans, their contact with Apsey, the records from the National Archives and the radio log and grid maps. They had already been talking with the Vietnamese embassy to help them locate provincial officials in areas where the Tiger Force operated. They wanted to retrace the steps of the Tiger Force so that they could find people who could have witnessed any atrocities. Sallah said, " 'We need to know what happened. There may have been a cover-up, the mother of all cover-ups."

Why go back and write about something that happened 30 years ago right now, someone asked. The reporters expected that question, and they were ready. "This was one of Mitch's finest moments," Sallah said. "He was very passionate about this. He said the United States is in another engagement right now and that is all the more reason to do this story. In a day and age when our troops are supposed to be on their Ps and Qs, and we [the government] need to make sure this doesn't happen again."

No one raised a question about the cost, Sallah recalled. "John would have been insulted if you had brought that up to him." Block mostly sat quietly and listened. Sallah recalls the way the publisher ended the meeting. "He just shut it down when he said: 'All right, when are you going to Vietnam?' He was great."

They left in late June and found 11 villagers who knew precise details of three killings. One was the niece of a 68-year-old carpenter who was carrying two geese in baskets attached to the end of a shoulder pole when he was shot several times by Tiger Force members. The niece said she helped carry his body back to their village in the Song Ve Valley. Sallah and Weiss would later write about her:

> Incense smoke rose over the grave as Tam Hau knelt on the grassy mound. Hands trembling, she prayed quietly to the uncle who stumbled upon the soldiers so long ago.
>
> Like so many others, he didn't survive. Torn by bullets, the body of Dao Hue was found near the river, a mile from the hut he shared with his niece. The elderly carpenter was one of the first civilians killed by Tiger Force soldiers in a chain of atrocities that forever changed the Song Ve Valley.
>
> The reminders are everywhere: the unmarked graves along the trails, the bend in the river where the men tried to hide from the soldiers, the rice paddy where the bodies were pulled from the mud. The stories of the troops firing on unarmed civilians in the summer of 1967 are told in schools, communal centers, and prayer services.
>
> . . . The details of his death are still recalled by people in the Hanh Tin hamlet, a cluster of huts and concrete homes with clay roofs where people share narrow dirt roads with water buffalo. His grave is passed every day by farmers heading to the rice paddies and children walking to school.
>
> . . . Kneeling at the grave of her uncle, Tam Hau shook her head slowly as she talked about Dao Hue, a widower with no children . . . "He never hurt anyone."[22]

Another was a man, Kieu Trac, now 72, who watched as Doyle and the Tigers began firing at 10 elderly farmers working in a rice paddy, because they "put" their heads up and looked at the soldiers. Kieu Trac's father, Kieu Cong, was among the victims. Sallah and Weiss wrote about the lingering impact:

> Years later, the attack on July 28 continues to define the war years for the people of the Song Ve Valley. Every year, relatives pray for the victims at Buddhist ceremonies and light incense and candles at their graves. Villagers say the assault has become the most recognized atrocity of 1967—one they still talk about when the topic of the war arises.
>
> . . . But more than farming, it changed lives. Suddenly, Kieu Trac became the head of the family—in charge of caring for his mother, four siblings, and his own young family. Every year, he gathers his family—16 members living in the same concrete and bamboo home—to remind them of the man who taught him to farm. Kieu Cong was a gentle provider who spent long days in the fields, with little time to share with his five children. But when he did come home, he often sat with his son and gave advice about living a moral life.[23]

No Gun Ri Shadows Work as Deadline Looms

Many times the reporters found villagers who knew many details that matched the records Sallah and Weiss had, but not enough to satisfy both of them that the villager was talking about a Tiger Force case. At times, the two reporters disagreed on the validity of a witness account, which meant they would not include it in the story.

For Sallah and Weiss, the experience of the Associated Press reporters who wrote the No Gun Ri stories weighed heavily on them. Questions about the credibility of several sources prompted a long controversy over the No Gun Ri reporting. The *Blade* reporters did not want that to happen to their story. In one case, a Vietnamese woman's account was strikingly close to the facts they had already found, but her memory of when the event occurred did not match where the records placed the Tiger Force's location at that time. One reporter thought the details were close enough and that the one discrepancy could be attributed to fading memory over time. But the other vetoed the case. "Even if there was just one discrepancy, we were not going to use it," Sallah said. "We didn't want another No Gun Ri." Weiss agreed. "We were being so certain that both of us felt good about it. We knew when this story came out we were going to be attacked. We saw that in No Gun Ri. We had to be able to defend everything."

They returned to the United States in the second week of July and soon discovered the trip would bring an unexpected bonus—more documents, this time from Gustav Apsey. Sallah and Weiss had been talking to Apsey, the lead investigator, for weeks by phone. He had already been a tremendous source. He would read from pages of his investigative reports about a specific incident, Weiss said. But they needed to see his entire file. Sallah is convinced that the Vietnam trip finally persuaded Apsey that they were serious about the story, which prompted him to make the complete file available. "When we came back from Vietnam and told him we had found these witnesses, it made him feel so good to know that all those years he had put into this case were worth it."

Apsey's files filled in the blanks found in the National Archives records. The information covered up by the Archive's redactions or lost in the missing pages now were in their hands. They had more names, more statements and evidence.

It also meant that they had a lot more work to do. And, by then, they were feeling deadline pressure. Almost as soon as they returned from Vietnam, Franck, the managing editor, told them he wanted the story by September. But by then, the reporters had interviewed only a fraction of the more 60 soldiers they would meet, and they still had to work the military bureaucracy to find out what happened to Apsey's criminal recommendations. Moreover, Apsey's records had opened a journalistic gold mine, and "it held the mother lode," Weiss said. The reporters realized they had no chance of meeting Franck's deadline. They lobbied for more time. They got another month, plus another reporter—Joe Mahr, a 31-year-old general assignment reporter—to help them down the stretch.

They sent Mahr to Washington state to get Apsey's records, while they started outlining the main stories and writing some of the sidebar stories for which the reporting was complete. They also used him to help wade through the Pentagon and military bureaucracy to determine the disposition of Apsey's investigation. Apsey had used more than 100 agents and interviewed 137 people. The investigation was the longest of those involving the Vietnam War, and, the reporters needed to find out what happened to Apsey's case. He had substantiated 20 war crimes committed by 18 members of the 40-plus Tiger Force platoon.

As they sifted through the new batch of documents, they continued interviewing. The Doyle interview came during this period. They also found the leader of the platoon, Lt. James Hawkins. The reporters, by then, knew much about Hawkins. Their investigation found that he had given the platoon virtually free rein to kill any civilians in the Song Ve Valley who had not obeyed American orders to evacuate and move to an American relocation camp. Witnesses had told the reporters that he ordered the platoon to open fire on 10 elderly and unarmed farmers working in a Song Ve Valley rice field. And Apsey had formerly accused him of killing an elderly carpenter carrying a shoulder pole. Nevertheless, the reporters were prepared to ask him about it.

Sallah made the call to him at his Orlando, Fla., home, and all three reporters listened to his chilling comments via speakerphone. Using what had become a customary approach, Sallah eased into the interview slowly with softball questions about some of the "great victories" of the Tiger Force, its history and about what it was like for Hawkins himself. Sallah let him tell "war stories" for about a half-hour before he moved in.

I know there was some controversy there, he continued. There actually was an investigation. Do you remember it?

Yes, I sure do, Hawkins said.

Wasn't there a time that you killed this guy, this old man? Sallah asked, referring to the elderly carpenter with the shoulder pole in the Song Ve Valley. The terrified man was pleading loudly for mercy, when he was first clubbed with a rifle and then shot. The reporters knew Hawkins had denied to Apsey 30 years earlier that he shot the man. But this time, he talked about it.

Oh hell, I had to shoot that old man, Hawkins answered, saying his loud pleading threatened to give way their position.

Sallah moved on to the farmers working in the rice paddy. Apsey had not accused Hawkins of that incident, but the reporters' sources said he had ordered it.

Did you order the shooting of the farmers? Sallah asked.

Well, yeah, Hawkins said. They were not supposed to be there. It was a free-fire zone. Any living thing there could be eliminated.

Were they armed?

No.

OK, why did you kill somebody in a free-fire zone?

They weren't in the relocation camps.[24]

The camps were facilities set up to house Vietnamese civilians in the Song Ve Valley, which the military had declared a free-fire zone. In researching the definition of a free-fire zone, the reporters found that it did not sanction killing unarmed civilians.

Hawkins went on to give a peek into the thinking of top Pentagon officials about the case. The Pentagon summoned him to Washington in November 1975, where he was told they had concluded wrongdoing occurred. He told the reporters they concluded, however, that "basically it's not in the best interest of this, that and the other to try to pursue this," Hawkins said. "This was after My Lai, and the Army certainly didn't want to go through the publicity thing."[25]

The interview was crucial and provided a capstone to their investigation. Hawkins had admitted to a killing he had denied to military investigators and to ordering the platoon to open fire on unarmed elderly farmers. First with Doyle and now through Hawkins, the *Blade* had two of the platoon's leaders articulating basic marching orders to their men that essentially gave carte blanche to kill anyone. "Anything in that area was game," Hawkins said. "If it was living, it was subject to be eliminated."[26] To complete the picture, they had dozens of soldiers in on-the-record statements and in the records of Apsey's interviews repeatedly admitting to committing or witnessing atrocities. And finally, Hawkins essentially acknowledged the military knew about his wrongdoings but consciously chose not to pursue the cases to avoid another round of My Lai–type controversy.

By the time Sallah, Weiss and now Mahr had finished the investigation, they had contacted more than 60 former Tigers, and dozens of others, including Vietnamese civilians and government officials. One commander acknowledged he verbally reprimanded Hawkins in the field for one killing, but never filed charges. Other Tigers said commanding officers knew about the atrocities, but never acted. Although the office of Secretary of Defense James Schlesinger and Army Secretary Bo Calloway received Apsey's report, Schlesinger refused to comment and Calloway said he didn't remember the investigation.[27]

When a Key Source Takes a Hit

The reporters also came to one conclusion that they found particularly disappointing: Their star source, Gustav Apsey, had omitted some serious charges when he wrote his final report. Both reporters had come to respect Apsey considerably. The minute detail in his reports was compelling. His final report had substantiated 20 war crimes by 18 soldiers. Much of the progress Sallah and Weiss had made in their own investigation was due to Apsey's help. But, they could not deny what their own investigation revealed to them about Apsey's final report to his superiors: It failed to include some serious crimes that Apsey had substantiated.

They saw the enormity of what their investigation had uncovered and felt they could not hold back anything. Sallah felt strongly about the issue. "You've got to be a hard ass, now," Sallah said. "You are doing investigative reporting. You are not there for a he-said/she-said story. You have already established that war crimes had occurred, because these guys admitted to it."

They had discussed these cases with Apsey during their investigation. At one point late in the project, Sallah talked to him again. "We called him, and I said, 'Gus, you may not like some of this story,' " Sallah recalled.

"We were tough on him," Sallah said. "Gus gets his ass kicked in the story, because we felt he didn't dot all of his I's and cross all of his T's. We had to hold him accountable for that." Here is how they did it in one passage:

> In the 1975 final report for possible prosecution, lead investigator Gustav Apsey presented incomplete or inaccurate information about the crimes— casting doubt on key cases. For example, no one disputed that Tiger Force soldiers fired on 10 elderly farmers in the Song Ve Valley in July, 1967. The only debate among the four soldiers who talked to investigators was how many farmers were struck by bullets.
>
> But in the report, Mr. Apsey inexplicably said he couldn't prove the atrocity took place. Missing from his report were the worn statements of four

soldiers who were eyewitnesses to the event. Spec. William Carpenter: "We killed about 10 of the farmers, then stopped firing."

Sgt. Forrest Miller: "We had received no incoming fire from the village and the people in the field, about 10 persons both male and females, were shot." The statements of the other two were basically the same: the farmers were shot without warning.

Sallah and Weiss found that Apsey had substantiated atrocities by five other soldiers, but the report did not include them. Four soldiers also said they had witnessed the killing of unarmed women and children in three underground bunkers near Chu Lai. But the final report said investigators had been unable to determine if they were combatants.

"We were indebted to him, but the truth is larger than one person," Sallah said. "We never promised him a rose garden; that we would go light on him. You take no prisoners on these stories. You've got to be relentless; you've got to be cold; you have got to let the bodies fall where they may. This is too important now. There is a greater good to be served. Life is unfair, but that is our job."

In the story, Apsey conceded he made mistakes. "When I think about it now, it bothers me," he said. "I screwed up. I don't know what else to say. The killing of women and children in the bunkers was a war crime. There's no doubt about it. I don't know why I wrote what I did."[28]

Clash Over Tone

To Sallah and Weiss, being "hard-nosed" had to be the dominating tone in the story. That would cause a clash with editors over whether the story should try to explain why the soldiers did what they did. Sallah feared the editors were going to give too much emphasis to that angle. Royhab said he just wanted a sidebar on that topic. But Sallah feared he wanted more of that element in the main stories. To him, it was a story about what causes soldiers to cross the line; to Sallah and Weiss it was "going crybaby," making excuses for the inexcusable.

Mundane, but routine and usually healthy tensions hover around reporter–editor relations: editors pushing the reporters to get the story done "yesterday" and reporters wanting more time; editors cutting stories for space and reporters wanting more space; editors wanting to borrow a project reporter for a quick Sunday story and the reporter needing to focus on the project. The most difficult period comes in the writing phase where creative minds and egos often clash.

In the Tiger Force project, conflicts were relatively mild—until near the end, when passions surfaced. Originally, the project included two full stories devoted entirely to atrocities. That was cut to one story. But the "crybaby" dispute also was difficult. Although it is a common example of an exchange between creative people, this, by all accounts, had an edge to it. "Part of it was the emotion of the time," Sallah said, noting that he sensed a chill between him and Royhab for several weeks afterwards. Royhab, although he said he did not sense the chill, said Sallah adamantly objected to doing the sidebar and to having only one story on the atrocities. "There were some heated discussions," he recalled. "But it means a lot to me to hear what reporters are thinking [during in-house deliberations].

Mike is passionate about his work. What makes him sometimes—I don't want to say difficult—difficult to manage, is what makes him the best of the best."

But Royhab felt strongly that a story that depicts such unimaginable actions by human beings against other human beings needs to attempt to explain how and why that can happen. He said he did not want to make excuses for the culprits, but he did want to try to give readers some knowledge about what can make people commit such inhuman actions.

For his part, Sallah said Royhab's idea "scared the hell out of me." He said he and Weiss believed his insistence on explaining why the Tigers crossed the line would "fuzz up" what the soldiers had done—commit atrocities. "There's a point where you've just got to stand up for your story, and you don't back down," he said. "We put so much into this. The story was bigger than me; it was bigger than him and everybody else. We didn't want them [the editors] to go crybaby, because we knew we were in a military conflict and we didn't want them backing down." Sallah said their work had identified at least two soldiers who faced the same dangers and pressures that the abusers faced and still chose to risk their lives trying to stop their comrades from killing noncombatants.

In the end, Sallah was pleased with the outcome of the disagreement. Mahr was assigned to do a sidebar headlined "Why Did Some Soldiers Target Civilians But Others Did Not?" on the final day of the series. He also did a sidebar ordered up by John Block reporting that today's military had made adjustments to prevent abuses. The main story by Sallah and Weiss for the final day explored the emotional problems Tiger Force veterans were experiencing after the war. The fourth day also explored post-traumatic stress disorder.

Postscript

The project ran as a four-day series from Oct. 19–22, 2003, with more than two dozen stories, including four main stories. The series provide a photo slideshow, audio that included seven excerpts from interviews with three former Tiger Force members, including Doyle, and a Vietnam map that showed the platoon's areas of operation and provided a list of specific cases of atrocities. All together, the reporters documented 81 specific killings, but reported strong evidence that hundreds more occurred. It documented 28 specific incidents, 15 of which the reporters uncovered themselves through interviews and records from the military investigation. The opening day story began this way:

> QUANG NGAI, Vietnam—For the 10 elderly farmers in the rice paddy, there was nowhere to hide. The river stretched along one side, the mountains on the other. Approaching quickly in between were the soldiers—an elite U.S. Army unit known as Tiger Force. Though the farmers were not carrying weapons, it didn't matter. No one was safe on July 28, 1967.
>
> *No one.*
>
> With bullets flying, the farmers—slowed by the thick, green plants and muck—dropped one by one to the ground. Within minutes, it was over. Four were dead, others wounded. Some survived by lying motionless in the mud. Four soldiers later recalled the assault. "We knew the farmers were not armed to begin with," one said, "but we shot them anyway."

The unprovoked attack was one of many carried out by the decorated unit in the Vietnam War, an eight-month investigation by *The Blade* shows.[29]

The story reported how the incident illustrated the type of brutality and murder that they had documented in their hundreds of interviews and review of thousands of pages of documents. After briefly summarizing several more examples, it revealed Apsey's investigation and how its findings had been ignored and the atrocities covered up for three decades. Warrant Officer Gustav Apsey, the investigator, who—in Sallah's words—"took a hit" in the story, found solace in the project. "You know, I'm going to bed peaceful as hell," he told the *Blade*. "Justice has been done."

The *Blade*'s stories were picked up across the country, and ABC News' *Nightline* followed up with its own interviews and gave credit to Sallah and Weiss. Notably, NBC and CBS News ignored the story, as did *The New York Times*, until it came under fire from the then–public editor of the *Times*, Dan Okrent, and Seymour Hersh, the Pulitzer Prize–winning investigative reporter who broke the My Lai story. Hersh heaped praise on the story and repeatedly denounced the *Times* for ignoring it. On Dec. 28, the *Times* weighed in with a story confirming the *Blade*'s findings.

Reader reaction at first was negative, with readers condemning the paper for running the story when America was again at war. "Why do you have to do this," one reader wrote to the *Blade*. Weiss answered that question eloquently during the in-house meeting with Block and editors, and Executive Editor Ron Royhab wrote a long note to the readers when the series started. It read in part:

> One reason is that the public has a right to know that American soldiers committed atrocities and that our government kept them from the public. We would have been party to a cover-up if we had knowledge of these war crimes and did not publish the story.
>
> Wrongdoing on this grand a scale is always significant. It is important to know what happened and why it happened because that's how a democracy functions. The people need to know what is being done in their name and who is responsible.
>
> . . . This country has a long and proud tradition of behaving honorably on foreign soil. It is because of that tradition, and because of the finest traditions of American journalism, that we are compelled to publish this report about American soldiers failing to live up to the proper standards and our government's failure to hold them accountable.[30]

Eventually, as the series began revealing the extent of the atrocities and the impact they had on people's lives, the reaction from civilians and veterans turned more positive.[31]

In April 2004, the series captured the coveted Pulitzer Prize for investigative reporting and several other awards. Among those other awards, was a $10,000 Taylor Family Award for Fairness in Newspapers administered by the Neiman Foundation at Harvard University.

In the meantime, Sallah and Weiss took a leave and expanded the series into a book, *Tiger Force: A True Story of Men and War,* which was published in May 2006 by Little, Brown and Company. Sallah went on to become investigations editor for the *Miami Herald*, and Weiss became business editor at *The Charlotte Observer*.

After the series, the Pentagon announced it would reopen the case by interviewing former soldiers of the Tiger Force under the direction of Army Secretary Les Brownlee. But more than three years after the *Blade's* series, no action had been taken against any of the officers. As of this writing, there still had been no dramatic action by the government that can be traced directly to the series.

Although the significance of an investigative project often is judged by its "impact"—the degree to which the work brings about reform or rights a wrong—*The Toledo Blade's* series perhaps will have a more intangible but deep-seated and thus long-lasting impact. In the painstaking work of Sallah and Weiss, readers can find more than an exposé of the "buried secrets," which are the atrocities and their cover-up. They also find a solid base of information for healthy public discourse on the "brutal truths" that lie beneath the shocking quotes and horrible images and all of the facts and figures.

One truth that emerges is that totaling the cost of war requires more than counting expenditures and casualties. Does this story also show that war takes a toll on a society's humanity? On an individual level, the soldiers who committed the atrocities depicted in this story were not the same people who left home and hearth equipped with the values and morality that their parents probably instilled in them. War did something to their humanity. One mother, for example, told Weiss her son came home from Tiger Force during a leave and showed such unrecognizably scary behavior that she thought maybe it was best that he did not survive the war. Meanwhile, the leaders of our society—military and government officials—knew about the atrocities but were not alarmed enough to take action.

Although the *Blade's* reporting, in the literal sense, only applies to specific soldiers in one military platoon and one specific war, a reasonable extrapolation suggests the story's "brutal truth" is more universal. Not long after the series was published, the military, now engaged in a war on terror, again had to deal with more accounts of American soldiers brutalizing noncombatants, most notoriously in prisons at Abu Ghraib and Guantanamo Bay. But even in civilian society, the inhumane treatment of these prisoners, which included torture, brutal treatment, rendition and denial of basic human rights, is now openly discussed and defended in a civilized society by national representatives as a justifiable action in a time of war. That reflects a deterioration of our culture's respect for humanity and should be toted up as part of the cost of the ongoing war on terror.

If the public in a democratic society is expected to rule wisely, it needs to hear that "brutal truth" even during war. Because the public has to tell its leaders when the cost of war gets too high, journalists have a responsibility to uncover those costs. That takes the kind of diligent, probing and careful investigative work that Sallah and Weiss provided in "Buried Secrets, Brutal Truths" and in *Tiger Force: A True Story of Men and War*. Although their impact is intangible, they will inform the public discourse on the current war and those that follow.

Lessons

INVESTIGATIVE REPORTING A MATTER OF NEWS CULTURE

Lesson Learned: Investigative reporting is the province of all journalists at news organizations of all sizes; the biggest obstacle to good investigative reporting is not the lack of money, but the failure of the news organization's leaders to establish a culture of investigative journalism in their newsrooms.

How It Applied: *The Toledo Blade* has a small staff and budget and small circulation. Just as Zusman and Meeker at the even smaller *Willamette Week* have instilled the notion that all of their reporters can do investigative work, the *Blade*'s reporters have the idea that their publisher believes his paper can "run with anybody," as reporter Mike Sallah said. Sallah's observation suggests that the publisher has made that attitude part of the paper's belief system. Sallah's partner, Mitch Weiss, said good investigative projects often start routinely: someone calls to complain about a perceived abuse; a suit is filed; an alert beat reporter who knows his or her specialty sees the bureaucracy deviate from its normal procedures. Tips are only as good as the reporter who knows what to do with them and the news organization that will let them do it.

THE TIGER FORCE BEAT

Lesson Learned: A daily reporter covering a beat should be like an investigative reporter in the sense that both become experts on their topic and develop a sense for recognizing when—in Weiss's words—"something is out of place."

How It Applied: Once Sallah and Weiss launched the investigation into Tiger Force, they practically became experts on many topics related to the story: military code of justice, the Geneva Conventions, war crimes, Vietnam culture and society, the Vietnam War, the meaning of the term free-fire zone, post-traumatic stress disorder. Likewise, once daily reporters are assigned to a beat or a specialty, they have to become experts. Sallah says a beat reporter covering government, for example, has to learn the laws of the state, county and municipal government and all of the normal procedures that government uses to carry out its duties. To hold people on a beat accountable, reporters have to know when the authorities' actions violate law or policy or deviate from normal procedures. They should keep dossiers on the principal elected and appointed officials. They should begin immediately building databases that track major functions of government to help spot trends.

A daily reporter covering a beat has to be aggressive and maintain a critical eye toward what people on their beat do as they carry out their duties. Weiss cited his partner's "due diligence" in painstakingly picking through the Tufts papers in search of a story to illustrate the difference between a good reporter and all other reporters. Even spot news reporters who have the investigative mentality would have eventually plowed through every Tufts document. It would take them longer and they might have to knock out a daily or a week-ender first, but their curiosity about what the military's top cop had stashed away in his personal papers would have driven them to eventually get through them all.

PERSISTENCE

Lesson Learned: Reporters have to be persistent.

How It Applied: In investigating Tiger Force, the reporter hit a number of early roadblocks. Sallah had to sift through 25,000 pages in the Tufts papers and deal with the frustration of repeated disappointments as one story idea after another fell through. Weiss said Sallah's persistence with those boxes of papers exemplifies "the difference between a good reporter and other reporters; other reporters would not have read through every single document, but Mike took time to read through them and to call me from the University of Michigan to check out leads. There a good chance a daily reporter would have just scanned a few and concluded it was all old stuff," he said.

He and Sallah confronted other early obstacles. The military refused to release records of the investigation, and sources initially said there was "nothing to it." But they found other ways to get the information through the National Archives and a source. In their case, resistance only served to whet their curiosity.

ANONYMOUS SOURCES

Lesson Learned: Although anonymous sources are valuable in the reporting process, they undermine the credibility of a story when information is attributed to them. For that reason, investigative reporters stress getting anonymous sources on the record or getting information through on-the-record sources or documents or, as is the usual case, a combination of both.

How It Applied: Although some stories such as the *Willamette Week*'s "30-Year Secret" simply cannot be done without the help of anonymous sources, Sallah says he does not like attributing information to them in a story. In his first interview with Pvt. William Carpenter on the Tiger Force story, Sallah backed away from Carpenter's request to go off the record even though he sensed that the ex–Tiger Force member was about to tell him the entire story. Nevertheless, Sallah was taking a risk. A reporter never knows whether he can go back to a source, whether he will be willing to open up again. In this case, a few subtle messages on the Tiger Force website might shut down potential sources. In a situation like the one Sallah faced with Carpenter, the temptation to take the information and find other sources to independently provide the same information is almost overwhelming. Sallah's snap decision had to take all of that and more into consideration. Sallah and Weiss later found records and other sources and then went back to Carpenter, who eventually became one of the most quoted sources in the story. He eventually admitted to something that he had refused to tell the military investigators 30 years ago—that he had participated in at least one killing. Sallah says he is sometimes successful with sources by simply being up front in explaining how much he dislikes using anonymous sources in a story. If the source still insists on anonymity and the information is critical, Sallah consents, but with the explanation that he would like to try to discover some new information and come back to the source to talk further about going on the record. Sometimes, revisiting the source when you have other sources talking on the records helps, he says.

DEVELOPING SOURCES

Lesson Learned: Learning to develop sources does not come with a five-step recipe, because it is like developing a relationship, only this one has to be developed quickly. Eventually, the value of that relationship depends on uniquely individual qualities. Relationships with sources in many ways requires what any might require, such as common courtesies, keeping in touch, periodically show-ing serious interest in the source and being respectful and nonjudgmental.

How It Applied: In their investigation, Sallah and Weiss had to develop sources with people who were hiding or trying to forget very dark events in their past—committing or witnessing war crimes. Although both learned a lot about post-traumatic stress disorder, much of what they did was simply "keeping them in the loop." That often meant talking with sources when they got new information to see what they thought of it. Sometimes, they simply, as a matter of courtesy, conveyed news about a long-lost comrade in arms. Weiss often turned inter-views into conversations by sharing things about his own life. Both reporters demonstrated sensitivity toward their interviewees and learned when to back off on the questioning and wait for another day.

Lesson Learned: Working sources sometimes is like a dance between two peo-ple who have different motives or agendas and both are trying to be the lead partner. Whatever metaphor is used to describe the process, the ultimate goal is to gain enough control so that you get the kind of understanding you need dur-ing your interviews with the source.

How It Applied: Mike Sallah's metaphor is the card game. He will show an ace or deuce, and sometimes both, but never all five of his cards—at first. In other words, he doesn't reveal everything he knows about the topic of his investiga-tion in the beginning for a variety of reasons. But you have to play the game to win. "Working sources is one of the toughest things for reporters, but it is the most crucial."

INTERVIEWING

Lesson Learned: Skill in persuading sources in particularly sensitive situa-tions such as war crimes or sexual abuse to open up derive from a complex mix. It usually is a combination of tricks of the trade and an instinct that forms from an individual reporter's unique character and evolves over the course of countless interviews, phone chats and conversations. Many intangibles—the reporter's demeanor or phrasing and tone of voice or type of question, or the interviewee's mood, vulnerability, anger, defiance or longing for vindication—come into play in interviews, and they may work differently from one reporter to the next.

How It Applied: Soldiers who had committed war crimes or witnessed them presented Sallah and Weiss with a complex range of emotions and attitudes. They often found the soldiers' attitudes and moods changing sharply from one interview to the next. Both learned as much as they could about post-traumatic stress disorder, and, in describing their approaches they both talked about trying to avoid pushing too far too fast for fear that the sources would "shut down." Both tried to keep interviews conversational, and they tried to remain nonjudg-mental.

Weiss said reporters are part journalist and part psychologist. He tries to ease tensions sometimes by bringing something personal about himself into the conversation. The routine preparation—drawing up a question list, developing an overall strategy and goals, researching the interviewee—help, but Weiss and

Sallah say interviewing requires instantaneous adjustments. You never know what you are going to confront in an interview or when a question or the tone of your voice will shut the interviewee down. "It comes with experience," Sallah once said, trying to explain the complex mental machinations he made in one tough interview. "You get better at it in time. The more people you meet, the more people you talk to, the better you get at thinking on your feet."

Lesson Learned: Although the ultimate goal of interviewing is to gather credible information and snag a sharp quote, the best means of accomplishing that is to treat the interview as a conversation in which you are trying to understand something. If interviewees believe you are trying to trap them, or merely get a "good quote," or bully them into acknowledging something, the discourse switches from an open conversation to a cold journalistic interview in which your subject is going to be more concerned about saying "something wrong" (something that makes him or her look bad or foolish) than in conveying information.

How It Applied: Although Sallah and Weiss are hard-nosed reporters, their interviews clearly had that "let-me-understand-this" quality to them. In one conversation with Carpenter, Sallah said his phrasing was something akin to: "Bill, we've got this information now and can you enlighten us on this?" Weiss, in getting Doyle to bluntly say he killed elderly farmers because they looked at him wrong, did not attack Doyle as a prosecutorial reporter would. In a disarming tone, he said, "So they were killed because they looked at you guys, is that what happened?" Weiss put the introductory phrase in the passive voice and expressed it in a soft passive manner so that the short ending question loses its damning punch. The question is blunt and clear, but Weiss delivers it in a way that does not figuratively shout "Doyle, you are about to hang yourself." Instead of sounding prosecutorial, his tone of voice sounds as if he is just casually repeating for the sake of affirmation what Doyle has already acknowledged.

Lesson Learned: Interviewing people in person provides many advantages to reporters. Besides helping you build rapport and trust, it helps you gauge the interviewee's reactions, giving you useful clues in a number of areas. Reporters are often stereotyped in negative ways. Many people have never met a reporter, and their knowledge is based on daily lambasting from radio and television talk-show hosts or caricatures in movies and television shows. A personal contact gives you an opportunity to disprove the myths and show you are not an ogre.

How It Applied: Sallah and Weiss were confronted with very challenging and often sensitive interviews with a corps of people often viewed as being suspicious of the press. So building trust and rapport was essential for them. They put a lot of stock in interviews that—in Sallah's words go "face-to-face, eyeball-to-eyeball," a cliché that nonetheless conveys the concentration he applies during interviews to reading the intangibles. Sallah once appealed an editor's ruling to gain permission to fly across the country to interview Medic Rion Causey in person. Then they went to Vietnam to talk to people face-to-face. These kinds of interviews provide tangible advantages, such as allowing you and your source to examine documents together and giving you the opportunity to gather descriptive details of the person and the setting of the conversation. Personal interviews yield many intangible benefits that help you sense when your questions strike a nerve with the interviewee. For example, if a person sits up straight and leans forward for most of the interview but then suddenly slumps when you ask a question, that is a clue for you to follow up either right then or to come back to the issue later. The same is true with watching eye contact. A look away, or, conversely, sudden direct eye contact, conveys messages that provide invaluable guidance in assessing and reacting to what the interviewee is saying. You also can employ your own body language, eye contact and gestures in an unlimited number of tactical ways; that is, make subtle points, test ideas or show special interest or casual interest.

Lesson Learned: Frequently, reporters, for tactical reasons, do not want an interviewee to know the intensity of their interest in a subject, or, that they have developed expertise. Nor do they want to show their excitement or interest when an interviewee makes an earth-shattering comment.

How It Applied: In interviewing Carpenter for the first time, Sallah did not want to show all five of his cards. At that point, he was not sure how Carpenter would react if he knew Sallah was in the investigative mode. There are many other reasons for keeping your cards hidden for a while. Just for writing purposes, you often want sources to use their own words to say something you already know, because you are always fishing for good quotes. But there are many more substantive reasons. For example, you may want to test your knowledge, get a confirmation of something you are not yet sure of, hear a fresh articulation of what you already know or use your expertise to test the expertise or honesty of your source.

Notes

1. The interviewees listed here are the sources for their direct and indirect quotes; reconstruction of interviews between themselves and their sources; and depictions of their conversations, thoughts and actions that are not referenced in the text:

Michael D. Sallah, *Miami Herald* newsroom, July 19, 2006; August 18, 2006, by telephone; June 22, 2007, by telephone.

Mitch Weiss, *Charlotte Observer* newsroom, July 17, 2006; August 15 and August 17, 2006, by telephone.

Ron Royhab, executive editor of *The Toledo Blade*, July 2, 2007, by telephone; July 12, 2007, e-mail.

John R. Block, editor in chief, Block Communications, June 25, 2007, by telephone.

Allen Block, board chairman, Block Communications, June 25, 2007. Some material from these sources is individually referenced where necessary to ensure clarity.

2. *Public Agenda*, "Public Agenda Special Edition: Terrorism, Public Supports Action on Iraq—Depending on the Situation." February 14, 2003. Publicagenda.org/specials/terrorism. Public Agenda is a nonprofit, nonpartisan research organization founded by social scientist Daniel Yankelovich and former Secretary of State Cyrus Vance. This edition reported a majority of people favored going to war against Iraq and believed the U.S. could not prevent another terrorist attack. About 70 percent felt the nation as whole was still suffering emotional pain from the terrorist attacks

in New York and Washington, D.C., and 87 percent had come to appreciate their country more since Sept. 11, 2001.

3. George W. Bush, January 28, 2003, "State of Union," The U.S. Capitol, Office of the White House Press Secretary.

4. Questions about the credibility of several sources prompted a long controversy over the No Gun Ri reporting.

5. Interview, John R. Block, June 25, 2007.

6. Ibid.

7. Interview, Ron Royhab, July 2, 2007.

8. Interview, Michael D. Sallah, June 22, 2007.

9. Interview, Mitch Weiss, July 17, 2006.

10. Ibid.; Interview, Sallah, July 19, 2006.

11. Michael D. Sallah and Mitch Weiss, *Tiger Force: A True Story of Men and War* (New York: Little, Brown, 2006), 262–63.

12. Ibid., 156, 350.

13. Ibid., 101.

14. Ibid., 194–95.

15. Interview, Sallah, July 19, 2006.

16. Sallah and Weiss, *Tiger Force.*

17. Ibid., 3, 313.

18. Ibid,313; Interview, Weiss, July 17, 2006.

19. Sallah and Weiss, *Tiger Force,* 11.

20. Sgt. William Doyle, interview by Mitch Weiss. Audio posted online at www .toledoblade.com with four-part series, "Buried Secrets, Brutal Truths," *Toledo Blade,* October 19–22, 2003.

21. Sallah and Weiss, *Tiger Force,* 292–95.

22. Michael D. Sallah and Mitch Weiss, "Pain Lingers 36 Years after Deadly Rampage," *Toledo Blade,* October 21, 2003, p. 1.

23. Ibid.

24. Interview, Sallah, July 19, 2006.

25. Michael D. Sallah and Mitch Weiss, "Inquiry Ended Without Justice," Day two of four-part series, "Buried Secrets, Brutal Truths," *Toledo Blade,* October 20, 2003, p. 1.

26. Ibid.

27. Ibid.

28. Ibid.

29. Sallah and Weiss, "Rogue GIs Unleashed Wave of Terror in Central Highlands," Day one of four-part series, "Buried Secrets, Brutal Truths," *Toledo Blade,* October 19, 2003, p. 1.

30. Ron Royhab, "Massacre Story Needs to Be Told," *Toledo Blade,* October 19, 2003, p. 1.

31. Sallah and Weiss, *Tiger Force,* 320.

Selected Bibliography

Articles

"Public Agenda Special Edition: Terrorism, Public Supports Action on Iraq," *Public Agenda,* February 14, 2003.

Sallah, Michael D., and Mitch Weiss. "Buried Secrets, Brutal Truths," four-part series, *Toledo Blade,* October 19–22, 2003.

Book

Sallah, Michael D., and Mitch Weiss. *Tiger Force: A True Story of Men and War*. New York: Little, Brown, 2006.

Interviews

Block, Allan, chairman, Block Communications (includes *The Toledo Blade*), June 25, 2007.

Block, John R., editor in chief, Block Communications (includes *The Toledo Blade*), June 25, 2007.

Royhab, Ron, executive editor, *The Toledo Blade*, July 2 and July 12, 2007.

Sallah, Michael D., former reporter, *The Toledo Blade*, June 19, 2006 (tape recording held by author).

Sallah, Michael D., August 18, 2006.

Sallah, Michael D., June 22, 2007.

Weiss, Mitch, former reporter, *The Toledo Blade*, June 17, 2006 (tape recording held by author).

Weiss, Mitch, August 15 and 16, 2006.

News Archive and News Search Service

Access World News, NewsBank, Inc., Naples, FL.

Website

The Pulitzer Prize website, http://www.pulitzer.org.

Speech

Bush, George W. "State of the Union," The U.S. Capitol, transcript, Office of the White House Press Secretary, January 28, 2003.

CHAPTER 4

Soft Touch Shows Shipbreaking Kills, Maims

He Just Needed Copy[1]

Early one evening in 1995, *Baltimore Sun* reporter Will Englund motored about Chesapeake Bay with a marine historian. He was trolling for a feature on old shipwrecks. At low tide, the remains of some of the ancient wrecks break the surface. Near Curtis Creek, you can see parts of the *Emma Giles*, the once famous side-wheel passenger steamer, whose ghost has inspired paintings and poetry.[2] Out from historic Fort McHenry, where Francis Scott Key once saw "the rockets' red glare," the historian launched into a captivating tale about the last act of piracy on the Chesapeake Bay near where they were floating.

As he talked, they cruised around the corner of the old fort. Quite by surprise, a jarring sight pulled Englund's attention away from pirates and shipwrecks. Looking across the Middle Branch toward the Fairfield pier in South Baltimore, Englund's eyes were drawn to a 45,000-ton ship, the *USS Coral Sea*, a diesel-powered aircraft carrier once hailed as "The Ageless Warrior."

"It was not in a very happy condition," Englund recalled.

It had once plowed the seas during the height of Cold War tensions with the Soviet Union. It had launched fighter jets from its flight deck into the skies over Vietnam and Libya and helped rescue 39 crewmen of the *SS Mayaguez* from the clutches of the Khmer Rouge in Cambodia. But by 1995, the Cold War had long since ended, and nuclear power was replacing diesel power in America's war fleet.[3]

Now, the *USS Coral Sea*, whose motto was "Older and Bolder and Better," was lashed to a pier in a sad state of deconstruction, and Will Englund sat in a bobbing little boat out in the harbor wondering about the once-proud warship.

What's that doing there, he asked the historian.

It was just a passing question, perhaps born of idle curiosity, the type that might occur to any reporter on any story.

Some guy got a contract to break the thing up, the historian said. It didn't work out and he ran out of money. The ship has been moored there ever since.

The scrapping had ceased about a year ago, and latest word was that the ship would be towed to India. There, workers were to swarm this once-hulking symbol of American power and finish the job.

Well, that's kind of interesting, Englund thought to himself: *USS Coral Sea*, history, local businessman and a big project that didn't go right. He wondered what went wrong and why it was being sent to India. It might be a decent story, he thought. Besides, he needed waterfront copy. Englund, then 44, had just finished a long stint as the *Sun's* Moscow correspondent, and he was trying to establish a beat specializing on the waterfront.

So began an adventure that would become a career event for him.

"It was nothing more profound than that," he said. No light-bulb moment, no insightful analytical revelation, no compulsion to drop every thing—nothing to hint that he was on the brink of something big. It did not even stir him to immediate action. He had a shipwreck story to do. The old warship would have to wait. "So, I sort of stuck it in my back pocket," he said.

There it remained for a spell, while he did the shipwreck piece and several other stories over the next several months. In December, he heard that a Chinese tug had pulled into the harbor to tow the battered carrier to India. He called the scrapper, Kerry Ellis, owner of Seawitch Salvage. The project had turned into a nightmare, Ellis told him. He had tried hard to "make a go" of it, but the government's environmental regulations had scuttled the effort and blocked plans to tow it to India. The interview produced a simple feature "about a man with a bright idea that didn't pan out," Englund said.

No sooner had it run than Englund got a call from an anonymous tipster. He called it one of those tips that essentially says "How can you write about so and so and not mention such and such?" In this case, the "such and such" was a host of environmental problems, including the handling and disposal of asbestos and polychlorinated biphenyls (PCBs), which are hazardous compounds used in ships' electrical and hydraulic systems. The tipster gave Englund a name. He followed the tip and "chipped away" at it and a couple of other stories.

By mid-March in 1996, Englund finished a story that had sent him to California to write about the last commercial sturgeon fishery, and he had turned his full attention back to the *USS Coral Sea*. He had learned that Seawitch was in bankruptcy court, where he found boxes and boxes of court records. They revealed a tangled story and a bitter dispute among Ellis and his partners. As in a messy divorce, the principles lambasted each other, exposing industry problems publicly.

The records and experts he consulted showed the financial problems arose primarily because the U.S. Environmental Protection Agency (EPA) was trying to regulate the way they were handling PCBs and disposing of insulation. He devoted all of March and part of April to the story, and on April 28, 1996, the story opened like this:

> With the end of the Cold War, the Navy has begun selling off its huge fleet of surplus warships for scrap—and the handful of businesses cashing in are leaving a dismal trail of toxic spills, mishandled asbestos, worker injuries and tangled lawsuits in port after port across the country.
>
> The Navy program has spawned a new type of ship-scrapping business, led by men who see opportunity where older shipyards see only risk and

liability. Veterans of the business have largely refused to take part, convinced that the only way to turn a profit is to cut corners and break the law.

The newcomers are not so squeamish. Unencumbered by high technology, capital investment or even permanent places of businesses, they say they are ready to handle as many ships as the Navy wants to sell—as many as 150 over the next few years.[4]

In another few paragraphs, Englund's story sweeps the national scene—out to California, up to Rhode Island and down to North Carolina—before it turns back to Baltimore Harbor and the *USS Coral Sea*. It explained how the industry works, the environmental problems, the business side and its run-ins with regulators. It was primarily a phone-and-records story. In the 15th paragraph, Englund powerfully described working conditions that clearly suggested a compelling human element to this story.

Ship-breaking is a dirty, dangerous, low-tech line of work. The primary tools are cutting torches and sledge hammers. Crews break and cut their way down through a ship, often in complete darkness, the rusty decks sloshing with chemically contaminated water and sometimes overrun with rats.[5]

But that was about the extent to which Englund's story explored that angle. Nevertheless, it was a good story. It ran on a Sunday and led the front page, the best possible play for a story.

Editor Wants More

The top editor of the paper, John Carroll, was so fascinated by it, he wanted more. Carroll, who had been in journalism since 1963, was surprised by the story. "I did not know it had been in the works, and I had not seen it before," Carroll recalled.

Carroll, then in his mid-50s, had come to the *Sun* in 1991, from the *Lexington Herald* (then the *Herald-Leader*), where he led the paper to a Pulitzer Prize for stories about cheating and payola involving the basketball team at the University of Kentucky. Several years earlier, as a metro editor at *The Philadelphia Inquirer*, he oversaw Pulitzer-winning stories on police brutality. In his reporting days, he had covered Vietnam and the White House for the *Sun*.

As much as he liked Englund's story, Carroll sensed there might be a bigger one. On the surface, it fit some of the criteria that he looks for: that it is "gettable" and that it has importance and meaning in a "visceral" sense. The best stories are literally about life and death, and certainly this one had said people were getting hurt and killed in the shipbreaking industry. Moreover, Englund's story had said shipbreaking was hurting the environment. He summoned the editors to discuss it. Carroll called attention to the fact that lawsuits had been filed, which meant there would be public records, court documents and depositions. He also thought the fact that workers had been hurt and that the environment was damaged gave the story enormous importance.

What struck him most, though, was that the subject was new. So many projects explore topics that people already know about, like nursing home abuses. "We've told that story a hundred times," Carroll said. "But this was a story I had never heard of before. I had never even heard the term 'shipbreakers,' so it could take the readers into a world they did not know about."

Englund said he understood Carroll's basic message to be this: There might be more to this story than phone calls and bankruptcy records, and that the key to finding that story would be through workers who scrapped the ships. "I thought it was a good idea," Englund said. Carroll ordered Englund to take some time to look into it some more and then to write a memo on how the paper could pursue it.

Investigative reporting was not entirely new to Englund, although he never considered it his specialty. The story was investigative, but it also was about the environment. Yet, he doesn't consider himself an environmental reporter either. "I don't see any clear distinction on any of these categories," he says. He had been a foreign correspondent for most of the previous five years for the paper and had done different types of reporting. "It is a little bit investigative, a little bit of being thoughtful and analytical and a lot of just keeping your eyes and ears open. I felt it was very easy to go from Moscow correspondent to working on shipbreakers."

Englund, the son of a mechanical engineering professor at Columbia University, studied English at Harvard, but he traces his journalism career even further back to high school, when his father gave him a printing press and a box of type. He and a friend used it to start a high school magazine. At Harvard, he was more interested in acting than journalism and wanted to go to New York to be an actor when he graduated. However, lacking the nerve to suggest to his parents that they pay for him to study theater, he decided to enroll in the Graduate School of Journalism at Columbia, where tuition would be free because of his father's position there. Although he talks about his passion for the theater, mention of a love for journalism is noticeably absent in his conversation. When asked about the omission, Englund smiled and said, "That still could happen."

He started his journalism career at the *Sun* in 1977 as a copy editor before becoming a reporter covering local government and education. As a Fulbright Fellow in 1988, he worked for *The Glasgow Herald* in Scotland. He and his wife, Kathy Lally, were in Moscow for the *Sun* from 1991 to 1995. He was in his early 40s when they returned to the states and Carroll asked him to cover the waterfront.

He said Carroll didn't give a lot of direction on what he expected, but Englund thought the beat should be more than just a local beat, and he liked Carroll's vision for the shipbreaking story. Englund took about two weeks to write the memo Carroll had ordered. It covered the national and international implications and how the paper could investigate the industry. Carroll apparently liked it. He called in Rebecca Corbett, his assistant managing editor in charge of projects, to direct the effort. He also pulled in Gary Cohn, one of his top investigative reporters, who, just a few months earlier had become a finalist for the Pulitzer.

The Partnership

Englund and Cohn were virtual strangers to one another. Still, down deep, Englund felt a bit of apprehension at first. On the day after he submitted his memo, Carroll told him he was going to assign Cohn to work on the story with him. "It was explained to me that Gary was very good with records," Englund said. Nevertheless, Englund was wary. As a longtime *Sun* man, he had noticed that a distinct trend had been emerging since Carroll took over: The *Sun* was taking on an *Inquirer* personality. Managing Editor Bill Marimow had come from Philadelphia, where he had once worked with Carroll on the Pulitzer-winning police abuse story. Jim Asher, another editor, and investigative reporter Wally Roche also had come from the *Inquirer*, and now, Gary Cohn, another Philly alumnus, was glomming onto his project. Plus, Cohn had worked for Carroll at the *Lexington Herald*. "So, I was concerned," Englund said. "Mostly, it was from the fact that Gary was from Philadelphia, and I thought he would be this tough-ass guy who would just take over the project and wouldn't really understand all of the layers of it."

But Englund soon lowered his guard, and came to the conclusion that Cohn was an enormously resourceful and energetic reporter and nothing like the stereotype he had feared. "It turned out that although he had this reputation as this 'Philly investigative reporter' . . ., he turned out to be an extremely sweet guy," so mild mannered, in fact, he makes Columbo the disarming television detective, look like a pit bull.

In every other respect, though, Cohn, who was in his mid-40s at the time, is the quintessential investigative reporter. Investigative work is about all he has ever done, and Carroll and Marimow are just two editors in a long line of highly successful and respected journalists who have guided his work ever since he graduated summa cum laude from the State University of New York at Buffalo in 1974. After a year of law school at the University of California at Berkeley and three months as an investigator for the Southern Regional Council, he began a five-year reporting stint with famed investigative columnist Jack Anderson. Anderson was much feared in Washington, and he made an impression on Cohn. "His style was very persuasive," Cohn said. "He was flattering, good at convincing them he was sincere." Cohn reported on a range of topics such as white-collar crime, congressional corruption and wrongdoing in the federal judiciary.

In 1980, he began his long relationship with John Carroll at the *Lexington Herald-Leader*, where he added to his credentials as an investigative reporter and did some breaking news stories. The *Herald-Leader* was a small- to medium-sized paper with a circulation of about 120,000, which Cohn felt is a good size for starting young newspaper reporters. Frequently, they have some terrific young editors on their way up who can spend more time helping young reporters learn the business, he said. At the Lexington paper, he had two: a city editor and Carroll. "The paper was small enough that, even though John was the top editor, I got to spend a lot of time working with him on stories." That is where Cohn discovered how demanding Carroll was. He was a perfectionist," Cohn recalled. "If he took an interest in my story, I knew I had good material." He investigated Kentucky's black-lung benefits program and the quality of the scientific research at the tax-supported tobacco and health research institute.

His next stop took him to the Miami bureau of *The Wall Street Journal*, where he did a two-year stint as a business reporter. Although not particularly enjoyable, that experience gave him useful knowledge about the corporate world and business finance. "In fact, I would advise any journalism student to take a course or two of business," Cohn said.

In 1986, Cohn joined *The Philadelphia Inquirer,* which brought him into contact with some of the profession's most respected journalists, starting with the legendary editor Eugene Roberts, who guided the paper to 17 Pulitzers. At the time, Cohn considered that a pinnacle in his career, because he always wanted to be a reporter for the *Inquirer,* which enjoyed a stellar reputation under Roberts' leadership. Cohn investigated and documented corruption by the president of the city's municipal union, examined why Philadelphia residents paid the highest auto insurance rates in the country, and explored how crimes against Hispanic citizens in Philadelphia go unsolved and Hispanic defendants in court were not given interpreters.

He worked closely with investigative editor Jonathan Neumann, who had been Marimow's partner in the late 1970s on the police abuse project. "He was a great, great editor," Cohn said, referring to Neumann. "Jon taught me that you never give up, that if one thing doesn't work, try something else and keep going back, keep digging. He also had a passion for stories that make a difference in people's lives." Cohn also learned from Wally Roche, who he would see again later at the *Sun.* He and Roche did the story on the corrupt union boss. "We spent a lot of time following him; Wally taught me how to do that," Cohn recalled.

But a larger, more abstract lesson came from Roberts. There had been rumors about the union boss corruption for quite sometime, but no one had proven anything. Cohn said Roberts' marching orders were pleasingly, neutrally simple: Let's find out everything we can about him and put it all together to see what's there. Cohn felt as if there was no agenda or hint that the only good outcome would be to nail the union boss. In essence, his orders were "Let's find out the truth once and for all, whatever it might be," Cohn said, with the emphasis on "whatever."

A few years later, Roberts left the *Inquirer.* Cohn remained for a while. Although the *Inquirer* was the paper he long dreamed of joining, Cohn had a chance to work with Carroll again in 1993 at the *Sun,* so he took it. He soon went to work on "Battalion 316," a four-part series that won some of the most prestigious investigative journalism awards in the country—the Selden Ring, Overseas Press Club and Goldschmidt Prize—and placed as finalist for the Pulitzer. The story revealed how a special unit of the Honduran army tortured and executed hundreds of suspected subversives with U.S. knowledge and complicity during the 1980s. Carroll and Marimow had been deeply involved in that project.

In early 1996, while Carroll was pondering the shipbreaking story idea, Cohn and his "Battalion 316" partner, Ginger Thompson, were still working on follow-ups on that project.[6] But Cohn was looking for another big project to start. "I had been talking to John about doing something on campaign finance," Cohn recalled. "But his reaction was that it 'had the feel of being done before.'" Carroll told Cohn that he liked the idea in Englund's memo and that he wanted him to work on it with Englund.[7]

Cohn had read Englund's story on the shipbreakers. "At most papers, that would have been it on that story," he said. But his longtime mentor thought "it was new and different," and needed more attention. Having worked with Carroll for years, Cohn respected Carroll's judgment. "John has this unbelievable knack for seeing possibilities in stories and recognizing big stories a little bit quicker than most people do."

Cohn did not know Englund, but he had been reading his work from Moscow and had come to respect his writing skills and breadth of experience. "He could churn out stories, but he also could really dig into them," Cohn said. He sensed that others in the newsroom may have felt that Cohn was the investigative force in the partnership because of his background. But he and Englund never worked the project in that manner. "In working with him, I thought Will was a terrific investigative reporter," Cohn said. "I probably had more background in documents and court records and things like that. Will is very analytic and a good writer. Will was the one who discovered this story, and I really felt fortunate to be a part of it."

Charting the Path

Englund's story and pitch memo became the outline for the investigation.[8] Companies were scrapping ships all over the country, including Brownsville, Texas, Wilmington, N.C., Terminal Island, Calif., and Quonset Point, R.I. Except for a Wilmington paper's coverage of shipbreaking in that city's harbor, the press had written little about the subject. Englund learned that countries the world over were sending retired ships to India for breaking up.

Englund and Cohn met with their editor, Rebecca Corbett, to map out a strategy. "We had hints from the Baltimore case that there were problems," Corbett said. They needed to determine the scale of the problems and consequences, and whether the shipbreaking industry was "a rogue industry." The regulatory agencies had paid little attention. Although the strategy included exploring the Alang, India, connection, Corbett said the first step had to be in-country. "We needed to figure out where the abuses were occurring, who the people in the industry were and where the dilatory oversight had been."

Cohn and Englund said Corbett immersed herself in every aspect of the project from planning, strategizing and influencing the direction of the story. "Rebecca and I didn't know each other, and maybe we were a little wary initially," Cohn recalled. "But she turned out to be unbelievable. He described her as "tough" but also said "she had a sense of when to leave us alone." Cohn discovered that Corbett had what he called "a real keen appreciation for the readers." For example, if they reported a pollution level as a number of parts per million, she wanted to know the consequences of that concentration on people.

For his part, Englund thought of her as a calming force. "She was very careful that we kept our feet on the ground. Every time we had a sense of finding some very important information, she would say, 'OK, good. Now, what else?'" Yet she still gave them the freedom they needed. "Rebecca let us go where our noses took us," Englund recalled. "She gave us a free rein and we checked in every other day or so." He also described her as meticulous in managing a project, in that she wanted to be kept abreast of their reporting and asked a lot questions. "There was a lot of 'Are you sure it is this and not this?'" he said.

Corbett, who in 2004 would move on to supervise investigative projects in the Washington bureau of *The New York Times*, got her start in journalism at a small weekly in Pittsfield, Maine, in 1973. After stints of reporting, editing or both at the *Central Maine Morning Sentinel* in Waterville and the *Manchester Journal-Inquirer* in Connecticut, she moved on to *The Baltimore Sun*. Corbett worked her way up the ranks from copy editor to night metropolitan editor and to city editor in three years, where she directed a staff of 25. She became the paper's first writing coach in 1989 and supervised projects and enterprise stories at the same time. By 1993, she rose to assistant managing editor in charge of projects. At the time of the shipbreakers investigation, she was supervising projects throughout the newsroom as well as specialist writers covering science, medicine, technology, environment, religion and nonprofits.[9]

The reporters' observations of her fit the way she describes her style and goal as a project manager. Corbett says she likes to get deeply involved in projects she manages, while still trying to keep an overview of the direction in which the story is heading. "I view my role as the person to keep an eye on what the story is, what are we after, how do we get there and how do we determine what we have." In the shipbreakers investigation, she visited the *USS Coral Sea* to get a sense of the story and did some independent research. "I want to immerse myself so that I will have a better sense of the subject matter," she said.

When she is supervising and editing projects, Corbett said she worries more about what is not in a story than what is in it. She has to be certain that she understands the context of the information and that all pertinent avenues have been explored. "As an editor, I try very hard to play devil's advocate . . . to not let the desire to have a great story blind the reporters to the reality that may require reframing the material and make it less dramatic and sensational." The questioning themes include the following:

- Is this really the way it is?
- Is there another explanation for this?
- What am I not seeking out?

Corbett says she wants to know how her reporters got the information they are presenting, whether it is reliable and complete and whether the sources were authoritative and in a position to know about the information they are giving the paper.

Cohn and Englund kept Corbett in the loop, so she never found herself doubting whether they were getting the complete story. They had meetings once every week to 10 days, and Corbett said she would ask "zillions" of questions. Cohn arranged to establish a handy computer "share basket" so that all three of them knew everything that was going on. The reporters' notes from every interview went into the basket. Memos to each other went in there, as did anything touching on the subject. They had hundreds of files divided into categories such as scrap workers, deaths, asbestos violations, court cases and others.

Site Visits, Paper Trail Reveal Sights, Sounds

Their visits to the scrapyards filled that basket with details of mayhem and sights and sounds from a half-dozen yards. But the most frightening details came from Wilmington, N.C., on the Cape Fear River, where they found what one source described as "one of Dante's levels of hell."[10] In Brownsville, Texas, they saw poorly trained and equipped laborers working in dangerous conditions and talked to a yard super-intendent wearing a hardhat with a "SAFETY FIRST" logo. Their observations pro-duced descriptions that almost overwhelm the senses. They told how they "felt suffocating heat" and how cutting torches "burn with a sort of back-of-the-throat roar." They described how "sparks fly where steel is being burned" and "acrid, choking smoke billows when a torch sets off insulation." Sometimes they found workers could give the most compelling descriptions. Twenty-two-year-old Jorge Corpus described how "you'd blow your nose and black stuff would come out from all the smoke you'd be inhaling." Such details and telling insights illustrated the overall picture they drew from visits to other yards, from interviews with hun-dreds of laborers and from court filings and records. "It's not an ice cream factory," one owner said, describing his own scrapyard.[11]

Although onsite visits and interviews became the most important parts of the reporting, the reporters gleaned graphic details and facts from public records. One record revealed that a Department of Defense inspector once refused to inspect a ship because he thought it was too dangerous to board; the next day a worker fell through a deck plate that was partially cut but was not safely roped off and marked to prevent the type of accident that happened. He lived, but was seriously injured. In California, the reporters learned from records that a ship-breaking company fired workers for telling inspectors about some violations. That tidbit came from the work notes of an inspector for the U.S. Occupational Safety and Health Administration (OSHA). Other records from the same agency revealed that a company sent its employees to an asbestos-handling class and then, when they went to work, ordered them to ignore everything they had learned in the training to save time. The agency inspected the yard when serious accidents or deaths occurred, and the reporters used the inspectors' reports to learn about conditions at yards.[12]

Cohn said he learned about the health and safety agency's records from oth-ers. He learned about the inspectors' work notes from another reporter who once did a project involving the agency. That same reporter told him that the complete file on an accident investigation becomes public when the investiga-tion is complete. A college professor who did research using the agency's records explained the databases and how they could identify salvage yard accidents by using another document that he had obtained from the Navy—a list of all the salvage companies scrapping Navy ships.

Wherever Cohn and Englund traveled, they checked federal and state crimi-nal and civil court records and bankruptcy filings for legal actions involving the shipbreakers. They frequently found the names of workers in these filings, as well as complaints, answers to complaints and interrogatories, and depositions, all of which often provided vivid details about accidents and dangerous condi-tions at the sites. Bankruptcy records at the federal courthouse in San Diego provided background on the difficulties shipbreakers had trying to adhere to environmental regulations when scrapping warships.

The Shipbreakers' Side

At the outset of the investigation, the journalists talked to the people at the cen-ter of the scrapyard problems: the shipbreakers. Typically, reporters build their cases first and then go to the subjects of the investigation. In this probe, however, Cohn and Englund decided early that they could not wait until the end of the reporting to go to the shipbreakers. The ship scrapping industry was complex and young. They would have to rely on them to learn about the industry. Moreover, they wanted to get into the salvage yards and onto the ships. So, they had to start talking with them early.

Cohn and Englund believed the strategy added two important dimensions to the project: By getting to know them early, they became real-life figures rather than usual stick-figure culprits in investigative stories; the owners brought the government's culpability in the issue to the reporters' attention early so that they had enough time to investigate it. As terrible as the plight of the workers was, they realized they had to investigate whether the Navy and the Department of Defense were disclosing how dangerous and dirty the ships were. "It would have been a mistake for us to assume that those were the only bad guys and wait to the end to interview them," Cohn said. "Moreover, there were some [salvage operators] who were genuinely interested in cleaning up their industry."

Cohn and Englund approached the shipbreakers as individuals genuinely intrigued by the business and wanting to understand their perspective. "This was a weird, arcane business, and they loved talking about it," Cohn said. "My theory is that they probably bored their wives to death talking about it, and here come these two reporters hanging on every word they were saying." More important, the shipbreakers wanted to make sure the reporters understood their defense. "They did not think they should take the whole rap, that the defense department did not tell them how toxic the ships were," he said.

In approaching the shipbreakers, they sought a neutral, nonjudgmental stance. In joint interviews, Englund characterized their individual roles as "good cop, better cop," an approach that seemed to play well with the shipbreakers. It set the tone and probably weighed heavily in some of the shipbreakers' willingness to let them into their salvage yards. "We were not badgering any of these guys or trying to trick them into saying something incriminating, Englund recalled. "We always had our notebooks out, and we would go back over something that looked or sounded kind of astonishing." Englund says their interviewing tactics with shipbreakers drove home a good lesson for interviewing some subjects of investigations: "If you are willing to say to them, 'look, let's set down and you tell me about what you do here,' and then listen to them and follow the conversation and their thinking, you can learn an awful lot more than if they are getting the feeling that you are just waiting to pounce. In all of these cases, we had to try to see the world through these guys' eyes."

Although the shipbreakers were not especially sympathetic characters in the story, Cohn and Englund still sought to show their personalities, particularly the verbose and sometimes ornery Richard Jaross. Englund first interviewed him by phone for the original story in April 1996, and, later, he and Cohn talked to him in person in Wilmington. "He spent the first 30 minutes telling us how he wasn't going to talk to us," Englund recalled. Then he talked. "Jaross was wittingly flamboyant," Englund said. "His psyche was out there on display all of the time, and you couldn't help but be taken by the guy. We wanted to write about him as a human being rather than as a cardboard villain."

Scenes, Human Stories Emerge, Carry Project

But Jaross' flamboyance and the personalities of the others sank in the wake of the death and environmental destruction the reporters found at their scrap sites. From the outset, they figured the real story would be down where the sparks from the cutting torch flared. There, they would find more than flamboyant personalities. That's where the color and texture of the story would be, where the tragedies recorded in dry court files and inspection reports unfolded, where the gritty reality of shipbreaking assaulted the senses. At the same time, they could not build a credible case just on shock and tears. The individual cases had to accurately illustrate specifically how the systemic failure played out on the ground so that readers could see the consequences of what the shipbreakers, the military and the regulators were doing or not doing. That would take more than two or three cases, more than 10 or 15; it would take dozens.

That would not be easy. First, they had to identify the salvage workers. Then, they had to persuade these mostly poor, undocumented, Spanish-speaking Latinos to talk to English-speaking white people from social and economic life-styles the workers could only dream about. But they had to try. Talking to them on site was difficult. When salvage company owners let them in, they often sent someone to follow them around, a practice that had a chilling effect on the workers, Cohn recalled. In Baltimore, Cohn waited at the salvage yard gates when workers quit work and followed them to the rooming houses and rundown hotels where they lived on the edge of the city. Later that night, he showed up at their door steps. In other locations, they found names of workers in court records when suits had been filed involving an accident. Often, success with one worker led to names of other workers. In still others, they went to areas of town where they lived and went door-to-door.

Intermediaries Open Doors

Identifying the workers was just one problem; getting them to open their doors and talk were two more. It was not uncommon for Cohn to knock on their door with a big pizza in hand. If their interpreter happened to be a pretty female and the workers opened their doors to her, or a union organizer looking for new turf, as was the case in Brownsville, well, whatever works.

In Brownsville, a hot and dusty Texas town of about 100,000 along the Rio Grande, Englund knew he would need a special interpreter, one who would be more than just a translator.[13] Englund learned from years of using interpreters in Russia the importance of finding a person who can also serve as an intermediary, who can understand what you are trying to do and connect with the workers. "If I had spoken perfect Castilian Spanish and gone to these colonias on the out-skirts of Brownsville and started knocking on the doors of their mobile homes, no one would have talked to me." He started by contacting Texas environmental advocates, and one referred him to David Elizondo, a longshoreman who was also a union organizer. Elizondo was eager to help, partly because he wanted to develop some union interest at the scrapyards. "We went to door after door after door," Englund recalled. Many would say they didn't know anything, but Englund would go back to them later to try again. Many of the workers either knew Elizondo or had heard of him. "He would vouch for me, and the workers seemed comfortable talking to him."

In Baltimore, the interpreter again proved to be the key to access. They first used another reporter, an American who knew Spanish. "They just were not opening up at all," Englund said. "They were slamming doors in our faces." So the reporters found a young Mexican law student at a Hispanic rights advocacy group in Baltimore who agreed to help. She was attractive, a fact that probably ended the door slamming, the reporters said. But if her appearance opened doors, her skill kept them open. She quickly established a rapport. "She was a Mexican from San Antonio, and she sort of spoke their lingo," Englund said. "They felt comfortable with her, unlike with the Anglo who spoke Spanish as a second language. She let these guys know, 'Look, you are not as isolated as you think you are out here.'" To those wanting anonymity, she could comfortably argue for Englund and Cohn, saying, "they think men don't have to be treated like you are, but they are not going to use your story unless you tell them who you are," Englund said. She assured them that they were not going to be alone, that other workers were talking to the reporters. These workers were the type of people her organization was trying to reach and serve. So, while trying to help Englund and Cohn, she was telling them about her organization, that she was there to help them. She gave them her card, told them about a good place to buy groceries and where they could find a church that held services in Spanish. All of that, Englund said, was extremely important in gaining their trust.

Interviews Mount, Case Builds

Cohn thought the key to access in many of his interviews was to be open, willing to listen and sincere about trying to understand the workers' situations. Cohn said he did not use a tape recorder in his interviews; he feared it might intimidate the workers. "I think they talked to us, because they had seen problems and no one else would ever talk to them about the problems." In Texas, the government inspector from the Navy rarely showed up. "He didn't speak Spanish, and he was afraid to go on the ship."

A few did not want their names used. Nevertheless, even those who wanted to remain anonymous were useful, because they provided new names and their accounts of what happens in the yard helped the reporters evaluate the validity of what others were telling them on the record. "The more people we had telling us the same thing, the more we could have confidence in what was in our notes and the more we could write with authority," Cohn said. "By the time we finished, we had talked to hundreds of workers."

After hearing from those workers and shipbreakers, it was clear their story was panning out. Moreover, Cohn sensed that it was coming together differently from any other project he had investigated. "There was something unique about this story," he said. Cohn usually expects a more amorphous situation to emerge in the reporting, some ups and some downs. "You expect to find clear problems in three places, 'sort-of-problems' in three others and everything being fine in three others. But in this case, every place we went, we found serious problems."

Cohn and Englund recognized multiple confirmations were crucial to the credibility of the story. The words of the workers, even when they provided firsthand accounts, are often insufficient in an investigative project that has to get beyond he-said/she-said reporting. Cohn referred to their confirmation efforts as a "triangulation," which involves the interview, public records and independent interviews in which they hear the same account recited.

The case of Raul Mendoza provided an example of the power and functionality of well-researched and documented anecdotal evidence. On $200 weekly from the Brownsville scrapyard, Mendoza supported a wife and three children and sent money to his parents in Matamoras, Mexico. Just before Christmas, he climbed into the pitch-black hold of a Navy ship and fell 30 feet. For more than three hours, he pleaded for help before rescuers reached him. He died on Christmas Eve. The reporters gathered incredibly graphic details, but they didn't come from a single interview or source. They came from several workers. They found details in a court file among interrogatories and depositions, and they interviewed people who had given depositions as well.[14]

In Wilmington, the reporters used the same tactic to learn about Lorenzo Lopez. They described him as a "soft-spoken 28-year-old who doesn't speak English" and was here to send money home to Guanajuato, Mexico. He survived an accident and told the reporters about it. Combining his account with details from the OSHA inspector's handwritten and typed notes, they wrote an anecdote that took the reader on board the ship and beyond to make key points about training and the government's role:

> The yards waste little time on training. Lorenzo Lopez, an illegal immigrant hired in Wilmington, said: "They didn't explain anything. They told me to look at what the others were doing."
>
> On Oct. 14, 1995, Lopez and another worker were told to cut steel pipes in the engine room of a destroyer, the *USS Dewey*. A flame from one of their torches ignited vapors that had accumulated overnight in a condenser.
>
> The explosion was felt three miles away. Lopez was knocked down. He was temporarily blinded, broke his leg, and burned so badly he spent six weeks in a hospital burn center. His eyesight was permanently damaged and he was disfigured. . . . Now, unable to work, he has few prospects.
>
> The Occupational Safety and Health Administration cited the yard for safety violations. The company failed to have an experienced employee check that no gases were present before any cutting began. Lopez was the second serious accident at the North Carolina yard in less than a year. . . . Like most efforts to enforce safety and environmental laws in the shipbreaking industry, the OSHA actions were taken only after the harm was done.[15]

Although one American shipbreaker said his scrapyard was not an ice cream factory, laborers in India's scrapyards would gladly trade places.

Working and Dying or Starving and Dying

The *Sun* sent Englund, Cohn and photographer Perry Thorsvik to see why. "From the get-go, there was India," said Rebecca Corbett, the line editor on the shipbreakers investigation. In the beginning, however, she was not sure of its link to the United States. Englund's memo had shown the shipbreakers were part of an international industry, and she had seen a documentary about Alang and the shipbreaking conditions there.

Retired merchant and warships from all over the world made their final voyages to huge scrapyards in Pakistan, Bangladesh and a beach on the Arabian Sea in Alang. There, unusual tides and currents cooperated to let the shipbreakers simply run these huge hulks high onto the shore, with no piers or dry docks needed. With close to 200 plots, loose government regulations and desperate men eager to work for $1.50 a day without fussing about dangers, Alang had become the shipbreaking mecca. Still, to make a story about Alang, India, effective for readers in America, they needed a strong link. "There was a huge so-what factor in that it was happening so far away," Corbett said. "That lots of egregious things happen in faraway places doesn't make it a story necessarily."

The reporters, however, soon found the answer to the so-what question: The U.S. EPA had recently decided to exempt the Navy and the U.S. Maritime Administration from rules that prohibited them from exporting hazardous materials. The warships and commercial vessels were filled with asbestos, PCBs, lead and other toxic materials. Caught between conflicting federal demands that they profit from the sale of mothballed ships but adhere to all environmental and worker laws, the Navy and maritime authorities saw India, Pakistan and Bangladesh as the perfect answer. With low wage scales and governments that turned blind eyes to environmental and safety problems, shipbreakers in those distant lands were happy to take this country's ships with their high-grade steel and pay handsomely for them. Cohn said the break started with a secondhand tip originating from someone inside the EPA. Nevertheless, the Navy and the EPA confirmed the tip.[16]

Before Cohn, Englund and Thorsvik could pack, they did advance work. Cohn traveled to London to meet with brokers and shipbreaking businessmen. "The shipbreaking business may have been in Alang, India, Cohn said, but the money part of the business and the brokers were in London. "My approach was straightforward: 'We are doing a comprehensive story on the shipbreaking industry, that we wanted to identify American ships and look at the environmental and labor situation,'" Cohn said. He found a businessman who had agreed to help identify the specific locations of American ships in Alang. He wrote or called contacts to urge them to cooperate with the reporters. To get preliminary information, the paper hired Sharmila Chandra, an Indian journalist from New Dehli, who had been referred to them by one of Cohn's former colleagues at *The Philadelphia Inquirer*. They asked her to go to the scrapyard in Alang to see what was possible. "She wrote us a report that was like something out of Charles Dickens and described all the ships, the living conditions and the accidents and injuries," Cohn said. Much later, they learned that the EPA had never been where they were about to go.

Journey to Hell

Their journey into shipbreaking hell started with a cup of tea.

"We would walk up and down that awful beach in Alang, and knock on the door of a scrapyard," Englund recalled. "We were ushered in. They would invite us on to the porch or the headquarters . . . then they would bring tea around," Englund said. "The breaking would be going on in front of us." They let the reporters run virtually free to talk to the workers and observe life on that distant beach. Here is some of what they saw:

> The workday begins, no different from the day before or the day after. A cutter takes a torch to an engine room pipe and residual oil inside bursts into flame. Nearby, smoke rolls from a smothered fire, mixing with acrid fumes of burning steel and paint. A little farther off, a ship's deckhouse is pushed off its perch and plunges 70 feet to the hold below, with a crash that sends a huge dust cloud swirling.
>
> Pairs of workers carry oxygen canisters on their shoulders, cushioning the load with their all-purpose safas, traditional Indian scarves. Gangs of a dozen or more men, plastic sandals on their feet, chant in unison and hoist heavy plates of steel on to their shoulder. Others heft cutting supplies alongside the beached ships, wading through muddy sand saturated with oil, dust, sludge and human excrement.
>
> The scrapyard owners look on from their porches, sipping sweet milky tea. Walking to and fro from the yards, the men of Alang seem listless, worn out, beaten down. But they are diligent workers. At Plot 66, two men, facing each other, pull on the ends of a large hacksaw, like lumberjacks, cutting the copper pipes of a boiler. They've been at it since 3 p.m. the day before. They expect to finish toward sundown the next day. Back and forth, in a patient trance, with an unvarying stroke, they pull the saw. "It's how we earn our bread," says Ram Sanwrey, 38.[17]

Day in and day out, for almost two weeks, the three journalists and Sharmila Chandra, their Indian interpreter, arose early in the morning to watch the workers emerge from the cardboard boxes or scrap-wood shelters that served as their homes. The reporters stayed all day, wandering up and down that five-mile stretch, talking and observing, watching the men work in the grime, listening to deafening noise, feeling the heat, smelling the stench, and, on one day, recording a simple Hindu funeral procession to a pyre fueled with lumber from one of the scrapped ships, a scene that would later become the conclusion to their final story. Cohn and Englund talked to the workers about the conditions of their lives and work, the accidents, how they felt about things, the dangers and the money they were making. One worker dies everyday, they were told, but they could not find anyone who kept track of the dead. "We talked to one worker after another," Cohn recalled. Although uneducated and very poor, Cohn found them to be, in their own way, extremely articulate. "There is a shadow of death on this place," one worker told them. "This place is haunted by death. But it is better to work and die than to starve and die."[18]

The access they received to find such quotes and gather so much storytelling detail amazed the reporters; they are not sure why they got it; perhaps the shipbreakers just figured an American newspaper couldn't do them any harm, Englund speculated. Cohn's London contact had opened some doors to some owners. And, to the workers, the three American journalists were a novelty. "They had never seen Americans before," Cohn said. "When we talked to one worker, 20 more would gather around; they all wanted to be interviewed."

And then, there was Sharmila Chandra—their interpreter, guide, fixer and journalism colleague. She is a tall, patrician, Brahmin. Englund said she spoke fluent Hindi, the language of the lower caste workers, who held her high in respect. She also charmed the two reporters with her street knowledge, the work she did for them in preparing the scouting report weeks earlier and her engaging sense of humor. Her husband was a news magazine editor, and Chandra liked to joke how she married beneath her caste.

She knew the customs and the bureaucracy, and she didn't mind being pushy when it was called for. Cohn and Englund recalled one meeting with some local officials responsible for overseeing the industry, when she forcefully shamed them into being cooperative. The reporters, adopting the role of polite foreign guests and sticking to their "good cop, better cop" interviewing style, were running into resistance when they asked for some documents about an accident at a shipyard, Cohn recalled. "I remember her standing up and slamming the table with her hand and saying: 'I can't believe you are not helping them; you are embarrassing our entire nation in front of our guests,'" Cohn recalled. Then she pointed at Will and me said, 'Let's go.' One of the officials stopped and pleaded, 'Please don't go, stay and have a Coke. . . .' Two minutes later, the Cokes came out and so did the documents."[19]

Before Alang, the reporters felt they were getting a very good story; afterward, they sensed it was over the top. "We felt this could be something really special," Cohn said. Alang, he felt, gave it a signature that would separate it from the usual exploited worker and greedy businessman story. "We were really excited when we were over there and when we were coming back."

Editing Gets Messy, Trying

"This story reads well—for an encyclopedia on shipbreaking"—was the reaction Cohn heard from Rebecca Corbett on one draft after they returned from India. Cohn recalls the comment with amusement, not even sure whether she meant it as a criticism. But he knew for sure it was just the beginning of what he expected—a memorable editing ordeal. The paper's top editor, John Carroll, was excited about the project, and Cohn, having worked for Carroll at two other newspapers, knew what that meant: He would take a two-fisted role in the editing process. In fact, Cohn had just weathered a Carroll edit in "Battalion 316." He knew what was about to happen and he knew what the outcome would be. "He told us the material in this story was very powerful, and he wanted to make sure we presented it in the best possible way," Cohn said.

It was powerful because Englund and Cohn had immersed themselves in the details, in the world of the scrapyard workers and in the personalities of the characters in the story. The shipbreakers and the workers had fascinated them; the quotes and facts had required exhausting and sometimes frustrating work. Their material was not just powerful, but plentiful, which meant they and their editors would have to make some tough, subjective choices.

That story had to convey several essential themes. The key ones included:

- Hell on earth exists in the shipbreaking scrapyard.
- The Navy and the Maritime Administration were retiring hundreds of warships and merchant vessels loaded with dirty and dangerous materials such as asbestos, PCBs, oil and fuel.

- They were selling the ships to shady contractors in the budding shipbreaking industry for as much money as they could make.
- The shipbreakers were exploiting the legal vulnerabilities of immigrants and violating safety and environmental regulations trying to turn a profit from the scrap metal.
- The work was killing and maiming scrapyard workers throughout the United States and fouling the harbors and beaches with the ships' hazardous wastes.
- The government was running into so many problems with domestic shipbreakers that regulators had officially decided to let the Navy and Maritime Administration ship their discarded vessels to overseas scrapyards. There, they could make more money, because businesses can exploit workers and pollute the environment with almost total freedom to disregard environmental or worker safety concerns.

In addition to those issues, the reporters saw several other subthemes: asbestosis killing the workers who built ships decades ago and now killing the workers who were ripping them apart; businesses firing workers to cover up violations of government regulations; the failure of the Navy and the Maritime Administration to oversee the scrapyards; and the failure of government regulators to enforce workplace safety and environmental laws.

Englund, drawing on his writing experiences as a foreign correspondent in Moscow, summed up the writing task succinctly. "You can't do an inverted pyramid on Russian politics," he said, referring to the organization of story material in descending order of importance. "We were doing more than relaying facts," he said. "We were trying to tell a story. You construct a picture with the way you put a story together." In telling that story, the writing has to show readers why they should care about your material.

When reporters impose a big project on their readers, they are asking for more than a few minutes of time; they are asking for a commitment. In shipbreakers, the reporters were looking for a three-day commitment. The first day would focus on the death and injuries that came with ship scrapping while introducing the readers to the main issues that the project would explore. The second would be the shipbreakers and the record of their workplaces' shameful histories, and the third day would take the reader to the scrapyard beaches of the Arabian Sea at Alang, India. The initial drafts on all of them underwent major cuts, each about twice as long as the versions that were published.[20]

At one point, they spent three days drafting a fourth story focusing on the *USS Coral Sea* in Baltimore Harbor. It was going to be a business investigative piece on the wreck and how its scrapping project went so awry. Cohn and Englund mined every note and record they could find and tediously constructed a detailed chronology of the *Coral Sea* scrapping. But in the end, neither Corbett nor Carroll liked it, and Cohn and Englund said they didn't put up any objections to spiking it.

A big project's day-one story is, in some ways, like a first date. It must intrigue, yet show substance and hint that there's plenty more to come, and you will get it all if you let me take you out again for a second date and a third date. So day one has to do lot of work in a graceful way. It has to be sweeping yet specific; thematic but compelling. It has to educate, yet it cannot lecture or preach; it must, as Englund said, tell a story.

For the shipbreakers story, Englund and Cohn wrote the draft and joined Corbett at a computer. As the frontline editor, Corbett's editing had to be detailed, and it was. "She was going over every word," Englund said. She questioned everything from the power of a particular adverb to whether the reporter meant asbestosis or mesothelioma. "There is always a danger with that really close editing that you will lose all the energy and spark in your prose, and it was something I was very concerned about. To effectively convey the conditions at the scrapyards, he wanted the stories to carry a strong sense of place. "You don't want to lose the sense of what Brownsville was like, of what Alang was like, and I was on the guard against that." In the end, he was pleased with Corbett's work. "She was good," he said.

The first edit would be just the beginning of what is an unpredictable editing process. After the first edit, a draft can skate through the next phase, but run into a gauntlet at the next, stall indefinitely at the final and fall into the dreaded "black hole," never to be seen again. When "The Shipbreakers" got to Carroll, he wanted to experiment with various approaches to day one, some that Corbett said "would have required a real left turn with the material we had." They rewrote the opening dozens of times, reworking and fine-tuning the top paragraphs and the bullets.[21]

Some of their strongest material covered workplace deaths and accidents. But they discussed whether opening with an anecdote about a death in the scrapyard would be effective because people are not surprised that accidents and deaths occur in the workplace. At one point, Carroll wanted to try a lead about asbestosis killing workers who built ships decades ago and killing workers that were ripping them apart now. They toyed with leads on the "dignity of a ship," how ships are built and the history of *USS Coral Sea* and its missions. "Day after day, I would come in and write another top and John would say he didn't like it and then I would write another. One day I came in and he said, 'Will, why don't you try sitting down and write out 10 possible leads?' So I did. We tried all sorts of different ways to get at it."

Most reporters readily acknowledge how much they value the editing process, but, in their heart of hearts, they will probably concede it is not fun. It is messy. It is unpredictable. It is ego battering. It is frustrating. Sometimes sparks fly.

Corbett remembers a period when Cohn and Englund "were in despair" trying to find a passable lead. One day, after weeks of experimenting with different drafts, Carroll said, "I don't know why this is so hard," Corbett recalled. "I just wanted to leap across the desk at him and say it is so hard because you keep wanting something that won't work." But she didn't. At times, the frustration pushed Englund to the brink as well. Once he let loose, and Corbett bore the brunt. "I wasn't quite brave enough to go in and yell at John," he said, laughing. "It wasn't a planned outburst. I just suddenly got so frustrated, I was shouting at her." Repercussions? None. "The next day, John was again saying, 'why don't you try it this way, Will?'" And so it went.

Carroll recognizes he is demanding. Working on such a project "is a very human thing," he says. "It is unavoidably an emotionally trying process.

I frequently tell them how much I like the story and wouldn't be subjecting them to such grief if it wasn't a great story, that if it wasn't a great story they wouldn't be hearing from me."

By the time a major project crosses Carroll's desk, it has lurched through many drafts, several edits and often, several lower level editors.

Carroll describes an editing routine that seems part methodical, yet airy enough to allow his journalistic instincts some sway, and his first step is to get out of the office. "I usually sit down at home where there will not be any interruptions," he said. "On the first read, I don't make any notes, and then I read it again."

Sometimes he takes a yellow legal pad and writes a one-phrase summary of every passage, such as "shipbreaker hurt." But his routine varies. "Sometimes I don't do it quite that assiduously. I may just put a check mark by anything that really hits me, that is a riveting piece of information, that we may want to bring up [to higher position in the story] and play that up."

At that point, he starts thinking either about the structure of the story or about "what's not there, whether something jumps out at me that is not there. If it feels complete, I start thinking about structure. After the people who write them and do the first editing, a fresh pair of eyes can see structural things that make it a better story."

The structural changes range from major such as making the last part the first part or reducing the project from five parts to four parts to reducing or expanding individual passages or adding a few quotes on a subject. "In essence, I try to get the overall structure of the piece figured out. Then I start tightening and rewriting leads. I try to get an opening passage, like the first 20 inches, to do a lot of things for you: grab your attention, give you sweep and human interest."

To Englund, the outcome made that trying period worthwhile. "Once we had the opening, it was like how else could it have ever been," he said. Here is how it went:

> Raul Mendoza knew that scrapping ships was dangerous, knew about smoke and the fumes and the accidents. He'd worked in Baltimore, where asbestos clouded the air, and North Carolina, where oil spilled into a river, and California, where workers were told to lie to government inspectors.
>
> But he needed a job. So, on Dec. 22, 1995, in Brownsville, Texas, he climbed into the hold of the *USS Yukon*, an old Navy tanker. Working in total darkness without safety equipment, he walked across a girder. Then came the scream.
>
> Mendoza had fallen 30 feet into a tank, straddling a cross beam in a blow that split his pelvis. He flipped off the beam and landed on his chest. He was pleading for help. Untrained in shipboard emergencies, rescuers took three hours to extract him. By Christmas Eve, he was dead.
>
> Raul Mendoza is just one of the casualties of a little-known industry called shipbreaking. Spurred by the Navy's sell-off of obsolete warships at the end of the Cold War, the business has grown up overnight in some of America's most economically depressed ports. And almost everywhere the industry has arrived, harm to human health and the environment has followed.[22]

Starting with the first suspenseful eight words, this painful, gut-wrenching and terrifying opening does everything it needs to do to get a three-day commitment from the readers. The outrage factor is high. The writing was superb. And the story captures major project themes: the problem was nationwide; the military had a responsibility; the regulators were not doing their job; and business and government were exploiting the vulnerable, allowing deathly dangerous working conditions and polluting the environment. The players, the problems, the victims and a hint of what needs to be done (i.e., make them wear safety harnesses and helmets with lights, trained rescuers) are packed into those few paragraphs.

Four, hard-hitting, efficient bullets, each from a different part of the country, came next: one summarized the multitude of health and safety dangers surrounding the workers; a second revealed that shipbreakers often make workers cover up violations of pollution laws; another told of workers killed and hurt in explosions, accidents and falls; and the fourth described the pollution of harbors, rivers and shores.

For a dozen more paragraphs, a fast-paced opening generally characterized the industry, the shipbreakers' mode of operation and the corruption. It summarized the system and its problems and the government's culpability and foreshadowed the trip to Alang, India. Then, just when the readers may start feeling overwhelmed, the story slows a bit, taking them on a little excursion, back to where Raul Mendoza worked, to let them get a feel for the locale and to meet one of the workers:

> The Texas border town of Brownsville, convenient to Mexican steel mills and Mexican labor, is the nation's ship breaking center. On the Rio Grande, Brownsville is a transit point for drugs and laundered cash as well as men and steel. Young men coming out of the Mexican countryside, desperate for any kind of job, settle in the "colonias" in the dry flatlands by the port. Over the past quarter-century, more than a dozen scrapyards have come and gone.
>
> Santiago Martinez, now 64, remembers the first day he showed up at a scrapping company called Transforma. The boss handed him a hard hat and some shoes (the cost of which was deducted from his pay) and told him to get to work.
>
> The boss, Martinez said, explained the job this way: "He told me, 'Give me a piece of the ship. Cut it.'"[23]

The day two story was easier to construct, but it also underwent major changes. It started primarily as a feature on one of the shipbreakers, Richard Jaross, but expanded into a story on several of the shipbreakers.[24] Cohn said he found the shipbreakers particularly intriguing, because they did not fit his preconceived notion about them. "Going in, I thought the owners of the shipbreaking companies would be rich guys in mansions, when in fact the opposite was true," he said. "They were small-time businessmen, and, in many cases barely eking out a living." Englund agreed, and said the shipbreakers were very accessible, particularly Jaross. "There was something winning about him," he said. Englund said he wrote an initial draft in a more "featury" way than the final version. But ultimately, he recognized that people had died working for them. "Terrible damage had been done," he said. "The Navy had been left holding the bag [reclaiming the old ships] time after time with these guys, and it was irresponsible what they were doing. So that's why we hardened it up," he said, noting the change was Carroll's call.

As for the Alang story, the editing was smoother. "The editing was not quite as annoying on day three, since the piece was more tightly focused on one element," Englund said. "That's not to say that they simply set it in type and put it in the paper; . . . but it came through the editing process with some of the spark still in it. Of course, it's easier to write vividly about an exotic place than it is about an ordinary place." Among the three parts to the project, it was the most graphic and disturbing of all, painting a picture where human beings seemed to be little more than burned-out welding torches, easily replaced when they could no longer cut steel. Its relevance to the United States was overwhelmingly apparent. Alang was, as the lead sentence said, "where the world dumps its ships, worn out and ready to be torn apart" and where the United States was prepared to dump its problems and score bigger profits at the same time.

When the editing and writing finally ended, the reporters read the final product and felt Carroll had brought the piece to its best form. "I've got to give him credit," Englund said of Carroll. "I have no regrets in the way it turned out."

Postscript

It turned out successfully for *The Baltimore Sun* and for the people involved in "The Shipbreakers." For Englund and Cohn, it won the Pulitzer Prize for investigative reporting in April 1998. Cohn remained at the paper for several years, and then again followed Carroll to his next paper, this time the *Los Angeles Times*. Carroll left Los Angeles in 2005 to teach and write as the Knight Visiting Lecturer for the Joan Shorenstein Center on the Press, Politics and Public Policy at the John F. Kennedy School of Government at Harvard University. Cohn resigned in 2007 from the *Times* to join Bloomberg News and to teach investigative reporting at the University of Southern California's Annenberg School of Journalism. Englund did another stint in Moscow, before returning again to Baltimore where he is an editorial writer. Corbett joined the *New York Times* in 2004. Two years later, she was promoted to deputy chief of the Washington bureau, where she supervises 38 correspondents. She supervised the reporting that exposed the National Security Agency's wiretapping practices and won the 2006 Pulitzer Prize for national reporting.

The *Sun*'s work also prompted some immediate and long-term changes in the shipbreaking industry. Within the month of publication, the U.S. Senate and House called for hearings on the problems the *Sun* revealed, and the Navy suspended plans to send its old ships overseas.[25] A month later, the Maritime Administration followed the Navy's example.[26] Moreover, rather than petering out as so many outrage reactions do as soon as the spotlight turns elsewhere, this initial spate of activity led to promising reforms and signs of fundamental change in policymaking and in attitudes toward shipbreaking.

The hearings and the legislative actions that those sessions produced eventually prompted the administration of President Bill Clinton to declare a moratorium on sending ships overseas. Congress launched a pilot ship-scrapping program designed to find new and better ways to break up vessels without killing and maiming workers and polluting rivers and harbors.[27] An inspector general's audit revealed what the shipbreakers and their laborers had learned the hard way: Business cannot profit from scrapping ships if they adhere to laws that are supposed to protect the lives and health of their laborers and stop the fouling of the country's waterways and harbors.[28] Overall, the government view of its responsibility for the mothballed ships started changing. Instead of seeing them as opportunities to make money by selling them to the highest profit-seeking bidder, government officials more and more are seeing that government has a basic responsibility for cleaning up its mess, just as it does when it closes military bases.[29] As a result, Congress started appropriating money to pay for scrapping the ships. Although a growing backlog of rusting vessels in the James River and elsewhere indicated that the money is woefully short,[30] the existence of subsidies at all represents a fundamental change in the way ship scrapping is now done.

In the summer of 2006—nine years after the series was published— Englund, who had become an editorial writer, offered a measure of the series' long-term impact. He says deaths and accidents in Alang, India, have dropped significantly because of reforms that came after the series, and the ship scrapping system in the United States clearly underwent some fundamental changes. But he fears that the old bureaucracy in the Navy and Maritime Administration still wants to retreat to the way ships were scrapped before, and some of the old shipbreakers are still in business. He says the Navy does not seem to care about its old ships, which at last count numbered about 100, because it budgets very little money for discarding them. The Maritime Administration was still trying to secure exemptions from federal environmental laws so that it could start sending its old commercial vessels overseas again. Meanwhile, its ships continued piling up in the James River and elsewhere, and Englund wonders what will happen if a hurricane slams through, cracking the ships open, spilling their fuel and ruining the James and Rappahannock Rivers.

In passing, Englund mentioned that the Maritime Administration was still doing business with Richard Jaross down in Brownsville. The year before, one of Jaross' laborers, Jesus Flores, who came north from Mexico to earn a living, died in an accident. Englund called Jaross to talk to him about it. He wrote an editorial and included an excerpt expressing his doubts about whether things had really changed:

> Mr. Flores' boss, Richard Jaross, says he should have known not to cut steel in a way that would place him in danger. Yet this accident stands out as both warning and rebuke to a government agency that should know better.
>
> Mr. Jaross has been in the shipbreaking business for three decades, and his history of accidents and environmental violations is dismal. He helped arrange the ill-starred scrapping of the USS Coral Sea in Baltimore in the 1990s—a project marked by fires, falls and cavalier disposal of asbestos that landed the local partner in federal prison. Mr. Jaross went on to set up a scrapping operation in Wilmington, N.C., that was described by a state official as looking like one of Dante's inner circles of hell, and that, after a fatal explosion, left the U.S. government back in possession of a dozen half-scrapped destroyers that it thought it had gotten rid of. . . .
>
> Before too much more history repeats itself, the government should get serious about how to do this job right.[31]

Lessons

INVESTIGATIVE PROJECT IDEAS

Lesson Learned: Beat the bushes and story ideas will fall out.

How It Applied: In typical beat reporter fashion, Will Englund was cruising the harbor looking for one story, but keeping his eyes and ears open for ways to develop his new waterfront beat. He did not explain it in those terms. Instead, he said: "I had to have copy; I had to come up with something." So he was beating the bushes, or "fishing for stories," which might be the more apt cliché here. The story he eventually reeled in provides a dramatic example of why the pressure on a beat reporter to "come up with something" is such a healthy exercise and evidence that the best and freshest investigative project ideas come off the beat.

Lesson Learned: Simple, fleeting thoughts about seemingly local story ideas on news beats can develop into major projects with enormous global implications. Journalism history is filled with examples of how beat reporting produces some of the most successful investigative projects, and reporters and editors who learn to analyze ideas from a broader perspective will see ways to develop ideas that others miss.

How It Applied: *The Baltimore Sun*'s newly established waterfront beat was the source of "The Shipbreakers," and reporter Will Englund discovered it while literally cruising his beat. Although he did not recognize it as an investigative project to the extent that it became one, it developed in a way that any reporter on any beat could easily experience. It started a flicker of an idea and grew from there thanks to a tip and another story or two.

With the hindsight wisdom that his and Gary Cohn's subsequent reporting gives us, we can now go back to his initial "feature" idea and imagine many "why-didn't-I-think-of-that" questions way back then. For example, that huge warship floating in its decrepit conditions now prompts us to think beyond the local feature and ask the broader story-idea question: What is happening to all of the other mothballed warships now that the Cold War is over? Because the Navy and Merchant Marine will have to mothball aging ships, how is the government ensuring that the process is done safely for workers and the environment? But for Carroll's intercession to pose such questions, the story of the shipbreaking industry may not have ever reached beyond Baltimore and its harbor. By looking globally at a local story, the saga reverberated powerfully.

Lesson Learned: Good reporters make their own luck.

How It Applied: Veteran reporters learn quickly that stories beget stories. After Englund wrote the feature on the *USS Coral Sea*, an anonymous caller suggested he should look into the environmental dangers of PCBs. Although some may say Englund was "just lucky" to get that tip, he made his own luck. In this case, he got the anonymous tip because his curiosity prompted a question about the aircraft carrier; and, he did not let his immediate preoccupation (the shipwreck story) bury the idea. When the tip came in, he followed it up. Tips, more often than not, lead to dead ends rather than to good stories. Reporters, preoccupied with that day's deadline or the weekend enterprise story that's coming due, often ignore such tips or put them off. But good reporters find a way to check everything out. The more tips, ideas and checks a reporter makes, the greater the chances he or she will find the big story. Englund wasn't lucky; he was a good reporter. He checked the tip out and landed a lead story for a Sunday front page. Not only that, his story caught the eye of the editor, whose broader perspective saw a story that went on to win the Pulitzer Prize.

Lesson Learned: A highly successful investigative project can be a follow-up story.

How It Applied: "The Shipbreakers" was a follow-up. Moreover, it followed up not to a spot-news, daily story, but a 2,500-word, very prominently displayed article that a talented veteran had already researched for more than a month. That original story—in the words of Englund, its author—"went nowhere," whereas the follow-up won awards and changed the industry here and abroad. There were many differences between the two stories, but one of the major differences is this: "The Shipbreakers" latched on to the original story's 15th paragraph, which graphically summarized the working conditions in the scrapyards, and forced the readers to feel those conditions and to meet the men who worked under them. In essence, the follow-up masterfully implemented the age-old journalistic saw, "Show, don't just tell." Carroll, who ordered the follow-up and whose record at picking winning project ideas speaks volumes, also recognized that, despite the *Sun*'s prominent display of the original story, it was still a new story. the original article simply told the *Sun*'s readers that this small, strange corner of the world existed; the project took the readers inside that world and showed that its problems had national and international human and environmental consequences. It was a human story with immensely important policy implications.

PRELIMINARY INVESTIGATIONS

Lesson Learned: Before asking a news organization to invest the time and resources in a major project, provide editors with preliminary evidence that you have a reasonable expectation that the work will produce a story.

How It Applied: John Carroll read Will Englund's original page-one story in April 1996 and saw the potential for an in-depth project. Yet, he still ordered Englund to spend a couple of weeks conducting a preliminary investigation and to write a memo explaining how the paper could pursue the story.

A preliminary or exploratory investigation is like test driving a car that you are thinking about buying; it should give you a feel for the story and a sense of whether the proposal will survive some of the most obvious challenges. The memo should clearly explain the primary idea and suggest secondary ideas and why they are important, interesting and new. It also should provide some evidence from interviews and records to show that the idea is more than some brainstorm that sounds good in your head, that it has substance. Finally, the memo should—in Carroll's words—show that the story is "gettable," that you will be able to find documents, records, statistics and a range of sources. Whether the news organization is big or small, editors will not devote a lot of time and money on a fishing expedition without a reasonable expectation that it will catch something.

Partnerships

Lesson Learned: Reporters thrown into a partnership on a project often have never worked together before, or they are strangers to each other. Yet, for months they will be practically joined at the hip and go through some trying times together. Because of the uncertainty about how the relationship will develop and affect the project, reporters have to be prepared to make the partnership work regardless of the quality of the relationship. When a reporter is assigned to work with someone with whom he or she is having problems, a nose-to-the-grindstone focus characterized by hard work, commitment to the story and being open and honest with the partner will make other problems seem moot.

How It Applied: Gary Cohn and Will Englund were almost complete strangers to one another when Carroll threw them together for about 18 months to work on a story. That is a common occurrence, especially at large newspapers. Nevertheless, partnerships more often than not produce the best projects.

On the surface, it would seem that Englund and Cohn were lucky to find themselves to be effectively compatible, especially given Englund's initial apprehensions about Cohn. He feared this "Philadelphia reporter would come in and take over the project." But like a reporter who must identify his or her preconceived notions about a story at the beginning and try to put them aside, Englund suspended his worries about Cohn and discovered him to be "an extremely sweet guy" in addition to being the resourceful and energetic reporter one would expect from someone with Cohn's previous accomplishments.

Despite his initial fears, Englund, as did most reporters who knew Cohn's background, respected his work. And Cohn, although he did not know Englund, knew his work and admired what he had been doing, particularly his writing and breadth of knowledge. From that starting point, it was only a matter of time before Englund learned his partner did not fit his preconceived notion. The hallmark of their partnership seems to be that neither had any desire "to take over the project," that they had the same vision of the project and each was driven by their common mission: to understand the shipbreaking story as thoroughly and as accurately as they could and produce the best possible project. Although they worked separately for considerable amounts of time, each always knew what the other was doing and discovering. They accomplished this through the "shared basket" and by talking to each other almost every day.

Not all partnerships work as well as Cohn's and Englund's. Most longtime investigative reporters probably have had at least one "partner from hell." Even in those situations, the single commonality—the story—forces reporters to put aside their differences. Young journalists working in such a partnership for the first time can make it work if they let the requirements of the story rather than their egos guide the way they deal with a difficult partner, even when efforts to talk through the differences fail.

Editor–Reporter Relationships

Lesson Learned: Investigative reporters get so deeply involved in a project and become so knowledgeable about the topic, that the line editor plays a crucial role in seeing the general direction of the reporting and ensuring that reporters do not become lax in viewing the evidence as objectively as they can.

How It Applied: Englund and Cohn and their line editor Rebecca Corbett described a working relationship that appeared to work well. Although Corbett did not get down into the reporting trenches like Zusman did in "30-Year Secret," the reporters recognized and apparently respected Corbett's "meticulous" management style and desire to know as much as they did about the work. In that respect, her style resembled *The Orlando Sentinel*'s Mike Ludden in "Tainted Cash or Easy Money?" She tended to ask "zillions" of questions and read their interview notes, she said. As I did with Ludden, Englund and Cohn particularly valued Corbett's "devil's advocate" way of testing their reporting. "If you can't convince your editor, you won't convince the readers," Cohn said.

ALL REPORTERS ARE INVESTIGATIVE REPORTERS

Lesson Learned: Although few journalists carry the title of investigative reporter, the investigative mentality should govern every reporter on every beat and assignment.

How It Applied: Although Will Englund won the Pulitzer for investigative reporting, he never thought of himself as a titled investigative reporter before or after "The Shipbreakers." Yet, in a seeming contradiction, he thinks "every reporter should be investigative." His partner, Gary Cohn, does consider himself an investigative journalist, and he has been working in that area throughout his career. Yet, in talking about his partner in "The Shipbreakers," he described Englund as "a terrific investigative reporter." So what's the difference?

Their answers go deeper than the general description we heard from Mark Zusman of the *Willamette Week* in Chapter 2, although Zusman, who described it as "connecting the dots" and "probing beneath the surface," probably would not disagree with their thoughts.

Here's Cohn's attempt to answer: "I guess maybe the difference is that you take longer and do everything possible to get the information; you don't just quote what somebody says; you become the expert; you analyze the information and you don't just do a he-said/she-said." He believes beat reporters are positioned perfectly to do investigative reporting, because they already have the sources established, know how the system works inside and out and have developed an expertise in their specialty. In investigative reporting, all of those tasks are part of the investigation.

Rebecca Corbett, the line editor for Cohn and Englund, offers a similar description. She describes it as "endeavors that require some significant amount of digging." It usually is targeted at "complicated, deeply held pieces of information and uses every tool necessary to get it." Corbett has dealt with both types of reporters for a long time, and her most insightful comment reflects on her experience with both. "Investigative reporters are more likely [than daily reporters] to be those who want to change the world." Cohn exemplified that trait in the practical sense when he said: "You can't change the world all at once, but you can change it a piece at a time; I've never bought into the idea that nobody cares."

Nevertheless, all three journalists believe all reporters should be "investigative" when they cover any story. Providing nuts-and-bolts elaboration, Corbett said, "Every reporter, should be using documents, interviewing multiple sources, and they should not be settling for stenography."

Cohn acknowledged that beat reporters do not enjoy the luxury of time and sustained focus on a story that he does. Nevertheless, if they have the investigative mentality, they will follow up the next day and the next and as many as it takes to get to the bottom of an important issue.

Englund, however, offered the most telling comment, one suggesting that a good beat reporter is an investigative reporter: "I found it very easy to go from Moscow correspondent to 'The Shipbreakers.'" Moscow had been his beat. It, like most beats, required him to do a little bit of everything, including a bit of investigative reporting.

The three journalists' approaches, methods and thoughts about investigative reporting begin to define reporters driven by the investigative mentality. They are intrigued by the how and why questions; wish to learn and understand rather than merely record and report; thrive on the challenge of complexity; are motivated to do whatever is necessary to get the information; desire to figuratively "change the world;" and are committed to trying to objectively gather and evaluate the facts and how they affect the premise of the story.

OBJECTIVITY

Lesson Learned: For investigative reporters, objectivity is not a state of being, in which robotic, unbiased neutrality is achievable by anyone with blood flowing through their veins. Rather, it is a reporting approach and a way of trying to get to the bottom of things.

It requires a disciplined, self-questioning process that is particularly important to investigative reporters who also have to draw conclusions from the facts gleaned from volumes of information they gather.

How It Applied. Chapters 1 and 2 examined the role of objectivity as a mental discipline for guarding against the big-story bias. Here, the value of objectivity emerges as a methodology that eventually led reporters to a set of conclusions. In talking about "The Shipbreakers," Gary Cohn discussed how reporters must avoid framing a story before the reporting is done. He said, "I've always been taught—from Jack Anderson to today—that you let the reporting tell you what the story is; you don't try to fit everything in a box. Sometimes, stories change."

That said, investigative reporters still must start somewhere, then gather all pertinent facts. At the end of the process, the reporters must "have the confidence to report what's in their notebook," Cohn said. His point was that conclusions are not opinions that contradict the effort to view facts objectively; they are the product of your reporting. "At some point in the investigation we had these many cases and this many deaths and accidents and many other facts." Based on such facts, they could conclude with confidence and authority that "everywhere the industry has arrived, harm to human health and the environment has followed." Cohn said, "You become the expert and from the facts you have gathered you can then say these conditions are dangerous, and that is not an opinion."

To get to that point in "The Shipbreakers," Cohn, Englund and Corbett had to try to be objective in their reporting and editing, and they pursued that objective in various ways. Corbett says she worries as much about what is not in a story as what is in it, which is a succinct expression of her approach to evaluating story material. She talked about a series of questions that run through her mind, and they generally deal with context, credibility of sources and alternative explanations for conclusions drawn from the reporters' findings.

Such questions depict an investigative mentality and provide an excellent guide for any reporter or editor trying to guard against biases and preconceived notions that are the bane of efforts to be objective. Corbett said objectivity is a "sensibility" trait. "To the reporters I see, it's like an inherent trait." She said Cohn, for example, was very scrupulous about gathering and then discussing exculpable information.

Cohn and Englund both said one of Corbett's most valuable roles in the project was the way she played the devil's advocate. It was a role they also played against one another, questioning the degree of certainty over facts and conclusions, discussing whether a situation is as bad as they are depicting it to be and in other ways. "That's one reason it is helpful to have two reporters on a project," Cohn said.

Finding Records off the Beaten Path

Lesson Learned: Although observations and interviews imbue a complex investigative project with color, life and energy, public records provide tangible evidence that undergird a project with a sense of substance and authority. Developing a records mentality helps find records off the usual paper trail.

How It Applied: If ever there was a story that needed the life and color that interviews and observations provide, the arcane and complex world of the shipbreaking industry was one of them. Cohn and Englund knocked on hundreds of doors (many of which were slammed in their faces) and recorded some terrible scenes at worksites to provide that life and color. Because of their success on that front and the quality of the writing, the role of public records in "The Shipbreakers" is easy to overlook. Cohn provided a detailed explanation of their value in the project and pointed to several specific examples of powerful and colorful information that emerged from records. Records provide more than boring statistics and mind-numbing databases. As Cohn revealed in discussing them, human stories are often buried there and prove the truth to the cliché that the records are the footprint of human activity.

Records are not always easy to find and use. There are many easy-to-get standbys like court and property records, meeting minutes, 911 audiotapes, audits and various regulatory inspection reports at nursing homes and restaurants and the like. Moreover, Cohn finds the popular *Investigative Reporters Handbook* from Investigative Reporters and Editors (IRE) a virtual encyclopedia of public records as well as a compendium of investigative techniques. It is just one of many such publications that the IRE and other organizations put out.

But such books simply cannot cover every exigency reporters confront in a story. Cohn seems to have an instinctive records mentality, one that constantly reminds him to be alert for opportunities to use records. In interviews, a standard question is "what records should I be looking for," he said. Records reveal other records, as do state and federal laws, regulations and policies that are related to the topic of investigation. In writing laws providing for new programs, for example, legislators consistently include language requiring administrators of the new program to compile statistics and write reports. Cohn said reporters should get in the habit of trying to figure out what inspections and licensing requirements might apply to any business or professional services provided to the public.

Finding other reporters or researchers who are familiar with an agency involved in an investigation was a valuable tactic for Cohn. He identified records by talking to another reporter and to a university professor who had worked with records of OSHA. The lesson? University faculty lists and the IRE library of investigative stories provide sources who may have traveled your path and can save you time and show new paper trails. The *IRE Journal* also provides how-we-did-it articles in which reporters frequently explain records and databases they found.

USE OF ANECDOTAL EVIDENCE

Lesson Learned: Although the value of anecdotes is usually illustrative in journalism, they can, when properly used, provide substantive evidentiary value. A well-reported and effectively written anecdote often has more impact on readers than unassailable, comprehensive findings based on thorough data gathering and hard evidence. But reporters primarily use them to illustrate broad problems and issues. However, when used properly, they also can have evidentiary value.

How It Applies: Anecdotes gain evidentiary value only to the extent that reporters can offer evidence showing that the circumstances and consequences depicted in them accurately represent common conditions. In this project, the story does not provide any systematic compilation of death and injury statistics from the dozen or more scrapyards that break up Navy and merchant ships across the country.

The three parts of "The Shipbreakers," however, are filled with enough well-documented examples of misconduct, mishaps and dangerous situations and references to others to make a solid case that the problems are common-place enough to warrant serious attention. At the same time, they successfully use records to document government laxity and disinterest by the Navy, the Maritime Administration, OSHA and the EPA. They also documented a degree of official amorality, particularly in the willingness of the government to send its shiploads of toxic problems and dangers to the exploited laborers in Alang, India.

GOING TO THE TARGETS

Lesson Learned: In addition to being fair to the people (or targets) who are the subjects of an investigation, investigative reporters have an obligation to readers to satisfy their natural curiosity for a detailed explanation of how those subjects react to the most egregious findings in a project. In such instances, detailed explanations rather than broad, sweeping responses are needed.

How It Applies: That lesson was a noteworthy shortcoming in "The Shipbreakers." They had early and repeated access to some of the shipbreakers, especially to Jaross. At one point, Jaross "acknowledged there have been problems over the years," and the stories explained and probed the shipbreakers' complaints against the government.

But the stories never made them explain how and why they could allow such deadly and environmentally harmful rule-breaking on their sites. Readers undoubtedly would be curious to know, for example, what the salvage company owner had to say about Raul Mendoza's fatal walk across a thin girder in a pitch black ship's hold, in the company of a foreman, without a safety harness. The stories do not provide such answers or force the owners to explain in their own words why they repeatedly allow so many workplace hazards on their sites. The owners also needed to openly and specifically address the very serious generalized allegation that they cut corners to make a profit and killed and maimed people in the process. Or the story should have given some explanation for the void.

Notes

1. The interviewees listed here are the sources for their direct and indirect quotes; reconstruction of interviews between themselves and their sources; and depictions of their conversations, thoughts and actions that are not referenced in the text.

Gary Cohn, Los Angeles, CA, May 23, 2006; May 24 and June 15, 2006, by telephone; July 31, 2006, by telephone; September 13, 2006, and Aug. 19, 2007, e-mail.

Rebecca Corbett, *New York Times* Washington, DC bureau, June 13, 2006.

John Carroll, September 27, 2006, by telephone.

Will Englund, *Baltimore Sun* editorial offices, June 27, 2006; August 17, 2007, e-mail.

Some material from these sources is individually referenced where necessary to ensure clarity.

2. Kent Mountford, senior scientist, Chesapeake Bay Progam, Annapolis, MD, e-mail message, August 7, 2007.

3. *Dictionary of American Fighting Ships* and *United States Naval Aviation, 1910–1995*, both published by the Naval Historical Center of the Department of the Navy. archive@navy.mil.

4. Will Englund, "Navy Sell-Off Leads to Abuses; Scrapping of Ships Leaves Wake of Spills, Double-Deals, Deaths," *Baltimore Sun*, April 28, 1996, p. 1.

5. Ibid.

6. Interview, Gary Cohn, May 23, 2006.

7. Ibid.

8. Ibid.

9. Rebecca Corbett, e-mail message, June 2006.

10. Will Englund and Gary Cohn, "Scrapping Ships, Sacrificing Men" (part one of three-part series), "Shipbreakers," *Baltimore Sun*, December 7–9, 1997, p. 1.

11. Ibid.; Interview, Cohn, May 23, 2006; Interview, Will Englund, June 27, 2006.

12. Interview, Cohn, June 15, 2006.

13. Englund and Cohn, "You're Going to Die Anyway," *Baltimore Sun*, December 7, 1997, p. 10A; Interview, Englund, June 27, 2006.

14. Englund and Cohn, "Scrapping Ships, Sacrificing Men."

15. Ibid.

16. Ibid.

17. Englund and Cohn, "Third World Dump for America's Ships?" *Baltimore Sun*, December 9, 1997, p. 1.

18. Ibid.

19. Interview, Englund, June 27, 2006; Interview, Cohn, August 19, 2007.

20. Interview, Cohn, May 23, 2006; Interview, Rebecca Corbett, June 13, 2006.

21. Ibid.

22. Will Englund and Gary Cohn, "Scrapping Ships, Sacrificing Men," p. 1.

23. Ibid.

24. Interview, Corbett, June 13, 2006.

25. Gary Cohn and Will Englund, "Broadsides Fired at Navy's Ship-Scrapping Program," *Baltimore Sun*, December 19, 1997, p. A1; Gary Cohn and Will Englund, "Navy Halts Plan to Scrap Ships Abroad," *Baltimore Sun*, December 23, 1997, p. A1.

26. Gary Cohn, "Agency Scraps Plan for Old Ships: U.S. Suspends Overseas Disposal of Cargo Vessels," *Baltimore Sun*, January 29, 1998, p. A1.

27. Gary Cohn, "Senate Votes to Fix Navy Scrapping—Pilot Program Would Test New Methods of Dismantling Vessels," *Baltimore Sun*, June 26, 1998, p. A1; Gary Cohn, "U.S. Halts Scrapping of Ships Overseas," *Baltimore Sun*, September 24, 1998, p. A1.

28. David Folkenflik, "Congress Impatient With Ship Scrapping," *Baltimore Sun*, May 19, 2000, p. A1.

29. Gary Cohn and Amanda J. Crawford, "Navy Picks Port Firm to Break Ships; Pilot Program Aims to Test Safer Ways of Dismantling Vessels," *Baltimore Sun*, September 30, 1999, p. A1.

30. "Shipbreakers, Revisited"(editorial), *Baltimore Sun*, April 13, 2003, p. C4.

31. Will Englund, "The Next Fatality" (editorial), *Baltimore Sun*, April 20, 2005, p. A20.

Selected Bibliography

Articles

Englund, Will. "Navy Sell-Off Leads to Abuses; Scrapping of Ships Leaves Wake of Spills, Double-Deals, Deaths." *Baltimore Sun*, April 28, 1996.

Englund, Will, and Gary Cohn. "The Shipbreakers" (three-part series). *Baltimore Sun*, December 7–9, 1997.

Naval Historical Center of the Department of the Navy. *Dictionary of American Fighting Ships*. Washington, DC: Naval Historical Center of the Department of the Navy. http://www.history.navy.mil/danfs/index.html.

Naval Historical Center of the Department of the Navy. *United States Naval Aviation, 1910–1995*. Washington, DC: Naval Historical Center of the Department of the Navy. http://www.history.navy.mil/branches/org4-5.htm.

Correspondence

Cohn, Gary, e-mail message, August 19, 2007.

Corbett, Rebecca, e-mail message, June 2006.
Englund, Will, e-mail message, August 17, 2007.
Mountford, Kent, e-mail message, August 7, 2007.

Interviews
Carroll, John, former editor, *The Baltimore Sun*, September 27, 2006.
Cohn, Gary, former reporter, *The Baltimore Sun*, May 23, 2006 (tape recording held by author).
Cohn, Gary, May 24, 2006.
Cohn, Gary, June 15, 2006.
Cohn, Gary, July 31, 2006.
Cohn, Gary, September 13, 2006.
Corbett, Rebecca, former assistant managing editor for projects, *The Baltimore Sun*, June 13, 2006 (tape recording held by author).
Englund, Will, reporter, *The Baltimore Sun*, June 27, 2006 (tape recording held by author).

News Archives and News Search Services
Access World News, NewsBank, Inc., Naples, FL.
The Baltimore Sun electronic archives

Website
The Pulitzer Prize website, http://www.pulitzer.org.

CHAPTER 5

Paper Trail Reveals Exploitation of Mentally Ill

It Came in With the Tree Plantings[1]

Investigative reporter Cliff Levy led the way into the cafeteria of *The New York Times*, took a seat at a table, and within 10 minutes he popped open his laptop and started talking about getting organized for a big project. Without organization, he said, how could you expect to control of the huge body of clip files, notes, documents and statistics you build when working a story?

He hates paper; his dislike for it almost sounds ideological: "I am extraordinarily opposed to paper," he says. When he gets it, he worries about losing it, at least until he can safely slide it into in the document feeder of his scanner so he can tuck it away in the hard drive. If you fax something to him, it will get e-faxed into his e-mail. Notes from the field? Straight from his notebook, right into a word-processing document that gets saved somewhere in his multilevel, meticulously categorized, chronologically organized note-taking system of yearly folders and monthly files and summary files and "best of" files, all of which he is very proud.

"The worst thing in the world is after six months on a project and you have 25 notebooks and you are scrounging around in them looking for stuff," he says. "It drives you bonkers."[2]

After listening to this bright, methodical, in-control Princeton graduate for 20 minutes, it seemed a bit jarring to hear how one of the most important investigations in his career originated. It came by happenstance, not from some telltale pattern that leaped out of his electronic note-filing system, or that emerged from the creepy work of a database management program that seems smarter than the rest of us.

"We came upon this by accident," he said.

It started in early March 2001 when the fax machine at the metro desk ground out a news release announcing that an advocacy group was suing an adult home for the mentally ill in Queens. The fax said Leben Home for Adults was putting some men through unnecessary prostate surgery. The news release was probably one of hundreds that flooded the news desk that day. "No one saw it, and we missed the story," Levy recalled.

Such is the fate of many news releases that drown in the daily wash of unsolicited material in most any newsroom. The same release apparently went to other New York City newspapers. None of their rivals wrote much about it. The *New York Post* wrote 219 words on March 10 and stuck it on page four.[3]

Somehow, the release landed in front of 47-year-old Joe Sexton, a deputy metro editor. "In one form or another, the possibility that an extraordinary outrage had taken place came in like every news release about the next tree planting in Brooklyn," Sexton recalled. At the moment, Sexton had no way of knowing the ramifications of the release, but within a few weeks it would send Levy into a bizarre world chasing a story for the next 12 months. But as he and Levy would soon learn, the situation at Leben Home and at others like it was not a secret story. It had been around for decades, and the details had long been in the public record. But few, including the *Times* had paid much attention to it.

This time, perhaps because a fresh pair of eyes was brought to bear, someone at the *Times* was paying attention. Sexton doesn't remember how this particular release among all of the others caught his eye, but he remembers why. "Once you sat down and absorbed the release, it was pretty ghastly."[4]

At that time, most of Sexton's *Times* background was in sports, and he was relatively new in the editing ranks at the paper. A native of Brooklyn, Sexton had been a journalist since 1984, when he helped establish *The City Sun*, a Brooklyn weekly. After stops at *The Bergen Record* in Hackensack, N.J., *The Syracuse Post-Standard* and United Press International, he joined the *Times* in 1987 to cover sports. He wrote about hockey and Major League Baseball. But he caught the eye of metro editors, and was lured away from sports in 1994. One gushing editor compared getting Sexton into Metro to the New York Yankees getting Babe Ruth, the legend who set the standard for baseball greatness.[5] Sexton became a metro news reporter, and after four years and a brief editing stint back in sports, he returned to metro in 1999 to supervise investigations and enterprise reporting.[6]

When the Leben Home item crossed his desk in early 2001, Sexton gave it to Levy, because he considered him an efficient, forward-looking reporter, who was well versed in the ways of government bureaucracy and public records requests. Sexton told him to hook up with the *Times'* reporter in Queens, Sarah Kershaw, and see if they could find any substance to the claims in the news release.[7] A few days later, Levy and Kershaw turned out a 2,000-word, page-one Sunday story reporting how a doctor performed questionable surgeries on 24 Leben Home men, six of whom suffered complications. No one, the story reported, had contacted the patients' relatives, guardians or primary care physicians.

Many were "listless and disheveled," Levy and Kershaw found. "Some were so bewildered they began to wander off" when they were driven up to the hospital and let out. One was 80 years old. The story said someone had persuaded them to sign forms allowing surgery for enlarged prostates, even though the condition had not been conclusively diagnosed. None had received a proper urological exam and few seemed to understand what they were signing. It said health officials found that the procedures had generated tens of thousands of dollars in Medicare and Medicaid fees for the hospital and at least one doctor.[8]

A Symbol of Dashed Hopes

Levy was intrigued by what he saw. He talked with Sexton, and they agreed to dig a little deeper. Levy and Kershaw looked at inspection reports and court records and talked to neighbors and to people who worked there.

The second story again made page A-1 on April 18, 2001, and one of the most startling findings was that abuses at Leben Home had been going on and documented in public records for 20 years. The story found that the state periodically inspected but rarely did much to force the home to correct serious deficiencies. One inspector said the situation "resembles those one was likely to see in the back wards of mental health institutions a decade or more ago." The reporters read reports of loan-sharking, drug trades, misappropriation of residents' funds and residents trading sex for money.

Three opening paragraphs reported a theme that threads through so many investigative projects—the sharp contrast between reality and the public pronouncements of business and government. In this case, Leben Home seemed to be a piece of reality that bore little resemblance to what the state had predicted decades earlier when it started releasing psychiatric patients from big state hospitals to small, community-based homes. At such homes, they were supposed to find proximity to loved ones, safety and independent livelihoods.

> In the years since that time of promise, Leben Home has amassed a record of neglect and misconduct. Last year, the home was forced by the state to evacuate its first floor, a warren of crumbling walls and fetid mattresses where 60 people lived before they were led out into the daylight, some clutching belongings in black trash bags.
>
> A few years earlier, the home overlooked the disappearance of a resident, crippling a police effort to find him. Seven months later, his family learned that he had been run over by a Long Island Rail Road train well before the home reported him missing, and had been buried, un-mourned and anonymous. A resident was raped at the home by a janitor in 1995, and two residents were killed, their culprits never found, in 1989.
>
> It all happened in a brick building with a barbed wire perimeter on 45th Avenue in Elmhurst, a place annually deemed by the state as acceptable quarters for 360 people with mental illness, some of whom can routinely be spotted panhandling on surrounding streets or picking through the garbage of the nearby Continental Diner.[9]

Levy was pleased with how the 3,000-word story turned out, but it was clear from several sources quoted in the story that Leben Home might not be the only home of squalor. He had learned that Leben Home was one of about 100 for-profit, state-regulated adult homes for about 15,000 mentally ill residents. Most of the homes were scattered about New York City and its suburbs, and about $600 million, mostly in Medicaid and Medicare funds, paid for the residents' care. Many of the homes had started as residences for the elderly, but later expanded to lure the legions of mentally ill state officials started releasing from the state psychiatric hospitals two to three decades earlier.

The most intriguing part of the story, however, was that the horrible situation at Leben Home was no secret. State government had chronicled the problems repeatedly in inspection reports for years but seldom did anything about the problems, and the *Times* had virtually ignored them.[10]

Sexton and Levy got together again. "I remember sitting down with Cliff and saying who knows how many folks actually died in these homes," Sexton said. Levy found the adult home situation fascinating and disturbing. "I was struck by how very little was written about this by the *New York Times* or by anyone else over the years. I had been a reporter since 1992, and I had never heard of this system. I had been in Albany for a year or two. I had covered City Hall. I knew about nursing homes, but I had no idea that there was this whole system set up . . . for mentally ill people released from psychiatric wards." The warehousing of human beings was supposed to have ended with the closure of most of the state psychiatric hospitals. But it was still going on at Leben Home. That consideration raised the broader questions, starting with these: What is happening in other adult homes? Were other homes in disrepair and unsanitary? Were the homes mistreating and neglecting their residents, using them for bogus Medicare and Medicaid claims? Was the state enforcing regulations? Or had it slipped back into the practice of warehousing human beings? "We didn't know," Levy said. "We had a very open mind, but we had a suspicion that the problems were not limited to this one home and that the system was in equal trouble. It seems unlikely that this one would be a striking anomaly."

Metro's Devotion to Home Turf

Levy said Sexton seemed as fascinated with the story as he was, and he told him to get going on it. The story provided the *Times* a good chance to show that it was just as committed to solid, thorough reporting in its backyard as it was nationally and internationally.

Some editors had long felt the paper had an undeserved reputation for ignoring its home turf, which is the metropolitan staff's responsibility, for the benefit of its vaunted international and national coverage. Indeed, metro is considered "the point of entry" for editors and reporters. Nevertheless, top editors starting with Bill Keller, executive editor, insist on its importance to the paper. "Even as the *Times* has acquired a national audience and global ambitions, Metro remains the paper's source and its soul," the paper told its staff in a Jan. 26, 2006, memo announcing Sexton's promotion to metro editor. "It is," they explained, "the mother lode of news that is as often of national interest as it is local."[11]

The word apparently had not reached its readers. In fact, a year later Sexton wrote a long, defensive missive to a reader complaint on that issue in a "Talk to the Newsroom" column in which he extolled the paper's coverage of New York back to 1995. "No fair reader of the paper—today, yesterday, last year, in 1995—could really make an argument that the paper does a poor job of covering New York. It's as tired a complaint as the Gray Lady moniker."[12]

Nevertheless, in early 2001, the paper was looking over its shoulder at the investigative successes of *The Washington Post*'s metro desk and drew inspiration to boost its investigative effort in its backyard.[13] They were particularly impressed with the work of investigative reporter Katherine Boo on the mentally retarded in Washington, D.C., and of reporter and then editor Jeff Leen. "They had methodically taken apart the District's broken government," Sexton said. "It was awfully good work, and I am always looking to learn a lesson and copy models." In the spring of 2001, New York's adult home system looked like fertile ground for some investigative digging.

Background, Experience Suited to Task

Levy brought a substantial amount of investigative and government reporting experience and a distinct reporting style to the assignment. Moreover, he had established a reputation as an aggressive and careful investigative reporter.[14]

His background in some ways seemed consistent with the theme of the project. First, he knows his state. A lifelong New Yorker, he was born in New Rochelle and, like his editor, was living in Brooklyn. His father was a psychiatrist, and his mother a sociologist. At Princeton, he had been managing editor of *The Princetonian*. His journalism education came from doing journalism and from "great mentors," he said, referring to editors and colleagues. Getting a well-rounded education in college, being curious and learning to write was all he needed to do good journalism, he says. "I don't believe in journalism schools. People should write for the high school and college newspapers and study whatever you want in school." For him, that was public policy and international affairs. His first job after graduation in 1989 was reporting in the New York bureau for United Press International. That lasted about a year, because he went to work as a news assistant on the foreign desk for *The New York Times* in 1990 at the age of 23.

The *Times* promoted him to reporter in 1992, and his early clips suggest that he, like most young reporters, had to pay his dues. Although he churned out a lot of stories in his first full year, most wound up inside. His most concentrated assignment had him writing 400- and 500-word dailies for three months on the newspaper's "Neediest Cases" charity drive. But starting in the spring of 1993, Levy's byline was making regular appearances, first on the local front and then, as the years went by, on page one. He was doing breaking and enterprise stories on a variety of topics such as former Mayor David Dinkins' budget cuts, the blizzard of 1993, a federal investigation into government fraud in Newark, Port Authority controversies, Romanian refugees who stowed away in shipping containers and the activities of Gov. George Pataki.

One set of stories stuck in his memory—some work revealing political patronage by then-Attorney General Dennis Vacco. As part of that run, he wrote a story reporting that Vacco's wife obtained personal information about the lawyers working for her husband and used it to try to raise campaign money from them for a close friend of the Vaccos.[15] It was the type of story that hit a chord with Levy. "It was classic shoe-leather reporting, and it ultimately led to intense criticism of his office and helped lead to his defeat in 1998," he said. "It was exciting, and I was very invigorated by it."

In the last half of the 1990s, Levy began to see that he enjoyed getting deeply involved in a specific subject. He saw that he liked to dig and was good at it. "It was one of my natural inclinations," he said. Starting in 1997, he was covering then-Mayor Rudolph Giuliani and City Hall and writing a lot of stories about lobbyists' influence on local government and campaign financing in the fall mayoral and city council election. That was the year he began learning to use computers to manage data.

By 1998, Levy moved up to chief of the Albany bureau, and again was writing major stories about campaign financing irregularities. He investigated fundraising practices and donor lists at the state-government level. His work prompted criminal investigations and in 1998 earned him the coveted George Polk Award awarded by Long Island University since 1949. His interest in campaign financing and the influence of lobbyists continued in 2000. In February 2001, Levy and another reporter published a hard-hitting investigative piece about a chairman of the Senate Insurance Commission profiting from insurance companies while often casting votes on legislation that favored insurers.[16]

Organize, Digitize or Go "Bonkers"

For Cliff Levy, the Leben Home story, which came to him a month later, would be a sharp turn in his reporting path. Sexton believes that it was the topical shift that appealed to Levy. "Part of what engaged Cliff was that after uncovering unsavory lobbying practices at City Hall and in Albany, here, with this story, you had, at heart, an incredibly human story and upsetting material."

Although the topic would be a departure from what had established Levy's credentials, it would not change his approach, which is methodical and thorough. He likes to do everything himself, and he doesn't often work with partners. Levy's preference for going solo fits with what he describes as "the most important" requirement for project reporting: organization. He organizes everything. If he makes a call or does an interview with a book author, he logs it into a Microsoft Word document: name, time, date, subject. "See here, 'I spoke to Steve at 11:50 a.m. on such and such,'" he said, referring to this author. "Without organization, you are going to collapse. If you get information in October [of one year], by March you will have already forgotten what you got in October," unless you are organized.

As for paper, "I don't use it. Every document I get, I get it digitized," he explains. To carry the project with him wherever he goes, he has found that a three-inch-long flash drive beats a briefcase. The paper itself is relegated to a paper folder as a backup and forgotten. "It becomes irrelevant," he said. All of the thousands of inspection reports on adult homes are on PDF files. "I scan it all, because then I don't have to worry about it again. His electronic folders are divided into years, and within each folder he has a Microsoft Word file for every month of that year and all the notes for that month are entered in chronological order. That is like a master file, from which he creates "summary files" and files that contain "my best stuff." Although the summary files are important, Levy says he also periodically reviews the longer monthly Word documents.

It is a system that appears to provide a structural way of freshening the original vision of the project idea as new information and interviews accumulate over the weeks of the project. "You can't ignore your monthly files," Levy said, "You have different visions of the project at different phases of the reporting. Something that can seem completely benign and useless at the beginning of the project can become very important when you look at it through the lens that you have at end of the project."

Levy frequently builds his own databases, plucking stats and information from his digitized documents into computer spreadsheets. Although the nonprofit investigative journalism organization, Investigative Reporters and Editors at the University of Missouri regularly runs boot camps to teach reporters how to use computers to manage and analyze huge amounts of information, Levy learned it on the job. While in the Albany bureau working on the campaign finance project, he enlisted a colleague to show him how to use Microsoft Access to store, manage and analyze the volumes of information he gathered.

He prefers doing all of his own database work rather than relying on staff who specialize in computer-assisted reporting. "You have to get a feel for all this stuff, and so you have to get immersed in it. This is the kind of thing that I will get up at 3 a.m. to work on, because you have to be kind of obsessively involved in it. Someone just trolling through the information on your behalf doesn't know the nuances and the background that you have and is not going to pick up on stuff." From this passion for computer-assisted reporting comes a bit of frustration with reporters who shy away from it. "This is not complicated stuff," he says, "And I grit my teeth when reporters don't want to learn how to do this. You miss out on some really good reporting."

Levy also prefers doing his own clip searches, even though many reporters, especially at large papers like the *Times* usually ask their in-house researchers to do that. "I looked at all the mental health reporting that had been done all over the country, and I put together this enormous clip file. Levy often starts with Investigative Reporters and Editors. Beside publishing *The Investigative Reporters Handbook*, which many journalists of all stripes consider a bible of sorts, it has been collecting investigative projects on virtually every subject since it was founded in 1975. The work of other reporters gives him clues and ideas on how to get information and the names of expert sources. He gets clues on how they tackled the subject and what types of problems and issues they explored.

Missed Stories Lurk in Darkest Corners

Levy found that the the *Times'* clips on adult homes were not very helpful. The file was pretty thin, but the archive contained enough stories on adult homes to show that the system had needed investigation long before the fall of 2001 when he started probing the issue. It showed that the *Times* had picked up on a number of clear signs during the two previous decades that adult home operators were exploiting and mistreating their residents. Yet, as Levy found, little was written. At times, there were stronger prompts in *Times* news columns 10 to 20 years ago than what Levy and Sexton saw in 2001.

A few stories about adult care homes (or adult boarding homes or residential care facilities, as they were called then) appeared between 1981 and mid-1990. But one on Feb. 8, 1981, in hindsight, provides an eerie harbinger and ample reason to suspect even then that mentally ill people assigned to community homes were in trouble nationwide. The story, appearing under the headline, "As 'Psychiatric Ghettos,' Boarding Homes Get More Dangerous," was prompted by three separate fires in boarding homes within six months that killed 74 people who were mentally ill, elderly or disabled in neighboring New Jersey. It pointed to the physical safety hazards common among such homes in New Jersey, New York and nationwide. It also warned that the release of thousands of mental patients from state psychiatric hospitals across the country had created a recipe for disaster.[17]

As Levy and Kershaw would discover 20 years later, the ingredients of that recipe produced neglectful conditions at Leben Home for Adults in New York from the early 1980s into 2001. Many of the residents at Leben Home had come from psychiatric hospitals in New York.[18] Like Leben Home, many of the adult homes discussed in that 1981 article were privately owned and operated for profit in structures originally built for every type of use from chicken coops and mobile homes to run-down hotels. Leben Home was built to house offices for an airline parts factory and then was converted to house elderly people before providing services to the mentally ill.

Levy and Kershaw discovered another old problem in 2001. The state could have closed Leben Home, they wrote, but for decades, the state was reluctant to take such actions against adult homes because of the expense of finding beds elsewhere for the mentally ill. They were right. Twenty years earlier, the 1981 *Times* story had reached the same conclusion and found that boarding home operators were virtually immune to government oversight, clearing the way for them to prey on this newly released hapless and helpless population. With the state releasing mental patients to save money, and the boarding home industry using them to make money, one source in that 1981 story depicted the states as a "fox in the chicken coop."[19] The states' desire to save money put them in conflict with the responsibility to enforce safety and health regulations, which Levy and Kershaw discovered was the crux of the problem at Leben Home.

Despite those early signs of trouble in the adult homes, the problem remained off the radar at the *Times* for another eight years, after which its coverage consisted of on-and-off spot news stories. In 1989, for example, the U.S. Congress noticed the growing problem when two congressional committees concluded that the federal government should immediately establish national standards for institutions that house mentally ill adults, the elderly and disabled. The *Times* wrote about that committee's findings.[20]

But then, the loudest alarms specifically for New York City sounded several times in the early 1990s and produced the same type of stories that would prompt Levy's investigation a decade later. In May 1990, the *Times* published a story about two suspicious deaths of mentally ill residents at Leben Home and the police department's propensity to close such cases after cursory investigations.

That was not all, though. Three months later, the paper published "Neglect Found in Residences," a story of about 2,000 words reporting how a state watchdog commission's inspection found that thousands of mentally ill patients and others were living virtually unsupervised in 28 adult care homes hiding dangerous, dirty and dilapidated conditions that mirrored what Levy reported 10 years later at Leben Home.[21] Moreover, there were four spot news stories about a Queens adult care home, Hi-Li Manor, for the mentally ill, where poor living conditions and alleged misappropriation of residents' money had prompted a suit and a license revocation effort by the state. That same home would surface again during Levy's investigation under a new name.

The dearth of coverage in the *Times* may have been due to competing subjects and issues on the editors' agendas. "I suppose there could be any number of explanations," Sexton said. "It has to do with the dynamics of the day. Journalism is an imperfect and human exercise."

The sparse attention to the problems in adult homes in prior years also illustrates in an ironic way how some of the best, most constructive and interesting stories originate in the hidden corners of society that have never earned a place on the public's agenda. Few segments of society are as quintessentially voiceless as the homeless mentally ill, the part of a community many journalists see as their special constituency. Yet, Levy said he found that most of the news coverage on the closing of psychiatric hospitals explored how mentally ill patients were winding up among the ranks of homeless people. And, indeed, the size of the homeless population exploded in big cities across the country. "I don't think anybody thought much about it beyond the homeless problem. What they didn't know about was this whole group of people who did not end up on the streets but ended up being warehoused in these privately run homes, and no one looked at that system. . . . So adult homes developed in an extremely haphazard way," he said.

Levy believes the New York press could have done a better job keeping tabs on the adult home system than it did, but he said the number of homeless people then was huge, and "they were more in everybody's faces. These others were not. They were out of sight, shoved off into a corner."

Getting Started

Although the adult home coverage was sparse, the clips helped give Levy and his editors reasonable grounds to believe an investigation would bear fruit. Sexton gave Levy free rein. "They said spend as much time as you need. It was an incredible luxury," Levy said, one that he found benefited the project in numerous ways. "I had no one saying I had to come into the office everyday and tell them what I was doing. They were very casual. Joe wanted to know a lot, because it was his project that he was chaperoning and also because he was very fascinated by what the reporting was turning up."

At the start, Levy knew nothing about adult homes for the mentally ill, except for what he had read in the clip files. He did not know what kinds of records and documents were kept on adult homes and which were public. Interviews with advocates, clip searches and other research helped him find the paper trail. The clip files had revealed a few suspicious deaths in years past, including a suicide in which the home was criticized for failing to provide sufficient security and properly administering the resident's medication.

He decided early that the story had to have a strong "statistical undercarriage" about deaths at the home, and that the story would focus on the largest homes with the worst conditions. An accounting of the deaths would be the best way to determine whether the homes were treating their residents humanely and whether the state was keeping tabs on them. Specifically, he wanted to find out how many residents of the homes died at each home and their ages at the time of death. Sexton agreed: "There are very few ingredients in any investigative story that are more powerful than when people are dying unnecessarily."

Getting the numbers would be difficult. A 1994 law required homes to report every death that occurred while the residents were under the homes' care. But

Levy discovered that the homes were ignoring the law, and the Department of Health, which is responsible for regulating the homes, was not enforcing that law. Death certificates were not public in New York. The coroner's records were secret. Eventually, someone told him that he could get the names of people who had died from Social Security Administration records. That would be a good place to start, especially if the Social Security Administration records listed the addresses of the dead people. He filed a public records request, launching what he described as "a four- or five-month crusade for me."

As that crusade dragged on, he pushed forward on other fronts. Although the statistics would be compelling, they would carry little power with readers unless Levy could take them inside the homes that produced the numbers and show them the human faces that they represented. He read the reports of state health department inspectors and pursued hospital records and Medicaid billings. He tracked down workers and visited the homes to observe their conditions and to interview workers.

After two or three weeks, Levy and his editors knew they were on to something. "We already knew from the first two stories [about Leben Home] that it probably would not be a bust," he said. "We did not know where it would it go, . . . but we just kept broadening it." As a month passed, then two months, they realized "there was a lot to this story." Levy worked at home a lot, but reported regularly to Sexton. "Sexton was very galvanized by this project," Levy recalled. "At one point, I came to Joe with a packet of notes like this," he said, holding up a sheaf of about 20 pages. "He read it and said, 'This is great; by the end of the reporting process I want you to have a pack this thick on each case.' He really wanted to do this one right."

For his part, Sexton did not believe he was articulating a standard of reporting that was new to Levy. He was trying to emphasize the importance and "richness" of the material that Levy was accumulating and that he realized that they had the "opportunity to do this story right and flawlessly with the greatest civic impact."

Reporting Turns Victims Into People

The reporting was revealing some horrid deaths: seizure-prone residents dying alone in the throes of a fit; people dying in their rooms from treatable illnesses like appendicitis and no one noticing until the stench of their decaying bodies became overwhelming; suicidal patients leaping from rooftops; a young man dead from a brutal knife at the hands of a roommate with a history of violence; and people dying from the ovenlike heat in their rooms during the hot summer months.

Levy wanted to show that people who died at adult homes were more than just victims, that they were sons and daughters with personalities and hopes. "It was very important to us to write about them, not as 'crazy' mentally ill people who no one cares about," Levy said. "We wanted to show them as real people who often have vibrant lives and that there are people who do care about them. To do that, you have to find their families."

Early on, Levy heard about Randolph Maddix, a schizophrenic, who died at the age of 51, while at Seaport Manor in Brooklyn. He learned about him from two workers at the home, and the case seemed to cry out for attention. After learning about Maddix's situation, Levy wanted to find his family.

It would not be easy. "I went to every 'Maddix' in the phone book," Levy said, scrolling down an activity log he kept in his electronic notes. For three days, he tried finding the Maddix family. "I was totally despondent," he said. But he kept dialing. "You never know that after the 15th call, the 16th call may be the gold mine," he said. He spent 10 to 12 hours over three days calling people, trying to find the right Maddix. "The average reader doesn't understand how you dig thousands of dry wells chasing leads," Levy said. Noting that daily reporters seldom have that much time to track down one source, Levy said, "There were just so many ways that the luxury of time benefited this project." Searching for a Maddix relative, Levy finally ran out of names to call and decided to give the two adult home workers another try. He had already interviewed them three times before. To his chagrin, they instantly remembered the street in Brooklyn where Maddix's mother lived.

Within 20 minutes, Levy was talking to her about her son. She said Maddix had no one to watch over him at night. "There wasn't anybody," she said. "Just him and God." Maddix started having seizures when he was a teenager. Thereafter he needed almost constant help, and had few joys. He liked cigars and going to the Coney Island boardwalk to drink coffee and gaze into the ocean.[22]

At Seaport Manor, Maddix's life came out in inspection reports and other records and through interviews with the two workers who had alerted Levy to his plight. Maddix had suffered more than 40 seizures at Seaport. In a July 1999 report, Levy saw that ambulances had been called 10 times to rescue him from seizures in the previous seven months. In one instance, Maddix broke his arm. In another episode—this one while at the hospital—he fell into a seizure and suffered what Levy described as a "finger-length laceration" on his face. A state inspection report on Maddix written in July 1999 concluded with this telling paragraph about a "PRI," a test to determine the level of care a patient needs:

> A PRI was conducted for this resident on 03/27/99 and indicated a higher level of care is needed. Persistent efforts were not documented and it did not appear these had been initiated. The annual case management evaluation was due in 10/98, but had not been done. As cited in violation 7 of this report, the case management notes and record-keeping . . . did not indicate follow-up or actions taken to address these problems. Interviewed staff were vague in describing what was being done and by whom.

Two months after the inspection, Maddix went to the bathroom at Seaport Manor, and like so many other times, he suffered a seizure, with no one there to help him. Twelve hours later, he was found dead, crumpled between the toilet and bathtub. Rigor mortis had already set in and his back had to be broken to get him into a body bag.[23]

Get Inside to Get "Inside-Story"

If the project was to show the deceased were more than just victims, it also had to show the adult homes were more than facts listed on an inspector's report.

Levy and a photographer had to get inside and see the day rooms, hallways and bedrooms in an unstaged state. To do so, they took advantage of the homes' laxity.

"I would go at night or on weekends when there were no administrators around, and the places were practically deserted of staff," Levy said. The doors were never locked, which meant he could walk in at will. Usually, a staff member sat at the front desk. To avoid a confrontation, Levy went in with a resident or an advocacy group representative. If anyone had asked for identification, he would have been required by policy to say he was a reporter for *The New York Times*. Journalism ethics and *Times* policy prohibit reporters from lying or posing as someone they are not. But no one bothered to ask. "You do not have to announce who you are," Levy said.

Throughout the investigation that year, his method worked. "I was never kicked out, and they never discovered me." He said he could wander around quite awhile without seeing a staff member. The photographer, Nicole Bengiveno, used the same tactic—befriending residents—to get access. She spent many months going around the phones taking photos. Levy said she wandered the long hallways and went into people's rooms with their permission and took pictures. "She didn't take that many photos in congregate areas. She would take a few quick snapshots and hide her camera." Bengiveno got caught once at Seaport Manor. Her camera was confiscated, but not before she extracted the film disc. Other than that, she escaped notice.

The visits were helpful to capture the ambience. They saw vermin and filth. Many residents wandered about unwashed, wearing dirty and torn clothing. Some packed into crowded smoking rooms and sat for hours rocking or talking to themselves. On the floors, lay cigarette butts and ashes, dropped food and spills. Televisions ran continuously, as residents sat slumped in chairs, many of them asleep or otherwise oblivious to what was on the screen.[24]

Getting Consent From the Mentally Ill

Often, Levy found that neglect turned exploitive. Most of the residents can legally sign consent forms. Levy's reporting had already discovered that home administrators and others had persuaded these vulnerable people to sign such forms to exploit them. Now, Levy, for a benevolent purpose—to find out whether patients were being exploited—was persuading mentally ill patients to sign forms to give him access to records. Some of the homes and health care providers saw these residents as gateways to Medicaid and Medicare funds. When Levy did the story on prostate surgery at Leben Home, he had heard that residents were later coerced into consenting to other questionable medical care and procedures, including eye surgeries performed by Dr. Shaul Debbi. "Although many of the residents told me they had eye surgery, they are mentally ill and very open to suggestion," Levy said. "There was no way I could quote this person as saying he had eye surgery from Dr. Debbi. I would never put that in the paper." He had to get their billing records first. But he needed their consent. "I picked 15 or so residents, brought them to a notary, and I got them to authorize me to get copies of their own psychiatric and Medicaid billings," Levy recalled.

One resident was of particular interest, because Levy had heard he was subjected to numerous procedures. Levy described him as "out of it," but he needed to look at his records. "I explained it very clearly to him who I was, what I was doing" and that Levy wanted to look at his records before asking him to sign a consent form. Asked if he was sure the man understood the explanation, Levy said he thought the resident understood some of it. "I think he knew I wasn't going to do anything to harm him and that I was going to help him." Moreover, he said his purpose was to find out whether the homes and doctors were taking advantage of vulnerable people. "The state gave me a bit of a hard time, but it eventually agreed, and they sent me his Medicaid billings." The records revealed that Debbi did four operations in four months. The resident also was charged $70,000 for therapy sessions and $20,000 for transportation to various appointments. "He had $200,000 in billings, and he wasn't sick at all," Levy said. The man's brother told Levy no one told him about any of the procedures.

Homes' Workers Tell All

Although Levy talked to many residents, he relied primarily on workers and former workers to get firsthand accounts of what was happening inside the homes. "Many of the residents often were not trustworthy narrators, because they were mentally ill. So it was very important that I talk to a lot of workers." Sometimes he would talk to 20 or 30 workers from one home, but usually not at the home.

"A lot of this was just classic shoe-leather reporting," he said. "You find the name of one and ask for the name of others and where they live and you look up their numbers. Usually a worker would know where other workers lived."

During the visits, he developed many sources, but usually talked to them away from work. "These were very low-level workers, who often were almost as mistreated as the residents," Levy said. "They were paid very poorly, didn't like the conditions of the homes, and they were more than happy to speak out." Although most former workers were cooperative, occasionally they wanted anonymity. Levy frequently appealed to "their sense of justice" by saying he was trying to "shine a spotlight on what was going on here." He also had time to build a relationship of trust with sources, who initially would only talk off the record and gradually speak to him for publication. "Again, that is another luxury you have on a long-term project," he said.

One worker at Seaport Manor, Toshua Courtham, revealed, without requesting anonymity, an astounding scene one night in the fall of 2000 when she and a group of workers were getting ready for the arrival of state inspectors. Their job was to falsify the records to persuade the inspectors that they were taking good care of their 325 residents. "We were told by the administrators at the home to be creative . . . or else we would lose our jobs," Courtham told Levy. Their creativity generated psychiatric evaluations for suicidal residents, case notes for manic depressives and therapy plans for women who sold sex for cigarettes and for men who preyed on others for their $4 daily allowances. The records carried the names of fictitious doctors, and frequently many received the same diagnosis. "Everybody, if you looked at their charts, they were all paranoid schizophrenic," she said. The ruse worked.[25] Levy confirmed the worker's account with several other former and current employees.

Usually, current employees asked that their names not be published, because they feared losing their jobs. Levy honored the request and did not pressure them. If they provided information needed for a story, Levy had enough time to get it elsewhere. Frequently, the source could give him the name and phone number of someone who would speak publicly.

Meanwhile, Back on the Paper Trail

Throughout the summer of 2001, he continued nagging the Social Security Administration (SSA) for death data from the homes. The administration would provide the names of the deceased and their dates of birth and death. Although it had the specific addresses in its files, that information was considered confidential. The SSA would only provide the ZIP codes where the deceased had resided when they died, Levy said. Although Levy could match the adult homes' ZIP codes with the ZIP codes of the names from the Social Security records, Levy wanted something that would prove more definitively that the deceased were residents of the adult homes.

So Levy took a different tack. He filed a public records request listing the specific addresses of the adult homes and asking for the names of the deceased who lived at those addresses. Surprisingly, the SSA did a special computer exercise for him to answer his request. "They sent me an Excel spreadsheet; and when I saw it I was jumping for joy. It just one day popped into my [e-mail] inbox, and I said 'Oh my god.' It turned out to be the Holy Grail of the whole project."

Levy called it the Holy Grail because, until he decided to count the deaths, no one knew how many people had died while an adult home resident. Relying heavily on those SSA statistics and other records, he documented 946 deaths of residents who lived in 26 homes between 1995 and 2001, with nearly one-third of them dying before reaching 60, and more than a third of that segment dying in their 20s, 30s, and 40s. The average death age was 63.[26]

Despite the disturbing numbers, Levy recognized that he would have to be careful in using them. Some of the residents' deaths were due to their mental illnesses, natural causes or circumstances beyond the control of the homes. Although he could not find a way to quantify those who died under such circumstances, he consulted an expert on mental illness and mortality who was familiar with the adult home system. The expert found Levy's statistics disturbing and confirmed that better and more skilled care would have extended life span figures. "This poor care leading to death is going to cut right across the age population," the expert told Levy. "It also means that people who are 70 are dying prematurely."[27]

Immersion in the Project Zone

With such expert interviews, court documents, inspection reports, medical billing records and other material, the parameters of the human story were taking shape: People were dying long before they should, even when allowing for the shorter life span normally associated with the mentally ill. His analysis examined individual homes and individual deaths. It found that one of every four patients who died under the age of 50 were residents at just two of the homes, including one whose name had come to the paper's attention before: Leben Home for Adults.

After six months on the project, Levy had made substantial progress. He, like many project reporters, was by that point so deeply immersed in his work he developed a tunnel vision that blocked out everything not related to the project. "When you are an investigative reporter, you have to put some blinders on and not worry about having your name in the paper," he said. "Investigative reporters have a choice: do they want to see their bylines on dozens of 600-word stories, or do they want to write a story that will have some a real impact on the community and affect people's lives?" For Levy, for most of the previous decade, the latter alternative was his choice.

Then Came 9/11

The reporting phase was three-fourths complete, and Levy was consumed by the project when the most horrific event in his lifetime occurred: The World Trade Center towers collapsed. Terrorists had flown two hijacked airliners into them, killing thousands, setting off what politicians started calling the war on terror and altering the course of history. He headed for the office. At the Manhattan Bridge, workers were teeming across on foot. Traffic backed up, and Levy was stuck. He called in and was told to interview some of the workers and pick up some color. He followed orders and then helped out on one or two other stories later. "But that was about it," he said.

That was the extent of his involvement in an event that changed the world. Sexton did not pull him off the project, and he kept working, mostly from his home. "I felt left out. I lived in New York, and I felt very personally affected by 9/11. I was sitting home working, wondering 'What the hell am I doing? Who cares what I am doing? New York City is coming apart. A terrible thing has happened, and I am one of the few reporters in the entire city not working on it.' It was an extraordinarily strange feeling, but somehow I found the will to keep going."

Deep down, Levy wanted to keep working his project. The temptation to pull off was strong. "I was torn," he said. "Although, I have got to tell you, I'm not a hard news guy. I am much more of a lone-wolf guy, so while it was tempting to do 9/11 stuff, I am not so crazy about doing stuff everybody else is doing."

Then Came Flight 587

Two months later, Levy was still trying to focus on his investigation and he, like the rest of New York, was still haunted by 9/11. Then, in early November, an airliner carrying 260 people fell over Queens, killing all aboard and some on the ground. By happenstance, Levy, who works quite often at home, had decided to go into the newsroom that day to talk to his editors about the project. "I had not spoken to them in six weeks. They had just ignored me [they were all working on 9/11]," he said. He got into the newsroom about 9:20 a.m., just minutes after the crash, and he had not yet heard about it. He saw a flurry of activity around the metro desk and asked a clerk what was going on. A plane had just gone down, she told him. "It was a huge story for several weeks," Levy said. "I thought to myself, geez, why do I even try?" Still, he stuck to the adult home story.

Sexton, Levy's editor, said he and then-metro editor Jonathan Landman (now deputy managing editor) agreed not to pull Levy off the project. "While you had this incredible and I-hope-once-in-a-lifetime story [about 9/11] unfolding around you, he was still capable of making strategic judgments that there were other deserving stories that the paper could not lose sight of regardless of how ambitious and authoritative we wanted to be on this biggest of all stories."

So Levy plugged along. Despite the long 9/11 preoccupation of his editors, Levy said he still relied on them heavily at other times, particularly assistant metro editor Christine Kay, who reported to Sexton, and joined the project around January. Sexton met once every week or two with Levy and Kay, who became Levy's primary editor and worked with him almost daily. She would get the raw copy from Levy, and they would draft and rewrite several times before sending the stories up the ranks.

Kay, 38 at the time and a 1985 journalism graduate from Pennsylvania State University, had been assistant metro editor since 1998 and had edited special projects and enterprise stories. She joined the *Times* in 1995, after working as reporter and editor at *The Pittsburgh Press* and then in a variety of assignments, including weekend editor at *Newsday*.

Editors Bring Perspective

Levy said he—and probably any good investigative journalist—values the role of editors like Kay and Sexton, because the nuts and bolts of an investigative project require reporters to get so deeply immersed in the details and nuances of the topic. "Any investigative reporter will tell you that you have no perspective because of that. If I have confidence in my editors, I throw myself at their mercy. I know when a fact is important, but if I have two facts, I can't tell you which is more important," he said.

Levy, who has since been promoted to cover Russia, said he valued Sexton and Kay as "sounding boards." He said, "Joe has a good story gut, and he gets very excited about good stories. Christine is one of the best story doctors and project editors in the business." He said Kay pushed him to get "more of a sense of what life is like in the homes," a suggestion that sent him back into the facilities late in the reporting. "I think this is an example of investigative reporters' lack of perspective."

Early in the reporting, Levy had heard about drug trading and women prostituting themselves in the homes for cigarettes, but he had never pursued that angle. "It just went completely over my head; I guess because I was so focused on people dying because of lack of care that selling drugs seemed kind of trivial," Levy said. Then Kay talked about the seriousness of drug sales and prostitution flourishing among people as vulnerable as the mentally ill. "It was one of those why-didn't-I-think-of-that moments," Levy recalled. "You have a lot of moments like that on these big projects because the amount of reporting you do is just so overwhelming you really need someone to come in say 'you did a good job on this, but we need more of that.'" His visits to Seaport Manor, records and interviews produced a section called "Ritual Turmoil."

> Residents and workers at the home call it payday. Once a month, Seaport's administrators hand out about $120 in allowance money to each resident from the disability checks they control. Then, the pandemonium begins.
>
> In-house loan sharks chase residents down the hall, intent on collecting their money, according to numerous current and former workers and residents. They said two crack dealers also opened for business, packing in an assortment of fellow residents, and even the police said they have made drug arrests at the home in recent years.
>
> Those residents unwilling to take part in either enterprise run to their rooms, fearful of the opportunistic and desperately in need of their tiny allowances. Inevitably, the strong at Seaport always know when the weak are in line to get their money.
>
> "It would be just one big mess," Angela Peters, a former housekeeper and dietary aide, said of payday. "We couldn't do any work on the floor because it was so crazy . . . ."
>
> Toward the end of the month, as residents start to run out of money, the atmosphere in the home turns even worse, workers and residents said. Used condoms can be found in the stairwells and hallways, as both male and female residents trade sex for spending money, drugs or cigarettes.[28]

By April 2002, Levy had compiled formidable evidence from records, statistics and individual case studies that adult home operators and some health care providers were neglecting and exploiting residents and that the state's regulatory enforcement effort was virtually nonexistent. After taking his findings to home operators and state regulators, he found his case was unassailable and his story was solid.

Solid Case Key to Power Writing

Although the case studies were heart-wrenching, to Levy, the death statistics and the state's knowledge of the problems and its inexplicable inaction were "stunning." When he finally wrote his story, three paragraphs near the top of the story captured the flavor of the mounds of statistics he compiled, the 5,000 pages of documentation he read, the 200 interviews he conducted and analysis he applied:

> But if the *Times* investigation found that the state's own files over the years have chronicled a stunning array of disorder and abuse at many of the homes, it discovered that the state had not kept track of what could be the greatest indicator of how broken the homes are: how many residents are dying, under what circumstances and at what ages. . . .
>
> The analysis shows that some residents died roasting in their rooms during heat waves. Others threw themselves from rooftops, making up some of at least 14 suicides in that seven-year period. Still more, lacking the most basic care, succumbed to routinely treatable ailments, from burst appendixes to seizures . . .
>
> In the end, whether the residents were in their 20s or 70s, it is impossible to know just how many of their deaths could have been prevented. The only

other accounting of the dead seems to be on Hart Island in the East River, where scores of adult home residents are buried in the mass graves of potter's field.[29]

The words are blunt, authoritative and powerful, and Levy boldly wrote them totally on the authority of his own work. Levy's personal outrage seeps through in the three passages, particularly in the last sentence of the final excerpt. Nevertheless, the conclusions preceding that line stand on a solid factual foundation as the readers will find as they plow through the next 18,000 words.

Confronting the Targets

The authority invested in that passage derives not only from the facts Levy gathered, but the test to which he submitted them when he presented his conclusions to the authorities and adult home operators being held to account. Levy wanted as complete and thorough responses as he could get, so his practice was to "lay it all out on the table—everything" to whomever was the subject of a particular finding. Sometimes, he would e-mail his findings. "My previous method was always to go in and question them in the form of an interview," he said. "I am now talking about laying it all out in a memo." Levy did not want to risk watching his yearlong effort wasted through a distracting postpublication correction, a long editor's note or debate over the fairness of his reporting. "I want to get as many responses as I can to our findings, because the worst thing in the world is when someone says you sandbagged me . . . , that we had no idea you were going to write that and not give us a chance to respond."

His top priority was the fact that New York State had not been keeping track of the hundreds of deaths at homes it had licensed and was supposed to regulate. He had put in a request for the department's death reports at adult homes. Although his investigation had documented close to 1,000 deaths in the previous five years, the state had only three death reports. Neither the governor, George Pataki, nor his top health officials would explain their failure to carry out the law, instead dispatching a deputy health commissioner in their place to respond. In mid-March 2002, the deputy promised to issue a regulation ordering strict enforcement of the law. Seven weeks later, Levy called him on his promise. The department still had not acted.[30]

That was not the only instance where Levy's questioning during the course of his reporting may have prompted action, or at least promises of action. He said the state Department of Health didn't learn of bogus eye surgeries on residents at Leben Home for Adults until Levy asked about them. The department promised to investigate. When he asked what the state had been doing to safeguard residents from exploitation, it could only point to a crackdown on part-time medical clinics, Levy said. He reported that the federal Centers for Medicare and Medicaid Services, which paid for the eye surgeries and other questionable health care costs, could not point to any efforts to investigate. The eye surgeon and home operator would not talk to Levy.[31]

Levy received similar reaction to his findings at Seaport Manor, where Randolph Maddix died. The state Department of Health began cracking down only after Levy began requesting government records and questioning officials. State officials said they had been reluctant to act before because closing the home would be too disruptive to patients. As with the Leben Home operators, Seaport's also declined to comment.[32]

When Reporters, Targets Cross Swords

Refusals to comment were common among home operators, but some did, and they disputed Levy's findings. In such cases, Levy attempted to provide enough evidence to give readers more than a point–counterpoint exchange of opinions. In one case, for example, Levy's investigation into the death of Ann Marie Thomas, a resident at Elm-York near La Guardia Airport. She died from heart failure, and his probe turned up evidence from numerous residents, former workers, and her sister and a report from an ambulance operator. The upshot was this: She had repeatedly complained about chest pains, and others tried alerting employees about her discomfort, but no one, including one doctor, treated her. "I think I'm having a heart attack and they don't believe me," she said in a phone call to her sister, Josephine, who tried fruitlessly to persuade the home's employees that she was in trouble.

When Levy confronted the operator, he denied that the home neglected her, but he refused to show records that it had been monitoring her.[33] "I did a lot of reporting on her death, and felt I had shown she had died out of neglect," Levy said. "They thought she was just hysterical." A state watchdog agency investigated and supported the operator, but Levy reported in the story it had not interviewed the sister or read the ambulance report that noted that her roommate told them she had tried to get help for Thomas.

Levy also asked the operator to explain a high number of deaths of people who resided at his home—110 in the last five years. The operator said he had only 10, and argued the others must have died elsewhere, but Levy reported that he refused to identify which ones.

At Park Manor, operators also denied any wrongdoing when Levy presented his findings from an investigation into the murder of Gregory Ridges, a lovable 35-year-old, once plagued by paranoia but gradually getting better. He was one of the few capable of holding down a job. He called his mother every morning to say he was going to work and every afternoon to say he had returned. With a bright sense of humor, he was a favorite among residents and workers, except for one person, his roommate, Erik Chapman, a man fascinated with knives. Levy summarized what happened this way:

> Sometimes at these homes, the greatest threat can be the person who sleeps in the next bed. Despite a history of violent behavior, Erik Chapman was accepted at Park Manor in Brooklyn.
> After four years of roaming the place with a knife, Mr. Chapman stabbed his roommate, Gregory Ridges, more than 20 times. At last, Mr. Chapman was sent to a secure psychiatric facility. Mr. Ridges was sent to Cypress Hills Cemetery at the age of 35 . . .[34]

In investigating this incident, Levy gathered the evidence and went to the operator of the home and to state officials. Introducing the response, Levy wrote:

"For now, there are only denials." It was language that clearly suggested that Levy was expressing an opinion, critics might allege.

Nevertheless, Levy would quickly establish that it was not bias, but a conclusion firmly established by facts. Even the seemingly editorial word "only" accurately depicted the relationship between their response and Levy's reporting. The response consisted of this: The operator told Levy that Chapman had no history of violence; the state Office of Mental Health said its investigation backed the operator's statement, but refused to release its report so readers could see how it reached its conclusion. In contrast, Levy laid out everything he found in his investigation to the readers and then displayed many of his documents on the website so readers could see for themselves. His evidence showed that Chapman's family feared him. Before he was accepted into Park Manor, Chapman had already stabbed his sister and stepfather, beat up a brother and put his father-in-law in the hospital for weeks after attacking him. He had been in and out of mental health facilities and psychiatrists' offices since the early 1990s. His violent behavior was well documented in official inspection reports and treatment records, which were some of the documents posted. The reports detailed Chapman's bizarre and paranoid delusions, his hostility toward Ridges, his desire to hurt those he perceived as his persecutors. "Patient remains very guarded and evasive," one psychiatrist at Kings County Hospital in Brooklyn wrote in a progress report. "This together with history of violent assaultiveness suggest he is a risk and dangerous to others. He should remain here." Moreover, Ridges complained repeatedly about Chapman, but the home did not move him or take action.[35]

Writing: Turning "Chaos Into Order"

By the time Levy had finished laying all of his evidence out to officials and home operators, he had accumulated what he described as a mass of material, and it somehow had to be converted into an organized, manageable series of stories. Readers, and probably journalists who have never been involved in a long-term project, do not know how much effort goes into the writing or the crucial role that editors must play at this stage of a project. "You end up with this mass of material, and it is hard to see what you have, because you were so inside of it all. All of that detail will make the story shine, but sometimes you can't see the larger picture because of it. You have to trust your editors . . . . Transforming it into a powerful piece of work is very hard, like transforming chaos into order," he said.

The transformation actually had started long before. For many project reporters, the writing starts at various stages. Some write daily by putting chunks of information into draft story form to help them analyze their material, to recognize unanswered questions or to alert them to emerging patterns. Sometimes, they can complete the reporting on sidebar stories and write first drafts early. Levy says he finds himself writing and reporting simultaneously after he thinks he is about halfway through the reporting. He may spend about one-quarter of his time drafting material, gradually increasing the proportion of time devoted to writing. Defining a cutoff point on the writing phase is impossible. The reporting—whether it is for tying up loose ends, making final efforts to get a response from a source or making another round of fact checks—continues. Editors often tinker with sentences and paragraphs until the last minute.

For Levy and his line editor, Christine Kay, the process started during the reporting when they met weekly to analyze his material. As the reporting drew near its conclusion, they began sketching outlines. The first of three days would cover the gamut of the death and misery Levy found in the homes. Day two would focus on patients at Seaport Manor, where problems in varying degrees appeared in inspection reports at other hospitals. The final day would show how the operators and health care providers, including doctors, exploited the residents with questionable surgeries and other medical procedures.

The first-day story is almost always the most comprehensive, and Levy's would eventually get in the paper at 7,500 words. His first draft was nearly twice that amount—more than 13,000 words, a count that was approaching the total for the entire three days. "You throw everything in there and then it becomes a process of tightening and tightening and reworking and reworking," he said, adding that after a year of reporting he could have written six times that amount. "It could have been a book," he said.

Initially, Kay looked at the first draft and made organizational suggestions. On later drafts, she focused on line and structural editing. She edited his editing and then he edited her editing, "and it would go back and forth." Sometimes, individual sections would go through that process. Eventually, a draft would go to Sexton. "He did the big thinking, and not so much of the line editing," Levy said. "The three of us rewrote the top of all three stories repeatedly—dozens of times." By the time they finished their work, the editors had cut day one by more than 40 percent, down to 7,500 words. The second- and third-day stories were down to 6,500 words each. Once Levy, Kay and Sexton were satisfied, the project went to the metro editor and then "up the masthead," Levy said, referring to top editors, including then-executive editor Howell Raines.

"It's a grueling and intense process," Levy said, and often, an emotionally painful one. Good material—such as information that reporters spent days searching for, quotation jewels, sentences that reporters spent hours crafting—get slashed. Levy says "It's a sign of good reporting if a lot of good stuff doesn't get in," which means that theoretically, even better "stuff" stays in the story. However, under the pressure of editing, showing such equanimity can be difficult, as Levy was about to find out.

Day one presented an overall picture of death and horror. It started on page 1 and filled four more pages inside. Day two on Seaport Manor and day three on the exploitation of residents by the home operators and health care providers were to start on the front page and fill up two full inside pages plus some spillover on a third page.

Out of the blue, however, after countless rewrites and just before publication, the top editors ordered more cuts to days two and three—10 percent on each story. "I was annoyed, really annoyed by that," Levy recalled. "Sexton told me the edict had come from on high. . . . It wasn't so much the amount of the cut, but more that it came so late," Levy said. In a well-written, cohesive story, everything is linked: sentence to sentence, paragraph to paragraph and section to section. "We were all exhausted at that point. The story had been so carefully edited, polished and fine-tuned, and then the order to cut it more came down." With that much crafting, cutting a hunk of copy is not easy and sometimes requires some difficult rewriting. But Levy was in no mood to fight. "If that is what it takes to get in the paper, it's like 'just do it.'"

Levy's reaction was heat-of-the moment grousing. The explanation for the cuts was that by the time readers reached the second and third day of the series, they would have a thorough understanding of the themes of the entire project, thus allowing the writing to focus more tightly on the new material. Later, Levy said he realized that the decision came so late simply because the top editors had been unable to get to it before then. And he found himself agreeing with the cuts. "It was sort of not being able to see the right perspective at the time. The story was powerful as is, and it did not need a lot of extra stuff," he said. Investigative reporters often risk testing the readers' patience by running stories that are too long. "When I spend a year on a project, I want it to run forever. An editor once told me 'Don't solve your problems at the expense of the reader.'"

Postscript

The series, headlined "Broken Homes," ran from April 28 to April 30, 2002, and spread from page one openings each day across a total of eight inside pages over the three days with text, photographs and charts. The website posted many of the state inspection reports, interviews and other material from Levy's investigation. The reader reaction was enormous, Levy said. No other story of his before or after the series prompted such a response. He continued writing about adult homes, and in April 2003, Levy won the 2003 Pulitzer Prize in the investigative category. The judges described it as a "vivid, brilliantly written series . . . that exposed the abuse of mentally ill adults in state-regulated homes."

The government response to the series was immediate. Federal prosecutors launched investigations; the administration of Republican Gov. George Pataki announced reforms; Democratic politicians challenging his re-election blamed him for the adult home tragedies. Although many of the proposed changes eventually faltered, a variety of promises and actions poured forth. Pataki vowed to revamp and eventually do away with the entire system, spend $8 million immediately on short-term improvements and spend another $65 million for longer range improvements for housing services, including the construction of 2,000 housing units immediately and thousands more later.[36] He promised to boost oversight, investigate deaths and hire nurses to administer medications and stop Medicaid abuses.[37]

Some officials did more than make promises. Federal authorities imprisoned the eye doctor who did questionable eye surgeries on adult home residents,[38] indicted the operators of Ocean House in Queens on fraud charges,[39] and subpoenaed records from nearly two dozen homes as part of a wide-ranging investigation. State officials removed the operators of Ocean House[40] and closed Seaport Manor in 2003, eventually barring its operators permanently from running homes for the mentally ill.[41] The Department of Health finally issued the long-promised regulation to force homes to start obeying the 1994 law to report to the state. The administration increased fines for violating state regulations, created a new office to investigate abuses at the homes and deployed state inspectors to make sure the homes install air conditioners and take other measures to prevent residents from suffering heat-related illnesses.[42]

The promises and initial actions seemed exciting, and some changes for the good came out of it, Levy said. "But there hasn't been the dramatic striking change that a lot of people hoped for." As for Pataki's $80 million budget proposal for doing away with the adult home system and replacing it with something better? "That has been much more incremental than expected. We still have the adult care system."

Before 2002 came to a close, more bad news competed with the promises of reform. Levy wrote in June that state officials moving to close Seaport Manor were moving its residents to a home with a record equally bad.[43] In another investigative piece in October, Levy reported that the Pataki administration had been taking patients out of state psychiatric hospitals and locking them up in unregulated and isolated special units in nursing homes.[44] He also discovered that the administration was exporting hundreds of other psychiatric patients to out-of-state adult homes and nursing homes that had no credentials for caring for the mentally ill. When Levy confronted authorities with this finding, they attempted to remove the sting of the story by saying they had brought most of them back. Levy, as he did in confronting other officials with his findings during the investigation, asked for proof of their claim and then reported either their inability or unwillingness to provide it.[45]

Many of the ambitious promises for reform faltered. The New York legislature rejected Pataki's plan to spend $8 million for immediate reforms that would have brought $7 million in federal matching funds and deployed nurses and social workers throughout the system to protect residents. Instead the legislature bowed to the adult home lobby and allotted most of the money to a bonus program for homes that earn good state inspection reports.[46] Efforts to pass new laws that would intensify oversight and clamp down on enforcements had bogged down in the state legislature by mid-2003.[47]

Legal advocates for the mentally ill, complaining that that little progress was being made and the legislature had lost interest in making sweeping changes, filed suit in federal court to try to force reform.[48] In early 2004, Levy reported that an invigorated enforcement effort fell apart in 2004 after two court rulings said inspectors had violated their own regulations and state law, forcing them to abandon 70 cases that had imposed fines as high as $55,000 against some homes for breaking heath and safety regulations.[49] In the meantime, reports of neglect and abuse in individual homes continued to filter out. Routine inspections at Brooklyn Manor in June 2002 found that decrepit conditions discovered a year earlier still remained.[50] In the summer of 2004, Levy discovered that the Pataki administration hired an adult home operator with a checkered past to take over a Queens home where two previous operators had embezzled funds.[51]

By then, the *Times*, in the previous two years, had written more stories about adult homes than it had in the previous decade, but coverage afterward practically disappeared although the problem it chronicled remained. In May 2005, a brief flurry erupted when a fire broke out at Brooklyn Manor, one of the most notorious homes, killing one man. One follow-up a week later reported that Brooklyn Manor had now accumulated enough violations to fill a 200-page state report, yet state officials bemoaned that after all the promises they still did not have enough power to close such homes. Echoing a response heard back in the 1980s, the state said that even if it could, it didn't know where to put the residents.[52]

To what extent the state kept its promise to build thousands of new community homes for the mentally ill as promised four years earlier remains unclear. But by the summer of 2007, adult homes for the mentally ill were rarely mentioned in the *Times*. They apparently had fallen off the public agenda.

Lessons

BEAT REPORTERS AND INVESTIGATIVE MENTALITY

Lesson Learned: Beat reporters must develop an investigative mentality that makes them public watchdogs who remain alert to possible investigative project ideas during their routine coverage of their areas of responsibility.

How It Applied: Literally, that is not how "Broken Homes" originated. An editor saw a news release about a suit that a legal advocacy group had filed, recognized it as a possible project and assigned an investigative reporter to check it out. But that is a hit-or-miss practice. As Sexton said, this one came in with tree planting announcements and all of the other news releases that flood a typical newsroom. Technically, the "Broken Homes" project idea fell on several beats, including at least four traditional beats: the courts, state government, the health beat or the cops, not to mention the beat of the people assigned to cover Queens. An alert and diligent court reporter could have picked up project ideas like this while routinely checking the daily civil suit filings, which is a common activity among many court reporters. Some often do it twice a day. A state government reporter could have picked up the story idea by keeping in contact with regulatory agencies that inspect facilities that have the most impact on citizens, such as restaurants, amusement parks, nursing homes, assisted-care homes for the elderly and disabled and adult homes for the mentally ill. Health reporters could pick it up by routinely checking in with advocacy groups that represent various health constituencies, particularly the mentally ill, and routinely checking health inspectors' periodic reports on health care facilities, including adult homes for the elderly. In these homes, people were murdered and drugs were sold, both activities that involved the police.

PROJECT OF NEWS ELITE HAS SMALL-TOWN FLAVOR

Lesson Learned: Although this was a project by *The New York Times*, the most respected, most well-known news organization in the world, "Broken Homes" was, in a figurative sense, a small-town newspaper project.

How It Applied: "Broken Homes" started with a civil suit, a routine event that occurs every day in every court system in the land. The basic paper trail consisted of inspection reports, which are accessible to any reporter or citizen, and court records. That is enough to get any reporter out and about on this assignment, where you can do as Levy did—learn more about other records and other sources. For example, Levy made use of a less well-known record on the paper trail—Social Security death data. But he did not know that source of information existed before he began this project. He learned about it while working the story. His discovery of that source had nothing to do with the power and resources of *The New York Times* or the special expertise of a reporter that only the *Times* could afford to hire.

In summary, Levy started this project with no knowledge of the subject and no list of records that he knew he could get. He—a self-described lone wolf—had no research assistants to do his bidding. He did everything himself. He started from scratch and learned what records were available. Any newspaper, including weeklies, could and should do these types of projects in their hometowns. These stories do not require the resources or the cachet of *The New York Times*. All they require is an investigative mentality. As Levy worked the project and met sources, victims and their families, he learned about other records, and through them, gained access to records that are not public, including highly personal psychiatric reports and medical records. Clifford J. Levy—the individual, not *The New York Times*—accomplished that.

However, the fact that huge papers like the *Times* and the *Los Angeles Times* do have the resources to hire talent like Cliff Levy who can pull off projects like "Broken Homes" provides any newspaper reporter at any size newspaper the opportunity to study the work they do and analyze how it can be done at their level. Many of these reporters frequently write short "how we did it" articles in publications like the *IRE Journal* that are helpful.

Although resources frequently do allow such big-city reporters professional luxuries that small-town reporters do not enjoy, they still employ essentially the same reporting basics available to anyone. "Anyone who says they cannot do this [type of work] is full of it," Levy said. The skills are the same that daily reporters have. "There is not that much of a gulf," he said. When resources are clearly a factor in the story, small newspapers can make adjustments, such as narrowing the scope of the project or tackling manageable pieces one segment at a time. Levy suggested that a smaller "Broken Homes" project is feasible in any town or county at most any newspaper, by simply reducing the period of study from the five years that his covered to whatever time period the papers believe is feasible under the circumstances and resources it can employ.

NOBLE MISSION YIELDS PRACTICAL RESULTS

Lesson Learned: Covering people and problems that do not get on the public agenda yields important and compelling stories while fulfilling the press's fundamental mission to give voice to the voiceless.

How It Applied: The problems in adult care homes for the mentally ill lurked in the corners and never got on the public agenda until 2001.

Such corners, hidden from view and spared from daily scrutiny, allow problems to fester and spread and grow increasingly complicated, until they finally catch the attention of the press.

Levy's depiction of the history of the coverage describes an age-old fact of life in covering the news: The loudest voices get the most coverage. The homeless population that Levy alluded to was penniless and sick and deserving attention. But, as he pointed out, they were not voiceless, because they were "in everybody's face," which guaranteed them a place on the public agenda. Those in adult homes, however, were herded into places that hid decrepit conditions that were not in everybody's faces; yet a basic journalistic mission that should be emphasized in every journalism education program is that the press' solemn duty is to give voice to the voiceless.

Aside from the nobility of such a mission, its pursuit also yields a very practical value for workaday journalists and, more to the point, for the readers. The adult home story offers a good example. The voiceless in those broken homes had incredibly compelling, albeit tragic, stories to tell. Levy's comment that he does not like to get involved in stories that everybody else is already working on is a common trait among good reporters and a good way of saying that the best stories are those not on everybody else's agenda. Good reporters do not join the pack.

Although reporters and editors feel tremendous pressure to give priority to covering the news that is already on the agenda, it is equally important to find the news that has not reached that point. As Levy and Sexton demonstrated in recognizing a good story when they saw it, news is news, regardless of whether it is on the public agenda. They latched on to an idea that a rival newspaper treated as a brief for the back pages and ran with it in pursuit of a good story and one of the noblest mission of journalism.

STORIES MISSED, PROBLEMS FESTER, SOLUTIONS FAIL

Lesson Learned: By failing to cover routine government operations such as regulatory inspections of institutions that purport to serve society, egregious misconduct festers until it becomes too complicated and entrenched to be corrected.

How It Applied: State government had been inspecting the adult homes for mentally ill people for years and had been writing reports about the tragic conditions they found. But few people read those reports, although they were public records. With little public scrutiny from the press, state government did nothing about the problems. When the *New York Times* learned about the conditions at adult homes for the mentally retarded, it launched an expensive, time-consuming and expertly done investigation to fully expose the problem. By all accounts, it was a tremendously successful project. The resulting package sparked expressions of outrage and promises of reform from politicians. However, the problems were so deep-seated and woven into the culture and customs of the bureaucracy, lasting reform was almost impossible without a long-term, concentrated focus. But the press moves on to other stories, and the politicians seek other offices, while the bureaucracy stays behind, as do the problems that prompted the investigation two years earlier.

Ironically, "Broken Homes" also reveals something about secrecy in government, even though the government's inspections were shining stadium lights on the problems at adult homes. Journalists often think of investigative reporting as revealing stories that public institutions are trying to hide, but Levy was investigating a problem that was not hidden. Because no one noticed the problem, corruption and negligence and laxity festered, and people died. The story of the *Times'* coverage of adult homes and the postscript to Levy's story illustrates that lack of public scrutiny, whether it is the product of a premeditated government cover-up or the failure of the press to do its job, produces tragic consequences that are not easy to rectify or to prevent from reoccurring. The government does a tremendous amount of work, particularly with its regulatory functions, that is public, yet unexamined. Its inspection reports should be as much a routine part of beat coverage as the thrice-daily cop-shop checks and as the routine publication of real estate transfers or birth and marriage announcements that small-town newspapers love so much. They are certainly much more constructive and beneficial to society, and they can make daily news reporting a regular exercise in watchdog journalism.

IF YOU SET THE AGENDA, COVER IT

Lesson Learned: Once a newspaper invests in a major investigative project, it is essentially putting the issue it investigated on the public agenda. That should give the paper an obligation to continue covering that issue until the problem is corrected and remains corrected.

How It Applied: The *Times* stayed with the problem that "Broken Homes" put on the public agenda longer than many news organizations do when they break a major story. The coverage tapered off considerably after the first year, even though it ran just enough breaking stories to show that the problems had not been solved.

HEED LARRY THE CABLE GUY: "GIT-R-DONE!"

Lesson Learned: Complex projects demand the full-time focus of a reporter and enough uninterrupted time to become educated about the topic (which is to develop expertise), track down sources and develop them, file public records requests and find confirmation sources. But whining about lack of ample time and resources does not relieve a news organization of its fundamental journalistic responsibility to do investigative reporting. That's our problem, not the public's.

How It Applied: Levy repeatedly pointed out examples of time-consuming efforts and mentioned how "the luxury of time" benefited the project. Unfortunately, fewer and fewer news organizations are willing to give their reporters that luxury. Editors and reporters, however, must find ways to make adjustments that will allow them to fulfill their investigative responsibilities.

Editors can alter their news judgments on what the news organization needs to cover so that they can give their reporter time and the opportunity to focus. They also can delay or simply forego nonessential, quick-hit, reader-friendly features so they can free other reporters to substitute for journalists assigned to a project. And finally, they can negotiate with a project reporter to spend at least one day per week in the daily mix.

For the reporters' part, they can search for ways to compromise with the editors, who still have "to feed the beast" as they call the daily news hole. For example, reporters can volunteer to pull off the project for an afternoon or a day whenever possible to do a daily story. Moreover, reporters frequently can work a project on an as-time-permits basis in the early phases of the project when they are waiting for public records requests or are doing desk research to learn about their topic. Finally, in a process sometimes called the "swiss cheese approach," reporters can nibble away at a project in small bites until they reach a certain point in the reporting when they can make an argument for devoting themselves full time for the remainder of the effort.

For both editors and reporters, creative thinking and planning sometimes reveal ways to report and write the project in a series of short-term stories. The same kind of creativity can reveal ways to divide the project into separate parts, with each assigned to one or more additional reporters.

BE BOLD, BUT CAREFUL

Lesson Learned: Investigative reporting requires bold editors and reporters, who cannot shrink from bluntly and authoritatively reporting conclusions that their facts support; it also requires great care and judgment to confine the conclusions to whatever the facts allow.

How It Applied: Publishing a front-page story that runs close to 20,000 words and accuses people of fatal greed, negligence or incompetence and the state government of turning a blind eye to such deeds takes courage. It gives even the cockiest reporters pause. In Levy's story, every conclusion was thoroughly documented either with official records or on-the-record sources whose information was confirmed by multiple additional sources and then submitted to challenge by the people and authorities that are their targets. Levy's editor, Joe Sexton, when asked what he expects of his investigative reporters, said, "I expect them to be honest. I am talking not just about day-to-day honesty about what you are finding, but total honesty with the material. You cannot force what is not there no matter how much time you have invested. But you also have to have the courage to say that what you thought was there was in fact really there."

RECLAIMING OBJECTIVITY

Lesson Learned: The ability to write confidently and bluntly with clearly articulated conclusions that serve the public derives from objective reporting that requires journalists to challenge and test the assertions of public officials as well as their own bias, findings and conclusions.

How It Applied: Levy could write with such power because he did the reporting as objectively as possible, a methodology taken as an article of commonsense journalism among professionals. Levy started to work on "Broken Homes" with a suspicion that the conditions he and Sarah Kershaw found at Leben Home in the spring of 2001 might be symptomatic of problems throughout the adult home system. In one part of his investigation, Levy checked out a lead that an adult home operator brought a new resident into a home filled with vulnerable people even though the resident had a long record of violent behavior. Afterward, the resident supposedly murdered his roommate. If that sequence of events proved to be true, it would make a terrific, albeit tragic, story.

In such situations, a reporter naturally hopes that the facts prove that the lead is true. Levy, however, would have been irresponsible and foolish not to recognize the big-story bias and subjected the theory to the most rigorous investigation and self-questioning before publishing it. He gathered a tremendous amount of documentation that established the resident's violent history.

However, when he asked the home operator about the case, he denied that the patient had a violent history. Moreover, state officials said their investigation supported the home operator's statement, but they would not release their investigative report. Just as Levy would have been irresponsible in publishing the story without a rigorous investigation, he would be equally irresponsible and unfair to his readers if he had backed down or failed to present his finding in a forceful and commanding manner that left no doubt in the readers' minds that his conclusions were correct and the assertions of the state and the home operator were incorrect. He did that in three ways: laying out the facts in great detail and posting his documentation on the website; reporting that the state refused to release its investigation; and transitioning to the official response this way: "For now, there are only denials." Although some critics may argue that statement reflects a bias, Levy had a higher duty not to let the official fuzz up the truth and to report that they apparently had not learned anything from this egregious situation. That six-word transition sentence accomplished all of that.

In a spot news situation, reporters usually do not have the facts necessary to challenge false statements of fact from officials with the power and authority that Levy could bring to bear. But they can demand, as Levy did in that situation and in others in the project, that the official prove his or her assertion and report the official's failure to do so. A diligent reporter in some cases that are especially significant to the public would follow up in the days ahead, giving the official more time to provide the proof, a scenario that eventually might warrant a follow-up story reporting that the official had earlier misled the public. In such a scenario, the journalist would be applying the demands of watchdog journalism on a daily basis.

Notes

1. The interviewees listed here are the sources for their direct and indirect quotes; reconstruction of interviews between themselves and their sources; and depictions of their conversations, thoughts and actions that are not referenced in the text:

Some material from these sources is individually referenced where necessary to ensure clarity.

Clifford Levy, New York City, June 6, 2006; August 25, 2006, by telephone. Joe Sexton, July 30, 2006, by telephone.

2. Interview, Clifford Levy, *New York Times*, June 6, 2006. Throughout this chapter, all direct and indirect quotes by Levy, depictions of his conversations with sources and editors, and thoughts and actions that are not referenced in the text originated from this interview and from a telephone conversation on August 25, 2006. Some material will be individually referenced to these interviews where necessary to ensure clarity.

3. Bill Sanderson, "Nursing Home Suit in Bogus Surgeries," *New York Post*, March 10, 2001, p. 4. The *Post* ran a 419-word follow-up the next day reporting a response from the doctor and a lawyer for Leben Home.

4. Interview, Joe Sexton, July 30, 2007.

5. "Memo from New York Times Editors," January 26, 2006, posted by Jim Romenesko to Poynter Forums on Poynteronline. http://poynter.org/forum/view.

6. "Talk to the Newsroom: Metropolitan Editor Joe Sexton," *New York Times*, April 2, 2001.

7. Interview, Sexton, July 30, 2007.

8. Clifford J. Levy and Sarah Kershaw. "Inquiry Finds Mentally Ill Patients Endured 'Assembly Line' Surgery," *New York Times*, March 18, 2001, p. 1.

9. Clifford J. Levy and Sarah Kershaw, "Broken Home/A Special Report: For Mentally Ill, Chaos in an Intended Refuge," *New York Times*, April 18, 2001, p. 1.

10. Ibid.

11. "Memo from New York Times Editors."

12. "Talk to the Newsroom: Metropolitan Editor Joe Sexton."

13. Interview, Sexton, July 20, 2007; Interview, Levy, June 6, 2006.

14. Interview, Sexton, July 20, 2007.

15. Clifford J. Levy, "New Attorney General Remakes Staff by Patronage," *New York Times*, November 10, 1995; Clifford J. Levy, "Lawyers Link Campaign Mail to Vacco's Wife," *New York Times*, November 10, 1995.

16. Clifford J. Levy and Christopher Drew. "In Albany, Ally of Insurer Profits from Them," *New York Times*, February 4, 2001, p. 1.

17. Edward A. Gargan, "As 'Psychiatric Ghettos,' Boarding Homes Get More Dangerous," *New York Times*, February 8, 1981.

18. Levy and Kershaw, "Broken Home."

19. Gargan, "As 'Psychiatric Ghettos.'"

20. Julie Johnson, "2 Committees Urge Congress to Stop Abuse at Adult Care Centers," *New York Times*, March 10, 1989.

21. Selwyn Raab, "Death Among the Disturbed: Were Police Inattentive," *New York Times*, May 24, 1990; Selwyn Raab, "Neglect Found in Residences for Disabled," *New York Times*, August 6, 1990.

22. Clifford J. Levy, "Broken Homes: A Final Destination; For Mentally Ill, Death and Misery" (part one of three-part series, "Broken Homes"), *New York Times*, April 28, 2002, p. 1.

23. Ibid.

24. Clifford J. Levy. "Broken Homes: Where Hope Dies; Here, Life Is Squalor and Chaos," *New York Times*, April 29, 2002, p. 1.

25. Ibid.

26. Levy, "Broken Homes: A Final Destination."

27. Ibid.

28. Levy, "Broken Homes: Where Hope Dies."

29. Levy, "Broken Homes: A Final Destination."

30. Ibid.

31. Clifford J. Levy, "Broken Homes: The Operators; Voiceless, Defenseless and a Source of Cash," *New York Times*, April 30, 2002, p. 1.

32. Levy, "Broken Homes: A Final Destination."

33. Ibid.

34. Ibid.

35. Ibid.

36. Clifford J. Levy, "Pataki Offers $80 Million Plan to Fix System for Mentally Ill," *New York Times*, January 30, 2003, p. 1.

37. Clifford J. Levy, "Tighter Rules for Housing Of Mentally Ill," *New York Times*, May 8, 2002, p. 1; Clifford J. Levy, "State to Survey Mentally Ill in Residences," *New York Times*, December 13, 2002, p. 1.

38. Clifford J. Levy, "Doctor Gets Prison for Fraud After Exploiting Mentally Ill," *New York Times*, September 4, 2003, p. 10.

39. Clifford J. Levy, "2 Accused of Looting Home for the Mentally Ill in Queens," *New York Times*, June 28, 2002, p. 1.

40. Clifford J. Levy, "New York State Fires Operators of 2 Homes for the Mentally Ill," *New York Times*, September 9, 2004, p. 1.

41. Russ Buettner, "Ex-Operators in Adult Homes Are Barred in Settlement," *New York Times*, December 29, 2006, p. 3.

42. Clifford J. Levy, "State to Check Heat Precautions Taken by Homes for Mentally Ill," *New York Times*, July 3, 2002, p. 5.

43. Clifford J. Levy, "Mentally Ill Go to Homes Seen as Little Better," *New York Times*, June 3, 2002, p. 1.

44. Clifford J. Levy, "Mentally Ill and Locked up in New York Nursing Homes," *New York Times*, October 6, 2002, p. 1.

45. Clifford J. Levy, "New York Exports Mentally Ill, Shifting Burden to Other States," *New York Times*, November 17, 2002, p. 1.

46. Clifford J. Levy, "Albany Spurns Plan to Rectify Adult Homes," *New York Times*, May 1, 2003, p. 1.

47. Clifford J. Levy, "As Clock Ticks, Albany Makes an Effort to Fix Homes," *New York Times*, June 1, 2003, p. 37.

48. Clifford J. Levy, "Suit Says State Is Segregating Mentally Ill," *New York Times*, July 1, 2003, p. 1.

49. Clifford J. Levy, "Crackdown Falters as 2 Rulings Favor State's Adult Homes," *New York Times*, January 14, 2004, p. 1.

50. Clifford J. Levy, "Despite Inspections by State, Violations at Home Continued," *New York Times*, September 15, 2002, p. 35.

51. Clifford J. Levy, "At Troubled Home, a Troubled Boss," *New York Times*, August 22, 2004, p. 1.

52. "Stuck in a Bad Place; With Few Options, State Lets Troubled Home Stay Open," *New York Times*, May 15, 2005, p. 37.

Selected Bibliography

Articles
Levy, Clifford J. "A Final Destination; For Mentally Ill, Death and Misery" (part one of three-part series, "Broken Homes"). *New York Times*, April 28–30, 2002.
Levy, Clifford J., and Sarah Kershaw. "Broken Home/A Special Report: For Mentally Ill, Chaos in an Intended Refuge." *New York Times*, April 18, 2001.

Interviews
Levy, Clifford, reporter, *The New York Times*, June 6, 2006 (tape recording held by author).
Sexton, Joe, former deputy metro editor, *The New York Times*, July 30, 2007.

News Archives and News Search Services
Access World News, NewsBank, Inc. Naples, FL.
The New York Times electronic archives.

Website
The Pulitzer Prize website, http://www.pulitzer.org.

CHAPTER 6

Daily Coverage Key to Hospital Horrors

Taking On Symbol of Racial Pride[1]

Martin Luther King/Drew Medical Center south of Watts was the proverbial sacred cow in Los Angeles in the summer of 2003.

Filled with immense significance in the city's racial history, it symbolized a hard-fought black victory against white oppression. The idea for King/Drew arose from the fire and anger of the 1965 Watts riots, and its advocates had to beat back white resistance before it finally opened in the early 1970s.[2] One of the wrongs King/Drew righted was a health care system that had forced many black residents to travel long distances to find a hospital that would serve their race.

As the pride of blacks for more than three decades, it was run almost entirely by black administrators and doctors, who had cemented deep relationships with community leaders. To criticize the hospital was seen as effrontery to the black community and anyone daring to do so risked being branded as a racist.[3]

That was the racial and political reality that summer when *Los Angeles Times* reporters Tracy Weber and Charles Ornstein began investigating the entire county-owned hospital system, and their probe took a turn they had not expected. The records they had been reading turned up enough horrendous medical mistakes at King/Drew that they realized their investigation should focus on it alone: nurses had been silencing or ignoring monitors and letting patients die; doctors were puncturing vital parts of the body; a pathologist erroneously told a patient she had cancer, because lab slides got mixed up. Committing a series of compounding mistakes, doctors and nurses killed a frightened little girl who went to the emergency room with a few scratches and some broken teeth from a minor traffic accident.

Although all of that may be shocking to newcomers, it had the whiff of stale news in Los Angeles, particularly when it is about King/Drew Medical Center. Ornstein and Weber understood that people had a general idea that King/Drew was and had been a patient-care disaster for decades; they had read the clips. People in its own community had been calling it "Killer King" since 1975, just three years after it opened. The *Los Angeles Times* had written about many of the incidents that gave birth to that cruel pseudonym. It had even done an impressive investigative project in 1989. So why do another? What about one of the other county-owned hospitals? Lord knows, County-University Southern California Medical Center had its share of problems, which are not as well-known as King/Drew's. Besides, it is the flagship of the county-owned hospital system and the largest in the system. It certainly could use some thorough, investigative scrutiny as well.

To Weber and Ornstein, though, what they had been reading in the inspection reports, inspectors' notes and court records trumped all of those considerations. King/Drew hospital—at that moment, even as they worked—was failing disastrously. So this was news again. It did not matter that it was the same story with new victims. People were dying. Beyond the immediate need for such a project, intriguing broader questions emerged: How could all of those cases of malpractice continue to happen despite the previous press attention, the state investigations and the promises to fix things? Why were they allowed to continue? Would another news package stringing together the latest medical horror stories change anything? Would it be too late? Had the problems and culture of negligence become so entrenched that nothing could save this revered symbol of hope and pride?

Setting the Goal: Finding Something Different

Investigative journalists are at their best exposing problems and laying out the consequences of those problems. The best can do that in precisely accurate, yet heart-wrenching, detail. Investigative journalism operates from the notion that society cannot make something better until its people know what is wrong. Ideally, the genius of the democratic system will work its magic; the public will demand corrective action by their elected officials, who, desiring re-election, will do the public's bidding, and things will get better. If they don't, the public will find new elected officials. Perhaps only the naively optimistic believe the free press and the other institutions of a democracy work with such civics-book efficiency.

Most journalists know better, however; they have run into too many stories like King/Drew. With King/Drew, the press *had* laid out the problems and consequences. The public *had* reacted. The elected officials *had* launched investigations and fired people and promised reform.[4] In short, the system, with its free-press component, had worked. Yet, after three decades, King/Drew was still "Killer King." This time the *Los Angeles Times* needed to do something more and something different.

For one thing, it had to advance the story. As in any project, the reporting itself would require diligent and thorough records work and sensitive interviewing. King/Drew was a public hospital run by elected officials, and their records were open and much of the records trail had been blazed before. But this time, Weber and Ornstein would have to find a new approach. Perhaps they could find a different trail of records and statistics, one that would help them investigate the conventional explanations of the past. Although the human toil at King/Drew was heartbreaking and needed to be laid out again as powerfully

and graphically as possible, they sensed that the political and racial considerations were a major part of the story, something no one had faced up to in the
past. Finally, somebody needed to be called to account, not for just another series
of medical misadventures and not for the failings of another administrator, but
for the entire, long-running mess.[5]

Partnership Joins Beat, Investigative Mentalities

To do this project, the *Times* would eventually assign two more reporters—
Steve Hymon and Mitchell Landsberg—and a photographer, Robert Gauthier.
A fifth reporter worked the project for a while but left about six months into
it. The paper's top editor, John Carroll, would bring his legendary hands-
on, line-by-line, word-for-word attention to the writing phase of the project.
Unlike many investigative projects, the writing would become as demanding
as the reporting.

Tracy Weber and Charles Ornstein made a good match to carry the lead roles
in the reporting. The 45-year-old Weber, who holds a master's degree in journalism from the University of California at Berkeley, had always gravitated toward
hard news and investigative work. "I couldn't do features," she said. "Every time
they would send me out do one, I would always find something bad to write
about. I even turned the religion beat into a crime beat," she said, laughing.

Ornstein says Weber has an uncanny knack for getting people to open up to
her. Part of the explanation is an ability to make people feel that she genuinely
wants to understand their situation. Indeed, Weber bemoans a seemingly uncaring attitude among many journalists that drives them to milk the victims in the
stories dry then forget about them. In some cases, Weber keeps track of key
sources after the project. You have to maintain your journalistic distance, she
says, but that does not require you to throw out your humanity.

Weber came to the *Los Angeles Times* in 1994 from the *Orange County Register*, where she was a senior projects reporter and wrote about religion and legal
affairs. At the *Times*, she worked for several years at the paper's huge Orange
County Bureau, an operation that was then as big as many midsized to large
metropolitan newspapers. There she met and worked with Julie Marquis, who
would later become the line editor on the King/Drew project.

Weber caught the attention of her peers and editors at the *Times* with several
investigative projects, including a long series of stories with another reporter
on parents' lavish expenditures in youth sports and another project on smuggling illegal prescription drugs from Mexico. She left the paper for a while in the
early 2000s and returned to the *Times* in 2003. She asked to work with Marquis
again and to write about public health issues, a request that was granted, which
brought her into the partnership with Ornstein.

Ornstein had been covering public health for a while. He knew the records
trail and had built up sources. Moreover, he was the numbers man on the King/
Drew story. From the earliest moments of the project, he worked to give the story
a strong statistical foundation, and he used the advice of experts to ensure that
the stories used hospital data accurately. "I took a couple of statistics courses
when I was in college, and I have always been comfortable with numbers," he
said. "I enjoy them."

Ornstein, 34, carries the quintessential daily news reporting mentality. Throughout the project, he worried about "all the stories we were missing" and battled a nagging urge to pull off the project to cover other stories on the public health beat. "In the beginning, it did drive me crazy," he said. "For a while, I was trying to do both at once, but you just can't," Ornstein said.

He came to the *Times* in 2001 after a five-year stint at *The Dallas Morning News*, where he spent most of his time covering health care business. A bright, boyish-looking journalist, Ornstein's tirelessness and productivity make editors want to clone him. Although he describes his career track as beat reporting, Ornstein talks about a touch of cynicism in his makeup, and a longtime tendency to question "why things are the way they are." It is a tendency that goes back to his college days at the University of Pennsylvania, where he led the campus newspaper as executive editor, studied history and psychology, and graduated summa cum laude.

He says he is comfortable in adversarial situations with institutional officials and others, which frequently goes with the territory in investigative reporting. Nevertheless, he said he does not enjoy that part of the reporting. "You are dealing with people's careers, livelihoods and reputations. It is not enjoyable to watch people stumble and lose their jobs. That is serious stuff. They have families and futures."

But in interviews, Ornstein is—in Weber's words—"unflinching" when questioning people. "Charlie will understand something way better than the people he is interviewing," she said, and will quickly challenge them if they proffer erroneous information. Ornstein agrees with that analysis, but says he is not trying to embarrass anyone in such interviews, or to sound as if he is trying to "catch them in something." But he said he does prepare thoroughly and when someone lies, he tells them: "I just say 'I don't think that's accurate' or 'that's not what the data show.'"

Julie Marquis, their line editor during the project, said Weber and Ornstein came into the project with their distinctive reputations and strengths, but to her, each of them also brought an overlapping quality that produced an effective partnership. Marquis, who was editor of health, immigration and growth demographics at the time, knows both reporters well. "Charlie had never really done 'investigative reporting,' but by temperament he is a wonderful investigative reporter. Tracy is an investigative reporter, but she is also a terrific beat reporter, in that she's great at building sources and getting people to talk, . . . and [like beat reporters] she kind of goes nuts if she is not in the paper."[6]

Moreover, each of them personified her concept of investigative reporting: every reporter is an investigative reporter. Marquis opposes the notion that investigative reporters should be "cordoned off" from the rest of the newsroom. To her, good beat reporters may focus on the who, what, when and where questions for the daily story, but, like Charles Ornstein, they have an insatiable curiosity that draws them back to that daily story in the days that follow to get to the bottom of the how and why.[7]

Early Evidence Points to King/Drew Focus

Shortly after Tracy Weber returned to the *Los Angeles Times* in April 2003, one of her first page-one stories with Ornstein carried the subheadline: "Sworn declarations allege instances when quicker care would have saved patients." A week later, they teamed up to write "Death Report Draws Probe," and then they immediately started working on a story published three days later under the headline "Hospital Problems Flagged by State."

Those stories were not about King/Drew Medical Center. They were about County-USC Medical Center, another hospital that is owned by the county government. In fact, it was troubles at County-USC that prompted Weber and Ornstein initially to look at the entire county-owned hospital system. A legal aid group had launched a suit against the county government to stop planned cutbacks at the hospitals, and some doctors had filed court papers alleging that emergency room patients were dying because of long waits and that care was substandard.[8]

The responsibility for ensuring that County-USC, King/Drew and the other government-owned hospitals operate as they should falls to the Los Angeles County Board of Supervisors. Those five men and women are elected officials, and they run the entire county. They are so powerful and politically entrenched that people often refer to them as the "five little kings." They exercise executive and legislative powers, and each represents sprawling domains that contain roughly equal portions of the county's 10.3 million people. They rarely face serious challenges to their re-election bids, and their tenures have ranged from 11 to 27 years. Yvonne B. Burke, a black woman who represents the district where King/Drew is, won her seat in 1992, after the retirement of her predecessor, Kenneth Hahn.[9] Hahn was a white man, who persuaded the state legislature to build King/Drew after Los Angeles County's mostly white voters rejected a bond referendum to pay for it.[10]

In the field of health care, the supervisors—being politicians—do not know much about running hospitals, so they delegate responsibility for administering the medical centers to the County Department of Health Services. When things go wrong at the hospitals, the health department director has to answer to the supervisors, who, in turn have to answer to the voters—theoretically.

In the summer of 2003, when Ornstein and Weber turned their attention to the county's hospital system, Weber drove down to the California Public Health Service's district office in Orange County and began digging through state inspection reports on the hospitals. Ornstein, while covering public health, had learned that the inspectors' notes are also public record, so Weber asked for those as well.

Ornstein looked at medical malpractice settlement amounts, and the reporters began talking to people about the county-owned system. "We were open-minded and wanted to know if the allegations being made in a lawsuit at County-USC were broader and indicative," Ornstein recalled. But it was soon clear to both of them that the inspection files on King/Drew were much thicker than the files on the others. The malpractice settlements were greater and more frequent, and the conversations of people they met focused on King/Drew. "It wasn't just that the volume of reports was so much greater," Weber said. "It was also the types of things that went wrong were pure crazy." She recalled the case of the little girl who survived a traffic accident with minor injuries but was killed by the incompetence of nurses and doctors in the emergency room. "The things that went wrong went across the whole program," she said. "It was just so bad."

Moreover, the hospital's physician training program at Charles R. Drew University of Medicine and Science was in trouble. Less than a year earlier, the nation's major accreditation council for medical schools, the Joint Accreditation Commission of Healthcare Organizations, withdrew its imprimatur from King/Drew's program for training diagnostic radiology residents. Four other physician training programs were on probation.[11]

Both reporters were well versed in the history of King/Drew and its place in race relations in Los Angeles County. They had examined the paper's previous coverage of the problems at the hospital carefully. The *Times* wrote stories in 1975 and 1977 about patient neglect, staff incompetence, doctors missing scheduled work hours, unsanitary conditions, employees coming to work under the influence of alcohol or drugs, and general disorganization.[12]

In the 1980s the *Times* paid scant attention to King/Drew. The paper's archives show that until mid-1989, there was almost nothing about patient-care problems at King/Drew hospital. The one exception came at the end of the decade. In September 1989, former *Times* reporter Claire Spiegel produced a three-day package called "Critical Condition." In more than 240 column inches, she described specific cases of malpractice, staff shortages, broken-down equipment, physician incompetence, and doctors moonlighting at other hospitals at the expense of King/Drew. She cited cases and reports going back to 1986.[13] "I've got a file folder labeled 'King/Drew-1980s,'" Mitchell Landsberg said. "It consists of Claire's story and not much else."[14] After her stories, the federal government threatened to cut off funds to the hospital. Investigators for the national accrediting agency recommended King/Drew lose its accreditation, and county supervisors vowed to investigate. But, in a seemingly miraculous development, within three months, government inspectors had declared there had been a "dramatic turnaround" at King/Drew. Accreditors gave the hospital a reprieve by putting it on probation, and less than two years later, the hospital had regained full accreditation.[15]

But Claire Spiegel's story on accreditation included ominous signs. Drawing from a confidential 18-page report by physicians on King/Drew's Quality Assurance Committee, Spiegel said doctors reported "serious outcomes, including deaths" had occurred because of inadequate staffing and lack of needed diagnostic and therapeutic services. "There is documentation to support deaths due to lack of resources . . . (and) a significant number of avoidable complications," the report said. Spiegel wrote that the report forecast "a progressive increase" in malpractice claims "as the limitations in providing the scope and level of care. . . have resulted in undesired outcomes, which include death."

Except for that story, King/Drew fell off the *Times*' radar for most of the early and mid-1990s. Then there was a scattering of stories between 1994 and early 1998 about staff turmoil, several stories about moonlighting doctors again and several more individual cases of malpractice, including one that dated back to 1992. The county supervisors again ordered up an investigation and called for a top-to-bottom overhaul.[16] But from spring 1998 through the end of 2002, King/Drew patient-care issues again disappeared from the coverage as reflected in the *Times*' online archives.

Several trends emerged from that coverage, Ornstein and Weber said. The county supervisors seemed to pay attention to the hospital only when the *Los Angeles Times* paid attention to it. When the supervisors reacted, the black community often rose up to oppose the supervisors' solutions and accused them of trying to shut it down. For example, the supervisors tried to fire the hospital administrator before Spiegel's 1989 package, but backed off when the community protested. After Spiegel's package, they fired him and the community again protested.[17] They also noticed that hospital supporters' defense followed several consistent themes: the supervisors were not funding the hospital sufficiently and the problems at King/Drew were no worse than the problems at comparable hospitals. Even as their investigation unfolded in late 2003 and throughout 2004, the same cycle—problems exposed, supervisors react, community objects, the civil rights significance is dredged up—was emerging again.

This time, the paper's investigation would try to break that cycle. "One of the reasons things never got fixed was because of the racial politics, and it always wore this weird sort of cocoon around it," Weber said. So they resolved that this time, they would question everything: the excuses such as lack of funding, the racial politics, the supervisors' efforts to fix the problems and the degree to which the black community itself was responsible for the troubles at King/Drew.

To Marquis, the two reporters' editor, they had to take on a mindset. "Every time you would say to the community that a patient had died, they would say to you that 'we had founded this hospital because the whites in the city would not take care of our people back in the 60s.' We decided we should take on this whole mindset that King/Drew deserved to be left alone, that they should be allowed to continue operating as they had, that this was a fair way to defend the hospital."[18]

Nevertheless, the project team recognized that—on the surface—the paper would appear to some as uncaring about the racial sensitivity of what it had taken on. The *Times* had deployed four white reporters and a white photographer under the guidance of a white line editor to look into the hospital. Throughout the project, they faced heated criticism. Two key black leaders—U.S. Rep. Maxine Waters, D-Calif., and community activist Lillian Mobley—refused to speak to them. But to Weber and Ornstein, the evidence they were uncovering made concerns about racial sensitivities pale in comparison to the life-and-death severity of the hospital's problems. "They didn't read what we read," Ornstein said, referring to their critics. "They didn't talk to the patients we talked to. They didn't read the state and federal inspection reports. They didn't talk to families who lost loved ones. They didn't look at accreditation reports."[19]

Soon after Weber and Ornstein began focusing on King/Drew, breaking news seemed to confirm their decision. In late August 2003, they learned about two patients dying at King/Drew hospital under unusual circumstances. Initially, the cause appeared to be that a faulty cardiac monitor had failed to alert nurses that the patients' condition had deteriorated.[20] Their story forced state officials to investigate. In the meantime, King/Drew news kept breaking. The day after their story, Ornstein and Weber reported that another one of the medical school's programs was in trouble: The accreditation council was withdrawing its approval of the training for general surgeons.[21] With that decision, one-third of the 18 doctor training programs were in trouble. Several related stories followed, and then, in September, the patient monitors were back in the news. Ornstein and Weber learned that state inspectors investigating the two patients' deaths blamed nurses and other employees, not faulty monitors.[22] In December, they reported on a far-reaching report on a surprise government inspection triggered by the two patients' deaths. It said "nurses shirk patient care, doctors allow problems to fester and county officials provide poor oversight."[23]

"News Comes First"

Although breaking news seemed to confirm the decision to focus on King/ Drew, it also made it apparent that this project would not unfold like most of the others. Often reporters' bylines disappear from the paper while they work on a project. Many investigative reporters like to plod along for weeks or months, hoarding their information until they have built a solid, compelling case before unloading the entire package in one huge series that will be the definitive piece on their topic. In a good investigation, however, exciting and exceedingly fascinating information emerges long before the day of publication. The urge to "save it for the project" is enormous. The reporters have devoted significant parts of their lives to the project, and they want to produce a story that does more than just inform; they want it to enthrall the readers just as it enthralled the reporters when they uncovered it. They want the project to be fresh and to pack a punch, to have an impact. To accomplish that, they cannot let the project turn stale.

With the King/Drew project, the story about the two patients dying because hospital staff failed to do their jobs demonstrated that they would have to do this project differently. "Until then, we were not planning on popping dailies before finishing the project," Weber said. From then on, the two reporters and Marquis weighed the urgency of each story: Can we hold this for the project, or do we need to publish now? They did not question the need to publish a breaking story, such as actions by the hospital accrediting agency or news of a government investigation. Early on, they also decided to publish a story any time they discovered a new act of negligence or any other story that had a direct bearing on public health.

It would have been hard for them or any of their editors at that stage to predict what was to occur. That simple decision would become a demanding one. Throughout the rest of 2003, developments on state inspections and accreditation news kept them busy. Soon after the turn of the new year, they learned that nurses had mistakenly given a patient a potent anticancer drug intended for another patient.[24] Their story prompted another round of investigations, which in turn prompted another round of breaking stories covering the impact of their initial story. And so it went for the rest of the year. From the moment their investigation turned to King/Drew, the reporters had to churn out daily stories, sometimes two or three times a week. Before the project series started, the *Times* produced 99 bylined, breaking stories about King/Drew, and one or more members of the project team wrote 75 percent of them, according to the paper's online archive index.

"As the months went on we did worry that events would overtake us and that maybe we had said everything there is to say about this hospital," Marquis, the line editor, said. "Our own impulses were fighting our other impulses, that there was a compelling need to make public immediately what was happening."

Weber also feared they were overwhelming the readers. "Yes, we were panicked, and worried that people were going to be sick of reading about King/Drew." Weber and Marquis were not the only ones thinking such thoughts. The newsroom buzz about the project was that Weber and Ornstein essentially were scooping themselves. "A lot of our colleagues [at the *Times*] thought the project was going to be a boondoggle," Weber said. "They told us this after the project was done."

But Marquis said John Carroll, the editor, was "a very calming force. He knew better than we did at the time that this story would retain its richness no matter what happened along the way." Carroll was aware of their concerns, but he never questioned in his mind whether to publish dailies when they became publishable or hold them for the project. He agreed with the decisions of his reporters and editors, because a fundamental journalism rule governs in such situations: "You cannot sit on breaking news, particularly on breaking news when life-threatening things are going on, to give you a better project. Tracy and Charles were very mature about that," he said. Carroll says he was not even worried when the county supervisors made two momentous decisions just weeks before the series was to run. The reporters were in the writing phase of the project when the board decided to close the hospital's trauma center and they appointed some turnaround experts to manage the hospital until they could fix its problems.[25]

Although their daily stories prompted the actions, it still appeared that the most important reforms had taken place before the project got into the paper. Most journalists outwardly consider themselves above thinking about winning awards with their stories, but most are keenly aware of the importance of "impact" in journalism contests. "It's not like we do these things for prizes," Marquis said, "but it would be disingenuous to say we didn't think about impact. . . . We thought we were running out of impact." But she credits Carroll for seeing the bigger picture.

Carroll says he wasn't worried. "I have been through this on other projects, and one breaking story is not going to change a 30-year-pattern." He was right. Although the two board actions seemed like a major effort to turn the hospital around, they would not work.[26]

Daily Stories Enrich, Crystallize Project Mission

Although the huge volume of stories sometimes rattled Weber, she soon learned early how much daily reporting during a project can make the project better than otherwise. The reporters unearthed sources they would never have discovered otherwise, she said. "Residents in the community contacted us; people in the hospital contacted us; doctors at other hospitals called." Each one provided new, richer information and a more in-depth understanding of the how-and-why explanations that had defied policymakers and elected officials for more than three decades. Moreover, the daily stories set the reader up for the gigantic package that began in December. The dailies could report another act of negligence, another investigation or another warning, but they could not adequately get to the root of the problems, explain the context or report how a hospital under the kind of intense scrutiny King/Drew was under in 2004 could not stop making such mind-boggling mistakes.

As the stories unfolded day after day, the readers may have indeed, as Weber and others realized, "become sick of King/Drew." But the mission of journalism does not allow those who might "get sick of a story" before it is complete to set the standard for practicing the craft. Journalism has a mission in a democratic society and a duty to the public interests to pursue a story to its logical conclusion, and public whim cannot determine when that has been accomplished.

In making news judgments, journalists carry a responsibility to think of those readers who care about public affairs, who understand their crucial role in a democracy, and who crave information that will help them fulfill that role. That is the niche of readers that modern-day journalism, in its confusion over 21st-century challenges and its marketplace obsession to be all things to all readers, has abandoned and must reclaim. The daily stories the King/Drew project team wrote in 2003 and 2004, the daily stories their predecessors wrote over the 30 years prior, the work of Claire Spiegel in 1989, and, indeed, the long history of negligence since the notion of "Killer King" took root in the public consciousness showed that the *Los Angeles Times* had to provide a definitive and thoroughly researched explanation, one that truly advanced the story and showed what needs to be done. Without it, there was no hope for a real solution to the troubles at King/Drew.

Working the Nuts and Bolts

As the project team's reporting progressed, it became clear, Weber said, that their project would be bigger than the entire body of daily stories. Their preliminary reporting strongly suggested King/Drew was the worst of the worst, but they would need more than anecdotes and inspection reports and accreditation evaluations to document that and to explain how and why it got that way and why it was allowed to wallow in such deterioration for so long. They also wanted to find out why the supervisors—"the five little kings"—acted more like the Cowardly Lion when dealing with King/Drew Medical Center. Finding the answers to those larger questions would have to begin with nuts-and-bolts journalism: researching records and statistics, interviewing, intrepid shoe-leather reporting.

Early on, Ornstein understood that statistics would become the foundation of any story that hoped to determine whether King/Drew was the worst of the worst. The reporting would have to remove the subjectivity from such a determination and give significance to the anecdotal evidence they were gathering from individual patient cases. Without that solid, objective base, their story would leave the *Times* vulnerable to charges that it was "picking on" King/Drew. Even statistics mean nothing without valid comparisons, comparisons that will give the readers tangible criteria they can use to evaluate King/Drew's performance and judge the validity of the project's conclusions.

Marquis, Ornstein and Weber brought in their colleague Steve Hymon to help with the statistics, workers' compensation records and public records requests. They filed over 100 public records requests.[27] Ornstein wanted statistics that would reflect the quality of care that is available at King/Drew and that would be comparable with other hospitals.

Malpractice settlements were a key statistic. The three reporters sent public records requests to every county-owned hospital in the state asking for data about the amount of money spent on malpractice suits by year and the number of cases they settled. He also devised a method to "level the playing field" by accounting for the number and types of patients the hospitals treated. King/Drew malpractice payouts were higher than those of 17 other public hospitals and six other University of California medical centers.

The reporters also compiled other statistics that allowed them to compare King/Drew's quality of care with that of others. For example, their research found that King/Drew violated state health regulations more often than 97 percent of hospitals statewide and more often than Los Angeles County's other three general hospitals. To the nation's main hospital accrediting agency, it was one of the worst in the country. The Joint Accreditation Commission of Healthcare Organizations, which accredits more than 4,500 hospitals, recommended that King/Drew lose its accreditation in 2004, one of only seven hospitals in the country to lose the agency's seal of approval. The hospital's medical school received the worst possible rating by the Accreditation Council for Graduate Medical Education twice in a row, a failure no other hospital in the country had suffered.

Next, the reporters had to deal with a decade-long refrain for every criticism of King/Drew: The county supervisors were shortchanging King/Drew, a charge that some hospital supporters directly linked to "racism and white supremacy."[28] Again, the reporters' research revealed that the opposite was true: King/Drew spent more per patient than the county's other three general hospitals and that it wasted more money. Harbor-UCLA, which is most similar to King/Drew, for example, has a budget similar to King/Drew's, but it treats 60 percent more people in the emergency room and nearly twice as many patients overall, the reporters found. King/Drew spent more on overtime and on temporary employees largely because of absentees.

The Stories Behind the Numbers

The reporters' painstaking number-crunching did what it was supposed to do: provide hard, measurable evidence that King/Drew had broken down.[29] Although such numbers are the meat and potatoes of a solid project, they usually make it bland reading fare, which is ironic in that the colorful, exciting, tragic, poignant, bizarre and generally complex tapestry of life usually lay beneath them. By capturing that human element, reporters turn the numbers into a story rather than a dust-gathering policy paper. Typically, in major medical malpractice projects, journalists usually roll out example after example of disastrous incompetence, complete with gory descriptions of its victims and teary depictions of grieving loved ones. The King/Drew project followed suit, although it did so to a depressing and perhaps superfluous extent. Although such anecdotes are necessary, they only show the consequences of a broken hospital: negligence and human tragedy.

The full story behind those malpractice anecdotes and the King/Drew numbers was much larger and the foundation for its narrative was deep-seated and solidly constructed. The reporters' digging revealed that behind the walls of King/Drew, a culture of fatal laxity had infected the staff. It emanated from the top ranks and permeated the staff at all levels, creating an environment where negligence and incompetence flourished and a sense of commitment to patients and public service had died. To create a journalism project that is a powerful story, Ornstein and Weber had to give the abstractions shape, form and action, because readers cannot understand what a culture of laxity is unless they can see and feel it through the words in the story.

The numbers and writing in the project smartly accomplished this in several ways. Mixed in with numerous depressing anecdotes about killed and maimed patients and grieving loved ones, the project fed readers numbers about absenteeism, high salaries and employee injury claims—a juxtaposition that seemed to amplify an uncaring attitude at King/Drew and perhaps made some readers think of Nero fiddling while Rome burned.

For example, to illustrate the chronic absenteeism, they reported specific days when patients filled the orthopedic clinic only to find there was no one— no doctors, physician assistants or doctor trainees—to care for them. Even the emergency room had to be closed for the weekend because so many nurses on every shift had called in sick or failed to show up. On occasion, Ornstein and Weber adopted a bemused writing style and used a bizarre topic to make the numbers more meaningful and palatable. In a section about wasting money in the second-day story, the reporters served up what could have been an exceedingly boring explanation of how the hospital spent exorbitant sums for employee injuries in comparison with other hospitals. Here's one passage chock-full of numbers in the middle but served up like medicine buried in chocolate pudding:

Vast sums at King/Drew go to workers injured in encounters with seemingly harmless objects.

Take, for instance, the chair.

Employees have been tumbling from their seats at King/Drew almost since it opened its doors. The hospital's oldest open workers' compensation claim involves Franza Zachary, now 71, who sprained her back falling from a chair in October 1975—costing the hospital more than $300,000 so far.

The bills for two other chair-fallers have topped $350,000 each, county records show.

Between April 1994 and April 2004, employees filed 122 chair-fall claims at King/Drew, more than double the number at Harbor-UCLA. And King/Drew has spent $3.2 million—and counting—to pay for them.

"Sitting down. Eating lunch. [Chair] broke" was how licensed vocational nurse Elizabeth Rugley described her mishap in a 1999 claim. "Fell to floor. Hit the floor. Landed on my buttock."

In the last nine years, records show, Rugley, now 51, has had three other on-the-job accidents at King/Drew: a second chair misadventure in which she slipped and banged her head on a wall, a tumble, and a trip over an elevator entrance. As a result, according to her filings with the state, she has strained her neck, wrenched her back and injured her right shoulder.

To treat Rugley's last three injuries and pay her when she has been unable to work, King/Drew has spent $364,435.[30]

Ordinarily, the fact that King/Drew spends more for workers compensation claims than other hospitals probably would not even register with hurried readers, at least not for long. But who could ever forget the chair falls?

For another example, consider the salary numbers in the project. Ornstein and Weber compared salaries for ranking doctors and found that 18 King/Drew physicians earned more than $250,000 in the last fiscal year, compared to nine earning that much at Harbor-UCLA. That would be a number that readers will quickly forget, but they will never forget Dr. George Locke.

Shoe-Leather Reporting Brings Stats to Life

Dr. George Locke was head of neurosciences. He directed neurosurgery and neurology at King/Drew, and he taught at the medical school. At age 70, he had been a mainstay at King/Drew. He is often the one who greets the dignitaries with hugs and handshakes when they show up to pay homage to the struggle that built King/Drew. And his million-dollar salary seemed to fit his stature. But not his work habits, the reporters discovered.

Ornstein's sources had told him Locke did not do much to earn his a huge salary, which included a teaching stipend. When asked, health department officials had difficulty justifying it. The reporters discovered that hospitals keep records of the number of surgeries each doctor performs and those records are public. They also researched his publications. Then they compared his productivity to a similar doctor at another hospital. Not only did the comparison doctor earn half of what Locke earned, but he performed about 100 surgeries compared to Locke's three in a year's time. While Locke was listed as an author in four journal articles in the previous 14 years, the comparison doctor was an author in eight in just two years.

Ornstein decided to check his daily work hours. A source slipped Locke's signed time clock cards to him, and they showed he repeatedly reported that he was at the hospital 12 hours a day and then continued to be on standby for another 12 hours, including one day that totaled an impossible 26 hours. Again, county rules stipulated that hours recorded on the time clock had to reflect hours at the hospital. Although such work habits probably would seem improbable to most readers, investigative reporters usually take the next step: determine whether the reported hours on the signed time cards match his actual work hours.[31]

Hymon took on that assignment. Armed with a photograph of Locke that the *Times* had in its archives and his license plate number, Hymon found where Locke parked his car at the hospital and staked it out. He spent weeks in November 2003 and another week in the summer of 2004 observing Locke's comings and goings at King/Drew. Hymon said Locke drove a recent model Mercedes, two-seat sports coupe. "I would drive down there every morning before he got there and wait," Hymon recalled. Locke routinely arrived at midmorning. A member of his staff would meet him and carry his belongings into the building for him. Four or five hours later, he would emerge—again with a staffer to carry his belongings—and drive home. Locke was routinely at the office four or five hours on days when he had clocked in for 12 hours.[32]

"It was a little weird," Hymon said, recalling the stakeout. "I had never done anything like that before. I felt conspicuous, because I am a white Jewish guy sitting in a parked car in an African-American part of town."

He also felt underused, bored and frustrated. Hour after hour, he sat there reading the *Los Angeles Times, The New Yorker* or a ski magazine, drinking coffee or calling friends on his cell phone. "I felt like I was doing real monkey work compared to what the other guys were doing," he said. "The tricky part was watching him come out and get in his car and then following him home to his subdivision in Orange County on a beach right on the water. It was not fun."

Such is the nature of investigative journalism. But it often pays off, sometimes in unexpected ways. During Hymon's stakeout, the project's photographer, Robert Gauthier, occasionally would join him. One day, luck played into their hands. Gauthier and Hymon were working on an unrelated feature story at King/Drew about a summer asthma camp for children. Standing in the parking lot near Locke's car, Gauthier was taking pictures of children enrolled in the camp boarding a bus, while Hymon interviewed a doctor connected with the camp. In the background, Locke pulled up in his car and got out to go into the hospital. Hymon spotted Locke, and discreetly signaled Gauthier. The photographer had already picked up on the unexpected opportunity, Hymon recalled. Although he aimed his camera in the general direction of Hymon's interviewee, Gauthier shifted the camera several inches and shot. "We just happened to be about 100 feet from Locke's parking space, and Rob just happened to be in the perfect spot," Hymon said. "It was pure luck."[33]

The Locke anecdote (without the photo-taking segment) became a section in the main story of day two. It illustrated extravagance and lax work ethics at the hospital and medical school whose supporters had claimed it was being underfunded. That story also compared the teaching stipends at Drew University of Medicine and Science with others and revealed county auditors' inability to unravel the school's incomplete financial records to figure out how many residents Drew trained, how its doctors spent their time or how the more than $13 million annual county appropriation was used.

Persistence Pays

Tracking down former patients or survivors of patients was more difficult. At times, Ornstein and Weber spent days looking for just one person. The addresses were old and cases of malpractice that emerged from state inspection reports deleted names. Some names came from malpractice suits and tips. They got many of them by asking the coroner's office to provide records of patients who had died of injuries at King/Drew from accidental causes, such as therapeutic misadventures.

Although patients and their families usually were surprisingly open, they often seemed overwhelmed by life, Weber recalls. Because the overwhelming majority of King/Drew patients were poor people, they often were totally consumed with day-to-day problems. "They had so many bad things happen in their lives, having a medication error at some point in the past wasn't really one of the bad things," she said.

Some, however, were the victims of severe, life-changing medical errors and were not aware of what had been done to them until the *Times* reporters told them. Weber said those interviews were the most difficult. Johnnie Mae Williams was one such case. For her, a minor gynecological examination mistakenly turned into a radical hysterectomy. A pathologist thought she had cancer of the uterine lining, but he was looking at the slides for a patient who had brain cancer. Williams, the mother of three children, had planned to have more children. The pathologist had made so many other mistakes, Weber and Ornstein eventually did a separate story on him. Finding Williams would be difficult. Moreover, when they began their search, they didn't have some crucial information: Williams was unaware of the mistake. Five doctors knew about it, but none told her.[34]

Weber and Ornstein spent days going to addresses that the newspaper library had provided through its searches of various public records databases. Weber said their final effort took her to an address that listed the name of her ex-husband. It was dark and pouring rain when Weber got there, but the address was in a gated community and she could not get in. When a resident drove up, Weber pulled close to the car's bumper and followed the car through the gate. She found the address, but the lights inside the home were turned off. She knocked on the door, as the rain drenched her. No one answered. She tried the doorbell. Still no answer. Weber kept trying, ringing the doorbell 10 more times. Finally, a man opened the door. He was big, perhaps in his late 40s, and he looked as if he had been asleep. He said he didn't know a Johnnie Mae Williams, but Weber strongly suspected he did. In the database searches, his name came up many times in association with Williams. So she pressed on.[35]

I have been writing about the problems of King/Drew hospital, she explained. The reason I want to talk to her is that she may have been involved in a medical malpractice situation when she was in the hospital.

I really don't know her, the man insisted, as he started closing the door.

Weber knew he had to be her ex-husband. In situations such as this one, Weber realized that the best tactic is to keep talking as long as you think the person can hear you. "I just started talking immediately," she recalled.

Look, I had a hard time getting in here and had to wait and follow somebody in, she told him. "I think he began to realize this was a serious thing and that it could make a big difference to her," she said. The man finally admitted Williams was his ex-wife.

But, I haven't seen her in eight years, he told Weber.

Again, Weber suspected that comment was not entirely true. They had been in a long relationship and had three children.

If you have any contact with her, would you have her call me, Weber pleaded. Here's my business card. It is really important.

The man took the card and closed the door. Weber left, thinking "It was probably going through his head that this is important and she is the mother of my children," she said. Nevertheless, Weber didn't count on getting a call. "I figured I had a 50–50 chance."

A day or two later, Williams called. "I was shocked," Weber said. Williams was living in a sober-living board and care facility, which probably explained the difficulty of locating her, and had called from a pay phone. Weber told her she was working on a story about King/Drew's problems and that she knew about her stay at the hospital two years earlier. Weber explained that she wanted to tell her something about her care and asked if she could come out to visit her and bring a photographer.

What do you want to talk about? Williams asked.

Weber hesitated. Williams was in a sober-living facility, and Weber worried that if she did not handle the interview sensitively, "I might trigger something."

I would rather talk in person, Weber told her. I want to bring some papers because there may have been a mistake in your care.

Williams agreed to the interview.

She and Gauthier drove out there. As she sat down at the table with Williams, Weber worried about Williams' reaction to the fact that the hospital had removed all of her reproductive organs "and no one cared enough about her to call and explain that it had all been a mistake. This whole interview was so horrible. Just horrible," Weber said. She eased into the bad news slowly.

Weber told her about the background of King/Drew and how they were looking into possible medical errors in various cases. She explained why they were doing the story and some of what they had been finding. Then she started talking about the pathology department and explaining that there had been some errors in cases, including hers. Finally, she told Williams that she had never had cancer.

I can't believe it, Williams said. I cannot believe it.

Her hands started shaking, and her eyes filled with tears. She had always defended King/Drew, she said; it had found cancer in her, removed it and saved her life, she thought. True, she had never felt like a "full woman" afterward,[36] and she blamed her "dependency" on the ordeal, but not on King/Drew.

Weber showed her all the paperwork she had. Williams recounted her experiences after the operation. "She took us through everything, the sidetracks in her life, her kids." Weber asked her for permission to examine her medical records. She agreed and rode to the hospital with Weber to retrieve them. During the trip, Williams continued talking about her life. At one point, she asked Weber for money to buy groceries and personal hygiene products. Weber explained why ethical standards prohibited her from granting her request, and Williams appeared to understand. After the interview, Weber kept in contact with her. Even after the project ran, she tried to keep up with Williams for nearly a year.[37]

Reporting the contents of private medical records of many cases became a key element of the story's credibility. Weber and Ornstein needed the files because the reporters had to submit them to independent doctors who would review the material and evaluate the care that was recorded in the files. Eventually, the project included new individual case studies showing malpractice. Although most were recent, some went back to the late 1990s, including one in 1993. By alluding to cases back to early 1990s and late 1980s, the project provided a clear message that the malpractice was long-term, continuous and systematic, even from the early 1990s when federal inspectors and accrediting agencies had assured the public that the trouble at King/Drew had ended.

Knowing the Past Reveals the Present

Tracking the history of officialdom's failures fell to Mitchell Landsberg. Landsberg, a quiet, versatile writer with a mild Clark Kent manner, is a veteran with a long history as an Associated Press reporter. He was a national editor for AP for several years, and did a fair amount of rewriting. Although he had done one or two long-term projects in his career, he had never been involved in a project like King/Drew.[38]

He joined the project in December 2003, several months after Ornstein and Weber had planned and initiated it. Initially, he was paired with Daren Briscoe, a black reporter, to examine the political angle and the community's role in shaping the hospital all the while it was being victimized by it. Briscoe left the paper about six months later when he landed a job in the Washington Bureau of *Newsweek* magazine. He left his notes and remained involved in the story for a while after he left.

Ornstein and Weber had already studied the history of King/Drew and had recognized the community's involvement when Landsberg started work. From that information, they sensed that the Board of Supervisors knew or should have known about many of the problems and had failed to solve them. Landsberg's job was to find out if the hypothesis was accurate. The black community's obstructionist reactions toward reforming the hospital also "were out there" when he started working on the story. The reporters had heard from county supervisors that every time the county tried to do something to fix problems at King/Drew, "they were besieged," Landsberg recalled. There had been strong feelings in the community that the county was trying to take power from the community and from the hospital leadership and to impose a public health administration.[39]

Landsberg decided to start at the beginning, and the beginning started this way in the final day of the King/Drew series:

> On the sultry evening of Aug. 11, 1965, a 21-year-old black man named Marquette Frye was pulled over by the California Highway Patrol at 116th Street and Avalon Boulevard for driving drunk.
>
> A crowd gathered. Frye resisted arrest. A patrolman struck him in the face with a nightstick.
>
> It was as if the blow knocked loose the cornerstone of a dam.
>
> What poured forth was a torrent of rage, propelled through the streets of Watts and South Los Angeles by the conviction that African Americans had lived too long with the contempt of a white-run society—denied respect, along with decent housing, education and medical care.
>
> That flood of anger led directly to the creation of Martin Luther King Jr./ Drew Medical Center, which opened in 1972. And the power of that feeling, rooted both in centuries of black struggle and in pride and hope for a better tomorrow, has always been as much a part of the hospital as IV drips and surgical gloves.[40]

That power also—as the project team's reporting had discovered—created a political and racial environment that helped give rise to the troubles at King/Drew. Landsberg did not have to chronicle those troubles; his colleagues had already done that. His job was to reveal when they started and how the power structure dealt with them. He went back to the reign of one of the five little kings, late 2nd District Supervisor Kenneth Hahn. Hahn was a white man, who ruled the district surrounding Watts since 1952, when his district was still predominantly white. After the 1965 Watts riots, Hahn sidestepped the predominantly white, countywide population that had voted down a bond referendum for a hospital to serve the black community. He went to the state legislature to find funding. When the hospital opened in 1975, Hahn became an icon in the black community. His portrait hung throughout the hospital.[41]

When he died, his personal papers went to a private library in San Marino, and Landsberg decided to plow through them.[42] It was not an easy process. The papers were only open to academic researchers. Using friends who were professors to vouch for him, Landsberg applied for readership privileges and gained access to Hahn's papers. "They made it pretty clear to me that I was very lucky, that they don't usually grant privileges to people like me," Landsberg said.

He spent a month going through them. "It was a glimpse of a master politician," Landsberg said. Hahn was a prolific letter writer to everybody from council members to presidents of the United States, and he saved everything. Landsberg said the archives contained a lot of information about the need for King/Drew hospital, and how the McCone Commission, which had investigated the Watts riots and was led by former CIA director John McCone, documented the lack of basic medical care for the black community.

Hahn's papers revealed that not long after the hospital opened in 1975, the supervisors started getting complaints about the treatment that hospital patients were receiving. "Those papers were a tremendous investment of time that led to little that we directly used in the story," Landsberg said. "But they helped confirm our thesis [that the supervisors understood the King/Drew problems from the beginning]."[43]

As a supplement to the Hahn papers, a confidential source provided Landsberg with "huge stacks of memos" from a former health department official to county supervisors that helped document the degree to which county supervisors knew about the troubles at King/Drew. In addition, county records revealed that the supervisors had to sign off on every major medical malpractice settlement between the county and plaintiffs. They found documents in which county officials had to explain to the supervisors why they might not win a suit. That background information was crucial, because the supervisors, throughout the history of the troubles at King/Drew, repeatedly expressed shock and outrage at any public disclosure of hospital misadventures. Repeatedly, they publicly ranted about not learning about the troubles at King/Drew until they picked up the morning newspaper. As late as December 2003, that was a common refrain.[44]

But 2004 was different from years past. Like never before, the drumbeat of press coverage was unceasing, and it had been since the previous summer. Even as the headlines spilled out, the *Times'* long-term project was no secret. As events unfolded through summer and fall, the supervisors continued in the same outrage mode, but this time they reacted differently. By 2004, they stopped claiming their staff was failing to keep them informed, and they frequently and publicly acknowledged their failure to solve the problem. At one point, in response to yet another story about a patient suffering at the hands of negligent King/Drew nurses, Supervisor Zev Yaroslavsky said he was running out of new ways to express outrage.[45] Another, Gloria Molina, at one point said, "We should be embarrassed, all of us collectively, because we have failed the community." Yvonne Burke, who represents the district where King/Drew is located, told the reporters, "I have to be very honest, I have existed from crisis to crisis over this whole 12 years."[46]

At the end of a colorful narrative about the history of the supervisors' dealings with King/Drew, Landsberg effectively used a single key vote by Burke in September 2004 that sums up that history and suggested that supervisors seemed ready to finally deal with the problem forcefully. On the board, informal protocol usually means supervisors defer to the district supervisor on matters that primarily concern that member's constituents. So they looked to Burke, and to Hahn before her, for leadership on matters concerning King/Drew. Twice in the mid-1990s, she had demanded action, and she got some, but not much changed as a result of it. More important, late in the year they began taking decisive action and stood firm. In October, the board voted to hire a turnaround expert to take control of the hospital and turn it around. To focus resources on the overall improvement of the hospital, all five members of the board had already publicly backed a proposal to close the expensive and resource-demanding trauma center. As expected, that proposal sparked massive community protests. When the time for a final vote came in November, Burke wilted.[47]

Reporting Burke's change of heart at the end of a long historical section on the supervisors and before a section on the power of the community spoke volumes. Her cave-in to the community was an action that—coming in the middle of a crisis when tough leadership was needed—seemed to symbolize the entire history of the supervisors' failure of leadership. In the past, the board usually would have followed suit. This time, however, the rest of the board stood firm and overruled Burke, voting 4 votes to 0 for the closure, with Burke abstaining.

Uncovering the full accounting of the black community's responsibility for obstructing reform at the hospital was more difficult to obtain. The clips from years past and the community's actions in the past 12 months provided some evidence. The supervisors sometimes blamed the community. Burke once publicly complained that she had been remiss in not pushing for the dismissal of some hospital administrators, but complained "any time anything is done, the community has become totally upset."[48]

However, the project never adequately explained why key community leaders failed to see that King/Drew could no longer be a civil rights battleground and that its problems were deeper than money. It never made them confront the "mindset" that the project sought to challenge, to get past the civil rights struggle and make them talk about the dead patients, the statistics, inspector's reports and the myth that the hospital was underfunded. Only in a brief passage, the series in the second-day story provides a brief comment, in which one hospital leader (depicted as representative of hospital supporters) disputes Burke's contention that funding is fine.[49]

Landsberg told of another pertinent passage that he said apparently was edited out. It was from a conversation with a top official of the health department who conceded to Landsberg that his department deserved some blame. "We wanted the community to get involved in the hospitals," the official told Landsberg. "That is a good thing. If they [the community] had the wrong idea about what was going on here, that was our fault for not getting the message across."[50] Although that passage did not get in the story, it was not a major omission, because the substantive answers needed to come from the community leaders. For example, there was no discussion from them about two of the major findings: that statistics showed that the hospital was not underfunded and that by objective measure of its patient care showed it fared much worse than comparable hospitals.

That was a major hole in the reporting, because the black community—particularly its leaders, such as U.S. Rep. Maxine Waters and community activist Lillian Mobley—take substantial hits in the *Times* project largely because of those findings. Landsberg and other members of the project team said they diligently tried to get them to discuss the troubles at King/Drew. "I talked to [Waters] at some length early on," Landsberg said. "But then she stopped talking." One day, Landsberg encountered her at a Board of Supervisors meeting. During a break in the meeting, Landsberg approached her.

Congresswoman, I would like to talk to you about King/Drew, Landsberg said to her.

She shook her head "no," Landsberg recalled.

Can you talk to me later, he asked.

Again, Waters shook her head "no."

Congresswoman, are you mad at me or are you mad at me because I am with the *Los Angeles Times*? Landsberg asked.

This time she nodded her head up and down, Landsberg said. It didn't matter whether she was answering one question or the other or both—she was not going to talk.

Landsberg said Lillian Mobley was not any more cooperative. He said she agreed to interviews a few times and then would cancel. Sometimes she would just say she was "too tired" to talk that day. "She just kept making excuses every day."[51]

Ornstein and Weber once encountered a bitter hospital supporter who sat behind them at public meetings and had a binder filled with clippings of the stories they had written on King/Drew. After she made some comments to the audience, the two reporters turned around and offered her their business cards. "She said, 'I know who you are,' and then she said she was going to 'whup' us," Weber recalled.

Community response reported in the series was like it had been before: The criticism leveled at the hospital reflected disrespect for the community, the supervisors were not sufficiently supportive of the hospital and that the hospital was being held to a higher standard than other hospitals because of where it was located and who it served.

Writing the Story

By the time the project reporters were ready to start writing the final drafts of the five-day series, the story count on King/Drew was already approaching 100. The rest of the newsroom wondered what else the project team could write, but the four reporters and their editors knew that the dailies were, ironically, the old story; their project was the new one. The dailies had only scratched the surface, and they essentially repeated the cycle that emerged in decades past: outrageous negligence–angry reaction–investigation.

This time, they had to reveal that cycle as part of the long-term story of King/Drew, because they had figured out what was turning it, and they had the facts, statistics, interviews and human stories to explain it. They could write something different from the past, because they could show that the excuses offered up—King/Drew was underfunded, King/Drew is no worse than other facilities—were just plain inaccurate. They also could show that hospital leaders, community leaders and the politicians let their own fears, self-interests, suspicions and territoriality stand in the way of doing what was best for the patients of King/Drew. Their investigation showed that supervisors should have cleaned house a long time ago, and the community should have demanded such action instead of fighting even the most timid proposals for reform. Instead, the project found, stagnation set in and the culture of laxity took root. Although the horror stories of patient care had been told before, this project had to tell them again to ensure that readers never lost sight of why it was important to diagnose the malady, to find the cure and to administer treatment without making any more mistakes.

Although the reporting had met some daunting challenges and revealed an incredible story, it would be for naught unless the writing measured up as well. By late summer, they had written so much and found so much that was new and complex and multilayered, the writing would prove to be as difficult and time-consuming as the reporting. For more than a year, they had been working sweatshop hours. But the story was too important to let it fail because of poor writing. They told their editors they were willing to do anything to ensure that the writing met the highest standards. "So often investigative reporters spend so much time and work so hard on the reporting that the writing is not given the same weight as the reporting," Weber said. "So it often falls a little flatter than it should be."

The "Book" on John Carroll

Every reporter has weathered grueling editing experiences, but few have weathered a John Carroll editing experience. Among reporters at the *Los Angeles Times* and other papers he led, the "book" on Carroll was thick, and the King/Drew project team had heard what was in it. Weber said she had decided she was going to send "my ego to Guatemala." They knew the rewriting would be endless, that haggling over words and phrases would be exasperating. "There were days we wanted to strangle him," Landsberg said. "But we had been told by others who had been edited by him that it was going to be the most grueling process that you have ever been through but that you would be glad with the way the story comes out when it is over." In the margins of one of the edited drafts of the fifth-day story, a midlevel editor scrawled the words "slit throat." "I don't know whether it was her own throat or John's that was going to be slit," Landsberg, the lead writer on day five, said laughing. "John Carroll is the most exacting editor I have ever encountered. He was a skinflint when it came to praise. There were days when we would slink out of his office, and if we got so much as a casual 'it's looking pretty good,' we were on cloud nine."[52]

Carroll, in discussing King/Drew and "The Shipbreakers" project he steered to a Pulitzer Prize a few years earlier for *The Baltimore Sun*, says that when his reporters turn in high-quality reporting, his goal is to make the project reflect the best that the news organization can provide. Despite the agonizing among reporters and other editors, the consensus said the story gets much better.

Carroll, who was then 63, is the son of the late Wallace Carroll, who was a well-respected editor and publisher of the *Winston-Salem Journal* in North Carolina, which long had been a state of aggressive, competitive midsize newspapers. He is a tall and slender silver-haired man, whose mild and courtly manner belies the demanding nature of his editing. In the *Los Angeles Times* newsroom, reporters viewed Carroll in at least two ways when he arrived at the paper in 2000 from its sister paper, *The Baltimore Sun*: as a rescuer from the turmoil that had beset the paper because of the Staples Center controversy,[53] and with a sigh of relief over the uncertainties that permeated the newsroom when that "second-tier" outfit from Chicago (the Tribune Company) bought Times-Mirror Corp. from the Chandler family.

When he took up his editing pencil on the King/Drew project in late 2004, he had already validated his reputation. By then, he had been a reporter or editor for 40 years and led news staffs to 13 Pulitzer Prizes at three different newspapers—the *Times*, the *Sun* and the *Lexington Herald-Leader*—and had been a metro editor at *The Philadelphia Inquirer*.

Weber said she knew she could learn a lot from Carroll, so she went to talk to him early about the editing process. "I told him that I wanted to be in on all the editing sessions, that I don't mind rewriting a gazillion times if that is what it takes to make it better, and that I could learn from this," she said. "He was really good about it." This project would be the first in her career where the writing received as much attention as the reporting.

Carroll edited closely, hated superlatives and insisted that the writing be tough, authoritative and as graphic as possible. "He challenged us on virtually every word, repeatedly questioning 'Do we really need this word?' or 'Is this the best word?'" Landsberg said. "Where some editors will always want to pull you back and tone down strong conclusions, John pushed us to be as straightforward as we could be, not to shy away from taking on issues such as race, to tell the truth as bluntly as we could."[54] Here's one example from day five:

> The Los Angeles County Board of Supervisors, which runs the hospital, was left with a political and moral dilemma:
>
> It could take tough, decisive action, which would surely bring protests and pickets. Or it could take the path of least resistance—issue ineffective reprimands, commission studies, fire an administrator or two—and hope the problems would go away.
>
> The political price of inaction was small. Members of the Board of Supervisors rarely face serious electoral challenges, and the people being harmed were not politically powerful or well-connected.
>
> So, given the choice—the distress of racial politics on the one side, the likelihood of more needless deaths on the other—the board chose to risk the latter.[55]

Five finely tuned sentences captured three decades of history and a complex choice and then struck with the succinctness of a bullet to the head: The commissioners risk lives for political expediency. Sometimes, Carroll would do that with just a word or phrase; sometimes it was a sentence or an entire paragraph. He turned "nursing negligence" into "fatal neglect." One of Landsberg's favorite lines in the story—"But the mistakes continued and, over the years, bodies piled up"—was typical Carroll. "He wrote that line," Mitchell said. Although Carroll doesn't mince words, he delivers his critique of a word, sentence or passage without an emotional edge. "He would say something like 'this is a terrible sentence' but he would say it matter-of-factly," Landsberg said.[56]

Carroll doesn't get as deeply involved in all page one stories as he did with King/Drew. The story struck a chord in him as soon as he learned about it. "I look for a story that has meaning and importance and, if possible, an emotional dimension, and one where you can see how to get it," he said. King/Drew fit all three criteria. "It was a visceral story, literally a life or death story," he said. "It was not about principle or procedures; it was about saving lives right then and it was about how people will die in the future if it is not fixed. And then it had the added dimension of the race and politics of the story." He also recognized the immense paper trail open to the reporters, because the hospital was owned by the government and its overseers were elected officials, whose files and correspondence also would be open for inspection.[57]

Carroll, his editors and the reporters generally agreed on the overall goal in the writing: to make the readers know right away that this was not going to be one more story about another bad case of malpractice at King/Drew. It had to persuade the readers from the outset that this series was going to be the definitive take on a decades-long tragedy. The writing had to show clearly and authoritatively what they had found: King/Drew was worse than anyone had ever suspected; the political and racial elements throughout the hospital's history played a key role in its problems; and the Board of Supervisors was ultimately responsible.

Although they agreed the board should be the focus of criticism, they recognized that the story needed to say there was plenty of blame to go around: the staff, doctors and top administrators at the hospital; the county health department and its director; accrediting agencies and inspectors who kept giving breaks to the hospital and the community, which seemed to fight reforms at every turn. However, the Board of Supervisors singly had the power to fix the hospital. It had let its guard down for long periods of time after the hospital opened in 1975, and its political timidity prevented the members from taking decisive action. To attempt to explain the responsibility of each entity would produce what Carroll described as an "incomprehensible mess" that would fail clearly and solidly identify who should bear responsibility for King/Drew's failures. Ultimately the supervisors were responsible, because they run the hospital.[58]

The opening day story had to capture all of those themes in a sweeping way, while driving home in compelling detail the human tragedy that is and has been the story of King/Drew Medical Center since the beginning. Because the opening had to incorporate so many interlocking themes while presenting a fresh story and clear demarcation from what had come before, it underwent the most rewriting. The first draft began with an anecdotal lead about Dunia Tasejo, a little girl who suffered minor injuries in a traffic accident but was killed at King/Drew. As powerful as it was, it presented several problems. An anecdotal opening about a case of negligence would seem to convey precisely what they were trying to avoid: the feeling that this was just another story about a broken hospital. Moreover, that particular anecdote was at least four years old. Why not use a more recent one, like the Sherry Ridley case, one of the most tragic and needless deaths:

> Sherry Ridley, a 43-year-old airport security guard, underwent elective surgery there for ovarian cysts in November 2002.
>
> First a doctor in training stitched through her colon in error, essentially blocking it, according to a surgical note in Ridley's medical records. No one caught the mistake for two weeks as her stomach painfully bloated. A second resident's belated repair job failed.
>
> Over the next couple of weeks, a senior surgeon opened the patient up eight times, trying to scrub out a worsening infection. More medical equipment sprouted from Ridley nearly every day; wires and hoses protruded from her like tentacles. Swollen with fluid, she ballooned from 187 to 321 pounds. Bands had to be looped around her abdomen to hold her incision together.
>
> Ridley, the mother of two sons and one of seven close-knit siblings, died five days after Christmas.
>
> "My sister went in there healthy," said Gail Gordon, her eldest sister. "She went from a human being to a monster when she passed."[59]

The reporters and editors considered the Ridley case, but ultimately the editors decided it was just too graphic to use as an opening. Carroll instructed them to try a more historical approach that encapsulated the political and racial background. They tried, but Marquis, Ornstein and Weber felt it made the story sound too much like an explanatory news feature piece rather than an investigative project that revealed the new discoveries they had made. Weber said Carroll was open to objections that any of them had to his suggestions. "He was fine with us coming back saying we tried it and it didn't work," Weber said. Sometimes, the reporters would spend a week rewriting a draft to try one of Carroll's suggestions only to hear him conclude the earlier version was better. "We had tried a lot of things John had suggested and we tried them again for him," Weber recalled. Eventually, they wrote drafts that experimented with every section in the long story as an opening. When they finally produced the version that got in the paper, the death of Dunia Tasejo again was the key to the opening paragraphs:

> On a warm July afternoon, an impish second-grader named Dunia Tasejo was running home after buying ice cream on her South Los Angeles street when a car sideswiped her. Knocked to the pavement, she screamed for help, blood pouring from her mouth.
>
> Her father bolted from the house to her side. An ambulance rushed her to the nearest hospital: Martin Luther King, Jr./Drew Medical Center.
>
> For Elias and Sulma Tasejos, there was no greater terror than seeing their nine-year-old daughter strapped to a gurney that day in 2000. But once they arrived at King/Drew, fear gave way to relief. Dunia's injuries were minor: some scrapes, some bruises and two broken baby teeth. The teeth would have to be pulled.

"They told me to relax," Sulma recalled. "Everything was fine." At least, it should have been.

What the Tasejos didn't know was that King/Drew, a 233-bed public hospital in Willowbrook south of Watts, had a long history of harming, or even killing, those it was meant to serve.[60]

There were many reasons for going back to that case, but the fundamental rationale was this: "Her case hit every note," Weber said. Because Dunia and her family were from Central America, they represented the new and growing minority in what was once a predominantly black community. Moreover, they represented the people who did not know about King/Drew's problems or about its historical and racial significance. The mistakes in her case broadly reflected the King/Drew environment because they were made in the emergency room and pediatric intensive care, by nurses, doctors, trainees and technicians, and each mistake compounded the previous one. Finally, the catastrophic magnitude of the mistakes—committed by people who were entrusted with a young, healthy life, which they then destroyed through sheer negligence—powerfully carried the theme that the troubles at King/Drew were no longer just a political controversy but a dire emergency needing immediate corrective action. It, like so many of the other segments of the anecdotal evidence in the stories, gave the entire project what Carroll saw as its "life or death" importance.

Carroll loves editing a story. "As an editor, it is a personal hobby for me," he says.[61] Among all the responsibilities of an editor at a newspaper, Carroll believes that editing stories, along with hiring good journalists, are the two most important duties of an editor.[62]

When Carroll personally delves deeply into a major project, his goal, like that of any respectable editor, is primarily to make the story better. But he says he has a larger and more long-term purpose, one that he hopes affects the entire paper and every reporter and editor working there. "It is good for the journalists and the paper to take a story and say 'this is going to be as close to perfect as it can be in headlines, photos, design, graphics—the whole thing, and it is not going into the paper until it is at its best.' It's a good, standard-setting thing," he said. With such stories, Carroll finds himself working side-by-side with everybody involved in the story. "It becomes a way of communicating to the newsroom what you want in terms of the way craft is practiced."[63]

Postscript

Immediately after the five-part series had run its course, Ornstein and Weber distributed it to experts across the country asking them for their suggestions on how to solve the King/Drew problems. There were many solutions, but the overriding answer was this: Take the hospital away from the Los Angeles County Board of Supervisors and hand it over to someone who knows something about running hospitals. The *Times* series, "The Troubles at King/Drew" went on to win the 2005 Pulitzer Prize public service award and several other honors. The judges described it as a "courageous, exhaustively researched series."

Later that year, Carroll, who had been fighting Tribune Company executives over a continuous series of cuts in newsroom staff, resigned, citing unhappiness over those cuts. He became a Knight Visiting Lecturer at the Kennedy School of Government in the Shorenstein Center at Harvard. In the fall 2006, he taught a course titled "Journalistic Values in a Time of Upheaval."

In the meantime, the *Times* did not let King/Drew fall off its radar. Ornstein and Weber kept writing about it, because the troubles there continued without any let up. They and other *Times* reporters continued covering the hospital's problems even as Ornstein and Weber worked award-winning stories about the problems in the nation's organ transplant program.

In the meantime, federal and state regulators and accrediting agencies continued applying pressure on the county to fix the problems, but their past pattern of issuing warnings and then backing off did not change. In 2006, the federal government decided to cut off funding, but it backed off when the Board of Supervisors agreed to drastically reduce the hospital from 233 beds to 42 and to give administrators at Harbor-UCLA Medical Center control of reshaping King/Drew. They changed the name of King/Drew to King-Harbor.[64]

Hospital staff continued mistreating its patients, including one case that captured national attention in June 2007. The hospital let a woman suffering abdominal pain writhe on the floor of the emergency room for 45 minutes and never treated her. She later died.[65]

Despite the massive coverage since 2003, the repeated expressions of outrage and intense eye of government regulators, the hospital could not fix three decades of neglect. The sustained scrutiny had all come too late. Several weeks after the incident of the woman suffering abdominal pains, the state of California initiated steps to take the hospital's license away.[66] In early August, federal regulators reported that the hospital still could not meet patient care standards. Finally, the county began shutting it down a few days later.[67] All that's left at this writing are outpatient clinics.

Lessons

INVESTIGATIVE PROJECT IDEAS

Lesson Learned: Like any good news story, a good project idea has to be important, interesting and new. But the King/Drew project provides a new dimension to what can be considered new, by showing that no matter how old a story may be, asking the how and why questions and revisiting the what question almost always yield new ideas, even about subjects journalists tend to cast off as "old news."

How It Applied: In Los Angeles County, a story reporting that Martin Luther King, Jr./Drew Medical Center was a bad hospital would be old news, especially among the two million residents who lived around it, to the law enforcement and health care communities and even to readers of the *Los Angeles Times*. It was a story that was three decades old. In fact, when its five-part series was published in December 2004, the *Times* had written close to 100 daily stories in the previous 17 months about the troubles at King/Drew. Nevertheless, the reporters and editors still found something different simply by asking the basic investigative reporting questions—how and why—and challenging the conventionally accepted answers. Despite the hundreds of stories that had been written, none had ever attempted to definitively answer those two basic questions: How could a hospital with a such a dismally tragic patient care history continue to operate for more than 30 years and why did those responsible let it continue? Their work revealed why this "old story" was still a story. Although not all "old news" subjects demand the attention that Tracy Weber and Charles Ornstein gave to King/Drew (lives were at stake in this story), it demonstrates that journalists need to re-examine long-running controversies from a fresh and long-term perspective. As Weber and Ornstein demonstrated, sometimes simply wondering why this is a long-running controversy can produce groundbreaking journalism.

WRITING

Lesson Learned: Because investigative projects usually require painstaking reporting that produces tremendous amounts of complex information, editors and reporters should be prepared to spend as much time on the writing as they do on the reporting.

How It Applied: Weber, a veteran investigative reporter, said the King/Drew project was the first in which she spent roughly equal amounts of time on the reporting and the writing. Although most of the writing was done after the majority of the reporting was completed, Weber's editor, Julie Marquis, said the writing process actually started in March when they started writing very rough drafts. Although the cynics may view that as writing before you have the facts, in reality it is an analytical process that requires the reporters to think about the information they have gathered at various stages in the reporting. It helps them understand what they know and do not know and what they need to know. At the end of the project, the reporting continued well after the writing had started. The most intense period of writing came after the reporting, but even then the reporters wrote dozens of drafts on some of the main stories. In King/Drew, John Carroll, the top editor of the *Los Angeles Times,* often asked reporters to experiment with many different openings, which sometimes required several days of additional reporting and rewriting. Then, he would reject the new version in favor of the original. In such situations, writing and reporting become simultaneous parts of the process and provide a concentrated way to analyze and test your information to make sure the story makes the best and most effective use of the material.

INTERVIEWING

Lesson Learned: To obtain the best and most revealing information in interviews, reporters must be thoroughly prepared and exude the notion that they are genuinely interested in learning and understanding the subject and the interviewee.

How It Applied: In interviewing, journalists often do little more than shag quotes. Such interviewing becomes a perfunctory exercise in asking the question and recording the response. In King/Drew, Weber and Ornstein each noted interviewing characteristics of the other that they felt made their partner a good interviewer. Ornstein knows "way more about the subject than the person he is interviewing" and is "unflinching" when he questions people, Weber said.

In short, Ornstein knows when someone is not giving him completely accurate information and quickly calls the person on it. The two traits combined means he has better a chance of getting credible, thorough and accurate information than those who do not have those qualities. For his part, Ornstein said Weber knows how to get people to open up to her. Although Weber keeps her journalistic distance from her interviewees, she noted that many reporters cavalierly get everything they can out of a source who has opened themselves up to their questions and then they dump them. Weber said she sometimes keeps in touch with a good source—as she did with Johnnie Mae Williams—even after the story is done, which suggests she is genuinely interested in the people who are providing information to her. That is a quality that interviewees or anyone in a conversation with Weber will sense. Not only does that quality foster trust, but it also makes subjects more open to explaining something to someone who is honestly trying to understand the topic or situation.

Is a Project a Beat, or Is a Beat a Project?

Lesson Learned: A project often can be treated as an ad hoc beat. City hall reporters become experts on municipal affairs in general, on their government in particular and on the people in government. In the same manner, project reporters become experts on their topic. However, project reporters often forget they are also daily news reporters who have an obligation to report breaking news concerning their topic when it is urgent and important to the public. For their part, beat reporters cannot forget that they are responsible for identifying projects that should be thoroughly investigated.

How It Applied: Between the summer of 2003 and throughout much of 2005, the *Los Angeles Times* wrote so many stories about King/Drew Medical Center it appeared to be a full-time beat, and Weber and Ornstein were the beat reporters. Like good, aggressive beat reporting, that concentrated daily coverage produced results such as state and accreditation inspections, the closing of the trauma center, the hiring of a turnaround consultant and government actions. Even without the project series, they were—to use a newsroom term of art—"kickin' ass."

Admittedly, Weber and Ornstein sometimes wondered whether they were "scooping themselves" or whether there would be anything left for the project. But the project team provided a journalistic clinic on how to cover a beat. In routine beat reporting, reporters are expected to produce dailies and weekenders, a routine that describes what Weber, Ornstein and their two colleagues did with King/Drew. But the group also took on a third mission on the "King/Drew beat": they worked a long-term project, which they steadily investigated as they covered their beat. In fact, Weber and Ornstein, and their line editor, Julie Marquis, said the daily beat coverage helped their long-term project immeasurably. Every good beat reporter should make that third mission a full-time part of the way they approach their beat. What Weber and Ornstein did fit neatly with Marquis' adamant belief that to be a good beat reporter, a journalist must be a good investigative reporter. "I don't differentiate the roles, except 'investigative reporters' have more time." Ornstein—the quintessential beat reporter—fit that belief, because his entire journalistic approach, he said, is driven by the need to find out how and why things work they way they do.

Marquis' logic seems unassailable. No one in a news organization is in better position than a beat reporter to sense trends, to know when a conflict of interest occurs, to notice systemic problems or departures from the normal policy, practice, and pattern or to be the first person a disgruntled employee thinks about when problems and misconduct arise. No one in the news organization knows the sources better than the beat reporter. If beat reporters do a good job reporting the news, they become the people with the most expertise who should be in the right place at the right time among the right people to identify the right projects to investigate.

The only missing elements for turning every beat reporter into a true investigative reporter are time—as Marquis points out—and the investigative mentality. The former is a solvable administrative issue. The latter requires a newsroom culture in which every reporter works every story with the investigative mentality. Developing that newsroom culture is neither a top-down nor a bottom-up process: It evolves from both directions. The editors must insist upon it and make that desire known by ensuring that a long-term investigative project becomes an integral part of each reporter's plan for covering his or her beat. Beat reporters must employ the investigative mentality in every interview, meeting or hallway conversation with sources. Although access to top officials is important, fear of losing it cannot prevent the reporter from asking tough questions or aggressively pursuing every story that arises without regard to whether it may offend a top official. Although the practice of tough, aggressive journalism may close up some sources on a beat, it opens up others.

NEED FOR PROJECTS SYMPTOMATIC OF DAILY REPORTING'S FAILURES

Lesson Learned: When news organizations fail to adequately cover institutions that purport to serve society, systemic weaknesses fester and misconduct often spreads and becomes more serious. Eventually, the problems become so egregious that a news organization takes notice and launches an investigative project. That is a scenario akin to calling the doctor when the patient is almost dead. In the journalism field, launching a project at that late hour is almost too late. The problem it identifies is usually deeply entrenched, and the bureaucrats who caused it are so numerous and powerful that the system can withstand the transient, elected leadership's effort to launch the sustained, aggressive reform effort that usually is needed.

How It Applied: Other chapters in this book have shown how investigative reporting frequently has to make up for failure of insufficient daily or beat reporting in the past. In "Troubles at King/Drew," we saw a similar pattern, but with a different twist that dramatically demonstrates the consequences of the failure of daily reporting.

Before Tracy Weber and Charles Ornstein turned their attention to King/Drew Medical Center, the *Times* had given the hospital spotty coverage despite the fact that its "Killer King" moniker attached not long after it opened in 1975. Early on, the paper broke stories about individual patient care disasters and produced a major investigative project in late 1989 that unearthed some serious systemic problems. The paper's online archives show—and the project team members confirm—that the paper did not devote sustained, watchdog coverage to a problem institution that purported to serve society.

A fundamental purpose of investigative reporting is to identify serious problems, such as a hospital that was killing and maiming the people it was supposed to serve. When a news organization brings such a problem to the public's attention, it is putting the problem on the public agenda. The news organization is then responsible for covering that agenda item aggressively by reporting to the readers how their government is correcting the problem and whether those corrections are working.

In Los Angeles County, the paper had many avenues to keep close watch on King/Drew throughout its history because it is a publicly owned hospital run by elected officials, which means that voluminous records are available. For example, the Board of Supervisors must approve malpractice settlements, state inspectors must conduct routine inspections, and accrediting agencies must do periodic reviews.

In stark contrast to that history, the *Los Angeles Times* aggressively covered King/Drew Medical Center after the publication of the series in late 2004, and it continued even after John Carroll left the paper and as Ornstein and Weber took on new and demanding projects. Other *Times* reporters were called in when necessary. Well into the summer of 2007, the paper's coverage was sustained and aggressive, keeping the pressure on state and federal regulators, accrediting agencies and, especially the Board of County Supervisors. At times, it maintained a special King/Drew link on its online edition for continuing developments.

Alas, it was too late. Although the Board of Supervisors had taken the most aggressive measures in King/Drew's history, hospital misadventures continued and patients kept dying unnecessarily. Finally, it was closed.

Notes

1. The interviewees listed here are the sources for their direct and indirect quotes; reconstruction of interviews between themselves and their sources; and depictions of their conversations, thoughts and actions that are not referenced in the text:

Tracy Weber, Los Angeles, CA, May 31, 2006; August 2, 2006, and July 5, 2007, by telephone.

Charlie Ornstein, Los Angeles, CA, May 31, 2006; August 23, 2006, by telephone.

Julie Marquis, *Los Angeles Times* cafeteria, May 26 and May 30, 2006.

Some material from these sources is individually referenced where necessary to ensure clarity.

2. "Brief History of Martin Luther King Jr. Multi-service Ambulatory Care Center," Los Angeles County Health Services. http://www.ladhs.org/history.htm.

3. Sue Fox, "County Set to Cut 79 Doctors at King-Drew," *Los Angeles Times*, June 5, 2003, p. B1. The story is about personnel cuts, and it discusses the hospital's role as a source of community and racial pride. Mitchell Landsberg, "Why Supervisors Let Deadly Problems Slide" (part five of five-part series, "The Troubles at King Drew"),

Los Angeles Times, December 9, 2004, p. A1. Tracy Weber, Charles Ornstein, " 'Killer King': County-run Hospital Mired in Poor Care, Financial Misdeeds and Empty Promises" *The Ire Journal*, May–June 2005, pp. 32–33. Interview, Marquis, May 30, 2006. Interview, Charlie Ornstein, May 31, 2006, and August 23, 2006.

4. Claire Spiegel, "Short of Staff, Funds Hospital: A Crisis in Critical Care" (First in a series, "Critical Condition: Martin Luther King Jr./Drew Medical Center"), *Los Angeles Times*, September 3, 1989, p. 1. This package is the most dramatic example of the scattering of articles about King/Drew's medical care problems that were published in the *Los Angeles Times* throughout its history before Ornstein and Weber launched their investigation in the summer of 2003.

5. Interview, Julie Marquis, May 26, 2006; interview, Tracy Weber, May 31, 2006.

6. Interview, Marquis. May 30, 2006.

7. Ibid.

8. Tracy Weber and Charles Ornstein, "County-USC Doctors Say Delays Fatal. Sworn Declarations Allege Instances When Quicker Care Would Have Saved Patients' Lives," *Los Angeles Times*, April 23, 2003, p. B1; Charles Ornstein and Tracy Weber. "Hospital Problems Flagged by State," *Los Angeles Times*, May 3, 2003, p. B1; Tracy Weber. "County-USC Faulted for Delays in Care. State Inspectors Report Staffing Shortages, Overcrowding and Incomplete Charts," *Los Angeles Times*, May 31, 2003, p. B1.

9. Los Angeles County website. http://lacounty.info/overview.htm.

10. Landsberg, "Why Supervisors Let Deadly Problems Slide."

11. Tracy Weber and Charles Ornstein, "King Drew Loses Its Right to Train Surgeons," *Los Angeles Times*, August 23, 2003, p. A1.

12. Landsberg, "Why Supervisors Let Deadly Problems Slide." This story mentions early 1970s coverage.

13. Spiegel, "Short of Staff, Funds Hospital."

14. Interview, Mitchell Landsberg, September 6, 2006.

15. Claire Spiegel, "King Hospital Faces Loss of Federal Funds," *Los Angeles Times*, September 26, 1989, p. A1. Claire Spiegel, "County Pledges to Correct Problems at King Hospital," *Los Angeles Times*, October 4, 1989, p. A1; Kenneth Garcia, "Turnaround by King Hospital Rescues Funds," *Los Angeles Times*, December 19, 1989, p. A1; Claire Spiegel, "King Hospital Passes Test, but Key Problems Remain," *Los Angeles Times*, November 27, 1991, p. A1.

16. Josh Meyer and Jeffrey L. Rabin, "Supervisor Urges Sweeping Hospital Overhaul: Responding to New Revelations of Problems at King/Drew, Burke Says She Will Seek a Major Shake-up to Try to Restore Confidence," *Los Angeles Times*, December 23, 1995, p. B1.

17. Claire Spiegel, "King Hospital Chief Removed from Post," *Los Angeles Times*, September 27, 1989, p. 1. The story says county supervisors considered firing hospital administrator William Delgado but backed off in the face of community protests and opposition from the NAACP and other black organizations. This article and the next three convey the tenor of the black community's reactions to criticism of the hospital. Claire Spiegel, "Angry Crowd Defends King Hospital," *Los Angeles Times*, September 28, 1989, p. B3. Supporters denounced inspection reports of King Hospital as biased and attacked the *Times* for "putting black leaders in the headlines only when they are accused of making mistakes." Geoffrey Mohan, "Defending a Beleaguered Hospital," *Los Angeles Times*, January 5, 1996, p. B1. This quotes hospital workers blaming racial bias and politics for the criticism and claim King/Drew's successes are ignored. Charles Ornstein and Tracy Weber, "Transfusion at the Top at King/Drew,"

Los Angeles Times, October 24, 2003, p. B1. The story quotes black county supervisor Yvonne B. Burke complaining about repeated community opposition preventing positive change. It also quotes a Drew professor opposing the appointment of a management team to seek solutions to the hospital problems, calling it a "power grab" by the county leaders who don't understand the hospital's history.

18. Interview, Marquis, May 26, 2006.

19. Interview, Weber, May 31, 2006; Interview, Charlie Ornstein, May 31, 2006; Interview, Marquis, May 26, 2006; Interview, Mitchell Landsberg, September 6, 2006.

20. Charles Ornstein and Tracy Weber, "2 Patients Die After Alarms Fail," *Los Angeles Times,* August 22, 2003, p. B1.

21. Weber and Ornstein, "King/Drew Loses Its Right," *Los Angeles Times,* August 23, 2003, p. A1.

22. Tracy Weber and Charles Ornstein, "King/Drew Patient Monitors Shut Off Following 2 Deaths," *Los Angeles Times,* September 10, 2003, p. B1.

23. Charles Ornstein and Tracy Weber, "Inspectors Rebuke King/Drew," *Los Angeles Times,* December 9, 2003, p. B1.

24. Charles Ornstein and Tracy Weber, "For Days, Potent Drug Given to Wrong King/Drew Patient," *Los Angeles Times,* February 26, 2004, p. B1.

25. Interview, John Carroll, September 27, 2006.

26. Ibid.

27. Weber and Ornstein, "'Killer King': County-Run Hospital Mired in Poor Care, Financial Misdeeds and Empty Promises," *The IRE Journal.*

28. Charles Ornstein, Tracy Weber, and Steve Hymon, "Underfunding Is a Myth, but the Squandering Is Real" (part two of five parts in "The Trouble at King Drew"), *Los Angeles Times,* December 6, 2004, p. A1. The story quotes a black former pediatric cardiologist, Dr. Ernie Smith, as saying, "I've been here 31 years and watched this hospital be yanked and pulled … shot and kicked. This is nothing more than racism and white supremacy."

29. Ibid.

30. Ibid.

31. Ibid.

32. Interview, Steve Hymon, September 1, 2006.

33. Ibid.

34. Tracy Weber and Charles Ornstein, "One Doctor's Long Trail of Dangerous Mistakes" (part three of five-part series, "The Troubles at King/Drew"), *Los Angeles Times,* December 7, 2004, p. A1.

35. Interview, Weber, August 2, 2006.

36. Weber and Ornstein, "One Doctor's Long Trail of Dangerous Mistakes."

37. Interview, Weber, August 2, 2006.

38. Interview, Landsberg, September 6, 2006.

39. Daren Briscoe, Charles Ornstein, and Mitchell Landsberg, "King/Drew Facing Major Overhaul," *Los Angeles Times,* December 10, 2003, p. B1. The story quotes County Supervisor Gloria Molina complaining about the hostility of hospital supporters toward her when she tried to get involved in the hospital, with supporters claiming she was trying to take over the hospital. The story said supervisors complained about the political sensitivities in an apparent reference to race and traditional political rivalries. Mitchell Landsberg and Daren Briscoe, "'Colorblind' Approach Urged for King/Drew," *Los Angeles Times,* January 14, 2004, p. B1. Black County Supervisor Yvonne B. Burke and Latino Supervisor Gloria Molina com-

plained about the racial sensitivities that have made reform difficult. Burke called for a "colorblind" approach, and Molina, alluding to the racial overtones, said there has been "this ghost or cloud" over King/Drew that interferes with change.

40. Landsberg, "Why Supervisors Let Deadly Problems Slide."

41. Ibid.

42. Interview, Landsberg, September 6, 2006.

43. Ibid.

44. Briscoe, Ornstein, and Landsberg, "King/Drew Facing Major Overhaul"; Landsberg, "Why Supervisors Let Deadly Problems Slide."

45. Charles Ornstein and Tracy Weber, "For Days Patient Given Wrong Drug," *Los Angeles Times*, February 26, 2004, p. B1.

46. Landsberg, "Why Supervisors Let Deadly Problems Slide."

47. Ibid.

48. Ornstein and Weber, "Transfusion at the Top at King/Drew."

49. Ornstein, Weber, and Hymon, "Underfunding Is a Myth."

50. Interview, Landsberg, September 6, 2006.

51. Ibid.

52. Ibid.

53. The Staples Center controversy was a newsroom revolt in the late 1990s that forced the resignation of the paper's top corporate executives. It erupted when journalists, including this author, learned that the executives had entered a secret, profit-sharing partnership with the developers of the Staples Center arena in the production of a special edition of the paper's Sunday magazine. The edition was devoted entirely to the opening of the new sports arena. The newsroom staff, especially the journalists who wrote the special edition, said the agreement compromised their integrity and the paper's independence, because the developers would help sell ads in the special edition and share in its profits.

54. Interview, Landsberg, September 6, 2006.

55. Landsberg, "Why Supervisors Let Deadly Problems Slide."

56. Interview, Landsberg, September 6, 2006.

57. Interview, Carroll, September 27, 2006.

58. Ibid.

59. Tracy Weber, Charles Ornstein, and Mitchell Landsberg, "Deadly Errors and Politics Betray a Hospital's Promise" (part one of five-part series, "The Troubles at King/Drew"), December 5, 2005, p. A1.

60. Ibid.

61. Interview, Carroll, September 27, 2006.

62. Leonard Downie and Robert Kaiser, *The News About the News: American Journalism in Peril* (New York: Knopf, 2002), 93.

63. Interview, Carroll, September 27, 2006.

64. Charles Ornstein, "How King-Harbor Has Stayed Alive; Defended by Its Community, the Hospital Hangs on to Certification Despite Repeated Lapses," *Los Angeles Times*, June 12, 2007, p. A1.

65. Charles Ornstein, "Woman at King-Harbor Died of Perforated Bowel," June 2, 2007, p. B3.

66. Charles Ornstein, "State Health Department Makes Case for Closing MLK-Harbor," *Los Angeles Times*, June 30, 2007, p. B1.

67. Charles Ornstein, Tracy Weber, and Jack Leonard, "King-Harbor Fails Final Check, Will Close Soon; The ER Is Shut Down, and the Rest Will Follow Within Two Weeks," *Los Angeles Times*, August 11, 2007, p. A1.

Selected Bibliography

Articles

Brief History of Martin Luther King Jr. Multi-service Ambulatory Care Center. Los Angeles County Health Services. http://www.ladhs.org/history.htm.

Spiegel, Claire. "Short of Staff, Funds Hospital: A Crisis in Critical Care." [First in a series, "Critical Condition: Martin Luther King Jr./Drew Medical Center"]. *Los Angeles Times*, September 3, 1989.

Weber, Tracy, and Charles Ornstein. "The Troubles at King Drew" [Five-part series]. *Los Angeles Times*, December 5–9, 2004.

Weber, Tracy, and Charles Ornstein. "'Killer King': County-Run Hospital Mired in Poor Care, Financial Misdeeds and Empty Promises." *IRE Journal*, May–June 2005, 32–33.

Book

Downie, Leonard, and Robert Kaiser. *The News About the News: American Journalism in Peril*. New York: Knopf, 2002.

Interviews

Carroll, John, former editor of the *Los Angeles Times*, September 27, 2006.

Hymon, Steve, reporter, *Los Angeles Times*, September 1, 2006.

Landsberg, Mitchell, reporter, *Los Angeles Times*, September 6, 2006.

Marquis, Julie, editor for health, immigration, growth, demographics, *Los Angeles Times*, May 26 and May 30, 2006 (tape recording held by author).

Ornstein, Charlie, reporter, *Los Angeles Times*, May 31, 2006 (tape recording held by author).

Ornstein, Charlie, reporter, *Los Angeles Times*, August 23, 2006.

Weber, Tracy, reporter, *Los Angeles Times*, May 31, 2006 (tape recording held by author).

Weber, Tracy, reporter, *Los Angeles Times*, August 2, 2006.

Weber, Tracy, reporter, *Los Angeles Times*, July 5, 2007.

News Archives and News Search Services

Access World News, NewsBank, Inc., Naples, FL.

Los Angeles Times online archives, http://pqasb.pqarchiver.com/latimes/search.html.

Websites

Los Angeles County website, http://lacounty.info/overview.htm.

The Pulitzer Prize website, http://www.pulitzer.org.

Conclusions

After spending hour after hour interviewing 25 journalists for this book, and after months studying the hundreds of articles written on their topics before and after their Pulitzer projects, a host of "what if" questions emerged. What if, for one example, a project of the magnitude and vision of "Troubles at King/Drew" had been written in the early 1980s when patients first started calling the hospital "Killer King"? How many lives would have been saved?

The questions are rhetorical; their point being that the type of stellar journalism seen in those stories and in so much investigative reporting we see today comes too late. Why does good journalism have to wait until people die?

In journalism education, that question and all of its ramifications for quality journalism must be on the front burner. It is especially important today as we navigate all of the adjustments that technology brings to us. If we are not careful, pressure to train multi-mediasts instead of journalists can distract us from the core mission of journalism to improve the quality of the information we provide to our readers, viewers or listeners.

In the profession, the easy excuse for waiting is that investigative reporting is too expensive to practice regularly; that the bottom-line pressures imposed by corporate chains are making good journalism increasingly difficult for every news organization; that newsrooms have all they can handle just getting the news out each day with decreasing resources. Newsrooms do, indeed, have full plates covering the routine news, and resources obviously play a role in determining to what extent newspapers can go beyond that role.

However, the work of the journalists in the preceding chapters and the origins of the projects they investigated suggest solutions and a new approach to daily reporting. Although both big media power and money help, the success of this work rested more on basic journalism and professionalism.

The fact that the word "project" commonly attaches to the word "investigative" suggests a solution by simply showing us what the problem is: Journalism waits until a community problem becomes "project sized" before reporters and editors take interest and unleash the full power of watchdog journalism. Traditionally, standard daily journalism has meant covering an event today for the next day's paper, then moving on to the next story while shoe-horning enough additional enterprise reporting on one of the dailies or on a feature topic to produce a weekender. It is indisputable that the routine provides an important and useful service to the public. Moreover, many aggressive, tough examples of watchdog journalism break out of that routine. In practice, though, it is a frenetic and exhausting pace, especially at small and midsized news organizations, and important stories often get lost in the rush and the flow of events.

When impressive investigative reporting projects do emerge, they do more than reveal deeply, entrenched long-standing problems. They also reveal the failings of daily journalism. Time after time, highly successful investigative work covers the stories journalists missed years ago or failed to cover adequately. Consider the first chapter in this book, which traces the 1992 investigative project by this author and Jeff Brazil. Three-and-half years before publication, in the winter of 1989, the *Sentinel* began publishing stories on Sheriff Bob Vogel's intriguing drug-interdiction program, in which his special squad pulled over I-95 motorists for picky violations and seized their cash on mere suspicion that it was drug money. As discussed in the chapter's Lessons section, those stories reported some immensely important events and practices that struck at the heart of American jurisprudence and at people's sense of racial justice. For example, those 1989 stories reported that the deputies had not proven that the cash was drug money or shown that the motorists had done anything wrong. They also reported how deputies used microscopic traces of cocaine on the bills as probable cause evidence of wrongdoing even though studies had shown money in general circulation was tainted with drug traces. They reported that noticeable numbers of those motorists were black or Hispanic.

Those apparent evidentiary and constitutional problems did not receive the journalistic scrutiny that a reporter imbued with the investigative mentality would employ, and those stories repeated those issues several times that year and afterward. The articles simply reported a law enforcement activity, and the dominant, more entertaining theme depicted the folk-hero sheriff doing battle with the forces of evil. Those reader-friendly but shallow stories never produced a major impact. Yet, in the summer of 1992—after the highway haul had reached nearly $8 million—the same newspaper carried "Tainted Cash or Easy Money?" which reported the same type of law enforcement activity and the same constitutional problems. But as Chapter 1 disclosed, that old story—now in "project form," because it had indeed become project size—prompted enormous popular and official reactions, sparked several investigations and reforms, won the Pulitzer Prize for investigative reporting in 1993 and gave all of our careers a big boost.

Skipping to the last chapter and jumping a dozen years into the future to the most tragic story in the book, a somewhat similar scenario played out at the *Los Angeles Times*. Prior to publication of "Troubles at King/Drew," the 2004 project by lead reporters Charles Ornstein and Tracy Weber the paper's cadre of experienced reporters and editors had covered the King/Drew Medical Center's problems sporadically since they first started surfacing in the mid-1970s. In 1989 the *Times* even published an investigative project revealing how the hospital was killing and maiming its patients because of negligence and incompetence going back over several years. In a dramatic and compelling way, then-reporter Claire Spiegel had taken the initiative and forced a life-or-death issue onto the public agenda. For a brief spell, the project received a flurry of attention and promises of reform, but then King/Drew fell off the radars of the *Times* and of county government, except for occasional blips here and there. Little or nothing changed at King/Drew. Sixteen years and several unnecessary deaths later, the *Times* again was reporting that King/Drew was killing and maiming people. As Chapter 6 reported, their stories prompted enormous reactions, sparking official investigations and real changes. The *Times* series was a tremendous success and won the 2005 Pulitzer Prize for Public Service.

In contrast to years past, the *Times* did not let King/Drew drop off of its agenda or that of the county supervisors. Nevertheless, all of the efforts came too late. The patient—the hospital itself—was practically dead. The follow-up coverage after the series ran produced more cases of negligence and negative inspections, and finally, authorities forced King/Drew to close in the summer of 2007. It is too early to write the epitaph for King/Drew, because supporters and county officials still promise it will rise again. If it does, its reincarnation will have its roots in the *Times'* late but exemplary and sustained coverage after the fall of 2003.

"Troubles at King/Drew" and "Tainted Cash or Easy Money?" became successful journalistically because they did what the previous coverage had failed to do. Besides exposing the problem and again documenting the human impact, the stories showed how, why and where the system broke down, placed blame and left a clear picture of what needed to be done to fix the problems. They covered issues and problems that the earlier coverage missed or simply failed to scrutinize. In short, they "did it right" this time, and got to the bottom of things.

These delay-push scenarios are not unusual. The "Broken Homes" project covered in Chapter 5 was not the first time that the *New York Times* wrote about the abuses of mentally ill residents in privately run adult homes. The coverage had begun not long after psychiatric hospitals across the country started dumping mentally ill people into those homes or into the streets. The paper's archives reveal clips from the 1980s and 1990s that addressed some of the key issues that Cliff Levy explored in 2001 and early 2002 to win the Pulitzer.

Highly successful projects that fit the traditional view of investigative reporting—revealing cover-ups, corruption and the like—also reveal the shortcomings of daily journalism. *The Baltimore Sun's* "Shipbreakers" project in December 1997 probably was the envy of reporters all over the country. The editor, John Carroll, and the reporters, Will Englund and Gary Cohn, had come up with the fresh story about a topic filled with human tragedy but so arcane that it never captured much attention. Even that project, however, showed that the *Sun* had overlooked a story that had been floating in Baltimore Harbor since 1993. Moreover, just two states down the coast, the much smaller and less prestigious *Wilmington* (N.C.) *Star-News* swung into action in 1994 after some of the shipbreakers in Baltimore got into trouble with federal environmental officials and set up their scrapping shop in Wilmington. The *Star-News* wrote dozens of stories about the scrappers' work in North Carolina, including one in 1994 about their problems in Baltimore Harbor. Moreover, just as the *Sun* was about to launch its probe into the shipbreaking industry, the *Star-News* published an investigative project of its own, revealing the environmental and safety hazards, worker deaths and injuries and other issues that the *Sun* would later cover in a much more powerful, thorough, revealing and global manner. That project—like the others—caused some immediate impact. By the summer of 2005, however, one of the authors, Will Englund—now an editorial writer—discovered the same problems had come back and some of the same culprits were still at work.

In Oregon, the journalistic issue in the revelation by an alternative weekly of former Gov. Neil Goldschmidt's sexual abuse of a 14-year-old babysitter is that it took the press three decades to discover and then report the sordid situation, too late for justice to render its verdict. Granted, government and business have mastered the art of secrecy, but as Chapter 2 discussed, the *Willamette Week*'s "30-Year Secret" was about a secret that actually was not so secret.

For years throughout the 1980s and early 1990s, Goldschmidt's victim frequently and openly blabbed details about the abuse to dozens of different people, including lawyers, when she got a little tipsy at the numerous bars she frequented. An *Oregonian* columnist and an editor and later the co-founder of *Mother Jones* magazine heard about stories in the 1980s or early 1990s. By the early 1990s, the victim's story was circulating in government circles. A former Goldschmidt speechwriter became disenchanted with his former boss after he learned about the abuse and began talking openly about it to numerous other insiders before he finally went to *The Oregonian* with names, places and dates.[1] Still, the truth did not emerge until Nigel Jaquiss, while working on an entirely different story about Goldschmidt in early 2004, heard about the rumor, found a scrap of an official document and went after the story with bulldog persistence.

Covering Beats as Investigative Projects

The reporting seen in these six projects and in several others researched for this book illustrate that journalism should not consider investigative reporting as a separate genre of the profession held in reserve until a problem becomes an expensive, resource-draining project that comes too late for substantive and long-lasting reform. Much of what these reporters did in investigating their projects mimics beat reporting. Their projects became their beats, and they had to learn their beats. As any beat reporter would do, they identified the major players, developed and nurtured reporter–source relationships, learned the bureaucracy, and sometimes wrote daily or enterprise stories.

"I always like to emphasize the similarities more than the differences," said Eric Nalder, a two-time Pulitzer winner and chief investigative reporter for the *Seattle Post-Intelligencer* at this writing.[2] Scott Higham, the son of a homicide cop and the winner of a Pulitzer in 2002 with Sari Horwitz for *The Washington Post*, started as a beat reporter in Florida, and found the similarities instructive. Higham said he did a lot of short enterprise and "quick-hit investigative reporting" while on the beat. "As a beat reporter, I started realizing that the whole reason to have a beat is to get deep into the subject matter and the community so you could start telling readers things that will make them sit up and pay attention."[3]

Sari Horwitz, his partner for their Pulitzer-winning series, "Lost Children," has long considered herself a beat reporter by nature. Joining the *Post*'s investigative team was strange to her. "It just seemed to me the best stories had always come off the beat," she said. Indeed, "Lost Children," was straight off a beat. But in her beats, particularly, covering law enforcement and later a self-developed poverty beat, she developed a signature style that was investigative in nature.

"I feel like there is so much reporting that is a response to the news: go to a crime scene, go to a president's briefing, write a story," she said. "I said I really want to get away from that. I wanted to get underneath a story, and I was doing this as a daily reporter."[4]

Of the six projects examined in the preceding chapters, "Troubles at King/ Drew" provided the best example of investigative journalism treated as a beat and a project. Ornstein and Weber probably could not have produced the King/Drew series without the luxury of focus. Although Ornstein considers himself a beat reporter and Weber an investigative reporter, both were the quintessential investigative/beat journalists, and King/Drew hospital became their de facto beat. They not only were investigating King/Drew for the five-part capstone package, but they and their two colleagues, Mitchell Landsberg and Steve Hymon, churned out close to 100 daily news and enterprise stories about the hospital during the 18 months leading up to publication of the series. As with any beat, the daily and enterprise stories generated tips and produced new sources. However, as Ornstein, Weber and their editor, Julie Marquis pointed out, the daily reporting contributed to the investigative project and gave it the texture and substance that would have been absent without it. Ornstein provided the beat reporter expertise and insider knowledge, and both he and Weber discovered new types of records, understood the hospital accreditation process, the state and federal inspection procedures and the complexities of patient-care statistics. In every way, they covered their beat thoroughly while they plugged along on a long-term project. That is beat reporting as it is intended to be.

The *Sun*'s Gary Cohn believes beat reporters are positioned perfectly to do investigative reporting, because they already have the sources established, know how the system works inside and out and have developed an expertise in their specialty. In investigative reporting, all of those tasks are part of what goes into investigating a topic.

The work of the journalists on these six projects shows how beat reporters can take their coverage beyond the basics. Beat reporters need to think of their beats as investigative projects in two ways. In a broad sense, they must become experts who understand how and why their beat works the way it does. In the more literal sense, they should be working on a long-term explanatory or investigative project while they are churning out their regular news fare. They have to do more than learn the bureaucracy; they have to learn the policies that govern the bureaucracy so that when it veers off track, they understand whether the deviation is an insignificant aberration, a systemic problem, a sign of someone gaming the system or otherwise serving the public poorly. They have to nurture reporter–source relationships with the minions in the bureaucracy, the ones who know how every gear and wheel in the machinery mesh. They should build factual dossiers on the key administrators and elected officials to help them remain alert to proposals, actions and decisions that serve self-interests as much as public interests.

Most important, beat reporters have to learn to analyze daily stories from a perspective that is broader and more comprehensive than what that day's 5 p.m. or weekend deadline would permit. A common theme among the investigative reporters and editors in these chapters is that—in Cliff Levy's words—"the luxury of time" provides them with the single most important advantage they have over the typical daily news reporter. The stricture of time naturally narrows the scope of the daily reporters' perspective, because they have to identify that little piece of the story that they can accurately develop in the time allotted for that day or week. Ironically, their only hope for relief from those strictures is the ability to see how their daily news story might be a microcosm of broader consequences, problems or developments that could be explored if they were not limited by the daily or weekend deadline. That is where the momentous ideas emerge, ideas that will persuade an editor to grant them "the luxury of time."

Nalder, the *Post-Intelligencer* investigative chief, believes that one of the most common reasons reporters miss good investigative stories on their beats is not that they fail to see the story, but that they fail to collaborate with people in their own newsrooms, particularly with editors, to have what he calls "an enabling conversation."[5]

Ideally, all of the projects are the type of topics that should emerge on a beat and can be spotted and investigated by a beat reporter imbued with the investigative mentality. "Broken Homes" could surface on several beats: the courts, police (because people were killed) or health and human services to name a few. "Shipbreakers" did emerge from a beat—the newly created and short-lived waterfront beat—but it also spanned several beats ranging from the federal courts to the environmental beat, business beat and immigration beat. *The Toledo Blade*'s "Buried Secrets, Brutal Truths" investigation into the Tiger Force's 1967 rampage covered a crucial issue in war coverage, military affairs and the defense beat, particularly at a time when the My Lai massacre had shattered American naiveté about this country's capacity for unthinkable brutality. In "Tainted Cash or Easy Money?" a police reporter, just as Weber and Ornstein did with "Troubles at King/Drew," could have launched a cash seizure investigation while churning out the periodic cash seizure dailies and covering other events.

"All Reporters Are Investigative"—For Real

The challenge to daily journalism that emerges in these pages is this: If the ability of editors to launch expensive investigative projects that affect public affairs continues to diminish, daily and beat reporters will have to take up the slack. They will have to assume more of the investigative responsibility in their daily routines if the media is to continue fulfilling the responsibility to serve as the public watchdog on government and all institutions that purport to serve society. Many hard-news reporters already argue that "all reporters are investigative." Now, more than ever, they must practice what they preach.

It starts with adopting an investigative mentality. Such a term defies definition in the dictionary sense, which is why the work of journalists in these chapters shows us rather than tells us what the phrase means. Cohn, the most senior reporter in the chapters and the most experienced, says his investigative attitude is more about understanding what and why something happened and who it affected rather than simply trying to nail a target to the wall with a barrage of prosecutorial questions. "It always scares me when I hear young reporters walk around the newsroom saying 'I'm going to get so and so, because he is the bad guy,'" Cohn said. "Life is not that simple." He and Englund began interviewing the captains of the shipbreaking industry near the beginning of their investigation, because, to understand the complexities of that business, they had to understand who worked in it. Deborah Nelson, a former investigations editor for the *Los Angeles Times*, whose 1996 work with Nalder won the Pulitzer Prize, said she also often went to the "targets" or subjects of the investigation very early in the reporting and revealed her mission. The early approach, she explained, helped her understand the project, and even opened up public records for her.[6]

In discussing the investigative mentality and what makes an investigative reporter, some of the journalists talked about a way of viewing their mission as journalists and of viewing a story. Rebecca Corbett, the former investigations editor at the *Baltimore Sun* and later an editor at *The New York Times*, said that whereas many reporters want to write stories that have a lot of impact, investigative reporters are more likely to be those who want to write stories that change the world. "Part of the difference," Corbett said, "is tenacity, perseverance and not having to have your name in the paper everyday." Deborah Nelson described investigative reporting "as nothing more than trying to figure out what really happened in matters of consequence." It's not just reporting what government officials say, but finding out whether what they say is the truth. "It's getting to the bottom of things," she said.[7]

Reviving the Pursuit of Objectivity

To get to the bottom of things, the mental and tactical effort to be objective was the most reliable path that the investigative reporters in these chapters followed, and journalism should reclaim it as its professional signature. The notion of objectivity is much maligned in academic circles, partly because the term and its application are often misused, sometimes by its own adherents. Used as a method of inquiry, objectivity becomes liberating rather than confining and turns into an instrument of reform rather than a roadblock. It is a process of testing one's perspective on facts and situations and challenging findings and conclusions. A conscientious effort to be objective leads reporters to the deepest understanding of a subject. As long as journalists understand that people cannot be truly objective but that reporters must never quit trying, they have a reasonable chance of producing stories that are as close to the truth as circumstances and human frailty will allow.

Stories grounded in that kind of effort produce the kind of powerful writing that cause reform, which is the goal of serious public affairs journalists. Lacing such writing with crusading, opinionated prose cheapens the work, because opinions—especially in this day of 24-hour cable talk, blogs and online reader reaction space—are, as they say, a dime a dozen. Moreover, relegating objectivity to the mindless he-said/she said style of reporting as many journalists and educators define it, reduces a valuable tool to a robotic ritual yielding a brand of journalism that frequently misleads more than it informs. Reclaiming it as a mind-opening and probing method of inquiry rather than as a perfunctory routine must define the journalists of the 21st century. That can be the key to renewing the journalists' ability and credibility as seekers of the truth.

In the pursuit of a news story, objectivity translates into a simple yet automatic question that investigative reporter Nigel Jaquiss was mindful of in "The 30-Year Secret": whether he was seeing a situation the way he wanted to see it or the way it really was. That is a question investigative journalists ask themselves repeatedly over the course of reporting a story. Granted, many observers find significance in the notion that one can never know the answer to that question in an absolute sense, and they are correct. But if journalists keep asking it anyway, they stand a better chance of getting closer to the truth than those who do not. Moreover, the effort to be objective in reporting stories will lead to the kinds of truths that will tell readers whether a politician statutorily raped a girl in Oregon, whether American soldiers murdered innocent people in Vietnam and whether the government failed to protect the mentally ill in New York City. Those kinds of truths are worth knowing.

In recent years, the purpose and value of journalistic objectivity has become fuzzy and controversial, because it is often confused with the notions of fairness and balance, especially when the three terms are intertwined or used interchangeably. To many people, including journalists, fairness to the innocent and to the scoundrel alike are commonsense imperatives. In journalism, the fairness mandate has a utilitarian value as well. It is another method of inquiry essential to the search for truth. Besides treating individuals fairly, it requires being fair to the facts, which is trying to understand what facts mean rather than making them reflect what you want them to mean or uncritically accepting what sources with agendas say they mean.

The increasingly common notion that stories must be balanced, however, has become one of the most serious challenges to fair and accurate reporting, and perhaps the primary contributor to confusion about the importance of objectivity in good reporting. Accuracy and truth—not balance—are the ultimate goals of reporting at any level, be it spot news or long-term investigative reporting. Balance becomes a distortion of reality when reporters pursue it as the mission of their work. The reporters in this book conscientiously tried to be fair to the subjects of their investigation and to the facts related to them. They talked about those efforts, but none of them stated that their mission was to produce a story that was balanced. Nor did they say their mission was to produce a story that was out of balance; it just did not come up in their conversations about their stories or about journalism as a profession. As many of them said, their primary mission was to understand the subject and to get to the bottom of things.

The omission of balance in their conversations is telling and proper. The requirement to be fair to the facts and to individuals in producing a thoroughly researched story usually will not produce a balanced picture. In fact, a requirement to balance all stories would be tantamount to a requirement to distort the facts. In "The 30-Year Secret," the *Willamette Week* set out to determine whether former Oregon governor Neil Goldschmidt had sex with a 14-year-old girl when he was mayor of Portland in the 1970s. If a body of evidence is of equal weight and 90 percent of that evidence had pointed to guilt and 10 percent pointed to innocence, a story balanced 50–50 would have required a distortion of the body of evidence. If a balanced story is the end product of objective, thorough and fair reporting, so be it. Even with that eventuality, though, the journalist should be suspicious of his or her own work, because it probably missed something. At best, balance can, in some carefully considered cases, function as a default standard of presentation for deadline reporting; but, again, it probably results in an inaccurate initial picture that should be fleshed out with additional reporting as soon as possible.

Balance may provide a useful reporting guideline, but only in the sense that a thorough investigation would require reporters to begin their work by examining all sides of a controversy rather than focusing on only one side. The evidence supporting some of those sides will be nonexistent or weak, and, thus can often be dismissed as frivolous rather quickly. Some sides will have more supporting evidence than others. News stories cannot burden the readers with every conceivable side to a controversy. So journalists must not flinch from making some evidence-based news judgments rather than give the frivolous as much authority as it gives to the credible. Making a news story balanced for the sake of balance is not journalism; it is presenting the world the way people may want it to be, not the way most of us have experienced it.

The practice of objectivity as a discipline in inquiry and self-questioning should be a primary part of journalism education and daily reporting on every story. That is what separates those who practice journalism as professionals from those who consider themselves journalists because they hold pen and pad or videocamera, witnessed an event and can publish on the Internet.

The New Newsroom Culture

Incorporating the investigative mentality in daily journalism will require editors and reporters to make adjustments to overcome some very real challenges. One of the challenges is the "beast." The beast is what some antsy editors call the gaping columns of white spaces that constitute the daily news hole. It is a ravenous monster, in their view, and its appetite for copy is never satiated.

The Washington Post's Scott Higham, in discussing why even large papers often fail to turn their attention to projects like his "Lost Children" until long after the problem has become entrenched, said it best: "A lot of city desks are set up to kind of feed the beast—give me stories, give me stories, give me stories. To do something like this you have to cut a reporter or two loose for a significant period of time."[8]

There are other hurdles that some journalists construct, such as fear of advertisers, reporters' fear of losing access to top officials, editors' pressure to make the newspaper a journalistic cafeteria that caters to the appetite of every conceivable reader desire, and, most worrisome of all, Wall Street pressure on corporate owners to show profit growth even in the face of declining advertising revenue. Until a new media business model emerges, profit pressures on newsroom budgets will remain. Some of the hurdles, like the beast, are real and necessary daily challenges. Hurdles can become impenetrable obstructions to watchdog journalism when editors let them become the sole definition of the culture of the newsroom. When feeding the beast becomes an obsession, the malady trickles down to reporters and line editors. Such a confining atmosphere dulls and narrows the vision of all who work there, blocking their ability to see the potential for a deeper story and killing their motivation to pursue it.

Many editors, including some in these chapters, see these hurdles as nothing more than interesting challenges, because they also have decided that the investigative mentality and the watchdog mission of journalism will define the culture of their newsrooms. In such a culture, the investigative mentality drives every editor and reporter on every story. One of the hallmark attitudes of the reporters in these chapters is that obstacles may delay the mission, but they don't stop it. "You never give up," The *Sun*'s Gary Cohn said. "If one thing doesn't work, try something else, and you keep going back, keep digging." Cohn was talking about specific efforts to get information, but his attitude defines an investigative mentality that applies to finding ways to get around administrative and budgetary obstacles to fulfill journalism's watchdog functions on a daily basis.

Editors, reporters and journalism educators, now, more than ever, must find ways to create a newsroom culture where this investigative mentality can flourish. Sometimes the solutions are nuts-and-bolts strategies as simple as establishing story priorities. Or, editors often can carve a project into manageable chunks and parcel them out. "I've occasionally seen beat reporters do investigative work in short bits, a column or column and half long," said John Carroll, the former editor of the *Los Angeles Times*, who played key roles in two of the projects in this book. "It can be very effective. It is an underutilized tool. You can do a comprehensive project in bite-sized pieces."

At the reporter level, reporters, especially those at small newspapers, have to learn to volunteer downtime in an investigation to feeding the beast. If a tight newsroom budget requires a reporter to pull off the project to help with the daily effort occasionally, he or she has to adjust to the disruption and find ways to minimize its impact on the project. These reporters do not have to allow such interruptions to dampen their investigative enthusiasm, because many titled project reporters earned their stripes only after spending years nibbling away at long-term projects in between dailies and short-term investigations. Other adjustments often emerge in the unique intricacies of any news organization.

The need to create a newsroom atmosphere amenable to watchdog journalism, however, requires a more fundamental solution. To provide the resources and "the luxury of time," journalism leaders must start rethinking the definition of newsworthiness. At minimum, refining news value could, in ad hoc situations, lead editors and reporters to consider abandoning less important stories or at least delaying them until the more serious work is done. In the long-term scenario, newsroom editors should start questioning whether serious public affairs journalism demands that Britney Spears' chaotic life deserves the same attention as the life-or-death issues that such frivolous stories keep pushing to the back burner. In fulfilling its role to serve the public good, does the definition of what is news in public affairs journalism really require turning news space into journalistic cafeterias? Is it time for serious journalism to develop its niche and define that niche by the battles it chooses to wage?

Finding a place for watchdog journalism may be difficult in today's media environment, but the mission, nevertheless, has traditionally been mandatory in the profession. It is a good, even noble, mission that should not be the preserve of big news organizations, I-Teams or individually anointed reporters. To carry this mission is no pipe dream. It is possible even at the smallest newspaper. "It all stems from the culture in the newsroom," said Mitch Weiss, who co-authored the Pulitzer series "Buried Secrets, Brutal Truths" for the modest-sized *Toledo Blade,* with a circulation of about 150,000. "You have to have curiosity, the drive, and the [investigative] culture. . . . If a reporter is persuasive and aggressive, they can get it in the paper."

The even smaller *Willamette Week* in Portland, Ore., started nurturing the investigative culture a long time ago. "All of our reporters are working on stories that they will not see for another six months," Mark Zusman, the *Week's* editor, said. "That's the idea. Every reporter has the ability to do that." They just need a newsroom culture where that ability can grow and be applied to journalism that is important to the public. In Zusman's newsroom, investigative work simply means probing beneath the surface, "to place things in context and to understand what's going on." His phrase for that effort is connecting the dots. "We use that term a lot around here," he said.

Notes

1. Nigel Jaquiss, "Who Knew, Long Before Neil Goldschmidt's Secret Became Public, Many Influential Oregonians Knew," *Willamette Week,* December 15, 2004, p. 1.

2. Interview, Eric Nalder, *Seattle Post-Intelligencer* newsroom, January 4, 2007.

3. Interview, Scott Higham, *Washington Post* newsroom, July 26, 2006.

4. Interview, Sari Horwitz, Washington, DC, July 26, 2006.

5. Interview, Nalder, January 4, 2007.

6. Interview, Deborah Nelson, *Los Angeles Times*, Washington, DC, bureau, June 26, 2006.

7. Ibid.

8. Interview, Higham, Jul 26, 2006.

"Tainted Cash or Easy Money?"

Copy of The Orlando Sentinel *series "Tainted Cash or Easy Money?" by Jeff Brazil and Steve Berry. The first three-day package began on June 14, 1992. The second package was published on August 23, 1992. It won the Pulitzer Prize for investigative reporting in April 1993.*

Tainted Cash or Easy Money? Volusia Deputies Have Seized $8 Million from I-95 Motorists. The Trap Is for Drug Dealers, But Money Is the Object. Three of Every Four Drivers Were Never Charged.

The Orlando Sentinel—June 14, 1992
Author: By Jeff Brazil and Steve Berry of The Sentinel Staff

Volusia County Sheriff Bob Vogel's elite Interstate 95 drug squad has taken tens of thousands of dollars from motorists against whom there is no evidence of wrongdoing nor any criminal record.

In one case, a woman lost part of an emergency loan to fix her hurricane-damaged home. On another occasion, grandparents lost part of their retirement nest egg.

And in virtually every case, the people stopped and stripped of their cash were either black or Hispanic.

Seizing cash from drug dealers is nothing new. But a review of records by The Orlando Sentinel raises questions about tactics and about the ethics of allowing this freewheeling drug squad to beef up the sheriff's budget with selective traffic stops of people never charged with a crime.

The findings:—In 199 of 262 cases—three out of every four—no charges were filed. Yet in only four cases did drivers get all of their money back.

Although Vogel contends that the stops are legitimate, nine of every 10 seizures involve blacks or Hispanics.

—Rather than go to court to defend seizures, the agency cuts deals with the drivers, drug dealers included. Motorists can get some of their money back if they agree not to sue the agency.

—If a driver won't agree to a car search, a drug-sniffing dog is standing by. But the Sentinel found evidence that most Florida currency carries traces of cocaine, casting doubt on the practice.

The "Tainted Cash or Easy Money?" series from the *Orlando Sentinel* is reprinted with permission.

—There are no written rules governing seizures. No higher authority outside the agency reviews results. There is no penalty for frivolous stops or seizures.

A broadly written state law allows the sheriff to keep whatever is seized, regardless of whether a crime was committed.

For the drivers, the realization hits like a hammer: The law allows their money to be taken, and there isn't much they can do.

"It's highway robbery," said David Vinikoor, a Fort Lauderdale defense lawyer.

Vinikoor, as a prosecutor, fought for passage of Florida's 1980 seizure law. "The concepts of guilt and innocence," he said, "have gone out the window."

Consider the case of Joseph Kea.

In March 1990 Deputy Bobby Jones stopped Kea for driving six miles above the speed limit. Kea, a 21-year-old black Navy reservist from Savannah, Ga., said he was going to Miami to school.

After issuing a warning, Jones got Kea's permission to search the car. Jones found no drugs, no evidence of wrongdoing.

But Jones found Kea's Navy uniform in the trunk, along with $3,989 in a nylon bag.

Jones said Kea was unusually nervous, that he had no luggage and had folded his money in groups of $100. He also noted Kea's wrinkled uniform and scuffed shoes, things no legitimate military man should allow.

Jones decided Kea was a trafficker and took the cash.

Through Jacksonville lawyer Willie J. Walker, Kea provided Navy pay stubs to show the source of the money and a resume showing a steady salary and work history.

A sheriff's investigator probed Kea's background but found no dirt, no criminal record.

At one point, even the investigator appeared to have doubts about the case. In the case file is a letter from Walker on which someone at the Sheriff's Office wrote: "Bobbie [sic] Jones doesn't care if the money is returned."

After eight months of fruitless demands, Kea agreed not to sue. He got back $2,989, of which his attorney got about 25 percent. The Sheriff's Office kept $1,000.

Since the practice started in 1989, the Sheriff's Office has seized almost $8 million. The agency has kept about half, after working out settlements with motorists' attorneys.

Vogel defends his seizures, saying deputies are hitting dealers where it hurts—in their wallets.

The stretch of highway where the enormously popular sheriff battles dealers is a key artery for tourists headed for Disney World. It's the fast track to Daytona Beach for bikers and spring breakers.

And it's the "mule" trail for drug couriers heading for South Florida, the entry point for most illegal drugs entering the country.

"There's no secret we live in the drug capital of the world," Vogel said.

The sheriff said his seizures should not be scrapped just because there might be "a few number of cases that there might be some legal questions . . . that I can't respond to.

"Are you suggesting then that we let them [drug dealers] go and not seize the illegal drug money?

"If you don't like the statutes . . . then you get the doggone statutes changed. We don't have to prove the fact that they are guilty."

A review of agency records shows that it is not simply a question of what officers can prove. Case files show that some motorists lost money simply because officers were suspicious.

Informal settlements

There is pressure to reform seizure laws at both state and national levels. Revisions to Florida's law go into effect July 1. They will force some changes in Volusia County's procedures, but critics say they don't go far enough to prevent abuses.

That leaves too much room for abuse, said Tom Guilfoyle, head of Metro-Dade's forfeiture unit. Instead, a judge must approve agreements.

In Volusia County, it's clear that most of the $8 million seized was drug money. In a quarter of the cases, arrests were made, mostly involving drugs. Many drivers had previous drug convictions. Some didn't even argue over the seizure.

But records show some drivers were stripped of cash simply because deputies—saying they were well-versed in the habits of dealers—didn't like something they saw.

One driver was deemed suspicious because he didn't carry enough luggage, another because he carried too much.

Deputies routinely said bills in denominations of $1, $5, $10, $20, $50 and $100 were suspicious because they are typical of what dealers carry. But that leaves few alternatives for others.

"If they can't prove it was involved in illicit activity," said South Florida forfeiture lawyer Sharon Kegerreis, "then why should they get to keep any of it?

"It's a new form of lawlessness."

Vogel disagreed: "I am totally convinced that the people that are working in our Selective Enforcement Team . . . feel wholeheartedly that those individuals are involved in drug activity or illegal activity."

Most shocking for drivers is the realization that the due-process provisions that protect criminal defendants' rights don't apply.

The presumption of innocence is gone. In this civil arena, drivers have to prove their right to carry cash.

Hiring an attorney to contest seizures can be expensive. To win a suit against the agency for legal costs, a driver would have to prove that deputies had no basis for seizure. That's extremely difficult; to take money, deputies merely have to show "probable cause" that a crime has been, or will be, committed.

Ultimately, that little-known trapdoor provision means that it's less expensive to settle out of court for the return of as much money as possible, even if the driver is innocent.

Presumed guilty?

Consider, for instance, the case of Jose Raposa, owner of Tri-Star Paint Shop in New Bedford, Mass. Raposa, 29, had $19,000 seized by Deputy Jones on May 2, 1991.

Jones didn't believe Raposa's story that he was headed to Miami to look for antique cars he had seen in a car-trader magazine or that he had gotten a home-equity loan because car dealers require cash.

Jones said Raposa was more nervous than the average person. Jones noted marijuana in the ashtray, although it wasn't enough to warrant a citation.

Raposa hired an attorney, who submitted bank documents showing the loan.

Volusia County investigator Paul Page followed up but found no criminal record.

A note to Mel Stack, the agency's forfeiture attorney, scrawled on one of Page's investigative reports stated: "Mel: Paul indicated pretty strongly that they can turn nothing up concrete on this guy."

After six months, Raposa accepted a settlement offer: The sheriff kept 25 percent; Raposa got 75 percent, of which his attorney collected $1,000.

"They should have given all my money back," he said, "but the lawyer said go for the deal."

It was the same for others who had no significant criminal record and against whom there was no evidence of wrongdoing.

Edwin Johnson—a 48-year-old black self-employed businessman and father of four—lost $10,000 in a settlement.

"If I had had the money, I would have fought longer," he said. "But it had gone on long enough. It caused me and my family a lot of pain."

Stack said the cases questioned by the newspaper were not "a representative sample" and likely would not cast the agency or the practice in a good light.

Ed Duff Jr., a former state assistant attorney general and son of former Volusia County Sheriff Ed Duff, said: "I don't think the Legislature intended the forfeiture law to be used this way."

It's one thing for a guilty person to lose 50 percent of his or her money, Duff said. But, "if you're innocent, even 1 percent is too much."

The objective: Cash

Chief Circuit Judge McFerrin Smith was dismayed by the Sentinel's findings and questioned whether the agency was more interested in curbing crime or collecting cash.

"At best, it looks borderline, doesn't it?" he asked.

Vogel disputed that analysis. As a whole, the agency is heavily involved in fighting drugs and makes numerous arrests, he said.

But for the drug-seizure squad, the bottom line is the bottom line. It has collected the equivalent of roughly $5,000 a day during the past 41 months.

Vogel said the squad tries to build criminal cases from its cash seizures.

Yet only a fourth of all seizures involve on-scene arrests. And although the agency conducted follow-up investigations when drivers contested seizures, it has never made an arrest as a result.

The follow-up does play a role, though, in further solidifying the decision to take money. In the case of Hersel Lawson, a 35-year-old Virginia businessman, two officers became suspicious during a visit to Lawson's used cycle shop in Roanoke.

Their report criticized the shop as dirty and lacking adequate parking and display space.

Lawson had no criminal record. Yet the agency said it would keep half of the $31,000 seized. Ultimately, Lawson's attorney was able to reclaim all but $3,750. But the settlement battle took seven months. Lawson's attorney got about 25 percent of the recovery.

"I was so stunned by it all, I didn't know how to react," Lawson said. "I've got a spotless record except for traffic tickets."

There are other ways in which records show that the emphasis is on collecting cash, not making arrests.

The five-man drug team works a combined 200 hours a week, stopping southbound cars.

It does occasionally stop cars in northbound lanes, where a drug dealer more likely would be carrying cocaine or marijuana. But records show that almost all cases were made in southbound lanes, where a dealer is more likely to be carrying cash.

A tally of roadside seizures shows that arrests for drug possession were highest in the beginning of the program in 1989 but have decreased significantly, while cash seizures have increased.

There was the case of two brothers stopped Jan. 29, 1989, on their way south. The two were asked to wait in the back of a patrol car during the search. In a secret recording made of their conversation, one says to the other that the drug-sniffing dog had "missed the reefer."

Deputy Frank Josenhans, who seized $9,540, said: "Look, I could arrest you for conspiracy to traffic cocaine, but it's not worth it."

Five months later, Josenhans again stopped one of the brothers and seized $36,864.

The officer kidded the driver about the dangers of his "occupation." Josenhans again noted that he could arrest him but wouldn't.

"He thanked me," Josenhans wrote.

The agency offered a settlement; the brothers accepted. The Sheriff's Office kept $24,249; the brothers got back $22,155.

"Think about that," South Florida forfeiture lawyer Carl Lida said. "Why would a police department give back what they think is drug money?"

Vogel said that he did not know, until interviewed in May by the Sentinel, that so many cases—three of every four—ended in settlements.

"I'm assuming those decisions are being made accurately," he said. "And if they're not, then we adjust the policy, we make corrections, we make changes."

Stack said that there might be questions about the propriety of negotiating settlements. But he said it's no different from plea-bargaining in criminal cases.

Stack said his job is to do what's best for his client, the agency. "It's a business. We don't want the wrong case to go up on appeal."

Circuit Judge Uriel Blount Jr., a 28-year veteran of the Volusia County bench, was dismayed to hear that two-thirds of the seizures involved less than $20,000 and that settlements occurred so frequently without judicial supervision.

"What you're telling me is somewhat surprising," Blount said.

The solution, according to forfeiture lawyer David Raben: "We need some congressman's kid to get stopped so people can see what this is like."

Memo: The series
Today: No one was charged in 3 of every 4 cash seizures by the squad. Monday: Nine of every 10 seizures involves a black or Hispanic motorist.
Tuesday: Sheriff Vogel spends more fighting drugs but hasn't fared better. See related stories on Pages A16 and A17
Page: A1
Column: Special report
Dateline: DELAND
Copyright 1992 Sentinel Communications Co.

Seizing Cash Is No Sweat for Deputies

The Orlando Sentinel—June 14, 1992
Author: By Jeff Brazil and Steve Berry of The Sentinel Staff

For Volusia County deputies, seizing money is simple.

They stop a car for following too closely, for instance, or for changing lanes without signaling. Then, if they are suspicious, they search the car.

Of 199 no-arrest seizure cases during the past three years, three-quarters of the stops were for one of four minor infractions: failure to maintain a single lane, following too closely, defaced license tag or broken taillight.

The most serious violation shown as a reason for a stop—driving more than 11 mph faster than the speed limit—occurred in six cases.

Not one of those speeders was ticketed. And of the 199 drivers, only 13 got tickets.

What happened after cars were ordered to the roadside is the key. Once the deputy issued a warning or—in rare cases—a citation, he would turn and begin walking away, according to dozens of drivers interviewed.

The deputy then would pause, return to the car and ask for permission to search. In most cases, drivers consented.

Records show that at least a handful of drivers initially refused to allow a search. They were told they would be detained until a drug-sniffing dog could be summoned. The drivers allowed the searches.

If they hadn't, the dog would have been led around the outside of the car. If he barked or wagged his tail, deputies would have had "probable cause" to believe that drugs or drug money were inside, and they could search without a driver's consent.

The decision to take money is left to deputies.

Their decisions are almost never second-guessed. Drivers got all their money back in only four of the 199 no-arrest cases, though a significant number of motorists had no criminal records and provided documentation that they said showed they came by their money legally.

Success counts. Seizure team supervisor Bobby Jones was promoted to sergeant after making several big seizures.

One-fourth of the drivers whose money was seized but who were not arrested got back into their cars and weren't heard from again.

In such cases, the agency lists the seizure as a forfeiture by default, meaning that the driver or passengers were assumed to be drug "mules" who would not risk further contact with authorities by contesting the seizure.

The other three-quarters of the drivers contested.

At that point, the agency initiated a background investigation.

In more than three years, the agency has never arrested anyone as a result. Yet in every case the deputy filled out an investigative report stating that the seizure was justified because, in his professional view, the driver or passengers, were "traffickers."

INTERPRETING THE LAW

- **Florida Contraband Forfeiture Act, 1980.** Legislature said police could take drug dealers' money and property without arrest.

- **Lobo vs. Metro-Dade Police Department, 1987.** State appellate court ruling: People with lots of cash must prove that they aren't going to commit a crime or haven't already. Paved way for seizures without arrest or proof of link to drugs. Allowed police to seize money with "other persuasive circumstantial evidence," such as signal by drug-sniffing dog or unusual packaging of cash.

- **Florida Department of Law Enforcement vs. Real Property, 1991.** Florida Supreme Court ruling: "Although we are concerned with the multitude of procedural deficiencies" in Florida's Forfeiture Act, it does not violate constitutional due process. Ruling added protections for property owners, including the right to hearing to determine if there was probable cause for seizure. If case went to trial, police needed "clear and convincing evidence" to support seizure.

Ultimately, the agency cut a deal with every "trafficker," usually keeping 10 to 50 percent of the money and returning the rest.

Settlements are handled by the sheriff's forfeiture attorney, Mel Stack, who uses his own discretion to cut deals. Stack was paid $44,000 a year as an employee to handle settlements. He resigned in mid-1990 to start his own firm. Sheriff Bob Vogel now pays him $48,000 a year as a consultant to decide how much to give back.

Stack said the deal often involves his "gut feeling."

In three years, only one no-arrest case has gone to trial. When the judge heard about Gregory Walton's lengthy criminal record, he awarded the sheriff the full amount seized, $22,520.

Walton initially filed an appeal with the 5th District Court of Appeal in Daytona Beach but didn't follow through.

Edition: 3 STAR
Section: A SECTION
Page: A17

"How Could They Say They Treated Me Fairly?"

The Orlando Sentinel—June 14, 1992
Author: By Jeff Brazil and Steve Berry of The Sentinel Staff

Jorge Nater and his wife would like to come back to America—six of their seven grandchildren live here—but it will be awhile.

The Puerto Rican couple's run-in with the cash-seizure squad has left them bitter.

Volusia County Deputy Sheriff Ray Almodovar stopped Jorge Nater, 48, and family friend Francisco Muriel for following another car too closely Feb. 4, 1991. Almodovar searched their car and seized $36,990, saying the pair were drug traffickers.

The deputy didn't believe Nater's story that he had sold an apartment complex in Puerto Rico three days earlier to a man in New Jersey. The deputy also didn't believe Nater when he said he was headed to Brevard County, where four of his sons live and that he was going to buy a home in Pompano Beach.

Pointing to Nater's guilt: He was more nervous than the average person, Almodovar said. When asked where he was going, he had to look up the address.

Finally when Nater and Muriel were asked to wait in a patrol car during the search, a hidden microphone recorded Nater saying to Muriel that, if they were allowed to leave, maybe they should hide the money "in a tire."

Pointing to his innocence: Documentation confirming his real-estate transaction, including a sworn affidavit from the buyer; no criminal record; testimonial letters from the mayor, police chief and a priest in his hometown.

After nine months of fruitless demands and the realization that he probably couldn't recover court costs, even if he sued and won back his cash, Nater agreed to a settlement.

The Sheriff's Office returned about 84 percent of his money, all but $6,000. Nater's attorney, Jose Perez of Orlando, got about 25 percent of the recovery.

Both he and Nater remain outraged over the seizure.

"It's a little shocking," Perez said. "In some of these cases, I'm sure they're doing a good job.

"But in others they're taking it from innocent people. And they have the money—you have to fight to get it back."

WHAT'S AT STAKE

From the 4th Amendment: "The right of the people to be secure in their persons, houses, papers, and effects, against unreasonable searches and seizures, shall not be violated . . ." From the 14th Amendment: "No state shall make or enforce any law which shall abridge the privileges or immunities of citizens of the United States; nor shall any state deprive any person of life, liberty, or property, without due process of law . . ." "As a citizen, I recognize their need to do something about drugs. But as a defender of the Constitution, and as a member of the group that comes out on the negative end of this, I object. When law enforcement is allowed to expand into constitutionally protected areas—and this is not because I am a member of a certain racial group—I have a problem with that." Willie Walker, a black Jacksonville lawyer who represented a driver whose money was seized

---

In a recent telephone interview, Nater struggled to check his emotions. "How could they possibly say they treated me fairly when they took my money?" he said.

Memo: Robert Perez of the Sentinel staff contributed to this report.
Page: A17
Series: Tainted cash or easy money?

Blacks, Hispanics Big Losers in Cash Seizures. A Review of Volusia Sheriff's Records Shows That Minorities Are the Targets in 90 Percent of Cash Seizures Without Arrests.

The Orlando Sentinel—June 15, 1992
Author: By Steve Berry and Jeff Brazil of The Sentinel Staff

When Volusia County Sheriff Bob Vogel's deputies stop a motorist and confiscate that person's money without making an arrest, you can almost be certain that the person is black or Hispanic.

An Orlando Sentinel analysis of agency records shows that Vogel's targets were blacks and Hispanics in the vast majority of cash-seizure cases.

Vogel's explanation is simply that whites are less likely to be involved in transporting drug money. He says that race is not a factor in deciding which cars to stop.

His five-man drug squad has been patrolling Interstate 95 looking for suspicious motorists since 1989.

But the Sentinel review produced statistics that strongly suggest the Sheriff's Office uses a "drug profile" to target whom it stops, even though the state Supreme Court ruled that use illegal.

Court rulings allow use of the profile only to detain a driver after a stop for a traffic violation.

All told, there have been 262 seizure cases since the practice began. Three-fourths of the time, in 199 cases, there were no arrests. Officers simply confiscated cash.

In those no-arrest cases, more than 90 percent of the drivers or passengers were minorities. Less than 5 percent were white, records show. In the other 5 percent of cases, officers had not noted race in their reports.

Most drivers got a good portion of their money back, but they first had to promise not to sue the agency.

The records also show that minorities lost the most money.

In the cases with no arrests, officers seized $3.8 million from minorities; whites lost $626,200.

"What this data tells me is that . . . the majority of money being transported for drug activity involves blacks and Hispanics," Vogel said.

Vogel said the stops are for traffic violations and that seizures are based on drug-courier indicators, such as nervousness, not race.

Vogel said the team stops plenty of whites, but most don't have drugs or drug money.

Paul Joseph, state president of the American Civil Liberties Union, called the statistics "startling."

"It would seem odd that nine of 10 people acting suspicious are black. It raises a question."

The program has been enormously successful, seizing almost $8 million and large quantities of drugs.

The Sheriff's Office kept half the money after settlements with drivers.

The Sentinel compiled data from every cash-seizure case in which no arrest was made.

Complete data for each of the 63 cash seizures involving an arrest were not available. After two reporters had spent more than a month reviewing seizure files, agency attorney Nancye Jones denied further access. Jones said the newspaper's review created liability for the agency, unless the cases first were purged of confidential information, such as drivers' criminal histories.

Data were collected, however, for 46 of the 63 arrest cases. It paralleled the findings in the non-arrest cases. The majority of motorists were black or Hispanic.

The sheriff said the newspaper's research was naive and a "liberal exploitation" of selected cases.

Married and the father of a teen-age daughter, Vogel carries out everything with gusto, be it his hobby, antique-collecting, or his anti-drug crusade. He counts himself among the toughest of the get-tough-on-drugs crowd.

As a Florida Highway Patrol trooper, Vogel had a knack for catching smugglers that earned him spots on *20/20* and *60 Minutes* and helped elect him sheriff in 1988.

Vogel had developed a set of characteristics, which he called the drug smuggler's profile: mostly young males driving four-door sedans or rental cars at a few miles an hour over the limit.

Vogel's profile did not include race, he said. But statistics showed that most of his seizures involved minorities.

Later, several court cases challenged the profile. In 1990 the Florida Supreme Court ruled against Vogel, saying that—as a trooper in 1985—he had improperly stopped Paul Clive Johnson, 29, of Paterson, N.J., on the basis of the profile. Vogel found four marijuana bales in the car.

In a companion case, however the court ruled that Vogel was justified in using the profile to detain Travis Harris Cresswell, 43, of Massachusetts for 45 minutes. The court said the detention occurred after Vogel had made a legitimate traffic stop—for following too closely.

As a result of the rulings, the profile is restricted, not outlawed. After stopping someone for a traffic violation, officers may use it, along with other indicators of criminal activity, to justify detaining the driver, the court said.

Nevertheless, records show that most stops by Vogel's deputies are for infractions so minor that they seldom interest officers enforcing traffic laws. In almost every case, deputies simply gave warnings.

It begins with officers who position their cars in the highway median, perpendicular to I-95.

At night, deputies shine high beams and floodlights across the road so they can estimate a driver's age and see the license plate and other indicators, Vogel said.

Colorado lawyer David Lane said he thinks it's to see skin color.

"Why else would they be shining their high-beam lights across the highway?" asked Lane, who filed a discrimination suit in Colorado, challenging similar profiles.

"Why do they need to look at the driver? It's because they wouldn't want to stop an elderly white couple with Disney stickers on their car," he said.

Carl Lida, the attorney who represented Paul Johnson before the Supreme Court, said minorities are particularly vulnerable.

"And if you're a minority, you're especially afraid to make him mad. The traffic laws are being used as an excuse to search," Lida said.

"Let me put it to you this way: How many times have you ever been stopped for a traffic violation and been asked to search your car?"

Memo: The series
Sunday: No one arrested or charged in 3 of every 4 cash seizures.
Today: Nine of every 10 seizures involves a black or Hispanic.
Tuesday: Sheriff Vogel spends more to fight drugs, but hasn't fared better. See related stories, A6.
Page: A1
Column: Special report

Series: Tainted cash or easy money?
Copyright 1992 Sentinel Communications Co.

Good Record Couldn't Save Man's Money. Hersel Lawson Jr. Says Calling Him a Drug Trafficker Is a "Joke." But Deputies Weren't Laughing When They Took His $31,000.

The Orlando Sentinel—June 15, 1992
Author: By Jeff Brazil and Steve Berry of The Sentinel Staff

Hersel Lawson Jr. told the Volusia County Sheriff's Office he would submit to a test—any test—to show that he didn't use drugs.

"I know it sounds silly," the 35-year-old Roanoke, Va., resident said. "But I never have. I've got a spotless record, except for traffic tickets."

Lawson's record was of little help April 15, 1991, when deputies seized $31,000, saying he was a drug trafficker.

Lawson told Deputy Ray Almodovar he owned a business in Roanoke and was taking the money, the proceeds of a bank loan, to Fort Lauderdale to open a bar with a friend.

AN ANALYSIS OF THE SELECTIVE ENFORCEMENT TEAM'S CASH SEIZURE CASES IN WHICH THERE WERE NO ARRESTS:

Age		Sex		Race / Ethnic Group		Car		Reason for Stop		Action		Number Persons in Car		Amount Seized	
18 to 29	52%	Male	73%	Black	85%	Out-of-state	56%	Failure to maintain single lane	35%	Warning	77%	One	20%	$1 to $5,000	18%
30 to 39	25%	Female	25%	Hispanic	6%	Rental	31%	Following too closely	27%	Citation	7%	More than one	78%	$5,001 to $10,000	18%
40 to 49	12%			White	5%	Florida	13%	Defaced tag	7%	No action	16%			$10,001 to $20,000	27%
50 to 59	3%			Unknown	2%			Speeding, 1–5mph over limit	7%					$20,001 to $30,000	14%
60 to 69	1%							Speeding, 6–10mph over limit	10%					$30,001 to $40,000	5%
69-plus	1%							Speeding, 11+ mph over limit	3%					$40,001 to $50,000	4%
Unknown	7%							Broken light	4%					$50,001 to $100,000	9%
														$100,001 and over	5%

Note: Some categories may not add up to 100 percent because of rounding off or incomplete agency reports.

Asked why he was using cash, Lawson admitted that his business was entangled in bankruptcy proceedings; he didn't want the courts to know about the money.

Pointing to his guilt:

The deputy thought that the story sounded suspicious. Lawson was nervous. He had the money in a Crown Royal whiskey bag, a popular carrying case among dealers. And there were four or five marijuana joints in the passenger side of his car, which Lawson said belonged to a hitchhiker he had picked up in Jacksonville.

Later investigators visited Lawson's used-motorcycle business and found it unkempt. And they said it lacked sufficient parking and display space, which they found incriminating, according to a report.

Pointing to his innocence:

Bank records showing a recent $25,000 business loan; no criminal record; corroborating statements from the friend with whom he planned to open a bar.

The Sheriff's Office made two settlement offers. Lawson first was offered $11,000, about 35 percent, of his money. Then he was offered $16,500, about 53 percent.

Lawson refused both, calling the assertion that he was a trafficker "a joke." Seven months later, Lawson, now a car salesman, agreed to do what no other seizure claimant has done: He let a mediator decide.

After hearing all the agency's evidence, the mediator ordered it to give back $27,250, about 88 percent, of his money. The sheriff's office kept $3,750. Lawson's attorney got a third of the recovery.

Memo: See related stories, A1 and A6.
Section: A SECTION
Page: A6
Series: Tainted cash or easy money?
Copyright 1992 Sentinel Communications Co.

You May Be Drug Free, but Is Your Money? Cocaine Is Found on the Cash of 8 Non-Users. The Test Suggests That a Drug Dog Would Detect Cocaine on Almost Anyone's Money.

The Orlando Sentinel—June 15, 1992
Author: By Jeff Brazil and Steve Berry of The Sentinel Staff

Uriel Blount Jr. is a circuit judge. He has never snorted cocaine. But his money has traces of the illegal drug on it.

Leesburg Police Chief Jim Brown hasn't snorted cocaine either. His money has traces, too.

The same is true of State Sen. Dick Langley, Sanford Mayor Betty Smith, Daytona Beach Community College President Philip Day and Orlando Sentinel Editor John Haile.

Each recently agreed to help The Orlando Sentinel test the theory that most currency in Florida is tainted with tiny amounts of cocaine. Without warning, reporters approached them and offered an even trade for money in their wallets.

The money was tested; most samples tested positive.

In Florida the presence of cocaine, even in microscopic amounts, is critical. It has been a key factor in justifying the seizure of tens of millions of dollars.

South Florida reigns supreme in seizing drug money. But no Florida agency north of Fort Lauderdale seizes more than the Volusia County Sheriff's Office. Under Sheriff Bob Vogel, it has earned a national reputation for cash seizures along Interstate 95.

One legal proof the agency uses is an "alert" signal by a drug-sniffing dog. If the dog wags his tail or barks when sniffing for drugs, it constitutes legal "probable cause" to believe that the money is tainted.

The newspaper's test, however, suggests that the odds are that a drug dog would detect cocaine on almost anyone's money in this state, according to toxicologist Wayne Morris.

Morris has testified in hundreds of criminal cases that as much as 90 percent of currency in some cities tests positive for cocaine. "If you took 10 samples from any major city in America, I'd be surprised if any one of them didn't come up positive," he said.

The reason: Cocaine adheres to what it touches.

The contamination spreads through a variety of means. Cocaine users roll up bills like straws to inhale the drug into their nostrils. Dealers hide money and drugs together. They "launder" cash profits by injecting the money into circulation. Seized money is deposited into banks, intermingling with other bills.

Besides Blount, Brown, Langley, Smith, Day and Haile, the newspaper obtained money from the Rev. Hal Marchman, founder of a Volusia County drug-treatment center, Orange County Chairman Linda Chapin and from a Publix cash drawer in DeLand.

Vogel was asked to participate but would not, saying: "That strikes me as somewhat offensive."

Vogel said the newspaper was "getting into personal and theatrical issues. We are not writing stories for the Sentinel or any other newspaper—at least I'm not."

Vogel would not allow the agency's dogs to be used in a sniff test of the samples.

"We're not going to call into question the credibility of our dogs by doing something like that," said Nancye Jones, Vogel's legal adviser.

In April the samples were taken to Morris, the toxicologist. He is a former crime-laboratory specialist for the Florida Department of Law Enforcement and now owns Morris Forensics Inc. in Winter Park.

The 57 bills—in denominations of $1, $5, $10 and $20—were tested with a gas chromatograph. To confirm findings, bills also were tested in a mass spectrometer.

The results: Six of nine samples carried detectable amounts of cocaine. The grocery-store sample was "borderline."

Samples from Marchman and Chapin were clean. Both were carrying new bills when asked to participate. Morris had predicted that they would test clean; the money hadn't circulated.

"The fact that you can get a negative on a new bill basically makes the argument," Morris said. "If it's been in circulation long enough, it'll be tainted."

Of six positive samples, only tiny amounts of cocaine—invisible to the eye—were present. But all were well within the range of a drug dog's detection ability, Morris said. Dogs' ability to smell is thousands of times more sensitive than humans.

Brown said, "I think you're on to a good story."

Haile, whose money had the most cocaine, said: "Based on what I've heard about tainting of money by drugs, I'm not surprised.

"The question is whether finding traces of drugs on money in Florida really says anything about who is dealing in drugs."

Blount said that many in law enforcement know that most money is tainted. That's why Vogel wouldn't "play the game," Blount said. "I think [he] knew what you were going to get."

Mel Stack, forfeiture attorney for the Sheriff's Office, said the agency has been downplaying the dog's role.

But dozens of lawyers interviewed for this series of reports said the agency continues to use dog alerts as grounds for confiscations and "as a legal hammer" during negotiations.

Memo: See related stories, A1 and A6.
Page: A6
Copyright 1992 Sentinel Communications Co.

"I Could Win the Battle but Lose the War" After 6 Months of Trying to Reclaim His Life Savings of $38,923, Edwin Johnson Quit Fighting and Agreed to a Settlement.

The Orlando Sentinel—June 15, 1992
Author: By Jeff Brazil and Steve Berry of The Sentinel Staff

The last people Edwin Johnson expected to take his life savings were law enforcement officers.

Returning to Florida from Georgia on April 15, 1991, Johnson, 48, was stopped on Interstate 95 for not signaling to change lanes.

After giving a warning, Volusia County Deputy Sheriff Michael Frederick asked to search the car.

Johnson agreed.

"If I thought it would lead to what it did, of course, I wouldn't have let him," Johnson said. "But I'm a law-abiding citizen."

When Frederick found $38,923 in a bag in the trunk, he told Johnson he thought it was drug money.

Johnson said it was profit from his business, Ed's Lawn Service in Miami, and a previous one, Thirst Quenchers Inc., a discount beverage distributor Johnson owned for eight years.

Johnson said he carried cash because he doesn't trust banks after being a victim of wage garnishment after a 1985 lawsuit.

Frederick found no drugs, no weapons and no evidence of wrongdoing.

Johnson, however, said Frederick told him he matched a drug courier profile.

Pointing to his guilt:

Johnson, who is black, was nervous. He didn't carry enough luggage. When asked to specify the amount of cash, he said, "30-some thousand," not the actual amount.

Pointing to his innocence:

Johnson's attorney, David Raben, provided accounting documents, tax forms, canceled checks, testimonial letters from Johnson's clients, records verifying the wage-garnishment story and a resume detailing Johnson's 28-year work record.

"Having experienced a writ of garnishment, . . . he was disinclined to subject himself to a similar seizure," Raben wrote.

The agency checked Johnson's criminal history and found only a very old misdemeanor, which was insignificant, according to Mel Stack, the forfeiture attorney.

After six months, Johnson agreed to a settlement. "It seemed like they could outlast you," he said. "I could win the battle but lose the war."

Johnson got back about 75 percent of his money, $28,923. The sheriff's office kept $10,000. Raben got a third of the recovery.

"If they gave money back to innocent people," Raben said, "they'd have given it back to Ed Johnson."

Memo: See related stories, A1 and A6.
Page: A6
Series: Tainted cash or easy money?
Copyright 1992 Sentinel Communications Co.

Confiscated Cash Bankrolls Fight Against Drugs. Critics Say the Seizure Law Encourages Police Agencies to Spend Time Looking for Drug Money Instead of Fighting Crime.

The Orlando Sentinel—June 16, 1992
Author: By Craig Quintana of The Sentinel Staff

Sheriff Bob Vogel spends hundreds of thousands more than his predecessor did to fight drugs, bankrolling his campaign with the confiscated cash of Interstate 95 motorists, most of whom were never charged with a crime.

State law allows the Volusia County Sheriff's Office to keep what it seizes from suspected drug dealers. Records show that Volusia's five-man drug squad has netted millions for the agency through selective traffic stops and car searches.

Yet, a review by The Orlando Sentinel shows that the sheriff has begun to use confiscated money to pay for routine operations. That appears to violate the law that allows cash seizures.

Where the sheriff gets his money—and how he spends it—is important because of what critics term "the profit motive" arising from the state seizure law.

Critics contend that the law encourages police agencies to spend their time looking for drug money instead of doing police work.

Vogel's drug team has been seizing cash from motorists for three years. Only one of every four from whom money was taken was charged with a crime.

A review of agency spending during Vogel's three years in office shows an increasing reliance on confiscated money. The largest share has been used to pay for the fight against drugs, the issue on which Vogel rode into office.

This year, the agency's entire $125,000 operating budget for drug investigations comes from confiscations. And it is 10 times what former Sheriff Ed Duff spent on average.

Last year, when seizures were higher, the drug investigations budget was 25 times what Duff spent.

Nevertheless, the agency made at least one-third fewer drug arrests last year than in 1989 when Vogel took office.

The sheriff says it is an indication of the effectiveness of his drug-busting programs.

However, the falling arrest rate is mirrored across the state and, locally, at the Daytona Beach Police Department. But experts say that can be misleading.

Numerous studies during recent years show less "recreational" drug use today. But "hard-core" users remain.

Focusing on arrests may, in fact, ignore the actual drug problem, said Ronald Akers, a University of Florida sociologist.

If overall drug use was already on the decline nationally, stepped-up efforts of local agencies may have had little real effect, said Akers, author of Drugs, Alcohol and Society.

"You have to judge it against what's going on elsewhere," he said. "Are there other agencies that are having similar decreases, which are not pouring in money?"

Locally, arrests for burglary and property theft, crimes closely linked with narcotics, remained steady since 1988, figures from the Volusia County Jail show.

"The [drug] arrests are down, but all the other crimes you'd associate with drugs are up," said John DuPree, Volusia County judicial services director.

When Vogel took over the Sheriff's Office, it was far behind the times, he said. It has taken millions to catch up. And the good news for Volusia County taxpayers, he said, is that drug dealers paid the tab.

That philosophy has its detractors, however.

"It's bad policy to give a police department a financial stake in law enforcement," said Paul Joseph, a law professor at Nova University and president of the American Civil Liberties Union's Florida chapter.

"Police should be out finding criminals, not out raising money for their department," he said.

The drug squad has confiscated almost $8 million since confiscations began three years ago. After arranging out-of-court settlements with motorists, the Sheriff's Office kept roughly half.

Not only has the windfall meant a beefed-up drug-investigations fund, it has paid for a new airplane, new Stetson-style hats and a laundry list of high-tech crime-fighting gear, such as motion detectors for agents and a system to detect hidden electronic bugs.

Total spending for the investigative fund: $400,000. It climbs to $723,637 if high-technology equipment for narcotics deputies—such as location monitors for undercover agents—is included.

Critics question the need for such spending.

"Bob is definitely the most expensive sheriff we've ever had," said Big John, a Volusia County Council member and Vogel's chief critic. "For what? My squabble is with the way we spend unprecedented sums of money."

Vogel dismisses the criticism as politically motivated.

"Big John doesn't know that it's a good sign to see a decrease in arrests," Vogel said. "It shows that the individuals are not out there committing the crimes."

Some council members have criticized his refusal to provide details of how the drug fund is spent. But state law lets Vogel keep that information secret. Vogel says disclosure would endanger deputies.

Vogel's use of confiscated funds has ballooned since he took office.

In 1989, Vogel operated with a $17,000 investigative budget furnished by Duff. No confiscated funds were used.

In 1990, Vogel budgeted $27,500 for investigations and beefed up the fund by adding another $50,000 in confiscated funds. Last year Vogel again began with $27,500 in tax dollars but added $225,000 in confiscated funds.

This fiscal year Vogel removed taxpayer support, except to pay for deputies' salaries and some basic expenses.

Vogel says that is smart management and saves tax money.

But it appears to run against the letter of the forfeiture law. It specifically allows police to pay for school-resource officers, equipment and various crime- and drug-prevention programs. It also lets agencies finance "protracted or complex investigations."

But the statute says confiscated funds "shall not be a source of revenue to meet normal operating needs" or other activities normally funded with tax money.

Under Vogel, nearly $9 of every $10 spent on undercover rentals, purchase of evidence and informants' tips comes from seizures, records show.

Without seized money, Vogel says, his narcotics program would be crippled.

Legislative staffers involved in recent revisions of the seizure law, who would speak only if not identified, confirmed that it was the intent of the law to ban such reliance. But there is no penalty for misappropriation of the funds, they said.

Although narcotics enforcement traditionally has been a normal operating expense, sheriff's officials say that their use is legal because they have expanded the drug squad's duties.

"The other point, too, is there is no penalty in the statute for—I won't say misuse—say, for the use of confiscated funds for something that maybe it shouldn't have been used for," sheriff's attorney Nancye Jones said.

"There's no criminal penalty, and I don't think the taxpayers are going to complain about us using that money for narcotics investigations rather than money out of their pocket."

Highlighting the Differences

Most state and federal law enforcement agencies seize property, but Volusia County distinguishes itself in several ways.

Many agencies don't make seizures without an arrest or, at least, finding drugs. Most don't have squads whose primary task is to seek and seize assets.

Volusia's practices are similar to those of the federal Drug Enforcement Administration, which seizes hundreds of millions of dollars a year at ports, airports and bus stations based on a "drug courier profile."

Alleged abuses by DEA prompted congressional hearings in May.

Where Confiscated Funds Went

$710,491—Computers, related equipment and software.

$154,582—Radio equipment, communications research, cellular phones.

$613,472—Uniforms, safety equipment, hats, name tags and gun holsters.

$723,637—Narcotics equipment/ investigations. High-tech gear Vogel said was needed to put his deputies on equal footing with drug dealers, including:

—A system that can detect hidden electronic bugs and recording equipment.

—A tracking system that can monitor the movements of undercover officers.

—Electronic bugs.

—Spy cameras to record meeting with drug suspects.

$695,592—Crime prevention / drug education, school resource officers in high schools and drug awareness materials.

$218,455—Other (safes, signs, cellular phones, legal bills, office materials and numerous pieces of equipment used in police work).

Total: $3,528,008

Source: Volusia County Sheriff's Office, *Sentinel Research*

Memo: See related stories on Page A4
The series:
Sunday: No one arrested or charged in 3 of every 4 cash seizures.
Monday: Nine of every 10 seizures involves a black or Hispanic.
Today: Sheriff Vogel spends more to fight drugs, but hasn't fared better.
Page: A1
Series: Tainted cash or easy money?
Dateline: DELAND
Copyright 1992 Sentinel Communications Co.

Sheriff's Drug Squad Gets the Bad Guys . . .

The Orlando Sentinel—June 16, 1992
Author: By Steve Berry and Jeff Brazil of The Sentinel Staff

Sixteen months ago, Volusia County Sheriff Bob Vogel's Selective Enforcement Team snatched a $10 million cocaine stash on Interstate 95.

Nine months later it seized almost $700,000 from a secret compartment in a minivan.

Of 262 cash and drug seizures along I-95, the two cases best represent the way Vogel likes to portray his anti-drug campaign.

Most of the team's cash seizures net less than $20,000, and there are few arrests, but it's clear that the seizure squad can hit it big.

The coke bust was in April 1991, when Sgt. Bobby Jones stopped a car going 35 mph in the fast lane.

His suspicions arose when driver Arquimedes Perez, 30, and passenger, Maria Carmen Florat, 26, both of New York, acted unusually nervous. Jones' search revealed a concealed compartment containing 88 pounds of cocaine.

Both were convicted of cocaine conspiracy and possession. A federal judge sentenced Perez to 14 years and Florat to 16 years.

In the $700,000 case, Jones made no arrest, although it was the largest cash seizure in the team's history.

Tommy Andres Filion, 29, of Miami was stopped because his van was weaving.

After warning him about careless driving, Jones noticed that one section of the van floor was higher than the other.

Beneath the carpet he found a concealed compartment containing $697,599.

Filion and a passenger said they knew nothing about it. They declined a receipt and never returned to dispute the confiscation.

Memo: See related stories on Pages A1 and A4
Edition: 3 STAR
Section: A SECTION
Page: A4
Series: Tainted cash or easy money?
Copyright 1992 Sentinel Communications Co.

. . . But Sometimes, Bad Guys Get Off Easy

The Orlando Sentinel—June 16, 1992
Author: By Steve Berry and Jeff Brazil of The Sentinel Staff

When Deputy Bobby Jones confiscated nearly $190,000 from Douglas Harbert and Thomas Pasco on Interstate 95, he did what Volusia County Sheriff Bob Vogel likes best.

He hit a drug dealer in the wallet.

But, as in many other cases involving motorists with drug-arrest records, he ultimately pulled his punch.

Although Jones found drugs in the car and lodged felony cocaine charges against both men, Vogel's staff ended up giving back $28,685.

When they learned that Harbert owed federal income taxes, they sent another $58,545 to the IRS.

Vogel's office retained $101,000.

It's a typical scenario. Vogel contends that every dollar he seizes comes from drug dealers. Nevertheless, he almost always strikes bargains with them, avoiding the need to prove his case in court.

In that case, Jones thought that he had found solid drug-courier "indicators." Besides the unusually large amount of cash, Jones found 7 grams of cocaine, 15 grams of marijuana, cocaine sifters still powdered with residue, a roach clip and rolling papers.

Both men acted unusually nervous and gave conflicting stories about their destination and plans.

Later in criminal court, the bargaining continued. Both men entered pleas that left them with misdemeanor drug convictions.

Memo: See related stories on Pages A1 and A4
Page: A4
Series: Tainted cash or easy money?
Copyright 1992 Sentinel Communications Co.

Lottery Winner's Luck Runs Out With Deputy's $37,970 Haul. Lottery Officials Confirmed Earl Fields' Winnings. But the Sheriff's Office Said It Had His Number—And His Money.

The Orlando Sentinel—June 16, 1992
Author: By Jeff Brazil and Steve Berry of The Sentinel Staff

One of Volusia County's quirkier seizure cases involves Earl Fields, who apparently is as unlucky with cops as he is lucky with the lottery.

Fields, 51, had $37,970 seized Feb. 4, 1991.

The Miami clothing maker told Deputy Bobby Jones that the money was lottery winnings.

But Jones decided Fields was a narcotics dealer because he was too nervous, too evasive and had wrapped the money in rubber bands, a characteristic of dealers.

Fields' attorney, Henry Davis, demanded the money back, providing a canceled check signed by then–Lottery Commissioner Rebecca Paul for $213,698.48.

Fields provided forms detailing his employment and finances. In those and a subsequent deposition, he described winning more than $400,000 in the lottery during an 18-month period.

The Lottery Department confirmed the winnings.

Nevertheless, officers developed a theory: Based on the view that no one could be that lucky, they speculated that Fields might be a money launderer.

For example, if someone had a winning ticket worth $50,000, Fields might buy it for $60,000 then claim the prize, transforming drug money into "clean" income.

No proof was offered. No further investigation was conducted. But the Sheriff's Office refused to return the money, saying that its suspicions were bolstered by Fields' 1973 conviction for conspiracy to sell cocaine, for which he served probation.

"Mr. Fields' decision wasn't irrational," Davis said. "The whole problem in these cases is you end up having to explain why a black man has $50,000 in his car. The fact is a black male who's got $50,000 in his car looks suspicious."

Finally, Fields agreed to a settlement. He got $23,000; the Sheriff's Office got $14,970; Davis was paid $8,000.

In an interview, the top investigator at the Florida Lottery, Colon Benton, scoffed at the notion of a black market for winning tickets. Common sense indicates that it would have to be widespread, Benton said, for Fields to have repeatedly bought winning tickets.

"The Florida Lottery is not investigating Mr. Fields, and I have no suspicions to investigate him," he said.

Memo: See related stories on Pages A1 and A4
Page: A4
Series: Tainted cash or easy money?
Copyright 1992 Sentinel Communications Co.

OLD LAW, NEW STANDARDS

The Orlando Sentinel—June 16, 1992

The Florida Legislature revised the state's controversial Contraband Forfeiture Law this spring, but critics say the changes are unlikely to prevent abuses.

Among the revisions, which will take effect July 1: OLD: Police have 90 days after seizing property to file a formal forfeiture request in court.

NEW: Police will have 45 days, but motorists can demand a court hearing within 10 days of the confiscation.

OLD: No restrictions on out-of-court settlements, in which police and the motorist split money or property.

NEW: All out-of-court settlements must be reviewed and approved by a judge or a mediator.

OLD: Agencies can spend seized funds essentially on any law enforcement-related function.

NEW: At least 15 percent of confiscated funds must go to crime prevention, school resources or drug education.

OLD: If a forfeiture goes to trial, police must prove their case by a preponderance, or majority, of the evidence.

NEW: Police must prove their case with clear-and-convincing evidence— a tougher legal standard than preponderance of the evidence but not as tough as the beyond-a-reasonable-doubt standard used in criminal cases.

None of the new provisions addresses what critics say they believe is the fundamental problem with forfeiture: that police can take money and property from people who are never arrested nor charged with a crime and against whom there is no evidence of wrongdoing.

Critics would like to see additional reforms:—Requiring police to meet higher standards of evidence before making a seizure.

—Forcing them to pay all legal costs and face punitive damages if they lose a forfeiture case at trial.

Mel Stack, the lawyer who handles seizures for the Volusia County Sheriff's Office, said: "Our deputies are aware of the new standard, and they will take it into account. It means they will have to take a harder look at their cases."

Memo: See related stories on Pages A1 and A4
Page: A4
Column: Reforms

Series: Tainted cash or easy money?
Copyright 1992 Sentinel Communications Co.

Color of Driver Is Key to Stops in I-95 Videos. The Tapes Show That Most Stops and Searches by Volusia County's Drug Squad Involve Minorities.

The Orlando Sentinel—August 23, 1992
Author: By Jeff Brazil and Steve Berry of The Sentinel Staff

Videotapes obtained by The Orlando Sentinel offer the most compelling evidence to date that Volusia County Sheriff Bob Vogel's drug squad uses skin color to decide whom to stop and search for cash on Interstate 95.

There is the bewildered black man who stands on the roadside trying to explain to the deputies that it is the seventh time he has been stopped.

And the black man who shakes his head in frustration as his car is searched; it is the second time in minutes he has been stopped.

They are among more than 1,000 people whose roadside stops are shown on videotapes obtained from the Sheriff's Office by the Sentinel through the state's public records law.

The videos, made by dash-mounted cameras in deputies' cars, show that the majority of stops—and searches—involve minorities.

To document the practice, Sentinel reporters watched 148 hours of videotape—nearly all that the department has. The findings included the following:—Almost 70 percent of the motorists stopped were black or Hispanic, an enormously disproportionate figure because the vast majority of interstate drivers are white.

—More than 80 percent of the cars that were searched were driven by blacks and Hispanics.

—Although deputies contend they stop cars only for legitimate traffic violations—as required by the Florida Supreme Court—only nine of 1,084 drivers stopped—less than 1 percent—received traffic tickets.

—Nearly 500 motorists who had committed no crime were subjected to detention and searches because they were suspected of being drug traffickers. Most were frisked, based solely on a deputy's suspicion, and then allowed to leave.

Ultimately, there is no way to determine how many people have been stopped in the three years the Sheriff's Office has been operating its freewheeling drug squad.

Presumably, there were thousands more, but for much of the time no videos were made. And it was the agency's practice to record over earlier recordings on tapes, thereby erasing the original recordings.

What is clear is the pattern that is repeated in tape after tape: In three of every four stops, the drivers are black or Hispanic.

Those numbers reinforce the findings of a Sentinel investigative report in June that focused on nearly $8 million the Selective Enforcement Team has seized, mostly from I-95 motorists.

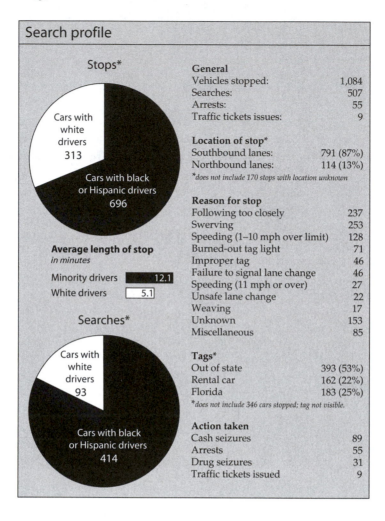

Search profile

Stops*

Cars with white drivers
313

Cars with black or Hispanic drivers
696

Average length of stop
in minutes

Minority drivers — 12.1
White drivers — 5.1

Searches*

Cars with white drivers
93

Cars with black or Hispanic drivers
414

General

Vehicles stopped:	1,084
Searches:	507
Arrests:	55
Traffic tickets issues:	9

Location of stop*

Southbound lanes:	791 (87%)
Northbound lanes:	114 (13%)

does not include 170 stops with location unknown

Reason for stop

Following too closely	237
Swerving	253
Speeding (1–10 mph over limit)	128
Burned-out tag light	71
Improper tag	46
Failure to signal lane change	46
Speeding (11 mph or over)	27
Unsafe lane change	22
Weaving	17
Unknown	153
Miscellaneous	85

Tags*

Out of state	393 (53%)
Rental car	162 (22%)
Florida	183 (25%)

does not include 346 cars stopped; tag not visible.

Action taken

Cash seizures	89
Arrests	55
Drug seizures	31
Traffic tickets issued	9

That analysis, based on a review of sheriff's records, found that no one was charged with a crime in three of every four cases in which money was seized.

Ninety percent of the drivers from whom cash was taken—but who were not arrested—were black or Hispanic.

Often there was no evidence of criminal behavior or criminal history when money was taken.

After reading the Sentinel report, Gov. Lawton Chiles formed a panel to investigate the tactics of Vogel's squad and others like it throughout the state. The panel will meet for the first time Tuesday.

J. Hardin Peterson, Chiles' general counsel and the point man on the panel, said the videotapes were "worse than (President) Nixon's.

"From what you've described to me, it's wrong. And I think the statute under which they're presently operating needs to be amended. That's what we're meeting for."

Expert: High court would "throw up"

Vogel would not be interviewed for this report. He issued a statement saying he wouldn't answer seizure-related questions until the panel's review ends.

The team he formed in 1989 to nab drug traffickers has had great success in using the Florida Contraband Forfeiture Act, a 12-year-old law that allows police to confiscate—and keep—money that they suspect is linked to drug trafficking. It is not necessary to make an arrest or even prove that a crime occurred.

But critics argue that the team's successes are merely the result of its widespread abuse of constitutional protections against unlawful search and seizure.

The idea, they say, is simple: Stop enough cars and you'll find a few drug traffickers.

The statistics show that only one of every 120 drivers stopped by the deputies was ticketed.

The Florida Supreme Court has ruled that deputies cannot stop a driver unless they witness a legitimate traffic violation.

Almost every stop was for a minor infraction: following too closely, having a burned-out tag light, making an unsafe lane change.

And, although the sheriff says that only the cars of suspicious motorists are searched, deputies found nothing and took no action in three of every four searches.

Casting further doubt on the practice is the overwhelming proportion of stops involving blacks and Hispanics.

Vogel has denied that the stops are based on skin color. He said in June that deputies stop "a broad spectrum of people."

The Sentinel asked to see records of stops. But several sheriff's officials said no records were made unless there were arrests or seizures.

The Sentinel learned of the existence of the videotapes through a Winter Park lawyer representing a defendant in a seizure case. The newspaper presented a legal demand to see the tapes, arguing that they are a public record.

At first, the Sheriff's Office refused, saying releasing the tapes would reveal confidential surveillance methods.

The tapes were made available after the newspaper repeated its legal demand through its attorney and after the Sheriff's Office was advised to release them by Volusia County Attorney Dan Eckert and the state attorney general's office.

Tapes show a pattern

Reporters spent six weeks at the sheriff's Operations Center viewing every tape the department had, except for a few involving pending legal cases, which the sheriff had the right to withhold.

The tapes showed that stops for black and Hispanic drivers lasted an average of 12.1 minutes; for whites, 5.1 minutes.

There were many cases in which black motorists said they had been stopped and searched before.

South Florida forfeiture lawyer Carl Lida reviewed a sample of the videotaped stops at the newspaper's request.

"If the Florida Supreme Court saw these tapes, they would throw up," he said.

It was Lida's argument before the Supreme Court that resulted in the ruling that prohibits the use of a "drug profile" to stop drivers.

Before being elected sheriff, Vogel was a Florida Highway Patrol trooper who made many drug seizures based on a set of characteristics he developed, called the "smuggler's profile." Essentially, it targeted young males driving four-door sedans or rental cars at a few miles over the speed limit.

Ruling in favor of Lida, the Supreme Court overturned a Vogel seizure and ruled that the profile could not be used to stop cars.

If a driver committed a legitimate traffic offense, however, an officer could use the profile, along with other suspicious characteristics, to detain a driver for a search, the court said.

"Benefit of the doubt"

Said Lida: "We want to give the police the benefit of the doubt when they say there is an alleged traffic violation. But when we put together 500 stops and you never get a ticket, wouldn't you conclude it's a ruse?"

On May 16, 1990, Sgt. Dale Anderson stopped a white motorist and asked how he was doing.

When the man said, "Not very good," Anderson replied, "Could be worse—could be black."

Anderson has since been promoted to lieutenant and head of the patrol unit for Spring Hill, a predominantly black area of DeLand.

In its earlier series, the Sentinel reported that records showed the drug squad focused primarily on seizing cash, rather than searching for drugs.

That emphasis on money also was apparent on the tapes.

Drivers who actually admitted to crimes—including drug and alcohol offenses—were almost never charged or cited.

A man who said he had a marijuana joint in his car was let go.

Another told a deputy—in slurred speech—that he had been drinking and probably shouldn't be behind the wheel.

"I'm sorry I'm in the condition I'm in," the New Smyrna Beach resident told Anderson in October 1989. "I do feel like I shouldn't be driving."

Anderson let the man go, saying: "You know, with all this Mothers Against Drunk Driving [expletive], I'm telling you, it's going to cost you two grand to get a lawyer."

Sixty-seven drivers had no driver's license or had a suspended license, in some instances because of convictions for driving while under the influence of alcohol. They were let go.

The vast majority of the stops, 87 percent, were in the southbound lanes, where any drug traffickers would more likely be carrying cash to Miami, the entry point for most illegal drugs brought into the country. Only 13 percent of the stops were in northbound lanes, where the catch more likely would be drugs.

In 179 stops, about 17 percent, it could not be determined which lanes were involved.

"Clearly an abuse"

After hearing about the information from the tapes, federal Judge Jim Carrigan of Denver said: "I have no objection to being tough on drug dealers. But everybody has to be treated the same."

Carrigan recently ruled that tactics employed by deputies in Eagle County, Colo.—tactics similar to those used in Volusia County—were illegal and racist.

Search Profile

An analysis of the Selective Enforcement Team's traffic stops and vehicle searches.

General:
  Vehicles stopped 1,084
  Searches 507
  Arrests 55
  Traffic tickets issued 9

Location of stop:*
  Southbound lanes 791 (87%)
  Northbound lanes 114 (13%)
  does not include 179 stops, location unknown.

Reason for stop:
  Following too closely 237
  Swerving 253
  Speeding 1–10 mph over limit 128
  Burned-out tag light 71
  Improper tag 46
  Failure to signal lane change 45
  Speeding 11 mph or over 27
  Unsafe lane change 22
  Weaving 17
  Unknown 153
  Miscellaneous 85

Tags:*
  Out of state 393 (53%)
  Rental car 162 (22%)
  Florida 183 (25%)
  does not include 346 cars stopped, tag not visible.

Action taken:
  Cash seizures 89
  Arrests 55
  Drug seizures 31
  Traffic tickets issued 9

Source: *Volusia County Sheriff's Office Videos, Sentinel research*
  By Brenda Weaver/Sentinel

Stops*
  Cars with white drivers—313
  Cars with black or Hispanic drivers—696
  does not include 75 stops in which driver could not be seen.

Average length of stop in minutes
  Minority drivers 12.1
  White drivers 5.1

Searches*
  Cars with white drivers 93
  Cars with black or Hispanic drivers 414
  does not include 78 possible searches/incomplete video. Brenda Weaver/Sentinel

---

NIGHT VISION

At night, deputies look for drug traffickers by shining headlights and spot-lights across Interstate 95. They say they're looking for traffic violations, driver's age, radar detectors, cellular telephones or CB antennas on out-of-state cars. Critics say they look for dark-skinned drivers. Whatever the object, there is little time. Headlights on their 1990 Chevrolet Caprices cast a 40-foot-wide beam at 50 feet. At 72 mph, average interstate speed, cars cross the lighted area in .38 seconds.

Source: Dr. David Moore, General Motors headlights specialist.

By MARK BOIVIN/SENTINEL

"It's more efficient to search everybody, but you can't do that when you violate the Constitution," Carrigan said.

Nancy Hollander, a nationally recognized authority on the issue of "profile" stops by law enforcement agencies around the country, said, "We've been saying these things for years, but this is the first proof.

"My reaction is that this is clearly racist, and it's clearly an abuse of the forfeiture laws."

State Sen. Jack Gordon, D-Miami Beach—who opposes letting police seize cash and property because it brings a profit motive to crime-fighting—also criticized Vogel's tactics.

The reasons for the stops, he said, sound like "it's whatever they can think of.

"I don't understand why the people of Daytona Beach tolerate it."

Memo: Henry Curtis, Sean Somerville, Lynne Bumpus-Hooper and Cory Jo Lancaster of the Sentinel staff and correspondents Linda Creesy, Cindy Finney and Ann Mikell contributed to this report. See related articles and charts on page A10 and A11. See microfilm for charts of Search profile and Night vision.
Page: A1
Column: Special report
Copyright 1992 Sentinel Communications Co.

Many Black or Hispanic Drivers Feel They Are Singled Out, Tapes Show

The Orlando Sentinel—August 23, 1992
Author: By Jeff Brazil and Steve Berry of The Sentinel Staff

Most of the time, when the Volusia County drug squad orders motorists to the side of the road, the drivers don't seem to mind.

Most don't even argue when the officers ask for permission to search their cars.

But videotapes show that many black or Hispanic drivers, the target of the vast majority of the searches, told deputies they believed that they were being stopped because of their skin color.

And, for a significant number, things got unpleasant when they tried to object.

On Jan. 22, 1991, Deputy Michael Frederick stopped two black men in a sedan for following too closely. The passenger got out to help the driver open his door, which was jammed, muttering something about being stopped "again" and something about the National Association for the Advancement of Colored People.

Frederick bristled and ordered him back into the car.

"I don't know what your problem is, pal," Frederick said.

When the man tried to explain that they already had been pulled over once by deputies on the trip, Frederick got tough.

"No, I'm just saying . . ." the man started to explain.

Frederick yelled, "No, you listen to me, all right? You listen to me right now. Do you understand that?"

"But . . . ."

Frederick said, "I'll tow the car, man. You'll be on foot."

The man said, "OK, all right. You win; you win. No problem."

Frederick said, "Yelling this NAACP crap . . . ."

When the man began to speak again, Frederick interrupted: "How far you going to walk today?"

The man backed down: "Hey, Mr. Frederick, you told me to shut up, I shut up."

The tape ends without revealing what happened.

Moments after stopping three young, out-of-state black men Oct. 19, 1990, and getting consent to search the car, Frederick found about $9,000.

The men said it was spending money.

Frederick didn't buy the story and began asking questions.

One man worked at Wendy's; another washed cars; and the other had earned $10,000 to $15,000 at a mattress firm.

Frederick placed the men into the back of his cruiser, where their conversation was secretly tape-recorded, and resumed his search of their car for drugs or other contraband.

The recording captured this conversation from the back seat: "He's just saying we can't have money to go on a trip because we are black. He's crazy, man. He ain't going to find no drugs in that car."

Frederick let them out of his car. As they started to get back into their own car, Frederick yelled something at them.

They protested. "We're just here to have fun," one said.

Frederick's voice drowned them out

"You nice men are liars," he said. "You are a liar. And so are you. And so are you. If I wanted to, I could keep this money and make you go to a judge and prove this is your money."

Frederick refused to listen to their response, warning them: "Don't piss me off, man, 'cause I'll take your money and put you in jail if I wanted. So let's not argue."

One of the men asked, "If we got something to hide, why would we say you can search our car?"

Frederick: "Because you know I'm going to search it one way or another, don't you?"

On Aug. 27, 1990, Sgt. Bobby Jones stopped a Hispanic motorist for swerving. During the 23 minutes he spent searching the car, Jones called in a second deputy to bring a tire tool.

Unbeknown to the motorist, who was asked to stand in front of the car, Jones let the air out of the man's spare tire before whacking the tire a couple of times with the tire tool. Finding nothing, Jones threw the tire back into the trunk, closed the lid, then sent the man on his way.

With a flat tire.

PHOTO: Search but no seizure Jan. 24, 1991—Sgt. Bobby Jones stops a van and tells its occupants, "I don't want to write you guys a ticket unless you want me to." They assure Jones they don't want a ticket. After a polite chat, he tells them they are free to go. As they turn to leave, Jones asks whether they are carrying drugs. Would they mind if he searches "just to make sure"? The motorists agree. Jones empties the van of luggage and searches underneath and throughout. He finds nothing. Time of detention: nearly 30 minutes. PHOTO SHOT FROM VIDEO BY PHELAN M. EBEN-HACK/SENTINEL [not reproduced]

Memo: See related article on page A1. See related charts on page A10.
Page: A10
Copyright 1992 Sentinel Communications Co.

Legal Experts Say Seizures Appear Illegal. A Sample of Videotaped Roadside Stops by Volusia's Drug Squad Gets Poor Reviews From 4 Lawyers.

The Orlando Sentinel—August 23, 1992
Author: By Steve Berry of The Sentinel Staff

Four legal experts asked by The Orlando Sentinel to review a sample of videotaped roadside stops by the Volusia County drug squad agreed that its seizures appear illegal.

All four viewed a videotape showing 21 stops in January 1991 by Sgt. Bobby Jones, head of the Selective Enforcement Team.

Videotapes of more than 1,000 traffic stops by the five-member drug team show that all of the officers follow a strict routine in dealing with drivers.

In the tape, Jones informs each driver that he or she has been stopped for a minor traffic violation and asks to see a driver's license. He is polite and chatty and returns the license before popping the surprise question:

"By the way, you're not carrying any drugs, guns or bombs, are you?" he asks. "You mind if I take a quick look?"

That approach would make it illegal to seize any contraband, according to the four lawyers who reviewed the tape: former prosecutor David Vinikoor, Miami lawyer Carl Lida, Nova University law professor Paul Joseph and Gainesville lawyer Robert Griscti.

Both Lida and Griscti won landmark Florida Supreme Court cases challenging seizures made under the Contraband Forfeiture Act. Vinikoor is now a Fort Lauderdale defense lawyer. Joseph is state president of the American Civil Liberties Union.

Their reactions: On the stops

Griscti: "The stops are illegal because they are made on a pretext to get into a dialogue with the driver to investigate the officer's hunch that illegal conduct is going on."

Lida: "The most significant factor is the pattern they show, a law enforcement strategy that is a ruse to investigate, question and search motorists."

Joseph: "In one stop, the officer stopped someone for traveling four car lengths behind a car instead of six. Now, would a reasonable police officer make that kind of stop? I doubt it."

Vinikoor: "The stops have absolutely nothing to do with the expressed reason for the stops."

Mel Stack, the lawyer who handles seizure cases for the Volusia County Sheriff's Office, responded: "I disagree they are stopping solely for searching. The purpose is to enforce the traffic laws. It doesn't really matter if they have an ulterior motive. It's an objective standard that they [the courts] use."

In more than 1,000 traffic stops, the drug squad issued a ticket less than 1 percent of the time.

Said Stack: "I don't believe that the fact that they don't write tickets makes this a pretextual stop. Writing tickets is up to the officer's discretion."

On consent to search

Lida: "I didn't see anything in the answers that warranted one person to be searched over another."

Joseph: "It's not always clear to me that consent is truly consent. It's very borderline."

"When the whites were searched, it was cursory. When a black driving an out-of-state car was searched, it was as if they [the officers] could not believe there were no drugs."

Griscti: "He crosses the line when he frees the driver to go, walks away and then turns and shoots an accusatory question. That catches the driver by surprise, and the officer follows that up with a request to search. The drivers are merely acquiescing to authority, to a cop on the side of the road."

Vinikoor: "Lawful consent is a knowing, intelligent consent. What I saw was submission to authority. People are acquiescing to a guy with a badge and a gun."

Volusia County Sheriff Bob Vogel would not be interviewed. In previous interviews, however, he has said the law allows officers to search a car when they suspect that a driver might be a drug trafficker.

The videotape, made from a dash-mounted camera in Jones' cruiser, was one of 128 examined by the Sentinel.

In it, Jones is seen stopping 11 white drivers and 10 black drivers. He searches cars driven by three whites and seven blacks, and he makes one seizure of $17,500. He does not write a single traffic ticket.

Memo: See related articles on pages A1, A10 and A11.
Page: A11
Copyright 1992 Sentinel Communications Co.

Statistics Show Pattern of Discrimination

The Orlando Sentinel—August 23, 1992
Author: By Henry Pierson Curtis of The Sentinel Staff

An overwhelmingly disproportionate number of black and Hispanic motorists have been the targets of Volusia County Sheriff Bob Vogel's drug squad.

Across the country, such patterns have been found to be strong evidence of racism or discriminatory policies.

The Orlando Sentinel found that minorities constituted 69 percent of the motorists stopped over the past three years by Vogel's Selective Enforcement Team on Interstate 95.

And blacks and Hispanics drove 82 percent of the vehicles deputies chose to search, according to a review of 1,084 stops videotaped by the drug team. Yet the vast majority of drivers on the interstate are white.

The Sheriff's Office contends that skin color plays no role in who gets stopped. Vogel says the drug team makes only legitimate traffic stops of drivers who commit a violation or whose cars have equipment problems.

A broad spectrum of statistical data, however, refutes the notion that random stops would result in a high number of blacks and Hispanics being stopped:

—A national survey by the U.S. Department of Transportation found that only 4.8 percent of all drivers taking highway trips of less than 75 miles are black. On longer trips, blacks constitute 6.8 percent of drivers.

—Blacks represented only 15.1 percent of the 973,000 Floridians convicted of traffic offenses last year, according to a computer analysis by the Fort Lauderdale Sun-Sentinel of 1.44 million tickets issued in 1991.

Statewide, blacks represent 11.7 percent of the driving-age population.

—National figures closely match those of the state. Blacks made up 12 percent of the population recorded by the 1990 census; Hispanics registered about 9 percent.

—On the stretch of Interstate 95 patrolled by Vogel, about 5 percent of the drivers of 1,120 vehicles counted during a five-day sampling in July and August were dark-skinned.

The Sentinel's review of traffic stops—and its analysis published in June of cash seizures by the drug squad—shows an overwhelming preponderance of black and Hispanic drivers.

Vogel critics have likened the results to those of a fisherman snatching the occasional mackerel out of a school of mullet. In the courtroom, statistical evidence of significant racial or ethnic disproportion has been repeatedly used to prove a pattern of discrimination.

In 1972 the U.S. Supreme Court ruled that the death penalty, as usually enforced in the country, was a violation of the Eighth Amendment prohibition against cruel and unusual punishment. In the decision, which struck down death penalty statutes in 39 states, Justice William O. Douglas wrote that the disproportionate number of minorities sentenced to death showed unconstitutional discrimination.

In a recent case involving issues nearly identical to the stop-and-search practices of the Volusia drug squad, a Colorado defense attorney recently had a cocaine seizure thrown out of court after showing statistical evidence of discrimination by the arresting officer. Of 200 traffic stops over 18 months, 188 cars bore out-of-state plates. More than half of the cars searched had drivers with Hispanic surnames.

The attorney since has filed a class-action suit against the sheriff of Eagle County, Colo.

Similar disproportion in arrests of out-of-state black motorists on the New Jersey Turnpike has prompted a lawsuit to overturn hundreds of traffic and felony convictions there.

To bolster their arguments, defense attorneys commissioned a study that showed out-of-state blacks represented just 5 percent of all drivers on the highway, yet they made up 69 percent of the arrests by a group of New Jersey state troopers.

In Volusia, critics scoff at the sheriff's contention that every stop his officers make is because of a traffic violation. "Any person upon viewing these numbers will know that whatever racial discrimination is, this is it," said Robyn Blumner, executive director of the American Civil Liberties Union of Florida. "Constitutionally and morally, you can't do this. Any police officer charged with protecting the public is obligated to be colorblind."

In an August 1990 videotape, Vogel's most successful deputy, Sgt. Bobby Jones, is talking about strategy. Jones stops a Hispanic motorist and spends 11 minutes searching his Chevrolet Blazer, without success.

"That guy was a good prospect, but nothing to it. He wasn't nervous or nothing," Jones tells a Florida Highway Patrol trooper.

"They haven't been looking that bad, but we just haven't been hooking up on nothing."

Nevertheless, Jones tells the trooper that he likes the roadside spot they've chosen to set up watch. "It's a good spot anyways. We like it because it weeds out local traffic. We found you're looking at less traffic and seem to look at them better."

Sheriff Vogel declined to be interviewed. He said previously that the preponderance of minority drivers caught in the drug squad's net simply showed that they were more likely to be drug traffickers.

"What this data tells me," he said, "is the majority of money being transported for drug activity involves blacks and Hispanics."

Yet, in this area as well, statistical data provide a marked contrast:

—For the last three years, whites and blacks in Florida have respectively accounted for an average of 47.5 percent and 52.4 percent of all drug cases, according to the Florida Department of Law Enforcement.

—A 1986 study by the national Bureau of Justice Statistics showed that whites committed 79 percent of all federal drug offenses.

Memo: Craig Quintana of the Sentinel staff contributed to this report. See related articles on pages A1, A10 and A11.
Page: A11
Dateline: DELAND
Copyright 1992 Sentinel Communications Co.

Court Record in Chapter 2

This copy of the Circuit Court Department of Probate records from Washington County, Ore., is the document that prompted *Willamette Week* reporter Nigel Jaquiss to launch an investigation into a rumor that former Portland Mayor Neil Goldschmidt had engaged in sexual relations with an underage girl while he was mayor.

Although the original document is a public record, the author has redacted the name of the victim, who is now an adult, and the court case number in an effort to minimize the chances that her privacy will be violated.

```
         IN THE CIRCUIT COURT OF THE STATE OF OREGON
               FOR THE COUNTY OF WASHINGTON
                    Department of Probate

In the Matter of the   )      No. C000000 PC
Conservatorship        )      ORDER APPOINTING
of                     )      CONSERVATOR
Jane Doe               )
_____
```

This matter came before the Court upon the petition of _____Jane Doe_____ and Doreen Stamm Margolin for the appointment of a conservator for _____Jane Doe_____

It appears to the Court from the records and files herein that:

(1) Venue is properly laid in this Court and no other Court in this state has acquired jurisdiction in this matter.

(2) Notice as required by ORS 126.007 and 126.187 has been waived. No interested person has requested notice pursuant to ORS 126.187.

(3) _____Jane Doe_____will be filing a personal injury lawsuit in relation to her claim for injuries sustained from 1975-1978, and is in need of protection because she sustained a psychological injury.

(4) Doreen Stamm Margolin is a qualified and suitable person to act as conservator and is willing to serve.

(5) The net proceeds of any settlement in any lawsuit filed will be deposited in an interest bearing account at Merrill Lynch, for the benefit of _____Jane Doe_____, and no disbursements shall be made from that account without Order of this Court.

(6) The need for accountings are hereby waived.

NOW, THEREFORE, IT IS HEREBY ORDERED,

(1) That Doreen Stamm Margolin be and she hereby is appointed conservator for _____Jane Doe_____.

(2) The bond of the conservator and accountings are waived.
DATED this ____2nd____ day of _____November_____, 1994.

_____

Circuit Court Judge

Conservator:

Doreen Stamm Margolin
OSB No. 81303
1020 S.W. Taylor St., suite 330
Portland, Oregon 97205
Telephone: (503) 222-9830

Attorney for Conservator:

Jana Toran
OSB No. 90398
621 S.W. Morrison Street, Suite 950
Portland, Oregon 97205
Telephone: (503) 225-0227

IN THE CIRCUIT COURT OF THE STATE OF OREGON
FOR THE COUNTY OF WASHINGTON
Probate Department

STATE OF OREGON   )   No. c000000 PC
) ss
County of Washington   )   LETTERS OF CONSERVATORSHIP

TO ALL WHOM THESE PRESENTS SHALL COME, GREETINGS:

NOW YE, that on the ___2nd___ day of _____November_____
____1994____, the Circuit Court of the State of Oregon for
Washington County, appointed ___DOREEN STAMM MARGOLIN___, as
conservator of the Estate of ____Jane Doe____; that the named
conservator has qualified and has the authority and shall per-
form the duties of conservator of the Estate of the named ward
as provided by law.

IN TESTIMONY WHEREOF, I have hereunto subscribed my name and
affixed the seal of the Court this __4th__ day of _____November_____
___1994___.

The net proceeds of any settlement in any lawsuit filed will
be deposited in interest bearing account at Merrill Lynch,
for the benefit of Jane Doe, and no disbursements shall be
made from the account without order of this court.

WASHINGTON COUNTY CIRCUIT COURT

By _____

Court Clerk

* *

STATE OF OREGON   )
) ss
County of Washington   )

I, a Circuit Court Clerk of the State of Oregon for Washington County, do hereby certify that the foregoing copy
of Letters of Conservatorship has been compared by me with
the original Letters on file and of record in my office and
in my custody in the above-entitled matter; that the said
copy is a true and correct transcript of said original and
of the whole thereof and that said Letters are now in full
force and effect.

IN TESTIMONY WHEREOF, I have hereunto set my hand and affixed the seal of said court this _____ day of _____, 19_____.

                         WASHINGTON COUNTY CIRCUIT COURT

                         By _____

                                             Court Clerk

            IN THE CIRCUIT COURT OF THE STATE OF OREGON
                   FOR THE COUNTY OF WASHINGTON
                      Department of Probate

In the Matter of the	)	C
Conservatorship	)	No C000000 PC
of	)	MOTION FOR ORDER
Jane Doe	)	AUTHORIZING EXPENDITURES

Conservator, Doreen Stamm Margolin, moves the Court for an order allowing her to withdraw sufficient funds to meet _____ Jane Doe's _____ usual monthly living expenses.

Net proceeds of a claim for personal injury and personal psychological injury will be deposited in an interest bearing account at Merrill Lynch for the benefit of Jane Doe. It will be necessary for the conservator to make monthly disbursements from the account for the benefit of _____ Ms. Doe _____ for her usual monthly living expenses.

The conservator moves the Court for an order authorizing her to withdraw sufficient funds to meet _____ Jane Doe's _____ usual living expenses, not to exceed $1,500 per month.

DATED this _____ 7 _____ day of February, 1995.

                         MARGOLIN & MARGOLIN

                         _____

                         Doreen Stamm Margolin, OSB 81303
                         Conservator for Jane Doe

APPENDIX C

Coy Allegation in Chapter 3

This appendix consists of a reduced-size copy of a 8½ × 14-inch crude spreadsheet containing 27 allegations of atrocities by the Tiger Force unit in Vietnam in 1967. The Army Criminal Investigations Division referred to it as "The Coy Allegation." The name comes from allegation 1 on the first sheet in which a Tiger Force soldier, whose last name was Coy, alleged that another member of the unit named Ybarra killed a Vietnamese infant by cutting the child's throat. The spreadsheet was prepared at the order of Col. Henry Tufts and was compiled from the reports of the ongoing investigation of Sgt. Gustav Apsey.

Toledo Blade reporter Michael D. Sallah discovered this spreadsheet among 25,000 pages of Col. Tufts' private papers. This document prompted him and his partner, Mitch Weiss, to launch an investigation into the allegations.

Allegation	Summary of Significant Statements	Remarks
1. COY alleged that YBARRA killed a Vietnamese Infant by cutting the infants throat.	COY related that he had executed false statements regarding this allegation, that he had not witnessed the killing but had been told of the incident by AHERN.	Investigation failed to disclose any evidence that the killing in fact occurred. Interviews of 120 former Tiger Force members failed to substantiate the allegation. AHERN was killed in action 16 March 1968.
2. COTTINGHAM alleged that during 1967, near Chu Lai, RVN YBARRA killed an 8–9 year old Vietnamese child by decapitating the child	COTTINGHAM stated that during a Tiger Force combat action an armed Vietnamese male was seen running into a hut. YBARRA and others entered the hut after YBARRA had thrown a grenade inside. COTTINGHAM did not witness what occurred inside the hut but was later told by the Tiger Force members that YBARRA had decapitated a 8 - 9 year old Vietnamese child. COTTINGHAM identified FISCHER as having been present. FISCHER related that he had been present in the village during the alleged incident and had been told by KERRIGAN that YEARRA had decapitated the child. KERRIGAN denied any knowledge concerning the incident. ALLUMS related that YBARRA had admitted to him (ALLUMS) that he had decapitated the child.	
3. CARPENTER alleged that prior to Feb 67, at an undetermined location in RVN, a Tiger Force medic mutilated the body of a dead Vietnamese male by severing the penis and sewing it between the body's eyes.	CARPENTER stated that he had been told by unidentified Tiger Force members as he joined the force in 1967, that a Tiger Force medic had severed the penis of a dead Vietnamese male and had sewn the penis between the body's eyes. Allegedly an unidentified news correspondent was shown the scene and subsequently refused to accompany the Tiger Force on future missions. HEANEY stated that he had heard a Tiger Force member had committed the body mutilation as related by CARPENTER. He considered this a rumor and to this knowledge such an incident had not occurred during his assignment with Tiger Force. PATTERSON stated that he had been told by unidentified Tiger Force members that a unit medic believed to have been DEFENBAUGH had committed such an act as described by CARPENTER, and had written words "dick head" on the forehead of the body. COOK stated that he had heard that the head had been cut from a body and mounted on a stake with the penis sewn between the eyes.	As of 9 July 1974, efforts to locate and interview DEFENBAUGH have been unsuccessful. On 20 Jul 74 DEFENBAUGH was interviewed and denied any knowledge or participation in body mutilations. He advised that he heard a "Rumor" regarding this allegation when he joined the Tiger Force in 1966.

Continued

Allegation	Summary of Significant Statements	Remarks
4. CARPENTER alleged that on or about 6 May 1967, west of Duc Pho, RVN, Tiger Force personnel captured a Vietnamese with explosives in his possession. The Vietnamese was shot as he followed their instructions to flee.	CARPENTER stated that Tiger Force members had captured a Vietnamese in possession of explosives who was suspected to be Chinese due to his large build. The prisoner was beaten and told to run. As he ran he was shot and killed. CARPENTER related that he did not witness the actual shooting, however, he had seen the prisoner alive and saw the body after he had been killed. BARNETT stated that the Tiger Force had captured a prisoner suspected to be Chinese due to his large stature. The prisoner was put to work, beaten and later killed. BARNETT denied knowing who killed the prisoner or the circumstances surrounding the killing.	During interviews of Former Tiger Force members, numerous individuals have alluded to the "Big Gook" that had been captured. Interviewees have mentioned prisoner killings by members of the Tiger Force. Investigation to date has not determined if they referred to this particular incident.
5. CARPENTER alleged that during June 1967, in the Song Ve Valley, RVN, HAWKINS, Tiger Force Platoon leader, killed an unarmed elderly Vietnamese encountered on a night patrol.	CARPENTER stated that HAWKINS, while crossing the Song Ve river during a night move ordered by HAWKINS, encountered an elderly, unarmed Vietnamese farmer. Hawkins grabbed the victim, at which time TROUT struck the victim with the barrel of his M-16 rifle. HAWKINS then shot the victim in the face with his CAR-15 rifle, blowing away half of the victims head. HAWKINS then shot the victim a second time. CARPENTER further related that at the time he had been assigned as HAWKINS RTO, and had been standing beside HAWKINS at the time the killing occurred. CARPENTER further stated that HAWKINS had been drunk on beer and there had been absolutely no justification for the killing. LEE stated that he crossed the river behind HAWKINS CP element when the victim was apprehended. HAWKINS, TROUT and CARPENTER arrived at the scene after being notified of the prisoner by LEE. Lee related he witnessed TROUT strike the victim with the rifle after the victim refused to answer a question posed by HAWKINS through his interpreter. LEE further stated that he then departed to return to his element. About three minutes later he heard a shot and concluded that the prisoner had been shot because he was screaming and giving away the units position. He stated that he later heard that HAWKINS had shot the prisoner and confirmed	HAWKINS initially denied the killing and later declined to answer further questions on advice of counsel. TROUT has declined to answer questions or make any statement on advice of counsel.

witnessed TROUT strike the victim with his rifle. He departed the area and later heard a shot and suspected that the prisoner had been killed. HEANEY, further stated that he had been told that HAWKINS had killed the prisoner and confirmed that HAWKINS and TROUT had been drunk on beer supplied the element earlier during the day. BARNETT stated that he had crossed the river behind the CP element and had heard a couple of shots fired. Later he passed the body of an old man lying on the trail. At the time he did not know what had occurred, however, later he was told that HAWKINS and TROUT were drunk when they crossed the river. BOWMAN stated that he witnessed the killing and had been standing within ten feet of HAWKINS when he shot the victim.

CARPENTER stated that a Vietnamese male had been wounded as he approached the Tiger Force night position. A medic was called for at which time TROUT advised that he would administer first aid. CARPENTER stated that he then witnessed TROUT shoot the Vietnamese male three times with a .45 cal pistol and place the body in a large hole in the ground. CARPENTER further advised that he thought the weapon used in the killing was assigned to BOWMAN. In a written statement BOWMAN related that he had heard the call for a medic and went to where the victim was lying. BOWMAN stated that TROUT had implied that he (BOWMAN) killed the victim with words to the effect "come on, break your cherry Doc." BOWMAN stated that he had refused to kill the victim at which time TROUT shot and killed the victim with BOWMAN's .45 cal pistol. BOWMAN further related that he thought the incident was a "mercy" killing as the victim would not have lived due to the seriousness of his injuries.

TROUT has declined to answer questions or make any statement on advice of Counsel.

6. CARPENTER alleged that during Jun - Jul 67, in the Song Ve Valley, RVN, TROUT shot and killed an unarmed Vietnamese male who had been wounded by Tiger Force members as he approached their night position.

Continued

Allegation	Summary of Significant Statements	Remarks
7. CARPENTER alleged that during Jun - Jul 1967, near Duc Pho RVN YBARRA killed a Captured NVA Soldier by cutting the prisoners throat with a hunting knife.	CARPENTER, in a written statement related that during Jun - Jul 1967, while conducting search and destroy missions near Duc Pho RVN, his team had departed a village on a mission. For unexplained reasons YBARRA had not accompanied the team. When CARPENTER returned to the village with the team, he stated he discovered a dead NVA soldier in his fighting position, killed by having his throat cut, YBARRA and GREEN were standing nearby. YBARRA related that he and GREEN had found the NVA outside the village hiding and had killed him by cutting his throat. CARPENTER stated that YBARRA specifically stated "I cut his throat." According to CARPENTER's statement BARNETT, JOHNSON, TROUT, BROCKL, EDWARDS, McDONALD and BOWMAN were aware of the incident. ALLUMS in a written statement relates that YBARRA had told him that he killed the NVA prisoner by cutting his throat and had scalped the body. ALLUMS advised he was unable to recall the details of his conversation with YBARRA, however, he did recall that YBARRA had the scalp in his possession.	GREEN was killed in action 29 Sep 67.
8. CARPENTER alleged that sometime during Jun - Jul 67, in the vicinity of Duc Pho RVN, YBARRA shot and killed an unarmed 15 year old Vietnamese youth. After shooting the Vietnamese, YBARRA severed the ears from the body.	CARPENTER stated that while on a patrol mission in the vicinity of Duc Pho, RVN, during the period of Jun - Jul 67, YBARRA while acting as flank security for the patrol shot and killed a 15 year old Vietnamese male. CARPENTER and the team leader, SGT EDGE, after hearing YBARRA fire two shots went to YBARRA's position where they observed the victim lying on the ground. CARPENTER stated that YBARRA was holding a hunting knife in one hand and a human ear in the other. CARPENTER further related that YBARRA, then in his (CARPENTER's) presence, severed the remaining ear from the body. YBARRA then placed both ears in a ration bag. EDGE in a written statement states that YBARRA had shot a Vietnamese male whom he (EDGE) estimated to be 22 - 23 years of age. EDGE related that he had assumed that the victim was VC due to the manner of dress and that the Vietnamese interpreter accompanying the patrol had told him the victim had been VC. He denied seeing YBARRA holding a hunting knife and advised that when he observed the body both ears were intact. EDGE did relate that a short time after this incident he observed YBARRA in possession of a container filled with liquid containing two human ears.	

9. CARPENTER alleged that during the period Jun - Jul 1967 in RVN, YBARRA was in possession of human ears and gold teeth	CARPENTER related that while bathing with YBARRA in the Song Ve River, RVN, he had observed YBARRA empty a ration bag which contained several human ears attached to a string and approximately 15 - 20 gold teeth. After washing the bag YBARRA replaced the ears and teeth and secured the bag in his jacket. SMITH stated that during Jun - Jul 67, on two occasions he had observed YBARRA wearing a string of human ears around his neck. FISCHER related that on one occasion he observed YBARRA in possession of two human ears. BARNETT stated that on two or three occasions he had observed YBARRA cutting the ears from bodies and that he had further observed YBARRA in possession of a string of human ears. COOK related that on one occasion he had observed a string of human ears lying next to an Army cot occupied by YBARRA. ALLUMS stated that on one occasion he observed YBARRA sever the ears from a body and had seen YBARRA in possession of a bag containing human ears and gold teeth.	During this investigation numerous individuals have related that the practice of severing the ears from bodies was common practice among members of the Tiger Force.
10. CARPENTER alleged that during Jul 1967, in the vicinity of Duc Pho, RVN, VARNEY and TROUT cut the throat of a Vietnamese prisoner.	CARPENTER stated that on one occasion after the Tiger Force had taken a prisoner, VARNEY allegedly bet TROUT that he could knock the prisoner out with one punch. VARNEY then struck the prisoner and after being unable to knock the prisoner down VARNEY held a knife to the prisoners throat. MORELAND then struck the prisoner's head behind impaling his throat on VARNEY's knife. CARPENTER related that he saw the prisoner's body but did not witness the actual killing. HEANEY related that he had been told by VARNEY that he had attempted to "knock out" a prisoner and had almost broken his hand. HEANEY denied any knowledge of the actual knifing. PEDEN related that he had witnessed VARNEY strike the prisoner and knock him to the ground. A Vietnamese scout who was present at the scene removed a bayonet from his pack and handed it to VARNEY, who held the bayonet against the prisoners throat. At this time either VARNEY or another person pushed the Prisoner's head against the bayonet at which time the prisoner fell to the ground. Later PEDEN passed the body of the prisoner as the unit was moving out. PEDEN advised that he did not know TROUT or MORELAND, and was unable to place either person at the scene.	VARNEY was killed in action on 26 Sep 1967. TROUT has declined to make any statement reference this allegation. MORELAND is currently in deserter status and has not been interviewed.

Continued

Allegation	Summary of Significant Statements	Remarks
11. CARPENTER alleged that during June 1967, in the vicinity of Duc of Chu Lai, RVN, KERRIGAN executed a prisoner by shooting him with a .38 cal pistol.	CARPENTER related that during Jun 1967, in the vicinity if Duc Pho, RVN, the Tiger Force had held a 20 Year old Vietnamese male prisoner. When the force broke camp, KERRIGAN shot the prisoner with a .38 cal pistol, CARPENTER stated that he did not witness the killing, however, he saw the body of the executed prisoner. TROUT is alleged to have told KERRIGAN that the unit was moving and couldn't be bothered with the detainee and that he would have to be killed. CARPENTER further related that he observed KERRIGAN walk the detainee a few feet away from the camp. He heard a shot and walked over to KERRIGAN and saw the body lying on the ground. CARPENTER further stated that he had heard TROUT order KERRIGAN to kill the prisoner.	TROUT has declined to be interviewed reference this allegatior No information has been developed to corroborate this allegation other than the statement of CARPENTER.
12. CARPENTER alleged that during Jun - Jul 67, in the Song Ve Valley, RVN, members of a Tiger Force patrol shot and killed several Vietnamese farmers.	CARPENTER related that during Jun - Jul 1967, in the Song Ve Valley, RVN, a Tiger Force patrol came under fire from a Hamlet located about 100 yards to the patrol's immediate front. The patrol then opened fire on several Vietnamese farmers working in the field located about 100 - 400 yards from the patrol's right flank. CARPENTER estimated that ten Vietnamese farmers were shot and killed. CARPENTER stated that the order to fire on the farmers came from HAWKINS ; however, he did not personally hear HAWKINS give the order, as it was passed down from the lead element. According to CARPENTER no attempt was made to ascertain if the dead Vietnamese had been armed. The enemy located in the hamlet to the front of the patrol departed leaving ammunition and canteens. CARPENTER denied having fired his weapon during this incident. Miller related that about ten persons, both male and female were shot by members of the the element. No enemy fire had been received from the village. The order to fire would have been given by either HAWKINS or TROUT, however, the persons were shot by mutual agreement of the patrol members involved. No one entered the field to as certain if the individuals had been armed. ALLUMS related that the order to fire was given as the persons working in the field to the right flank of the patrol has started to run away. ALLUMS did not know if the farmers were killed as a result and felt that they were out of firing range and escaped into the jungle.	

13. CARPENTER alleged that sometime during Jul - Aug 67, in the vicinity of Chu Lai, RVN, COGAN, shot and killed an elderly unarmed Vietnamese male.	CARPENTER stated that during Jul - Aug 67, in the vicinity of Chi Lai, RVN, during a combat action, a Tiger Force patrol entered a village and observed a 20 year old Vietnamese male running from a hut. The patrol opened fire, killing the Vietnamese male. A search of the body disclosed that the victim had been in possession of enemy documents. During a search of the hut an elderly Vietnamese male believed to have been the father of the victim was found inside the hut. TROUT ordered COGAN to kill the old man. COGAN walked the victim out behind the hut and shot him with a 45 cal pistol through the mouth and left him lying on the ground. CARPENTER stated that he saw the victim was still alive and so informed COGAN, who returned and shot the victim a second time through the throat killing him. CARPENTER related that he had witnessed COGAN shoot the victim the second time and had actually heard TROUT order COGAN to kill the victim. BARNETT related that he had been present during the action and witnessed the shooting of the Vietnamese male on whom the documents had been found. He stated that an old Vietnamese male had been found in one of the huts and had been taken outside and killed. BARNETT further related that he had been shot twice, however, did not know who did the actual killing. BOWMAN, corroborated that the incident occurred as alleged by CARPENTER. He advised that the old Vietnamese had been shot twice by a combat Engineer assigned to the patrol. BOWMAN was unable to further identify the individual. SAWYER stated that during the action he had observed COGAN guarding an elderly Vietnamese male whom he estimated to be 60 years of age. Later he was told that COGAN had shot and killed the victim. SAWYER denied having witnessed the actual killing.	COGAN has not been interviewed reference this allegation. Interview is being held in abeyance pending completion of investigative leads. TROUT has declined to make any statement reference this allegation.
14. CARPENTER alleged that sometime during Aug 67, in the vicinity of Chu Lai, RVN. SAWYER shot and killed a Vietnamese prisoner and beat another prisoner with a shovel.	CARPENTER related that during Aug 67, in the vicinity of Chu Lai, RVN, members of the Tiger Force captured two prisoners and detained them at a temporary camp where they were used to construct fighting positions. SAWYER, a combat engineer assigned to the Force, was placed in charge of the prisoners. CARPENTER related that he observed SAWYER tie both prisoners with detonating cord, then explode a piece of the explosive in view of the prisoners to demonstrate the effect CARPENTER further stated that he had witnessed SAWYER beat one of the prisoners with a shovel to the extent that the prisoner had to be med - evaced from the area. SAWYER subsequently shot the second prisoner	SAWYER has been administered a polygraph examination. In the opinion of the examiner SAWYER was truthful in his statement concerning the death of the prisoner, however, was deceptive concerning tying the prisoner with detonating cord.

Continued

Allegation	Summary of Significant Statements	Remarks
	with his M-16 rifle and justified his act with the excuse that the prisoner had attempted to escape. BOWMAN in a written statement related that he had observed SAWYER shoot a prisoner from a range of about 35 - 50 yards. BOWMAN confirmed that a prisoner had been severly beaten, requiring that he be med - evaced from the area. BOWMAN denied any knowledge concerning SAWYERS having tied the prisoners with detonating cord. He further opined that SAWYER would not have shot the prisoner unless directed to do so by someone with authority. SAWYER in a written statement admitted shooting a prisoner. He related that three prisoners had been brought into camp and that he had guarded the prisoners until the following morning. At about 1030 hours, during a work-break one prisoner ran down the hill. SAWYER stated that he fired a warning shot, then fired a second shot killing the prisoner when he refused to halt. SAWYER denied killing the prisoner without justification as alleged and maintained the prisoner was attempting to escape. He further denied having been directed by anyone to kill the prisoner, or having beaten a prisoner with a shovel, or tying the prisoners with detonating cord.	
15. CARPENTER alleged that YBARRA and GREEN had forced Viet - namese female to participate in an act of oral sodomy, after which YBARRA cut the females throat.	CARPENTER alleged that sometime after 17 Aug 67, in the Que Son Valley, between Tam Ky and Chu Lai, RVN, the Tiger Force had engaged in searching a Vietnamese village during which he (CARPENTER) had observed a 13 - 14 year old Vietnamese female. The Force moved out of the village, setting up camp on a nearby hilltop. Approximately one hour later YBARRA and GREEN "bragged" that they had forced the female to commit an act of sodomy, after which YBARRA had cut the girls body. HEANEY related that he had heard a rumor that someone had forced the female to commit sodomy and that her throat had been cut. He denied having heard YBARRA or GREEN discuss the incident. BARNETT stated that he had heard YBARRA had forced the female to commit sodomy and had cut her throat. COLLIGAN stated that he had heard a rumor that YBARRA had seduced a Vietnamese female, after which she had been "fired up", (killed). ALLUMS related that he recalled YBARRA having talked about a	Green was killed in action 26 Sep 67.

Continued

female he had seduced or forced to commit an act of sodomy and subsequently killed. ALLUMS could not recall if GREEN had been mentioned in connection with this incident.

16. CARPENTER alleged that during his assignment with Tiger Force body mutilations were a common practice. Tiger Force members severed ears from bodys and left playing cards inserted in the throat and ear wounds.

CARPENTER related that during his assignment with the Tiger Force several unidentified members of the Force had severed the ears from the dead bodies. Tiger Force members, after cutting the throats and ears of bodies inserted into the ear and throat cavities playing cards depicting the Ace of Spades and the words "Sat Cong" (kill Viet Cong). CARPENTER further stated that such body mutilations were common practice within the Force and had occured prior to his assignment with the Tiger Force. According to CARPENTER Tiger Force members talked openly about such mutilations. BARNETT related that body mutilations were committed by several members of the Tiger Force and condoned within the unit. Other than YBARRA, he was unable to identify any specific individuals. BARNETT confirmed that the the Aces of Spades were used and placed on dead bodies. He further advised that HAWKINS and TROUT were aware that acts of mutilation were being committed by personnel under their command. COBERLY in a written statement related that he had observed Tiger Force members, whom he could not identify cutting ears from bodies and in possession of collections of human scalps, ears, and gold teeth. BURRELL related that it was common practice for Tiger Force personnel to sever at least an ear or finger from the bodies and that the dismembered parts were left with the body or in the general vicinity of bodies. BURRELL further confirmed that the Ace of Spades playing cards were placed in the general vicinity of bodies. BURRELL further confirmed that the Ace of Spades playing cards were placed or dropped in the vicinity of bodies. During this investigation several individuals interviewed professed to have had knowledge or had heard rumors concerning body mutilations. HAWKINS and TROUT rendered written statements denying that personnel under their command had engaged in body mutilations. MERRILL related that while assigned to the Tiger Force he had observed unit members in possession of human ears. He further stated that he had seen mutilated enemy bodies which had the ears severed and throats cut. MERRILL denied having actually witnessed any body mutilations or having participated in such acts.

Allegation	Summary of Significant Statements	Remarks
17. COOK alleged that during his tour of duty with Tiger Force he had observed YBARRA in possession of a human scalp which he had affixed to the front sight of his M-16 rifle.	COOK related that during 1967, while the Tiger Force was stationed in the area of Duc Pho, RVN, he had observed YBARRA in possession of a human scalp which was affixed to the front sight of his rifle. CARPENTER related that on the occasion when YBARRA had cut the throat of a NVA prisoner, YBARRA had scalped the body (Allegation #7). It has not been determined if the scalp YBARRA allegedly removed from the body of the dead NVA prisoner is the scalp COOK subsequently observed affixed to YBARRA's rifle. CASSIDY related that on one occasion he had observed YBARRA cut some hair from the head of a Vietnamese female and tied the hair to the barrel of his rifle. The female had not been injured by YBARRA. ALLUMS advised that he observed YBARRA in possession of a human scalp. This is believed to be the scalp taken by YBARRA from the NVA soldier killed by YBARRA. KERNEY in a written statement related that YBARRA had a human scalp affixed to his rifle. He denied knowing how or where YBARRA had acquired the scalp.	
18. COOK alleged that HISE, a Tiger Force medic, was in possession of a liquid filled jar containing a human ear.	COOK related that while he was assigned to Tiger Force he had observed HISE, a Tiger Force medic, in possession of a liquid filled jar containing a human ear. It was rumored that HISE had been given the ear by KERRIGAN. COOK stated that he departed the Tiger Force during Dec 67, at which time HISE was still in possession of the ear. FULTON stated that he had observed a SP5 Medic assigned to Tiger Force in possession of a plastic bag containing a human ear. FULTON was unable to identify the medic as HISE. EDGE in a written statement related that at an undetermined time he had observed HISE in possession of a jar containing two human ears. MILLER in a written statement related that he had observed HISE in possession of a jar containing two human ears.	HISE declined to be interviewed concerning this allegation.

Continued

19. MAYHEW alleged that during Aug - Sep 67, in the vicinity of Duc Pho RVN, DOYLE beat a Vietnamese prisoner while questioning him and subsequently ordered the prisoner shot.

MAYHEW related in two written statements that sometime during Aug - Sep 67, in the area of Duc Pho, RVN, he accompanied a Tiger Force element consisting of 8 - 9 members and led by DOYLE. During the patrol two Vietnamese males, one pregnant female and two 3 - 4 year old children were observed in a village and questioned by DOYLE as to the whereabouts of the VC. DOYLE separated the two males and and began the questioning, through the interpreter accompanying the patrol. While questioning one of the males, DOYLE, apparently dissatisfied by the answers he was receiving, struck the male with his rifle. After the male continued to deny any knowledge DOYLE shot the victim in the forearm with his M-16 rifle. DOYLE subsequently ordered the victim executed. Several patrol members opened fire with M-16s and a M-79 grenade launcher, killing the victim. MAYHEW stated that he or the interpreter did not participate in the killing and that he did not see DOYLE take part in it. He (MAYHEW) was unable to recall who or how many members of the patrol were involved. MAYHEW related that the killing had been unjustified and a search of the area failed to disclose any evidence to substantiate the Vietnamese as having been associated with the enemy. MILLER related that he had been told of this incident by MAYHEW, the medic assigned to the element, after MAYHEW's return from the mission. BRUNER related that he had been present in the village as a member of a Tiger Force element led by TROUT. Later they were joined by an element led by DOYLE. BRUNER stated while in the village he observed DOYLE shoot a Vietnamese male in the forearm with his M-16 rifle. He (BRUNER) left the area to check on other prisoners taken by the patrol. When he returned to the scene he observed the victim lying on the ground with numerous body wounds. Prior to this he had heard a burst of gun fire and a M-79 being fired. BRUNER could not substantiate DOYLE having ordered the execution as alleged by MAYHEW. BRUNER was shown pictures of Tiger Force members believed to have been members of the elements involved but was unable to make positive identifications.

Allegation	Summary of Significant Statements	Remarks
20. ALLUMS alleged that during Jan 67, in the area of Duc Pho, RVN, GREEN tortured a tied and gagged prisoner, then killed the prisoner by cutting his throat.	ALLUMS related that during Jun 67, in the vicinity of Duc Pho, RVN, GREEN tortured a tied and gagged prisoner by inflicting several superficial lacerations on the prisoners throat with a knife. GREEN subsequently killed the prisoner by cutting his throat. ALLUMS stated that GREEN had been instructed by McGAHA to dispose of the prisoner. ALLUMS advised he was an eye witness to this incident and that there were additional persons who witnessed the killing; however, he was unable to identify additional personnel. During re-interview ALLUMS stated that he had been mistaken that it had not been McGAHA but NAUGHTON, the Tiger Force Platoon Leader from May - Jul 67 who had ordered GREEN to dispose of the prisoner.	McGAHA was killed inaction 28 Jan 68. No information has been developed to corroborate this allegation other than ALLUMS statement.
21. EDGE alleged that during Jul 67, in the Song Ve Valley RVN, YBARRA and GREEN killed a prisoner by cutting his throat. The prisoner was to have been evacuated from the Tiger Force area by Helicopter	EDGE in a written statement related that during July 1967 in the Song Ve Valley, RVN, a Tiger Force element had taken an NVA Prisoner. YBARRA and GREEN were detailed to escort the prisoner to a helicopter pick up for evacuation. YBARRA and GREEN departed with the prisoner and returned as the element was forming to depart the area. YBARRA displayed a knife with fresh blood stains. CRAFT asked YBARRA what he had done with the prisoner, GREEN replied that he (YBARRA) had cut the prisoners throat. EDGE stated that HAWKINS and TROUT were present during this incident and that HAWKINS had reported that the prisoner had been shot and killed while attempting to escape.	No information has been developed in corroboration of this allegation other than the statement of EDGE.
22. WOOD alleged that sometime during Jun - Jul 67, in the Song Ve Valley RVN, HAWKINS and other unidentified Tiger Force personnel fired on two elderly Vietnamese females as	WOOD in a written statement related that sometime during Jun 67, in the area of Duc Pho, Song Ve Valley RVN, a Tiger Force element had established a perimeter. Two persons were observed approaching by a perimeter guard. HAWKINS ordered the perimeter guards to open fire. WOOD stated that he attempted to countermand HAWKINS order; however, HAWKINS opened fire himself and was joined by the guards in firing on the individuals. A subsequent search disclosed the two persons to be Vietnamese females. One was wounded and both were evacuated from the area by helicopter. WOOD stated that he had reported this incident to the Executive Officer, 1st Bn, 327th Inf and	No information has been developed to corroborate this allegation other than the statement of WOOD.

they approached the Tiger Camp Perimeter.	to the Office of the Inspector General, XVIII Airborne Corps, Ft Bragg, N. C. WOOD was unable to identify the personnel other than HAWKINS involved in this incident.	HAWKINS has declined to be interviewed concerning this No information has been developed to corroborate this allegation other that the statement of JOHNSON JOHNSON has been administered a polygraph examination. In the opinion of the examiner JOHNSON was not deceptive.
23. JOHNSON alleged that HAWKINS shot and killed a wounded prisoner	JOHNSON in a written statement related that sometime during Jun - Jul 67, in a village located in the Song Ve Valley, RVN, he and other Tiger Force members were involved in a night ambush. After the initial fire fight a wounded male VC was captured. DOYLE was was asked what to do with the wounded prisoner. He replied to wait until HAWKINS arrived. HAWKINS arrived later and shot the prisoner with his M-16 rifle. JOHNSON stated that he had witnessed the actual shooting.	
24. MILLER alleged that DOYLE booby trapped a supply of food which was purposely left in the open unattended area. As a result four or five Vietnamese were killed	Investigation has disclosed that a quantity of "C" rations had been wired with explosives by DOYLE and other Tiger Force personnel as alleged by MILLER. However, this was normal combat procedure and the persons killed were in fact Viet Cong. MILLER did not arrive on the scene until the following morning and apparently was not fully aware of what had transpired.	No additional investigative effort contemplated.
25. MILLER alleged that during Jul 67, Tiger Force members had shot and killed two Vietnamese youths	MILLER in a written statement related that during Jul 67, in the Song Ve Valley RVN, a Tiger Force element had been sent to contact a CIDG Force adjacent to the Tiger Force area of operations. Upon entering the area a 12 year old Vietnamese male was found leading his two blind brothers. The two blind males were subsequently killed by the Tiger Force. The 12 Year old male was evacuated by Helicopter. MILLER advised that he did not witness the actual shooting or could identify the individuals responsible. He stated that the order to kill the victims would have come from HAWKINS or DOYLE.	For additional information refer to allegation No. 26.

Continued

Allegation	Summary of Significant Statements	Remarks
26. SANCHEZ alleged that two Vietnamese males believed to have been brothers were shot and killed by Tiger Force personnel.	SANCHEZ in a written statement related that on or about 28 Jul 1967, in the Song Ve Valley, RVN, while on patrol a Tiger Force element observed two Vietnamese males to the patrols front. The order to halt was given, however, the Vietnamese refused to halt and began to run. The patrol gave chase eventually catching them. The Vietnamese, a 25 year old and a 13 year old males were unarmed and the older was suffering from a shrapnel wound to his lower leg. After questioning by the Vietnamese Interpreter assigned to the patrol it was determined that the older male was a Viet Cong, and the younger male was his brother. The patrol queried the command element as to the disposition of the prisoners and subsequently received a radio transmission to the effect "What do you do with a horse with a broken leg". The prisoners were then shot and killed. SANCHEZ stated he witnessed the actual killing but was unable to identify the Tiger Force personnel who did the shooting. SANCHEZ was wounded later the same day and evacuated. The order to kill the prisoners was given by a 1LT or CPT in command of the patrol element.	This incident as related by SANCHEZ may be the same be the allegation made by MILLER (Allegation #25). Additional interviews have been requested to as certain if they are the same and the identify of the persons involved.
27. KERNEY, alleged that on one occasion several Vietnamese nationals to include children were killed by Tiger Force person	On 17 Jun 74, KERNEY orally related that during a Tiger Force combat operation Tiger Force personnel had killed several Vietnamese to include several children by grenading bunkers the victims had taken refuge in. KERNEY stated that the Tiger force had approached the village about dawn at which time the villagers had taken refuge in bunkers. Tiger force personnel had attempted to talk the villagers into leaving the bunkers however, an interpreter was not available to talk to the villagers. KERNEY stated that he did not recall	Investigation to date has not determined if the incident described by KERNEY and FULTON are the same or two separate occurrences. The facts as related appear to be the same, however KERNEY advised that the incident occurred near

nel when they refused to leave their bunkers.

an order being given to use hand grenades, however, this was not necessary as members of the Tiger Force "Knew what to do". KERNEY could not recall how many persons were killed during this incident but did recall seeing bodies being removed from the bunkers. According to KERNEY, a search of the bunkers failed to disclose any evidence of enemy affiliation, or that the villagers were in sympathy with the Viet Cong. No incoming fire had been encountered by the Tiger Force prior to this incident. KERNEY could not explain why it had been necessary to extricate the villagers from the bunker.

FULTON in a written statement advised that he had been involved in a village operation during which he and other personnel had been ordered to grenade bunkers located in the village. The incident had occurred near the end of the day. FULTON stated that he had been located near the rear of the column and had not seen anyone running in to the bunkers and did not know if the bunkers were in fact occupied. He advised that he assumed they were as the order to use grenades had been given by an NCO he thought to have been SSG HAUGH. FULTON related that after the incident the element moved on about 20–30 meters and established a perimeter. During the night human sounds were heard emanating from the bunkers.

dawn while FULTON stated that it occurred near the end of the day. It is possible that the length of time involved has made remembering difficult. Investigation continues.

INDEX